The Marriage Question

CLARE CARLISLE

The Marriage Question

George Eliot's Double Life

ALLEN LANE
an imprint of
PENGUIN BOOKS

ALLEN LANE

UK | USA | Canada | Ireland | Australia
India | New Zealand | South Africa

Allen Lane is part of the Penguin Random House group of companies
whose addresses can be found at global.penguinrandomhouse.com

First published 2023
001

Copyright © Clare Carlisle, 2023

The moral right of the author has been asserted

Set in 10.5/14pt Sabon LT Std
Typeset by Jouve (UK), Milton Keynes
Printed and bound in Great Britain by Clays Ltd, Elcograf S.p.A.

The authorized representative in the EEA is Penguin Random House Ireland,
Morrison Chambers, 32 Nassau Street, Dublin D02 YH68

A CIP catalogue record for this book is available from the British Library

ISBN: 978–0–241–44717–8

'*About marriages one can only rejoice with trembling.*'

George Eliot to Benjamin Jowett, 14 April 1875

Contents

Preface

There is something dazzling about marriage — that leap into the open-endedness of another human being. It is difficult to look directly at it, difficult to think that thought. A philosopher usually swoops on such things like a magpie: *Look!* a shifting, shimmering *question*, all indeterminacy and iridescence. Don't you just want to snatch it up, take it home, and sit on it for a long time?

Yet marriage is rarely treated as a philosophical question. Perhaps domestic life, traditionally a feminine domain, has seemed too trivial a subject for deep thinking. When I studied philosophy at university, most of the authors I read were unmarried men: Plato, Descartes, Spinoza, Hume, Kant, Nietzsche, Wittgenstein. Did they regard marriage as a hindrance to the serious work of philosophy, rather than a spur to thought? My friends and I were constantly analysing relationships — our own and other people's. We sat up late contemplating our parents' happy and unhappy marriages, and asked ourselves if we would ever get married. I loved the idea of choosing my own family — but how would I know I was making the right choice?

Beneath its conventional surface, marriage simmers with tensions between self and other, body and soul, passion and restraint, the poetry of romantic love and the prose of domestic routine. Each day our partners watch us cross the precarious bridge between our intimate and our social selves. Somehow we are supposed to make a happy home in these fraught, ambiguous double binds. For better or worse, the answers we find to our marriage questions — whether to marry, whom to marry, how to live in a marriage, whether to remain married — are often close to the heart of our life's meaning. Over centuries these questions have shaped religious, political and social histories. Of course, in such a culture choosing to be or become single is as significant as choosing to marry — just look at Kierkegaard, whose broken engagement was not just a personal drama but the catalyst for existentialism. As soon as we begin to reflect on marriage we stumble across great philosophical themes: desire, freedom, selfhood, change, morality, happiness, belief, the mystery of other minds.

In the middle years of the nineteenth century Marian Evans found her calling when she transformed herself into George Eliot — an author celebrated for her 'genius' as soon as she published her debut novel. During those years she also became a wife. Bruised by a series of messy romantic involvements, she had met the writer George Henry Lewes, whose wife was sleeping with his best friend. After 'eloping' to Berlin in 1854 Eliot and Lewes lived together for twenty-four years. They could not be legally married, but she asked people to call her 'Mrs Lewes' and dedicated the manuscript of each novel to her 'Husband'. George Eliot did not appear on my philosophy curriculum, and it was a long time before I discovered that she pursued her marriage question with the tenacity of a great philosopher, as well as the delicacy of a great artist.

Early in her relationship with Lewes she wondered at the 'great experience' of marriage — 'this double life, which helps me to feel and think with double strength'. These words hint at questions that would continue to shape her married life, over the years ahead: ambition, dependence, and the effort to connect thought and feeling which surges through her writing, creating a new philosophical voice. Precisely this combination, and the struggles it entailed, produced the extraordinary works of art — intense, intimate, experimental — that still open our eyes and stretch our souls. George Eliot's fiction searches the lives of ordinary people to uncover truths we can recognize as our own, truths at once intellectual and emotional. Her literary achievement was so immense that her successors felt bound to break the form of the novel in order to move beyond her.

Eliot's leap into life with Lewes was a crisis from which she never recovered, though she grew immeasurably within it. Their union was unconsecrated, outside the law: by daring to call it a marriage she was prising the concept from the grip of Church and State. To nearly all her contemporaries the relationship was a scandal, and for years she was socially ostracized. At the same time, her marriage helped her to become George Eliot. Lewes urged her to begin writing fiction, and gave constant encouragement as she laboured, full of self-doubt, over her work. He acted as her agent, publicist and secretary. For more than two decades 'Mrs Lewes' was a role she lived day to day — yet this name was a fiction: the woman she could not be. 'George Eliot', too, was an invented self, a male author who was entitled to be a serious thinker as well as a popular novelist.

Eliot belonged to a generation bereft of the old religious certainties. 'All around us, the intellectual lightships had broken from their moorings,' wrote J. A. Froude, an historian whose early career coincided with hers. Future generations would 'never know what it was to find the lights all drifting, the compasses all awry, and nothing left to steer by except the stars.' In 1851 newly-wed Matthew Arnold wondered if marital fidelity was now the only kind of faith and truth to hope for: 'Ah love, let us be true / To one another!' Eliot shared this sense of spiritual search, and likewise turned to long-term love for an anchor in a shifting, spinning modern world. Yet she experienced marriage quite differently from male acquaintances such as Froude, Arnold, and other eminent Victorians. From her youth to her last years she wrestled with what her generation called the Woman Question: how should a woman live in a patriarchal world? In Eliot's writing as well as in her public and private lives, the Woman Question became inseparable from the marriage question. She lived these questions, often painfully, caught in the tension between her longing for approval and her refusal to compromise.

'I don't consider myself as a teacher, but a companion in the struggle of thought,' Eliot wrote to a friend in 1875, as she worked on her last novel. Writing fiction, she found creative ways to address deep questions: rather than personifying ideas or telling didactic stories, she philosophized through her art. Her willingness to think in the medium of human relations and emotions, and to carry out that thinking in images, symbols and archetypes, expands the canonical view of philosophy that is embedded in universities — institutions that systematically excluded women until the twentieth century. Eliot once reflected that her friend Herbert Spencer, a prominent Victorian philosopher, had an 'inadequate endowment of emotion' which made him 'as good as dead' to large swathes of human experience, thereby weakening his arguments and theories. She might as well have been talking about philosophy itself. Her own philosophical style is compassionate, subversive, seasoned with humour, and enriched by an attentiveness in which fleeting moments — a glance, a touch, a flush of feeling — become significant.

*

Marriage is made of these intimate and ephemeral moments, yet it also has epic proportions. It stretches out through time, into the future, growing and changing: that is why George Eliot had to write grand novels such as *Middlemarch* to bring it into view. Like a plant, a long-term relationship has its phases of development, its cycles, its seasons, its changing weather. Under adverse conditions, it might wither and die; it might come close to death and then revive. When we imagine a marriage like this, we think about how it is connected with other living things — other people, other relationships — and rooted in an ecosystem. Victorian philosophers learned to call this ecosystem a 'milieu' or 'environment'. We could also call it a world: a mixture of natural, social and cultural conditions.

Getting together with another person means stepping into their world: their family, friendships, culture, career path, ambitions; the places they know and the possibilities they contemplate; their taste and style and habits. Being in a marriage — legal or otherwise — means living in a shared world. We might even say that the marriage *is* this shared world: again, something that grows and changes.

When Marian Evans met George Lewes in 1853, their worlds already overlapped. They moved in the same circles in London's literary scene. They had read many of the same books, immersed themselves in intellectual currents that were shaping their century — Spinoza's philosophy, Carlyle's histories and satires, Romantic literature. But when their worlds merged, a shared world began to grow.

The effort to understand growth was, in fact, at the heart of this world. Seized by the idea of development, the nineteenth century generated theories of progress and evolution which transformed the way people thought about nature, history, and themselves. From their study of Goethe, Marian and Lewes learned to see growth as a question at once scientific, philosophical and artistic. When they met Lewes was working on his biography of Goethe, and he finished it during their first year together. It was due to Goethe's legacy, he explained, that 'we are now all bent on tracing the phases of development. To understand the *grown* we try to follow the *growth*.'

Goethe's first scientific work was a little treatise titled *The Metamorphosis of Plants*. Echoing Spinoza, Goethe saw matter and spirit, body and soul, as the 'twin ingredients of the universe'. A plant, he argued, is not merely a physical thing. It is an archetype, an idea: a fluid pattern and rhythm of growth, expressed in visible form — root, stem, leaf, flower, fruit. George Eliot would carry Goethe's obsession with form and flux into her fiction, through her inquiry into the 'process and unfolding' of human character, and her increasingly daring experiments in literary form.

If we take a plant as our metaphor for marriage, this must be the plant as Goethe envisaged it: essentially in process, simultaneously ideal and real, symbolic and particular, inward and expressive. What I am calling 'the marriage question' should also be thought of as a living, growing thing, frequently branching in new directions, always rooted in and reaching out to a world. Eliot's marriage question was entangled with meanings of marriage expressed in customs, laws, works of art. It cannot be summed up in a sentence or a paragraph because it stretched through her whole lifetime. It shaped her sense of self, coloured her emotional experience, and continually found expression in her writing.

In pursuit of George Eliot's marriage question this book will move between biography, philosophy, literary interpretation, and histories of art and religion. It begins with a choice, a momentous day, and a honeymoon; it ends with death, mourning, and another choice.

Within this arc, its structure is thematic as well as chronological. Reading Eliot's works as she wrote them, we will see her wrestling, in life as in art, with themes that belong to a philosophy of marriage: sanctity and morality, vocation and voice, passion and sacrifice, motherhood and creativity, trust and disillusion, success and failure, destiny and chance, love and loss — and also the nature of philosophy itself.

With its desire to understand human relationships and feelings, its interest in the form and flux of a life, biography offers another means to expand philosophy into the territory Eliot herself cleared and claimed. By showing how Eliot's thought grew, biography becomes a medium for philosophical inquiry.

*

Though Eliot and Lewes socialized with many eminent intellectuals and artists during their later years together, the core of their double life was what she called a 'shared solitude'. Perhaps this description fits all marriages, though of course the experience of solitude can range from blissfully contented to desperately lonely. If marriage is a shared subjectivity, then its truth can only be known from the inside. This inwardness belongs to the sanctity of marriage; it is one of the things betrayed when a marriage is violated.

Phyllis Rose's 1983 book *Parallel Lives* peered inside the marriages of five Victorian writers — Thomas Carlyle, John Ruskin, John Stuart Mill, Charles Dickens and George Eliot — and concluded that Eliot and Lewes had by far the happiest relationship. Was it simply a coincidence that they were the only couple not legally married, and that in this instance the wife was more famous than her astonishingly supportive husband? Or did these exceptional conditions make their partnership freer, less compromised, more authentic? Eliot's story of marital success seemed the perfect match for Rose's second-wave feminism. And it is still seductive: we want to watch Eliot flouting convention and having it all — work, love, wealth, fame, even (by a certain definition) motherhood.

Other biographers have tended to share this positive assessment of George Eliot's unconventional marriage. But as I read her letters and reread her fiction, I feel more and more curious about the image of 'perfect love' that both Eliot and Lewes cultivated — at least in part, surely, to prove their critics wrong. How does this defiantly idealized public image connect to the very dark marital interiors portrayed in the novels, with their recurring scenes of ambivalence, brutality and disappointment? Do these scenes retaliate against the moralism that condemned their author, by smashing the façade of respectable marriage? Or do they transmit inward experiences that Eliot knew first-hand? And how did a woman who once declared that she liked 'to feel free' find life with a husband who kept her 'in a mental greenhouse', as the Scottish writer Margaret Oliphant once put it? Mrs Oliphant, a widow who churned out dozens of novels, biographies and histories to support her three children, rather envied Eliot's rarified literary life — but greenhouses can be oppressive as well as nurturing, and are not built for human habitation.

If there were moments when Eliot's marriage stifled or disappointed her, would she have admitted it? The narrator of *Middlemarch* suggests that it is 'not a bad thing' for wives and husbands to hide their domestic suffering. Our pride demands this, he explains — as if unhappiness were a failure — and Eliot was certainly proud. 'We mortals, men and women, devour many a disappointment between breakfast and dinner-time; keep back the tears and look a little pale about the lips, and in answer to inquiries say, "Oh, nothing!" Pride helps us; and pride is not a bad thing when it only urges us to hide our own hurts — not to hurt others.' *Daniel Deronda*'s proud young wife Gwendolen Grandcourt believes that revealing her 'disappointment' and 'sorrow' will bring 'nothing but a humiliation which would have been vinegar to her wounds'. I am not suggesting that Mrs Lewes was secretly as miserable as Mrs Casaubon, or abused like Mrs Grandcourt, but she might have tasted some of their feelings. At least we might wonder how many tears, how many compromises, how many days of depression and despair a happy marriage can absorb, before its happiness is called into question.

*

It is often said, echoing Plato and Aristotle, that philosophy begins with wonder. Thinking about other people's relationships tends to begin with wonder, and stay there. The world is full of couples, like it is full of houses: we are surrounded by these everyday mysteries, but we hardly ever get to go inside. Maybe a lighted window now and then lets us glance into the interior of a shared life; we might see a kitchen or a living room, very rarely a bedroom. In our own house, when we were children, we never saw what happened after bedtime when the grown-ups were alone. We didn't know what they felt when they touched each other — or when they found themselves far apart.

Some of Eliot's biographers have speculated about her sex life with Lewes, but we know almost nothing about it. One fourth-hand source has her saying something about birth control and sexual satisfaction — it is not clear whose — early in their relationship; twenty-two years later a close friend saw Lewes seize her hand and kiss it. Eliot seems to have possessed a certain sexual power, particularly over younger women, though it is impossible to say how deliberately she wielded this power, or how it made her feel. Much more certain is the interest in sexuality — its many modes, its fluctuations, its hidden depths, its complexity — that is indirectly yet unmistakably expressed in George Eliot's writing. Of course, this does not tell us what Eliot herself experienced. It tells us what she thought about, where her imagination could go.

The letters exchanged between Eliot and Lewes were buried with them in Highgate Cemetery. Although this puts the intimate details of their relationship beyond our reach, it is itself revealing. It suggests a deep commitment to the privacy of their marriage, which they nevertheless performed for friends and acquaintances — and increasingly, as George Eliot's fame grew, for posterity. We might be tempted to think that if we dug up those buried letters we could prise open the black box that recorded the inner workings of their shared life. And it is true that most marriages do contain secrets, which may or may not one day come to light. But they also contain questions, ambiguities, grey areas: zones of conflict and confusion that even the partners themselves struggle to understand, let alone resolve.

For example: how do you tell the difference between protectiveness and control, between love and selfishness, between loyalty and submission? Who has compromised more, sacrificed more, suffered more? Who has the most power? Marriages, like people, are not entirely transparent to themselves, and answers to these questions are perhaps more often decided than discovered.

I think that by a combination of close reading and empathy, and also a little imagination, we can lay our hand on Eliot's marriage questions. We might already inhabit some of them ourselves. If being 'Victorian' now seems synonymous with conventional marriage and its corseted moral codes, it may be surprising to discover that a novelist as solidly Victorian as George Eliot brings new elasticity to the concept of marriage. Many of the themes she explores in her art — desire, dependence, trust, violence, sanctity — could be transferred to wider, less traditional ideas of married life. In this way, Eliot can be our 'companion in the struggle of thought' even when this struggle encounters possibilities which she did not inhabit or imagine.

More biographically, too, Eliot's unusual circumstances brought her closer to a modern experience of marriage. She was involved with several men before settling down with a long-term partner in her mid-thirties. She chose not to have children, and navigated relationships with Lewes's sons. Within a few years of her married life she was earning much more than her husband. Living at once inside marriage and outside its conventions, she could experience this form of life — so familiar yet also so perplexing — from both sides. A successful marriage was never, for this woman, an easy lapse into social conformity, but a precarious balancing act — and people were watching to see if she would fall.

A Note on Names

George Eliot's biographers must wrestle with the question of how to name her. It is usual to refer to one's subject by their surname, but here this is a contested issue that bears witness to Eliot's complex, perhaps fractured identity — due partly to her ambiguous marriage. Calling her by her legal surname, Evans, during the period of her unofficial marriage would reject the title 'Mrs Lewes' that she claimed for herself (albeit inconsistently), while calling her Lewes poses the problem of distinguishing her from her partner.

Her name changed several times over her life, and she was known by different names to different people. She was born Mary Anne Evans in 1819, and adopted the name Marian when she moved to London, aged thirty-two. A few people, including Lewes, called her Polly, an affectionate variation on Mary. By the end of the 1850s she was signing herself Marian Lewes or Marian Evans Lewes; some people addressed her as Mrs Lewes, while others refused to do so.

As the voice that speaks through her novels and poetry she is, of course, George Eliot. Preserving the distinction between this purely literary voice and the woman formed by choices and experiences which do not lie on the surface of her pages, I want to call this woman Eliot, the surname she created for herself. I also want to register the shift from her lives as Mary Anne and Marian to her life as an artist, by using whichever name she was chiefly known by as we move through her story. But when did Marian become Eliot? Though she adopted her pseudonym in 1857, for more than two years her identity remained secret and she was George Eliot only to Lewes and her publisher.

I have decided to switch to calling her Eliot in the spring of 1859, when her friend Barbara Bodichon guessed that she was the author of *Adam Bede*. This moment of recognition was joyous for both women, though its triumph was laced with shame. Three months later she became George Eliot to the world.

Question and Answer.*

"Where blooms, O my Father, a thornless rose?"
"That I cannot tell thee, my child;
Not one on the bosom of earth e'er grows,
But wounds whom its charms have beguiled."

"Would I'd a rose on my bosom to lie!
But I shrink from its piercing thorn;
I long, but I dare not its point defy,
I long, and I gaze forlorn."

"Not so, O my child, round the stem again
Thy resolute fingers entwine—
Forego not the joy for its sister pain,
Let the rose, the sweet rose, be thine!"

* When she was twenty-one Mary Ann Evans translated this poem from German to share it with her friend Maria Lewis. It was sent in a letter to Maria dated 1 October 1840.

I

Setting Sail

She had decided, she had prepared, she had waited, and finally the day arrived. Light came into her room around five in the morning, and she rose early. It was Thursday, 20 July 1854: today she would *not* be married to George Lewes, and they would set off on their honeymoon.

She got ready for the journey alone. There were no sisters or bridesmaids to calm her nerves, no wedding dress to be helped into, no father to give her away — her father was dead — but no brother, either; Isaac Evans, like her sister Chrissey, was a hundred miles from London, and knew nothing about Mr Lewes. She had told no one about this day except her friends Charles Bray and John Chapman, who had lent her money for the journey. A secret elopement on borrowed funds was the sort of thing expected of a foolish seventeen-year-old. Marian Evans was not seventeen: she was thirty-four, and leaping into a new life. She was expectant, excited, nervous — what if he didn't come?

She left her Hyde Park lodgings with her belongings in a carpet bag and took a cab east through the city to St Katherine's Wharf, where the River Thames is very wide. They had arranged to meet on a steamer bound for Antwerp.

That night, in a lyrical mood, she marked the beginning of her marriage story in her diary. Their journey from London to the Continent was a 'perfect' passage into a 'lovelier' dawn — and also a passage from 'I' to 'we':

July 20th 1854.
I said a last farewell to Cambridge Street this morning and found myself on board the Ravensbourne, about ½ an hour earlier than a sensible person would have been aboard, and in consequence I had

20 minutes of terrible fear lest something should have delayed G. But before long I saw his welcome face looking for me over the porter's shoulder, and all was well. The day was glorious and our passage perfect . . . The sunset was lovely but still lovelier the dawn as we were passing up the Scheldt between 2 and 3 in the morning. The crescent moon, the stars, the first faint flush of the dawn reflected in the glassy river, the dark mass of clouds on the horizon, which sent forth flashes of lightning, and the graceful forms of the boats and sailing vessels painted in jet black on the reddish gold of the sky and water, made up an unforgettable picture. Then the sun rose and lighted up the sleepy shores of Belgium with their fringe of long grass, their rows of poplars, their church spires and farm buildings.

Life was merging with art: the crossing became a sequence of forms and colours, painted boats and skies shifting from day to night to day again. She was shifting too, not just an observer this time, but the figure at the centre of this 'unforgettable picture'.

Marian was also travelling through a literary landscape. Early in 1853 she had read Charlotte Brontë's new novel *Villette*, whose spirited heroine Lucy Snowe sails from London to Labassecour — a fictionalized Belgium — to begin a new life. She arrives in Villette in the middle of the night, finding a dreamlike town full of surprises, populated with faces from the past, like some region of the unconscious. In this uncanny, passionate place Lucy meets an eccentric little man who bears no resemblance to a romantic hero. They fall in love, but the world does not want them to marry. He is generous and kind; with extraordinary care he creates for her a life that is more truly her own. 'I am preparing to go to Labassecour,' Marian wrote elusively to Sara Hennell, her closest friend, a few days before she left England with Lewes.

Since she was a girl she had inhabited a world of books, which offered both refuge and adventure. She had taken lessons in German and Italian, taught herself Latin from a grammar book, and devoured thick volumes on history, philosophy, religion, art and science. The few books by female authors were novels, and novels were almost always about marriage. In 1852 she read Jane Austen's *Sense and Sensibility*, in which the challenge faced by the charming Dashwood sisters is to marry the right men. 'The Miss Dashwoods were young, pretty and unaffected . . . Elinor had a delicate complexion, regular features, and a remarkably pretty figure. Marianne was still handsomer ... her complexion was uncommonly brilliant; her features were all good; her smile was sweet and attractive.' Marianne Dashwood is sixteen, and believes that 'A woman of seven and twenty can never hope to feel or inspire affection again.' Like Austen's other stories, *Sense and Sensibility* depicts the brief, heady period in a young woman's life when she is conscious of her own power to shape her future — a power limited to accepting or rejecting a prospective husband, but nevertheless exhilarating.

Charlotte Brontë's novels also moved towards marriage, but they explored a different kind of challenge, closer to Marian's experience and rendered vivid by the intimate intensity of an autobiographical voice. Jane Eyre and *Villette*'s Lucy Snowe — plain, impoverished heroines more or less alone in a world made for prettier women — exist on the margins of eligibility, and do not feel entitled to hope for marriage. At eighteen Jane Eyre is clear-eyed and pure-hearted, accomplished and creative, yet she knows this is not enough. 'I sometimes regretted that I was not handsomer,' she confides to the reader — 'I sometimes wished to have rosy cheeks, a straight nose, and a small cherry mouth: I desired to be tall, stately and finely developed in figure; I felt it a misfortune that I was so little, so pale, and had features so irregular and so marked. And why had I these aspirations and regrets? It would be difficult to say: I could not then distinctly say it to myself; yet I had a reason, and a logical, natural reason too.'

Why does Jane Eyre, like so many women, want to be married? During the 1840s, when Brontë wrote the novel, radical voices were protesting that marriage deprived women of their legal right to own property, earn money, and keep custody of their children if they separated from their husbands. In 1854, the year Marian set sail to 'Labassecour', her friend Barbara Leigh Smith published *A Brief Summary, in Plain Language, of the Most Important Laws Concerning Women*, which explained that 'A woman's body belongs to her husband; she is in his custody.' Smith's fierce 'Remarks' on English marriage laws drew attention to the stark difference between single and married women: 'A woman of twenty-one becomes an independent human creature,' she wrote, 'But if she unites herself to a man, she finds herself legislated for, and her condition of life suddenly and entirely changed.

Whatever age she may be, she is again considered as an infant.' Having been 'courted and wedded as an angel', a wife is 'denied the dignity of a rational and moral being ever after.' When the philosopher John Stuart Mill prepared to marry Harriet Taylor in 1851, he had felt it his duty 'to put on record a formal protest against the existing laws of marriage'. This feminist husband made 'a solemn promise' never to use the controlling powers that would be conferred on him by law once Harriet became his wife.

Less progressive authors were also alert to the unequal dynamics between married couples. Sarah Stickney Ellis's popular guidebook for wives — dedicated to Queen Victoria — offered tips for dealing with husbands whose upbringing had nurtured 'their precocious selfishness' and accustomed them to 'the triumph of occupying a superior place'. Ellis counselled women to humour their husbands' egos. 'It is perhaps when ill, more than at any other time, that men are impressed with a sense of their own importance,' she observed sagely, and advised her readers 'to keep up this idea by little acts of delicate attention.' Any woman who had 'not yet crossed the Rubicon' into marriage should, Mrs Ellis urged, 'look the subject squarely in the face.' The longest chapter of her book is devoted to 'Trials of Married Life': most wives could expect to endure 'daily and hourly trials' of bad temper, idleness, profligacy, fussy eating and 'causeless and habitual neglect of punctuality'.

'"But why then,"' asks Ellis, ventriloquizing a young reader, '"all the fine talk we hear about marriage? and why, in all the stories we read, is marriage made the end of a woman's existence?" Ah! there lies the evil. Marriage, like death, is too often looked upon as *the end*; whereas both are but the beginning of states of existence infinitely more important than that by which they were preceded.'

Novels persistently portrayed marriage as a happy ending. Young female readers longed to be 'courted and wedded as an angel' — or, if already married, to reimagine this phase of life, so vibrant with possibility. Like Charlotte Brontë's heroines, Marian Evans struggled with these longings. She had read *Jane Eyre* in 1848, soon after it was published; then nearly thirty years old, she was, like Jane, conscious of falling far short of the feminine ideal. Though her figure was slender and graceful, she had a large manly nose, a long chin, 'evasive' grey-blue eyes, a formidable intellect and a brooding, sensitive disposition — a 'temperament of genius' as her friend Charles Bray put it.

All her life Eliot tended to transform thwarted desire and unspent anger into depression. In her early twenties she had 'felt a depression' that, as she wrote to her friend Maria Lewis, 'has disordered the vision of my mind's eye and made me *alive* to what is certainly a *fact* though my imagination when I am in health is adept at concealing it, that I am alone in the world.' At that time she was living with her father, and had several close friends; her loneliness revealed her longing for a husband. She could not quite say it outright. 'I mean,' she explained delicately, 'that I have no one who enters into my pleasures and my griefs, no one with whom I can pour out my soul, no one with the same yearnings the same temptations the same delights as myself.'

This need for intimacy was mixed with other yearnings, even harder to confess, for creative fulfilment. Throughout her twenties she had lived with the marriage question — not whom she *would* marry, but whether she *could* marry — hanging over her. This question seemed less an exhilarating uncertainty than an ominous cloud, growing heavier as the years went by.

*

Now she was with Lewes, and the sun was rising over Europe's 'sleepy shores'. But her marriage question, far from dissolving, had taken on a new and unexpected shape. Like Mr Rochester — Charlotte Brontë's first ugly, flawed, irresistible hero — Lewes had 'a wife still living' and could not divorce her, not least because divorces were prohibitively expensive. Agnes Lewes was no fiend locked in a gothic attic, but a pretty, plump, cheerful woman who had borne Lewes three sons, before having more children by his friend Thornton Hunt.

In 1853 Marian and Lewes had crossed paths in literary London; they became friends, then more than friends. Whatever the state of his marriage, *she* would be seen to be committing adultery if she lived openly with him. And for the Victorians, being seen to commit adultery was much worse than doing it in secret. Public transgressions not only humiliated those who were betrayed, but also — and this seemed to be the greater sin — threatened social codes of propriety.

When Jane Eyre contemplates her future with Mr Rochester after discovering, at the altar, that he is already married, she is resolute. Rochester begs her to travel abroad with him, but Jane chooses to wander into the cold night, homeless and heartbroken, rather than live unmarried with the man she loves. She is eventually rewarded with a large fortune, a blissfully happy marriage, and a baby boy with dark flashing eyes like Rochester's.

Marian disagreed with the marriage morality of *Jane Eyre*, and when she faced a similar decision she made the more radical choice. It was a cruel dilemma. Lewes offered a brighter future, and the daily companionship and affection she craved. He had chosen her; at last she could prove to the world that she was worth loving. But now the question of her worthiness would shift from her feminine charm to her moral character. The consequences of a public relationship with Lewes were uncertain, but she knew she might lose her friends. It would have been easier to defy convention if she was aristocratic, bohemian, insouciant — more like George Sand, in other words — and not a lower-middle-class woman from a conservative Anglican family, who harboured 'a desire insatiable for the esteem of my fellow creatures'.

Her resolve was strengthened by a new philosophy of marriage. During the first months of 1854, already involved with Lewes, she had translated Ludwig Feuerbach's *The Essence of Christianity* into English. This book argues that the union of a man and woman does not need a church or a priest, since natural human love is 'sacred in itself'. Like earlier generations of German Romantics, Feuerbach was inspired by a pantheist spirituality which refused to separate God from the world. He saw nature itself — and especially human nature — as divine, and he condemned narrow Christian moralism that treated sensual pleasure as unholy. 'Life as a whole is throughout of a divine nature. Its religious consecration is not first conferred by the blessing of a priest,' argued Feuerbach — and marriage should be 'the free bond of love,' not merely 'an external restriction'. This daring new philosophy made freedom and spontaneous love the essence of a 'truly moral' marriage.

'With the ideas of Feuerbach I everywhere agree,' Marian wrote to Sara Hennell at the end of April, as she completed her translation — but she did not tell her friend that she was planning to put these ideas into action. The book was published a couple of weeks before she set sail with Lewes, with her name beneath Feuerbach's on the cover, as if anticipating the censure to come by defiantly asserting her principles. Lewes was not desecrating marriage by leaving his legal wife, and she, Marian Evans, was not just running off with a married man. They were affirming a 'truly moral' radicalism.

And now she was entering an uncharted world. In this new dawn she was emerging as an unfamiliar, untested self — what kind of wife would she be? — and quite possibly renouncing her former life. Indeed, she had left more than one old life behind her.

*

She had turned sixteen in November 1835. A few months later her mother Christiana died after a long illness, probably breast cancer, and then her elder sister Chrissey left to marry a local man. Her brother Isaac, who had been her best friend and protector when they were children, was already living away from home in Birmingham. On Chrissey's wedding day Mary Anne and Isaac wept together 'over the break up of the old home-life'. They were mourning their mother as well as their beloved sister.

Mary Anne now became her father's chief companion, and mistress of Griff House, her childhood home in Warwickshire. As if to herald a shift in her identity, she altered the spelling of her name to Mary Ann. She was no longer a child; she was becoming a woman — and, at least in theory, eligible for marriage.

Though she had little control over her future, she was able to give literary shape to her inner life, chiefly in the form of letters to Maria Lewis, her former schoolteacher, a devout Christian and at that time her closest friend. Following Maria's example, she had become fervently religious. Her friend embodied one image of her own destiny: a spinster and a governess — a precarious profession, since the need for one's services was continually being outgrown. In 1839, aged nineteen, she sent Maria an inventory of her mental landscape: 'disjointed specimens from history, ancient and modern; scraps of poetry picked up from Shakespeare, Cowper, Wordsworth and Milton; newspaper topics; morsels of Addison and Bacon, Latin verbs, geometry,

Griff House

entomology and chemistry, reviews and metaphysics — all arrested and petrified and smothered by the fast-thickening, everyday accession of actual events, relative anxieties, and household cares and vexations.' Another day found her 'plunged in an abyss of books and preserves', snatching a few minutes in the midst of jam-making to write to her friend.

Her appetite for knowledge and ideas was voracious, yet the woman who would translate Spinoza's *Ethics*, edit the *Westminster Review* and write *Middlemarch* did not feel entitled to express her intellectual aspirations. Perhaps she was embarrassed by them. Confessing a desire makes a claim on the world — and surely only a woman grander, richer, or at least less plain could have the audacity to imagine herself becoming a great artist? Mary Ann did not tell anyone that she hoped to create an important work of philosophy, or that she wanted to be a writer, widely read and recognized for her genius.

Instead she approached these desires sideways, or in reverse. She could reveal her 'restless, ambitious spirit' only in reflecting on her failure to fulfil 'the duty of perfect contentment with such things as we have'. Nevertheless there was a grandeur to her half-spoken ambition, which protested against her 'walled-in world' by invoking Shakespeare, Carlyle, Wordsworth and Byron. Her sense of dwelling in 'a small room' that cramped her 'instinctive propensity to expand' often made her unhappy. Squandering her gifts in intensely literary letters to a Midlands governess clouded her heart with an anxiety she could not explain. Instead she made jokes to belittle herself, or wallowed guiltily in repressed frustration. 'I have a world more to say, and am very fertile in thoughts that like many greater productions are born to die in unregretted obscurity,' she wrote at the end of one letter to Maria — 'How is it that Erasmus could write volumes on volumes and multitudinous letters besides, while I whose labours hold about the same relation to his as an anthill to a pyramid or a drop of dew to the ocean seem too busy to write a few? A most posing query! Solved, after due thought, by the very recondite fact that your poor friend is considerably inferior in mental profundity, power and fertility to the said Erasmus.'

Stuck in her father's farmhouse, she internalized the constraints of her situation. Her letters to Maria played out an elaborate dialectical dance, offering a flash of her creative power in one sentence, before twisting and withdrawing into self-critique or self-mockery in the next. She denounced as 'ambition' her longing to exercise her talents. One day she sent Maria a melancholy sonnet mourning her childish pursuit of a sunlit future, where the grass seemed 'more velvet-like and green'. Her poem ended with a jaded glimpse 'Of life's dull path and earth's deceitful hope'. Not yet twenty, she was already aestheticizing disappointment, consigning her dreams to the past.

This disappointment was doubled by every glance in the mirror. Her disapproving reflection seemed to forbid even the ordinary feminine ambition to be fallen in love with, let alone her hidden hope to create something extraordinary. Finding a husband was a matter of making a home in the world, and she envisaged herself an outsider. On receiving news from Maria of a friend's imminent marriage, she cast herself as the Greek philosopher Diogenes the Cynic, a subversive performance artist who lived on the streets of ancient Athens in a clay barrel:

> When I hear of the marrying and giving in marriage that is constantly being transacted I can only sigh for those who are multiplying earthly ties which though powerful enough to detach their heart and thoughts from heaven, are so brittle as to be liable to be snapped asunder at every breeze. You will think I need nothing but a tub for my habitation to make me a perfect female Diogenes . . .

But she did not disdain marriage; on the contrary, she might have wanted it too much. Channelling her desires into an evangelical fervour, she found spiritual reasons to abstain from the 'earthly bliss' of human love. Perhaps others could 'live in near communion with God' while relishing 'all the lawful enjoyments the world can offer,' she wrote to Maria, 'but I confess that in my short experience and narrow sphere of action I have never been able to attain this; I find, as Dr Johnson said respecting his wine, total abstinence much easier than moderation.' Her complex, crowded sentences, blending earnestness and irony, evoke an inward struggle to keep desires deemed immoderate, unacceptable, under tight control.

In 1840 she was attracted to her tutor Joseph Brezzi, who taught her Italian and German: she found him 'anything but uninteresting, all external grace and mental power'. This plunged her into acute self-doubt and fear for the future, 'such a consciousness that I am a negation of all that finds love and esteem as makes me anticipate for myself — no matter what'. As she approached her twenty-first birthday, her sense of being excluded from marriage, and at odds with worldly ways, became less pious and more anguished. She remained painfully ambivalent, fearful of her own excessive passion:

> Every day's experience seems to deepen the voice of foreboding that has long been telling me, 'The bliss of reciprocated affection is not allotted to you under any form. Your heart must be widowed in this manner from the world, or you will never seek a better portion; a consciousness of possessing the fervent love of a human being would soon become your heaven, therefore it would be your curse.'

At a party she stood in a corner, unable to join in the dancing and flirting. Her head ached and throbbed, and by the end of the evening she had succumbed to 'that most wretched and pitied of afflictions, hysteria, so that I regularly disgraced myself'.

All this misery did not make her any more attractive to potential suitors. Through those years the possibility of marriage glowed and pulsed in her psyche, a danger zone, tantalizing and terrifying, exposing her longing for love and her dread of rejection.

*

Another fresh start came as she turned twenty-one and left her childhood home, moving with her father to a house near Coventry. Torn from her roots, she experienced this move as 'a deeply painful incident — it is like dying to one stage of existence.' But the new life that replaced the old one was more interesting, bringing new freedom and virtually a new family through friendship with Charles and Cara Bray, a wealthy couple who hosted many thinkers and artists at their home. They were rumoured to have an open marriage. Charles was chronically unfaithful and Cara, people said, was willing to promote her husband's happiness 'in any way that his wishes tend'.

In the Brays' cosmopolitan circle Mary Ann's talents were recognized and nurtured. Sara Hennell, Cara's clever, scholarly sister, became her closest confidante. Sara was a few years older, and unmarried; she shared Mary Ann's philosophical curiosity, her interest in religion, and her literary aspirations. Sara lived with her mother in Hackney, near London, and they exchanged frequent letters. Maria Lewis's predictable pious thoughts faded into the background as this new correspondence became Mary Ann's chief medium for exploring her ideas and feelings. Her sentences became more fluid and free. Writing to Sara, she could take her intellectual life seriously. 'I have had many thoughts,' she reported in one letter, 'especially on a subject that I should like to work out, "The superiority of the consolations of philosophy to those of (so-called) religion."'

Sara, who knew German, became Mary Ann's first collaborator. She helped her translate David Friedrich Strauss's monumental work *The Life of Jesus Critically Examined* — a task which took nearly two years, since the book was 1,500 pages long. As their intellectual and emotional intimacy grew, it formed the pattern for an ideal marriage. Mary Ann's letters addressed Sara as 'Dearly beloved spouse', or were signed 'Your loving wife'. For both women this intense friendship was a substitute

Sara Sophia Hennell, self-portrait

love affair. Usually apart, they looked forward to spending time together — 'I love thee and I miss thee,' she wrote to Sara in 1846.

Her freethinking Coventry friends and her wide reading quickly drew her to the conclusion that Christianity was based on 'mingled truth and fiction'. For a while she refused to go to church on Sundays. This angered her father, who made it clear that they had moved closer to town to improve her marriage prospects — a favour that would be withdrawn if she rebelled. She resumed her church-going, but marriage eluded her. The closest she came to finding a husband was in her twenty-fifth year, when a young artist who restored paintings for a living asked her to embark on a courtship. She said yes. 'She came to us so brimful of happiness,' Cara Bray wrote to Sara. Mary Ann 'had not fallen in love with him yet, but admired his character so much that she was sure she should.' Her only objection was that his profession was 'not lucrative or over honourable'.

Portrait of a young woman (with book), believed to be Mary Ann Evans,
and perhaps painted by the artist and picture restorer to
whom she was briefly engaged in 1845

Having rushed into this courtship, she rushed out of it. When she
saw her young man again a couple of days later, he 'did not seem to
her half so interesting as before.' The next day she concluded that 'she
could never love or respect him enough to marry him and that it
would involve too great a sacrifice of her mind and pursuits.' She
wrote to break it off, feeling guilty and upset, but her swift decision
when she thought her 'mind and pursuits' were threatened clarified
how much these things mattered. While she longed to be married —
and though her other prospects were wholly uncertain — she would
not compromise her literary ambitions.

The following year she wrote a satirical story about being proposed
to, merging these themes of mind and marriage that had clashed so deci-
sively during her engagement crisis. Her story took the form of a letter
to Charles Bray describing a surprise visit from a German scholar, Professor Bucherwurm of Moderig University,* author of a commentary on

* Professor Bookworm of Mouldy University

the Book of Tobit, a treatise on Buddhism, and 'a very minute inquiry' on an ancient Egyptian pharaoh. The professor has dirty skin and black teeth, and wears a threadbare coat. He hopes to write a new system of metaphysics — and is 'determined to secure a translator in the person of a wife'. The translator of Strauss's *Life of Jesus* seems an ideal match. Professor Buchenwurm explains that he requires,

> 'besides ability to translate, a very decided ugliness of person . . . After the most toilsome inquiries I have been referred to you, Madame, as presenting the required combination of attributes, and though I am rather disappointed to see that you have no beard, an attribute which I have ever regarded as the most unfailing indication of a strong-minded woman, I confess that in other respects your person at least comes up to my ideal.'

Mary Ann is surprised, 'having long given up all hope' of marriage. She accepts immediately — 'For you must know, learned Professor, that I require nothing more in a husband than to save me from the horrific disgrace of spinster-hood and to take me out of England.' She briskly sets out her terms:

> My husband must neither expect me to love him nor to mend his clothes, and he must allow me about once in a quarter a sort of conjugal saturnalia in which I may turn the tables upon him, hector and scold and cuff him. At other times I will be a dutiful wife so far as the task of translation is concerned.

She also vows to do her best to grow a beard. They consult her father, who consents, 'considering that it would probably be my last chance' — and so 'on Wednesday next I become the *Professorin* and wend my way to Germany — never more to appear in this damp atmosphere and dull horizon.'

Naturally, she has thought about clothes, and is planning a bridal look inspired by Joan of Arc: 'I have ordered a magnificent wedding dress just to throw dust into the eyes of the Coventry people, but I have gone to no further expense in the matter of trousseau, as the Professor prefers as a female garb a man's coat, thrown over what are justly called *petti*coats so that the dress of a woman of genius may present a symbolical compromise between the masculine and feminine attire.' She has asked Sara to be her bridesmaid, and hopes Charles will come to the wedding.

It is all there in three witty pages: her erudition, her scholarly accomplishments, her anxiety about looking masculine and *not* being beautiful, her wish to please her father, her sense of disgrace at being unwanted, her pleasure in intellectual companionship, her longing for new horizons, her defiant humour — all except love, which even in this fantasy she denies herself. The jaunty prose and brave self-mockery belie the old pathos: the marriage question still pressed upon her and now, entering her late twenties, time was running out.

*

She did not repeat her mistake with the picture restorer. The men she went on to fall more or less in love with were — like Sara Hennell — intellectuals who understood her ambitions and helped her to pursue them. Through the Brays she met John Chapman, a handsome young publisher who dealt in ideas, theories, philosophies. He published her translation of Strauss. In 1851 he acquired the *Westminster Review*, London's leading progressive journal, and invited Mary Ann to lodge in his house on the Strand and help him to edit it.

By then her father had died, leaving her a small income. She had travelled to the Continent with the Brays and stayed on alone in Geneva for a few months. She began to imagine making a living as a woman of letters. To mark her break from provincial life she changed her name to Marian Evans.

When she first moved into 142 the Strand, her intimacy with Chapman complicated an already fraught *ménage à trois* between the publisher, his wife, and his mistress. The other two women formed a brief alliance and she was cast out. But after this crushing start she was persuaded to return to Chapman's house — he needed her editorial skills — and settled into being his friend and colleague. He had opened the door to another new life, right at the heart of literary London.

At the *Westminster Review* she commissioned, edited and wrote reviews of new works of philosophy, science, history, politics, fiction and poetry. Soon she was effectively running the journal, holding its eminent contributors — and Chapman himself — to high standards.

She worked long hours, largely unpaid and unrecognized: at that time, articles and reviews were printed anonymously. Her admiring young colleague and fellow-lodger William Hale White later recalled how she spent her evenings correcting proofs, 'with her hair over her shoulders, the easy chair half sideways to the fire, her feet over the arms, in that dark room at the back of No. 142'. She conversed and corresponded, undaunted, with the most exciting thinkers of her generation.

Marian had moved on quickly from her short-lived romance with Chapman, but Herbert Spencer, a talented philosopher and editor of the *Economist* magazine — and promisingly unmarried — caused her deeper heartbreak. For several months they went out together all the time, to concerts, plays and the opera. In the spring of 1852 he wrote her a letter carefully explaining that he wanted no more than friendship, to which she equally carefully replied that she was not in the habit of imagining 'that anyone is falling in love with me'. Though she had read Pascal — who insisted that '*Le coeur a ses raisons*' — it was not so easy to learn her own heart's inner logic, which allowed hope to grow stubbornly, in spite of her protestations.

That summer, in a spiral of anxiety, she sent Spencer a passionate letter confessing her 'hopeless wretchedness' about him. 'I want to know', she wrote, 'if you can assure me that you will not forsake me, that you will always be with me as much as you can and share your thoughts and feelings with me.' If so, she would be 'always cheerful' and 'satisfied with very little' — rash promises, but she was desperate. 'Those who have known me best,' she told Spencer, 'have always said that if I loved anyone thoroughly my whole life must turn upon that feeling, and I find they said truly.' She did not ask him for marriage, or even for romance, but her own feelings were finally clear: 'If you become attached to someone else, then I must die, but until then I could gather the courage to work and make life valuable, if only I had you near me.'

She believed that her intellectual and creative powers rested on this relationship. Yet there was strength and even pride in her dependence. 'I suppose no woman ever before wrote such a letter as this — but I am not ashamed of it,' she declared, as if even in her desperation she perceived the beauty of a human heart that dares to open and reveal itself. This was not the sort of beauty Spencer was looking for. But despite finding the situation 'painful', he continued to see her as she asked. He even 'hinted at the possibility of marriage', though it would be 'without positive affection' on his part; 'this she at once saw would lead to unhappiness.' Perhaps to dilute the intensity of their time together, Spencer began to take his friend George Lewes along when he visited her.

She had known Lewes by reputation before meeting him, for the first time, in a tiny bookshop near Piccadilly Circus in the autumn of 1851. He had been in London for twenty years and was well known on the literary scene as a talented, prolific writer. He had published a book on the French philosopher Auguste Comte, a four-volume *Biographical History of Philosophy*, and numerous reviews and articles — on Goethe, on Spinoza, on Hegel. In 1850 he had co-founded the *Leader*, a radical weekly newspaper, with Thornton Hunt, the eldest son of Shelley's friend Leigh Hunt and, by then, Lewes's wife's lover. Lewes was also a playwright and amateur actor, and wrote a regular column for the *Leader* in the persona of 'Vivian', a bachelor, theatre critic and man about town. He lived 'in a whirl', as he put it, of 'manifold work and love of society.'

Lewes was both ambitious and pragmatic, and never seemed afraid to ask for what he wanted. As the illegitimate son of an absent father, he had made his own way in the world. Growing up, his family had moved around a lot, living in Jersey and Brittany as well as in London, and he attended several different schools. Instead of going to university he had apprenticed himself to Leigh Hunt and Thomas Carlyle, who regarded him as 'the Prince of journalists'. He became a friend of John Stuart Mill, William Thackeray and Charles Dickens. He spoke fluent French and had spent time in Paris, where he met the philosophers Victor Cousin and Auguste Comte, and the scandalous cross-dressing novelist George Sand. Vigorous, bright, tenacious, not inclined to doubt or nuance: his personality flowed into his literary style. Jane Carlyle found him 'the most amusing little fellow in the world', full of 'famous stories'. These virtues more than compensated for his 'immense ugliness' and his company was always sought in London's bohemian circles. Lewes was small and slight, 'whiskered and unkempt', with a face 'pitted from smallpox' and 'a lively audacious eye'. He had 'always preached a doctrine of free love — a sort of "we

Sketch of Agnes Lewes, George Lewes and Thornton Hunt by
William Thackeray, c. 1850

may each do as we like" morality', and according to London gossip 'he
certainly did very much as he liked'. With his scruffy charm, dubious
past, literary connections and bold ideas, he had a racy glamour.

When Marian and Lewes became friends, they were both struggling. She was heartbroken over Spencer, and he was in poor health
and low spirits, sunk in what he later described as 'a very dreary
wasted period of my life'. Lewes's wife Agnes was nursing her second
baby by Thornton Hunt; by 1853 Agnes had a third child from the
relationship, and Lewes had moved out of the family home. He felt a
special gratitude to Herbert Spencer: 'It was through him that I
learned to know Marian — to know her was to love her — and since
then my life has been a new birth.'

By the end of 1852 'Mr Lewes' was making regular appearances in Marian's letters to her friends in Coventry. She reported that her new friend was 'kind and attentive', 'a man of heart and conscience wearing a mask of flippancy'. She complained happily that his visits were distracting her from her work. When he fell ill she wrote his reviews for him. 'Mr Lewes has quite won my liking, in spite of myself' — and she liked the woman she became in his presence: loveable, desirable, needed, the kind of woman who makes a difference to a man's life. 'L'amour va son train,' Lewes wrote to a friend in the spring of 1853: by then, they were almost certainly a couple.

*

Apart from being irretrievably married, Lewes seemed perfect for her. Like Spencer, he was an original thinker; like Chapman he dealt in new ideas; like Sara Hennell he understood her aspirations and encouraged her pursuits. And like Marian, he was remarkable — 'a miracle', as one of their mutual friends put it: 'a most kindly, genial, guileless person, & with versatility & accomplishment'. He shared her intellectual appetite, her ferocious work ethic and her ambitious nature. He was also attractively different from her. While she was melancholy and earnest, he was cheerful and brazen; while she had grown up rooted in the Warwickshire countryside, his youth had been urban and itinerant. They were both steeped in Romanticism, but her hero was Wordsworth, with his spiritual reverence for Nature and Art, while Lewes followed Shelley's atheist gospel of free speech, free love, and radical politics.

Lewes also fulfilled her desire, expressed in her satirical sketch of Professor Bookworm, to travel to Germany. Lewes had visited the Continent several times, and their journey to 'Labassecour' was the beginning of a research trip for his half-written biography of Goethe. Partnership with this witty, sociable man, with his pioneering spirit and agile intelligence, exceeded the possibilities embodied yet withheld by Chapman and Spencer — though it was her friendship with Sara Hennell, more than those unrealized romances, that foreshadowed her life with Lewes, giving her a taste of shared projects and requited affection.

Marian had not chosen to remain alone for so long, but all those years without a husband produced a more varied experience of her own heart than most women gained before they married. Three years later, after she began to write fiction, she reflected that her years as a single woman with an elusive vocation had prepared her to do great work. Once again, intimate companionship and the life of the mind come together in her vision of fulfilment: 'I am very happy — happy in the highest blessing life can give us, the perfect love and sympathy of a nature that stimulates my own to healthful activity. I feel, too, that all the terrible pain I have gone through in past years has probably been a preparation for some special work that I may do before I die.' Those years were difficult, but her 'restless ambitious spirit' had been extremely successful in finding new life, wider vistas, more fertile soil. This spirit — and little else — had driven her forward, from Maria Lewis to Sara Hennell, from Spencer to Lewes; from Coventry to London, and on to the Continent.

On her wedding day a Victorian woman left behind her former selves, and the family that shaped them. Thirty years into her own marriage, long-suffering Jane Carlyle warned a young fiancée that marrying was 'a flying leap into infinite space'. At St Katherine's Dock Marian Evans had said goodbye to the walled-in girl at Griff House, the aspiring writer and philosopher in Coventry, the assertive unpaid editor of the *Westminster Review*. These shadow-selves would be waiting for her when she returned to England, clamouring to be redeemed and transfigured in her writing. But how her brother Isaac, her sister Chrissey, or Cara Bray and Sara Hennell — her adopted sister and her substitute spouse — would receive her back again was uncertain, since they had no idea she was going away with Lewes.

Years earlier, when she imagined donning a magnificent wedding dress to marry a grubby scholar who would 'take her out of England', she had made Sara her bridesmaid. Now she left her in the dark. All Sara possessed of Marian's future was a letter hinting about 'Labassecour' and one last scribbled note, addressed to her along with Cara and Charles: 'Dear Friends — all three, I have only time to say good bye and God bless you. Poste Restante, Weimar for the next six weeks, and afterwards Berlin.'

2

Honeymoon

Each morning she woke up, and Lewes was there. This unbroken intimacy was a new experience for her. From Antwerp they travelled east by train, stopping at Brussels, Namur, Liège and Cologne, staying a night or two in each place. They sailed south-east up the Rhine to Mainz, then on to Frankfurt, Goethe's birthplace.

There they spent a couple of days visiting works of art: two statues of Goethe; Julius Hübner's dramatic painting of Job; Cranach's portraits of Martin Luther and his wife. She was most moved by a white marble sculpture of Ariadne, abandoned lover of Theseus and wife of Dionysus. The artist, Johann von Dannecker, had spent eleven years making it. Ariadne was seated on a panther, perfectly poised, leaning forward and gazing ahead. She seemed determined, graceful, ready for the future, capable of anything. 'I never saw any sculpture equal to this,' Marian wrote in her diary: 'the feeling it excites is the essence of true worship — a bowing of the soul before power creating beauty.'

Late that afternoon they boarded a train: 'the second class carriage was so comfortable, and the weather so lovely after the morning rains.' They saw the sun set over the spires of Marburg before arriving in Weimar in the early hours of 3 August — two weeks after they had left England.

No tipsiness can be more dead to all appeals than that which comes from the fitful draughts of sleep on a railway journey by night. To the disgust of your wakeful companion, who has been smiling in envious pity upon you as you have stared wildly around at every stoppage of the train and then instantly sunk into dreamland again, you are totally insensible to the existence of your umbrella and to the fact that your carpet bag is stowed under your seat or that you have borrowed his books and have tucked them behind the cushion. 'What's the odds so long as one can sleep?' is your *formule de la vie*, and it is not till you have begun to shiver on the platform in the cool morning air that you are alive to propriety and to the necessity of keeping a fast grip upon it. Such was my condition when I reached the station at Weimar. The ride from thence to the town thoroughly roused me and as usual by the time I got into a bedroom I had no longer any desire for bed.

Marian was ready to be inspired. Magnificent ideas, art, literature had been born in this quiet town, and they were following a path trodden by other intellectual pilgrims — Romantic radicals who worshipped not the Catholic saints, but the miracle of Genius.

Goethe had settled in Weimar as a young man and remained there for nearly fifty years, until his death in 1832. They read an account of that time by Madame de Staël, the turban-wearing *femme de lettres* who conspired against Napoleon. Early in the nineteenth century she had travelled to Weimar to visit Goethe and Schiller, and encountered

Madame de Staël by Marie-Éléonore Godefroid, 1813

'devoted disciples' of art who spoke 'of the new literary works, as of the most important public events. They summoned the whole universe by reading and study; they broke free from the limits of circumstance through the expansion of thought.' Madame de Staël's imagination was 'constantly kept awake at Weimar by the conversation of poets'. Goethe himself, she enthused, was 'full of grace and philosophy ... even the defects of his character, moodiness, embarrassment, constraint, pass like clouds round the foot of that mountain, on the summit of which his genius is placed.'

Now Lewes was in pursuit of Goethe. Together they explored his grand house on Frauenplan in the centre of the town; Ottilie von Goethe, his daughter-in-law, allowed them into the study and bedroom, usually closed to visitors. 'Here our feelings were deeply moved,' wrote Marian, her imagination caught by relics of a literary life — a writing table, a bookcase, the small bedroom with its high writing desk and the armchair where Goethe 'used to sit and read while he drank his coffee in a morning'. In his library were 'bits of paper with philosophy history etc. written on them to mark the classifications of the books'. Here she 'breathed deeply', with tears in her eyes.

Whenever they walked up Schillerstrasse she was 'very much thrilled' to see the inscription *Hier wohnte Schiller** over the door of the little house once occupied by the great poet, philosopher, and friend of Goethe. Inside, she was again captivated by the study, with its writing desk by the window. This room also contained the poet's skull and 'an intensely interesting sketch of Schiller lying dead'.

They stayed in modest lodgings and watched their money carefully. Most of Lewes's literary earnings went straight to his wife Agnes and her children in London. But Thomas Carlyle had given Lewes a key to Weimar's high society: a letter of introduction to the Duchess of Weimar's private secretary, describing its bearer as 'ingenious, brilliant, entertaining, highly gifted and accomplished'. This gained them entry to Ottilie von Goethe's salon. They quickly befriended Franz Liszt, musical director at the Weimar court and a 'Grand Seigneur', Marian noted, within this elite circle. Liszt's romantic situation was not dissimilar to hers: he lived with Princess Carolyne von Sayn-Wittgenstein, a married

* Here lived Schiller

Roman Catholic who was separated from her husband. Marian recorded her 'startling' appearance: 'I had expected to see a tall distinguished looking woman, if not a beautiful one. But she is short and unbecomingly endowed with embonpoint; at the first glance the face is not pleasing, and the profile especially is harsh and barbarian, but the dark, bright hair and eyes give the idea of vivacity and strength. Her teeth, unhappily, are blackish too.' She was intrigued by Princess Carolyne's outfit: a white gauzy robe with an orange lining, a black lace jacket, and a 'piquant cap' trimmed with violet silk. As for Liszt — she felt 'genius, benevolence and tenderness beam from his whole countenance.' They were invited to his home, where they saw pianos once owned by Beethoven and Mozart, and a room 'filled with memorials of Liszt's triumphs and the worship his divine talent has won'.

When Liszt played the piano Marian watched him closely: 'I sat near him so that I could see both his hands and his face. For the first time in my life I beheld real inspiration — for the first time I heard the true tones of the piano. He played one of his own compositions — one of a series of religious *fantaisies* ... When the music expressed quiet rapture or devotion a sweet smile flitted over his features; when it was triumphant the nostrils dilated. There was nothing petty or egoistic to mar the picture.' She enthused about Liszt in her letters to London, as well as in her journal. He was 'the first really inspired man I ever saw,' she wrote to Charles Bray, a little star-struck: 'When I read George Sand's letter to Franz Liszt in her *Lettres d'un voyageur*, I little thought that I should ever be seated tête-à-tête with him for an hour, as I was yesterday.' Describing him to her friend Bessie Parkes, she implied a certain similarity to Lewes: 'Liszt is here, as you know ... He has that "laideur divinisée"* by the soul that gleams through it, which is my favourite kind of physique.'

*

These scenes of artistic inspiration — Liszt, Schiller, Goethe, Ariadne — posed a question for Marian: how might she make her own great work? Under what conditions could women, in particular, find

* Ugliness made divine

creative fulfilment? In Weimar that August she pursued this question in a long essay for the *Westminster Review*, titled 'Woman in France: Madame de Sablé'. It considered three recent studies of women by prominent male authors — Jules Michelet's *Les femmes de la Révolution*, Saint-Beuve's *Portraits de femmes*, and a big book on Madame de Sablé by Victor Cousin.

From 1655 until her death in 1678, Madame de Sablé hosted a philosophical salon in her apartment at the Port-Royal convent in Paris. The friend of Pascal, Arnauld and La Rochefoucauld, she was 'the animating spirit of a society whence issued a new form of French literature' — the *pensée* and the *maxime*, a reflective genre well suited to exploring the contradictions of the human psyche. Madame de Sablé and her friends spent hours debating the nature of *l'amour*. Her own *maxime* on this subject, written before La Rochefoucauld published his more celebrated collection of '*maximes morales*', defines love as the power that shapes and animates the human soul. Madame de Sablé saw love as a

Madeleine de Souvré, Marquise de Sablé

spiritual life force, the soul of the soul: 'Love, wherever it is, is always the master. Wherever it is found, it forms the soul, the heart and the mind . . . And it truly seems that love is to the soul of the person who loves, what the soul is to the body it animates.'

Meanwhile, at the Palais de Luxembourg, Anne Marie Louise d'Orléans, Duchesse de Montpensier, gathered her female friends to write 'portraits' of themselves and one another. These women described both physical and moral traits in fine detail — and 'from this pastime proceeded a complete literature.' They inspired Jean de la Bruyère to write his provocative *Caractères*, a collection of satirical portraits of his contemporaries published in 1688, borrowing its title from a similar book by the ancient Greek philosopher Theophrastus.

Marian was interested in the *salonistes* behind this literary innovation, so important for the development of the novel. She imagined them in their heavy silk gowns, huge sleeves billowing and soft hands stained with ink, 'great ladies transformed all at once into writers, and unconsciously inventing a new manner of writing, of which no book gave the slightest idea'. These were women who inspired men — and not simply as muses. She herself was among their literary heirs; she had written portraits of Liszt and Princess Carolyne in her journal.

What were the causes, Marian asked, of the 'earlier development and more abundant manifestation of womanly intellect' in France, compared with England or Germany? How had that country produced Madame de Sévigné, a great letter-writer, 'the single instance of a woman who is supreme in a class of literature which has engaged the ambition of men', and Madame de Staël, one of Michelet's *femmes de la Révolution*, whose name 'still rises first to the lips when we are asked to mention a woman of great intellectual power'? Her own favourite Frenchwoman, George Sand, was not only the most popular novelist of the early nineteenth century, but also 'the unapproached artist'.

While Marian saw no intellectual difference between men and women — 'Science', she declared, 'has no sex' — she believed that in literature, which demands the artist's 'entire being', women have 'something specific to contribute'. Women are physically, emotionally and psychologically different from men, she argued, yet it takes a certain kind of social order to allow these differences to be 'a source of variety and beauty' rather than grounds for inferiority.

One significant reason for the strong feminine influence in French literature and philosophy was, she concluded boldly, France's notorious 'laxity of opinion and practice with regard to the marriage-tie'. With more than a hint of irony, she presented this as the happy consequence of a regrettable state of affairs:

> Heaven forbid that we should enter on a defence of French morals, most of all in relation to marriage! But it is undeniable that unions formed in the maturity of thought and feeling, and grounded only in an inherent fitness and mutual attraction, tended to bring women into more intelligent sympathy with men, and to heighten and complicate their share in the political drama . . . Gallantry and intrigue are sorry enough things in themselves, but they certainly serve better to arouse the dormant faculties of women than embroidery and domestic drudgery.

Romantic suffering, too, could enrich a woman's soul. The prolific *vies amoureuses* of Madame de Staël and George Sand showed, no less than Goethe's love affairs, how 'the very sorrows — the heart-pangs and regrets which are inseparable from a life of passion' — deepen a woman's nature 'by the questioning of self and destiny which they occasioned, and by the energy demanded to surmount them and live on'.

Surely Marian was not thinking only of 'Woman in France', but recalling her own 'intrigues' and 'heart-pangs' over past loves. Perhaps she was anticipating more sorrows to come. Her future with Lewes was, after all, uncertain and insecure. Back in England, John Chapman and Charles Bray were wondering how long he would stay with her.

Drawing on her experience of Weimar society — and its contrast with boring English dinner parties — Marian praised European salons where men and women talked together as intellectual equals. At the gatherings hosted by Madame de Sablé and the Duchesse de Montpensier, men did not 'first lay themselves out to entertain the ladies with a grimacing "small-talk", and then take each other by the sword-knot to discuss matters of real interest in a corner'. These women were allowed to be 'intelligent observers of characters and events'. Female authors flourished in France, she explained, 'by being admitted to a common fund of ideas, to common objects of interest with men'. *This* was the essential condition not only of 'true womanly culture', but also of 'true social well-being' for all.

Her *Westminster Review* essay ended with a rallying cry to readers back home:

> Let the whole field of reality be laid open to woman as well as to man, and then that which is peculiar in her mental modification, instead of being, as it is now, a source of discord and repulsion between the sexes, will be found to be a necessary complement to the truth and beauty of life. Then we shall have that marriage of minds which alone can blend all the hues of thought and feeling into one lovely rainbow of promise for the harvest of human happiness.

She might be forgiven this utopian rainbow, blending thought and feeling, for something like it hung over those days in Weimar, as late summer passed into a golden autumn and she harvested her long-awaited happiness. She wrote to Charles Bray with news of her 'exquisite enjoyment', and her sense of having 'begun life afresh'. In her letter to Bessie Parkes she expressed both contentment and excitement: 'I am beginning to have that calm autumn feeling which has never failed to come at this season in my least happy years. This is a happy one — full of the seeds of future activity, in spite of age and grey hairs.' And how gratifying it was to tell John Chapman, her old flame, that 'I am happier every day and find my domesticity more and more delightful and beneficial to me. Affection, respect, and intellectual sympathy deepen, and for the first time in my life I can say to the moments "Verweilen sie, sie sind so schön.*"' Together, Marian and Lewes faced their future 'with new ambitions and new powers'.

*

Writing her essay on Madame de Sablé while Lewes worked on his biography of Goethe, they fell into a daily rhythm they would maintain for many years — writing in the morning, walking in the afternoon, and reading aloud to one another in the evening, if they were not out at a concert or dining with their glamorous new friends. Some nights they looked at Lewes's manuscript; on other evenings they read *Elective Affinities*, Goethe's experimental novel about illicit love. They might

---

* 'Let them last, they are so beautiful' — a quotation from Goethe's *Faust*.

not be legally married, but they enjoyed a 'marriage of minds' as they read and talked and walked together through the park in Weimar, along the River Ilm, 'overarched by tall trees, through which the golden sunlight played and chequered the path before us'. At the end of November she wrote up her recollections of those honeymoon weeks in the back of her journal: 'Dear Park of Weimar! In 1854, two loving happy human beings spent many a delicious hour in wandering under your shade and in your sunshine, and to one of them at least you will be a "joy for ever" through all the sorrows that are to come.'

Already she felt the shadow side of their happiness, the cloud gathering across their honeymoon. Scandal and shame lurked at a distance, as disapproving gossip back home was conveyed by letters from their friends. John Chapman and Charles Bray — the only people who knew she was with Lewes — were fending off questions about her. For a few weeks that autumn it seemed as if the finest Victorian minds were occupied with her sex life. Marian and Lewes were doing something unspeakable, and moral indignation gave everyone an excuse to talk about it. The very heat of the outrage suggests that overt moralizing was fuelled by covert prurience — as when modern tabloids censure celebrity affairs while feasting on the salacious details. George Combe, the famous Edinburgh phrenologist, was aghast. He had taken a paternalistic interest in Marian since meeting her at Bray's house: he had examined her 'very large brain', and found her 'extremely feminine and gentle' as well as the cleverest woman he had ever seen. 'We are deeply mortified and distressed,' Combe wrote to Bray, and inquired 'whether there is insanity in Miss Evans's family; for her conduct, with *her* brain, seems to me like morbid mental aberration.'

In Chelsea, Thomas Carlyle was also vexed. He thought Lewes was quite right to leave his unfaithful wife, who 'deserved it' — but there were mysterious reports of a letter from Marian Evans to the writer Harriet Martineau being passed around the Reform Club. Carlyle wrote to Lewes asking him 'to contradict, if he could, on his word of honour, the bad rumours circulating about a certain "strong minded woman" and him'. He was not impressed by Lewes's reply. Lewes confirmed that the letter to Miss Martineau was 'a pure, or impure, fabrication', yet avoided the substantive issue of his relationship with Miss Evans. 'On all private matters,' he told Carlyle, 'my only answer is *silence*.'

Meanwhile literary London was pressing Chapman for information, and he wondered what he should say. Answering him, Marian became haughty in her own defence, her sentences shrinking to a crystalline formality that barely contains her fury:

> I am sorry that you are annoyed with questions about me . . . About my
> own justification I am entirely indifferent . . . The phrase 'run away' as
> applied to me is simply amusing — I wonder what I had to run away
> from . . .
>
> You ask me to tell you what reply I should give to inquiries. I have
> nothing to deny or conceal. I have done nothing with which any person
> has a right to interfere. I have surely full liberty to travel in Germany, and
> to travel with Mr Lewes. No one here seems to find it at all scandalous
> that we should be together . . . But I do not wish to take the ground of
> ignoring what is unconventional in my position. I have counted the cost
> of the step that I have taken and am prepared to bear, without irritation
> or bitterness, renunciation by all my friends. I am not mistaken in the
> person to whom I have attached myself. He is worthy of the sacrifice
> I have incurred, and my only anxiety is that he should be rightly judged.

Declaring herself 'entirely indifferent' to her own reputation, she fiercely defended Lewes. He was 'in constant correspondence' with his wife, she explained, and 'nervously anxious' about the welfare of his children. She had seen Lewes's letters to Agnes, which confirmed that he had been honest with her about their marriage; she found his 'conduct as a husband in the highest degree noble and self-sacrificing.' Revealing that their future together had been undecided when they left England, she alluded to new 'circumstances', not involving her, that had made Lewes 'determine on a separation' from his wife. This probably meant that Agnes was pregnant by Thornton Hunt for a fourth time.

A week later she wrote a similar letter to Charles Bray, repeating this account of Lewes's relations with Agnes and emphasizing his generosity towards his family. She closed with a stiff little paragraph about Cara Bray and Sara Hennell — to whom she had not yet written, though they had both written to her:

> I am ignorant how far Cara and Sara may be acquainted with the state
> of things, and how they may feel towards me. I am quite prepared to

accept the consequences of a step which I have deliberately taken and
to accept them without irritation or bitterness. The most painful consequence will, I know, be the loss of friends. If I do not write, therefore,
understand that it is because I desire not to obtrude myself.

Her words were grown-up and perfectly articulated; her unwritten
feelings were not so far from a child's dread of withdrawn love. In
fact, the sisters were more upset by her silence towards them than by
her 'running away' with Lewes. Clever, empathic Cara had seen Marian rush into entanglements with several men, not all of them single.
Having received enthusiastic letters about 'Mr Lewes' in recent
months, she must have guessed they were now a couple. Yet she had
responded to an inquiry from George Combe's wife with a cool dis-
missal of rumours about her friend — 'We have not heard of anything
dreadful happening to Miss Evans,' she wrote to Mrs Combe; Marian
had simply 'travelled to Weimar under Mr Lewes's escort'.

Sara answered Marian's indirect question about 'how they may feel
towards me' with a hurt, angry letter accusing her of 'boasting' about
how serenely she could give up their friendship. This letter arrived in
Weimar on the last day of October, and so consumed Marian that she
wrote nothing in her journal that day. Her passionate reply to Sara
bears no trace of the wary stoicism she had expressed to Charles Bray.
Instead she explained how much she needed her friends:

When you say that I do not care about Cara's or your opinion and
friendship it seems much the same to me as if you said that I didn't care
to eat when I was hungry or to drink when I was thirsty. One of two
things: either I am a creature without affection, on whom the memories
of years have no hold, or, you, Cara and Mr Bray are the most cherished friends I have in the world . . . I wish to speak simply and to act
simply but I think it can hardly be unintelligible to you that I shrink
from writing elaborately about private feelings and circumstances. I
have really felt it a privation that I have been unable to write to you
about things not personal, in which I know you would feel a common
interest, and it will brighten my thoughts very much to know that I
may do so. Cara, you and my own sister are the three women who are
tied to my heart by a cord which can never be broken and which really
pulls me continually . . .

I have written miserably ill, and I fear all the while I am writing that I may be giving rise to some mistake. But interpret my whole letter so as to make it accord with this plain statement — I love Cara and you with unchanged and unchangeable affection, and while I retain your friendship I retain the best that life has given me next to that which is the deepest and gravest joy in all human experience.

Marian Evans.

If this was a difficult letter to write, it was also difficult to receive. While Marian declares her love for Sara, she also reminds her that she is no longer her confidante, and no longer her closest friend. Her final sentence insists that her affection is unchanged, yet spells out precisely what *has* changed: their friendship is now in second place to a new intimacy which brings 'the deepest and gravest joy in all human experience' — a superior happiness that her unmarried friend cannot understand.

For Marian's birthday on 22 November, Sara sent a warm letter signed 'Your ancient friend', which restored peace. Sara's birthday was the day after hers; this year Marian was thirty-five and Sara forty-two. They had often celebrated this auspicious 'junction' together, but perhaps their stars were not so aligned as they had once believed.

Sara praised the 'elegance and profundity' of the essay on Madame de Sablé she had read in the October issue of the *Westminster Review*, and guessed that Marian had written it. This issue of the *Westminster* also contained a 'disgraceful' review of the Feuerbach translation, on which they had collaborated earlier that year — 'But all these things are ante-diluvian to you,' added Sara, making a joke of it. It was only five months since she had helped her friend finish the Feuerbach book, but she knew how much had changed. Marian, with her biographer of Goethe and her new European connections, had entered a different epoch of her life — and Sara, her 'ancient friend', suddenly belonged to a distant past. 'Your letter to Charles today seems to show you very happy now,' she wrote — 'But I have a strange sort of feeling that I am writing to someone in a book, and not to the Marian that we have known and loved so many years. Do not mistake me, I mean nothing unkind.'

*

By this time Marian and Lewes had moved on to Berlin, and were settled in lodgings on Dorotheenstrasse, between Unter den Linden and the River Spree. As in Weimar, they lived cheaply among piles of books and mixed with interesting people. 'We rise at eight; after breakfast read & work till between one & two; walk in the Tiergarten or pay visits till dinner, which is at 3; come home to coffee, and, when not at the theatre or in society Miss Evans reads Goethe aloud to me & I read Shakespeare aloud to her,' Lewes reported to their new friend, Princess Carolyne.

Here Marian's most memorable encounter was with Christian Rauch, a distinguished German sculptor, whom she thought 'the finest old man I ever saw'. At Rauch's atelier she was fascinated by his works in progress. This was a different experience from marvelling at a finished work, like Ariadne, or communing with the remnants of finished lives, like those of Goethe and Schiller. She was drawn to the 'little clay models' that prepared the way for immense works of art: here were human forms emerging, searching, half-made, responding to the artist's call. Rauch had been commissioned to create a towering statue of Immanuel Kant — whom he had met in 1789 — to send to Königsberg, the philosopher's native city, and he was working on a small prototype. 'My heart leaped,' she wrote, 'at the sight of old Kant's quaint figure.'

On 8 November, within a week of arriving in Berlin, she had embarked on a new intellectual adventure: translating Baruch Spinoza's *Ethics*. Spinoza was Madame de Sablé's contemporary, though they moved in very different circles. During the 1660s and 70s, while the *saloniste* was penning her elegant maxims, Spinoza lived frugally in obscure lodgings in Leiden and The Hague, earning his living as a lens-grinder. It took him at least nine years to write the *Ethics*. Though he was quiet and modest, his pursuit of truth made him a troublemaker. As a young man he was expelled from his Jewish community in Amsterdam; after he died in 1677, leaving his *Ethics* to be published posthumously by his devoted circle of friends, the Catholic Church added his works to its Index of prohibited books. For the next hundred years Spinoza was widely denounced as a heretic and atheist.

Late in the eighteenth century, philosophers and poets in Weimar and Berlin seized on the *Ethics*, thrilled by its claim that God is not separate from nature, that everything is in God. Madame de Staël described how Spinozism offered a new religious possibility: human feeling, desire, creativity were not sinful but natural, with 'a philosophical meaning and a religious aim'. For the Romantics, 'the love of beauty, the elevation of the soul, the joys of devotion' were signs of God within us: 'when the existence of man is expansive, it possesses something divine.' This idea guided Feuerbach's belief that human love is sacred, needing no consecration by official marriage rites.

Spinoza's *Ethics* could have offered Sara Hennell a metaphysical explanation, had she wanted one, for the deep changes in her friend's life. This book — the greatest work of European philosophy since Plato's *Republic* — shows that our lives are thoroughly interconnected, always parts of larger wholes. According to Spinoza, human beings are not discrete, self-sufficient substances, as Descartes had thought, but amorphous, impressionable 'modes' that are continually being formed by their encounters and relationships. Marian's experience bore this out: her new partner, new experiences and new milieu were making her a new person. Translating the *Ethics*, she learned that if two like-minded people live together, they will become 'a double individual more powerful than the single'.

Spinoza was already an important part of Marian and Lewes's shared history. They had both read him closely in the 1840s — she questioning her faith, he confirmed in his atheism, both of them welcoming Spinoza's critique of moralistic doctrines that figured God as a kind of super-human judge who rewards good behaviour with a place in heaven and punishes sinners with the torments of hell. Long before they knew one another, the same currents of radicalism and Romanticism, channelled from Germany to England by Carlyle and Coleridge, had delivered Spinoza's works into their eager hands.

During his youth Lewes discovered Spinoza's philosophy in a dark, smoky pub in Holborn, where he used to meet with other intellectuals to exchange new ideas. In 1843 he wrote an article on Spinoza for the *Westminster Review*, one of the first sympathetic accounts of the philosopher to be published in English. Like the Romantics, Lewes presented Spinoza as an intensely religious thinker who 'sees in the universe nothing but the manifestation of God.' All this was too metaphysical for Lewes himself, a strict empiricist as well as an atheist. But he admired Spinoza as the bold freethinker who had shaped modern German thought. His biography of Goethe describes the great poet's 'reverence' for Spinoza as 'one of his best teachers', and shows how Goethe drew a 'poetical Pantheism' from Spinoza's austere system.

The *Ethics* had been translated from Latin into German and French, but not English. Lewes saw an opportunity: he secured an agreement with the London publisher Henry Bohn to produce the first English edition. Marian would do the translation, and this would bring them a much-needed £75. She began work on it a few days after they arrived in Berlin, while Lewes pressed on with Goethe. The city was cold and already snowy in November, but, she informed Charles Bray, 'we work hard in the mornings till our heads are hot, then walk out, dine at three and, if we don't go out, read diligently aloud in the evening. I think it is impossible for two human beings to be more happy in each other.'

Their intellectual labours were entwined more closely than ever. When they walked together in the Tiergarten each afternoon, they compared notes on the morning's studies. She read Jacobi's *Letters on Spinoza*, which, as Lewes noted in his biography, had influenced Goethe. One day they took 'a delightful two hours' walk in the frosty air towards Charlottenburg', and talked about Spinoza. As she rendered his dense, intricate Latin text into elegant English prose, Lewes developed his own interpretation of Goethe's dynamic Spinozism:

> Science tells us that the world is always becoming. Creation continues. The world was not made, once and forever, as a thing completed, and afterwards serenely contemplated. The world is still a-making. The primal energies of Life are as young and potent as of old, issuing forth under new forms through metamorphoses higher and ever higher, as dawn broadens into day.
>
> Goethe's religion was eminently concrete, and devout in its worship of realities. He believed in fact; he thought reality in itself holier than any fiction could make it. Human nature was to him a holy fact, and man's body a temple of holiness. This is Hellenic, but its kinship with Spinoza's system is obvious. Spinoza had no sympathy with those

philosophers who deride or vilify human nature: in his opinion it was better to try to understand it . . . And this did Goethe. He strove above all things to understand Fact, because fact was divine manifestation.

Here Lewes's positivist zeal moulds — and somewhat flattens — both Spinoza and Goethe in accordance with his own devotion to 'Fact'. He was right, however, to observe that the *Ethics* urges its readers to understand themselves. Spinoza explains that human beings, like all finite things, constantly strive to continue existing. We want to be ourselves, to flourish, to express our true nature. While God is an eternal fullness of being, our existence always fluctuates, sometimes growing stronger and sometimes waning — and our emotions are the feeling of this fluctuation. This means that understanding our emotions gives us knowledge of our existence. Joy, as Spinoza defined it, is the feeling of an increase in power, while sadness or depression is the feeling of diminished power. Rejecting the traditional Christian values of humility and pity, Spinoza argued that expressing our powers of acting, thinking and making naturally brings joy, an infallible sign that we are living well. And because we are always dependent on others, we flourish best among people who help us to cultivate our powers, and to see our thoughts and feelings more clearly.

As Marian translated the *Ethics* she discovered a philosophy of dependence and empowerment that perfectly reflected her situation. Being free, Spinoza explained, does not mean being autonomous or self-sufficient. On the contrary, free human beings 'are united to each other by a great need of friendship'. Though Spinoza never married, he cautiously approved of marriage so long as 'the love of both the man and the woman is not excited by physical attraction alone, but is chiefly caused by freedom of soul.' Spinoza's philosophy also shows why a partnership might diminish our power, rather than enhance it. Our porous boundaries and susceptibility to influence can be both a blessing and a curse.

One day Lewes was unwell, and Marian wrote in her diary that this 'makes us melancholy', as if they were one body, afflicted with the same pain. Sharing their thoughts, absorbing each other's ideas and emotions, their minds grew together.

*

Lewes bore witness to their double life in the chapter of his biography devoted to *Elective Affinities*, which they had read together in Weimar. In Goethe's hands, Spinoza's rational analysis of human relationships was transformed into a tragic mess. *Elective Affinities* tells the 'painful story' of a marriage torn apart by desire for other people, likened to an attraction that binds chemical elements into new compounds. Lewes judged it comparable to 'the masterpieces of Miss Austen', yet he felt impatient with its detailed descriptive passages and regretted Goethe's 'expanding the *novella* into a novel'. Marian disagreed, and Lewes invited readers to consider her opinion: 'A dear friend of mine, whose criticism is always worthy of attention, thinks that the long episodes which interrupt the progress of the story . . . are artistic devices for impressing the reader with a sense of the slow movement of life; and, in truth, it is only in fiction that the dénouement usually lies so close to the exposition.'

Elective Affinities is morally ambiguous on the conflict between duty and passion. 'When critics rail at it, and declare it saps the whole foundation of marriage, and when critics enthusiastically declare it is profoundly moral because it sets the sacredness of marriage in an entirely clear light,' wrote Lewes, 'they have done no more than put *their* interpretations on what the author had no intention of being interpreted at all.' Goethe was, he insisted, 'an Artist, not an Advocate': he dealt with truth rather than judgement, permitting readers to draw 'those opposite conclusions which might be drawn from reality itself'.

Reading and discussing Goethe with Lewes, Marian was forming her thoughts about how to render life in art. Her own world was, in Lewes's words, 'still a-making'. In their Berlin lodgings and on their walks through the city, their shared life was daily reshaped by books and conversation, spinning between German, English, French and Latin, and inspired by Spinoza and Goethe, two of the most expansive minds European history had produced. In this wide, sparkling intellectual landscape she could gather her creative powers.

Three years later, filled with excitement and apprehension that her first work of fiction was in press, she would recall these honeymoon days with Lewes. For many years — at least since the 1840s — she had contemplated writing a novel, but had got no further than an 'introductory chapter' describing a Staffordshire village. She had

George Henry Lewes, 1850s–1860s

taken this chapter with her to Germany — it just 'happened to be among the papers I had with me', she explained airily. One night in Berlin she read it aloud to Lewes.

His verdict was disappointingly lukewarm. 'He was struck with it as a bit of concrete description, and it suggested to him the possibility of my being able to write a novel, though he distrusted, indeed disbelieved in, my possession of any dramatic power.' But sharing these treasured pages brought her dream into their shared world, where it gained a fuller reality. 'Still, he began to think that I might as well try, some time, what I could do in fiction, and by and bye when we came back to England and I had greater success than he had ever expected in other kinds of writing, his impression that it was worthwhile seeing how far my mental power would go towards the production of a novel, was strengthened. He began to say very positively, "You must try and write a story."'

3

Sanctity

Before Lewes, both marriage and art were distant objects of longing. Marian had imagined the blurred outlines of an elusive husband, and cherished a 'vague dream' to write a novel. Now these things were the elements of her existence, like water, like air, and they posed insistent questions. When would she begin her novel, and what would it be? Would she ever become Mrs Lewes in the eyes of her family and friends? How could she write herself into being as an author and a wife?

By the summer of 1855 they were settled in rented rooms in East Sheen, a village near Richmond on the south bank of the Thames, 'writing hard, walking hard, reading Homer and science and rearing tadpoles'. Their lodgings were small and they worked in the same room; Lewes's scratching pen 'nearly drove her wild'. They let the neighbours assume they were married, and she asked her friends to address their letters to 'G. H. Lewes Esq'. In the autumn they moved to lodgings in the centre of Richmond.

Now they were back in England, Marian was no longer considered a suitable guest at parties and dinners. Her friendships with women shifted according to their attitudes to her new life with Lewes. Her younger, progressive friends Bessie Parkes and Barbara Leigh Smith accepted her situation warmly, and became close confidantes. Bessie, a poet, was the daughter of radical Unitarians. Barbara, a painter and activist, came from a wealthy family of reformers, and had a striking bohemian style. She wore loose simple clothes, refusing to follow the fashion for crinoline, corsets and ribbons.

Marian still corresponded with Sara Hennell, but they had less in common than before. Her relationship with Cara Bray was differently altered. Cara, the wife of an unfaithful man, had reason to be sensitive to the threat posed by women willing to sleep with other people's husbands. Perhaps she thought men were unable to resist the temptation to stray, if given the opportunity. Writing to Cara in September 1855, Marian defended herself: 'if there be any one subject on which I feel no levity it is that of marriage and the relation of the sexes — if there is any one action or relation of my life which is and always has been profoundly serious, it is my relation to Mr Lewes.' Her views on this 'momentous subject' were, she insisted, 'truly moral' — yet she was ostracized while secret infidelities went unpunished. 'Light and easily broken ties are what I neither desire theoretically nor could live for practically. Women who are satisfied with such ties do *not* act as I have done — they obtain what they desire and are still invited to dinner.'

Her letter to Cara explored the rift between them — 'how difficult it is to produce a true impression by letters, and how likely they are to be misinterpreted even where years of friendship might seem to furnish a sufficient key.' She was angry that Cara had not used this 'key'

Cara Bray, watercolour by her sister Sara Hennell

to understand her new life, though she expressed her fury by disavowing it: 'I indulge in no arrogant or uncharitable thoughts about those who condemn us, even though we might have expected a somewhat different verdict. From the majority of persons, of course, we never looked for anything but condemnation.' Cast out of respectable society, she retaliated by excluding Cara from the small circle who could discern her life's moral truth. Cara's disapproval, she implied, placed her among the conventional 'majority' who could not be expected to comprehend her 'relation to Mr Lewes'.

Yet her initiation into marriage also made her feel closer to Cara, better able to understand her life. The following year, she returned to the metaphor of an interpretative key after receiving a 'sweet letter' from her old friend, which was, she replied warmly, 'really something my soul thirsted for'. Now 'the key' was something they shared:

> I think we are nearer to each other than we could ever have been before, for I am able to enter into your feelings and understand your life so much better. It is a great experience — this marriage! and all one's notions of things before seem like the reading of a mystic inscription without the key.
>
> I can't tell you how happy I am in this double life which helps me to feel and think with double strength. I shouldn't say these things unless I loved you very dearly, as I do.
>
> Ever your old
> yet new
> Marian

This letter claims marriage — an 'experience' rather than a legal, social, public matter — as something she and Cara have in common. In declaring herself 'able to enter' Cara's feelings, holding the key to the meaning of her life, she asks her friend to use this same key to enter into *her* inner life — and not to see her as an outcast, a trespasser, a thief. Marian wanted Cara to receive her on the hallowed ground of marriage, to 'read' her as a wife.

*

While she reflected on marriage in her personal letters, her public writing turned to the subject of art — that other sacred thing. When they returned from Germany in the spring of 1855, John Chapman had asked her to take on the *Westminster Review*'s poetry and fiction pages. She had also begun to write regular reviews for the *Leader*. She was becoming versatile, like Lewes: she wrote pieces on Carlyle and Goethe, on Greek drama and German mythology, on Ruskin's *Modern Painters*, on feminist works by Margaret Fuller and Mary Wollstonecraft, on the poetry of Milton, Young, Gruppe and Heine, and on new work by Matthew Arnold, Alfred Tennyson, Robert Browning. She had left England an editor and translator, and returned a professional writer and critic.

In her diary she carefully recorded her literary earnings and added up the totals: £119 and 8 shillings for 1855. That year Lewes earned £430, including £250 for *The Life and Works of Goethe*, which came out in the autumn. Marian sent a copy to Charles Bray: 'I can't tell you how I value it,' she told him, 'as the best product of a mind which I have every day more reason to admire and love.' The biography sold well and received enthusiastic reviews, though some English critics complained that Lewes refused to condemn Goethe's womanizing.

Marian shared Lewes's tolerant view of Goethe. She disagreed with readers who demanded moralizing attitudes from literature — especially now she was confronting such attitudes in her life. Reviewing a new English translation of Goethe's *Wilhelm Meister's Apprenticeship*, she declared that this controversial novel 'appears immoral to some minds because its morality has a grander orbit than any which can be measured by the calculations of the pulpit and of ordinary literature.' Reviving an argument that stretches back to Plato's *Republic*, she shone philosophy's fierce light on conventional mores, exposing them as petty, partial, and blind to a 'grander' moral vision.

At the end of her review these reflections veer from literature to life. Only a few people, she suggests,

> are taught by their own falls and their own struggles, by their experience of sympathy, and help and goodness in the 'publicans and sinners' of these modern days, that the line between the virtuous and vicious, so far from being a necessary safeguard to morality, is itself an immoral fiction.

She was by now halfway through the translation of Spinoza's *Ethics* she had begun in Berlin, and its critique of moralistic religion had crystallized her thinking. Echoing Spinoza, Marian informed readers of the *Westminster Review* that a moral system based on rewards and punishments — whether human or divine — 'undermines all true moral development by perpetually substituting something extrinsic as a motive to moral action, instead of the immediate impulse of love or justice, which alone makes an action truly moral'.

Her review of *Wilhelm Meister* applied these insights to literary moralism. She dismissed 'the so-called moral *dénouement*', in which a novel's characters are rewarded or punished according to some presumed moral code. As a reader, she disliked bossy authors who pronounced judgement on their characters — 'We don't want a man with a wand, going about the gallery and haranguing us. Art is art, and tells its own story.' Yet she believed that literature could — and should — teach virtue by refining and enlarging moral perceptions. Goethe led his readers by example: looking at the world through his tolerant eyes, their own vision would expand. 'Every great artist is a teacher,' she declared, 'by giving us his own higher sensibility as a medium, a delicate acoustic or optical instrument, bringing home to our coarser senses what would otherwise be unperceived.'

She was honing her philosophy of art. 'In making clear to ourselves what is best and noblest in art, we are making clear to ourselves what is best and noblest in morals,' she wrote in the *Westminster Review* in the spring of 1856. Like the pre-Raphaelite painters, she was inspired by John Ruskin's 'realism' — 'the doctrine that all truth and beauty are to be attained by a humble and faithful study of nature'. She argued that art should 'amplify' experience rather than invent or falsify it, just as Ruskin urged artists not simply to copy what they observed, but to 'come between this nature and me, temper it for me, interpret it for me.'

Marian fused this new realist aesthetics with the Romantic spiritualization of art she had encountered first-hand in Weimar. She urged artists to the 'sacred task' of truthfully portraying the lives of ordinary people. Falsification would be a 'serious' betrayal of this task — a choice of word that echoed her insistence, to Cara Bray, that she held marriage to be 'profoundly serious,' not to be violated or treated lightly.

Being truthful, however, did not mean conforming to what others saw. For the Romantics it meant being faithful to your own heart, your own vision, your own feeling. Marian had learned to believe that the truth of art, like the truth of her marriage, lay not in social convention or in some objective fact, but in an inward experience — and the question was how to express this truth in the world.

*

In Germany with Lewes, in pursuit of Goethe's relics and in the company of Liszt, Marian had glimpsed genius. She had returned to London with a new authority, and in her literary criticism she claimed her place as a priestess in the temple of art. But it was one thing to guard the shrine, to proselytize, to point out false idols — and another to lay her hand on the deity within. It is one thing to have a doctrine of truth and beauty, quite another to bring them into being.

Lewes wanted her to begin a story, now convinced of her literary 'genius'. He knew from his own experience that the spirited prose and intellectual brilliance displayed in her journalism were no guarantee of success in fiction: many years earlier he had published two mediocre novels. Lewes encouraged her to approach fiction-writing in an experimental spirit, not too oppressed by great expectations. She had 'wit, description, philosophy,' he told her, and though there was 'no telling' how her story might turn out, it was worth a try — not least because they needed more money. Fiction could be much more lucrative than non-fiction. They were at this time 'very poor', and Lewes was liable for his wife Agnes's frighteningly large debts. When he later recounted George Eliot's humble beginnings, he emphasized financial need rather than artistic inspiration:

> Our friends — Herbert Spencer and others — used to say to me — Why doesn't she write a novel? and I used to reply that she was without the creative power. At last — we were very badly off — I was writing for Blackwood — I said to her 'My dear — try your hand at something. Do not attempt a novel — but try a story. We may get 20 guineas for it from Blackwood and that would be something.'

On this account, Lewes held — against the encouragement of their friends — that Marian could not write a decent novel, and it was Lewes who then decided that she *should* write fiction, and determined the form this should take. Within these tightly circumscribed conditions, Lewes's unromantic change of heart offered Marian an opportunity. She was now, at last, not just permitted but urged to pursue her literary ambitions — *and* gain Lewes's approval at the same time.

In May 1856 they set off for the seaside. As with their travels to Weimar and Berlin, this was a research trip for Lewes, who had decided to put his empiricist philosophy into practice. Like other Victorians curious about the origins of species, he was keen to take his researches out of the study and onto the seashore. The rock pools of Ilfracombe, on the north Devon coast, were an ideal hunting ground for collectors of shells, fossils, and primitive life-forms. Armed with a borrowed microscope and glass jars for specimens, they embarked on the twelve-hour train journey 'all the way to Exeter', then travelled on, the following day, to Ilfracombe. Lewes would write up these zoological expeditions in a popular series of 'Sea-side Studies' for *Blackwood's* magazine.

Marian had articles to write for the *Westminster Review*, but she threw herself into Lewes's new project and clambered over rocks with him in her scruffiest dress. Soon her diary was filled with exotic new acquaintances, natives of a strange and ancient world:

> We had a glorious hunt this afternoon on the rocks and found two specimens of the Anthea Cereus and a red and blue spotted anemone — treasures to us ... Brought home a rich store of Actinia Crassicornis ... Saw some splendid anemones, some Eolids and Corallines ... Found some specimens of the Alcyonium Digitatum, the Clavellina and the Stag's Horn Polype as well as abundance of Laomedeae and Actiniae ... Saw for the first time a Lophius, or Fishing Frog.

'I never before longed so much to know the names of things,' she wrote in her diary. This desire was not simply a collector's zeal, but a philosophical passion, 'part of the tendency that is now constantly growing in me to escape from all vagueness and inaccuracy into the daylight of distinct, vivid ideas'.

After six sunny weeks in Devon they took a boat across the Bristol Channel to Tenby, on the Welsh coast, where they continued their zoological investigations. Marian finished her translation of Spinoza's

Ethics, but Lewes promptly fell out with Henry Bohn, who was supposed to publish it. Lewes was convinced that Bohn had promised him £75, while the publisher stuck at £50, which Lewes angrily refused. Marian's fine translation would remain unpublished and unread for more than a century. She made no comment on this disappointing conclusion to eighteen months' work in her diary or her letters.

With no more pressing deadlines, she allowed her mind to relax, even rest a little. She found herself writing a descriptive essay, almost a story, about their happy weeks in Ilfracombe. There was a new ease in her narrative voice, full of feeling and impressions. She had, in fact, learned this immediacy from Romantic poets, while reading Goethe had sensitized her to colour, light and form. She eulogized the 'lovely' algae on the beach; the moment in late spring 'when the trees are in full leaf, but still keep their delicate varieties of colouring and that *transparency* which belongs only to this season'; the 'pale stars' of primroses on the hillside. The rocky tors rising from the sloping green hills reminded her of 'some noble animal that has reared itself on its forelegs to look at something — as if the land had lifted itself up in amazed contemplation of the glorious sea'. Ilfracombe itself was an uninteresting tourist town — 'the lines all rectangular and mean'— yet what is it, she asked, 'that light cannot transfigure into beauty?'

As Marian and Lewes explored these coastal towns, they philosophized about how all creatures — including humans — are shaped by their surroundings:

> In a flat country a house or town looks imposing — there is nothing to rival it in height, and we may imagine the earth a mere pedestal for us. But when one sees a house stuck on the side of a great hill, we begin to think of the strong family likeness between ourselves and all other building, burrowing, house-appropriating and shell-secreting animals . . . Look at man in the light of a shell-fish and it must be admitted that his shell is generally ugly, and it is only after a great many more 'steps or phenomena' that he secretes here and there a wonderful shell in the shape of a temple or a palace.

These sentences found their way, hardly altered, into Lewes's first 'Sea-side Study', revealing their intellectual intimacy and, perhaps, his willingness to copy her writing. The passage also shows how the adventures of amateur zoologists on Britain's beaches — during a decade that would end with Darwin's *On the Origin of Species* — provoked seismic theological questions about human beings and their place in nature.

One evening they strolled to the beach to watch the sunset. 'How lovely,' she thought, 'to look into that brilliant distance and see the ship on the horizon seeming to sail away from the cold and dim world behind it right into the golden glory! I have always had that sort of feeling when I look at sunset; it always seems to me that there, in the west, lies a land of light and warmth and love.'

She was still searching for her first story, with Lewes telling her to 'begin at once'. At last she wasn't simply gazing through a shroud of review proofs at the 'vague dream' he had helped to sharpen. Now she could inhabit the dream, occupy its uncertain space; she could sense the contours of the work she hoped to create. Her longing to know the names of things stretched out, and one morning at Tenby, some-where between sleep and waking, she discovered the name of her story.

> As I was lying in bed, thinking what should be the subject of my first story, my thoughts merged themselves into a dreamy doze, and I imag-ined myself writing a story of which the title was — 'The Sad Fortunes of the Reverend Amos Barton.' I was soon wide awake again, and told G. He said, 'O what a capital title!' and from that time I had settled in my mind that this should be my first story.

Back in London at the end of the summer she wrote a scathing *West-minster Review* essay on 'Silly Novels by Lady Novelists'. She began her own story in September. She had decided it would be the first in a series of 'Scenes of Clerical Life'. Marian wrote a few pages, then read them to Lewes. He thought her dialogue was good, and 'no longer had any doubt' about her ability to write fiction. Yet she still had to prove herself to him: 'there remained the question whether I could command any pathos' — and this was 'to be decided' by Lewes.

Although — or perhaps because — he was so closely involved in her writing process, she needed time alone to write. She did not find it easy to ask for this time. Years later, Lewes recalled how she secured a solitary evening to tackle her first tragic scene, the death of Amos Barton's downtrodden wife:

> One day when I was going to town she said 'I wish you would dine in London today.' I was all astonishment to hear such an extraordinary wish expressed as that we should be apart and eagerly enquired the reason — but she would not answer. Presently she said again 'I *wish* you would stay and dine in town today.' And then on my pressing for a reason, it came out. She said she felt she had something she must write that evening. And I always objected to her working at night. But so it was this time — she said she felt she *must*. And that evening she produced the scene of Milly's death.

She read the scene to Lewes when he came home that night — 'We both cried over it, and then he came up to me and kissed me, saying "I think your pathos is better than your fun."'

'Finished my first story', she wrote in her diary on 5 November, and the next day Lewes sent *The Sad Fortunes of the Reverend Amos Barton* to John Blackwood in Edinburgh, who had just published his series of 'Sea-side Studies' in *Blackwood's* magazine. The story was, Lewes explained, 'submitted to me by a friend' — a male friend, not a Silly Lady Novelist. Confessing his own 'considerable doubts of my friend's power as a writer of fiction', Lewes described how reading the story turned those doubts 'into very high admiration'. He praised its 'humour, pathos, vivid presentation and nice observation' and, with a critic's authority, declared that this story accomplished 'what has never before been done in our Literature, for we have had abundant religious stories polemical and doctrinal, but since *The Vicar of Wakefield* and Miss Austen, no stories representing the clergy like any other class with the humours, sorrows and troubles of other men.'

Within a week they received a reply from Edinburgh: 'My Dear Sir, I am happy to say that I think your friend's reminiscences of Clerical Life will do ... If the author is a new writer I beg to congratulate him on being worthy of the honours of print and pay.' Blackwood offered a few criticisms, and some moderate praise.

Marian was, as Lewes put it, 'unusually sensitive' to comments about her writing — though at this time she was sending Sara Hennell 'brusque' critiques of an essay on Christian belief. It felt different to be on the receiving end. Blackwood's comments on her first story occasioned 'a little bilious attack' that lasted a few days. Lewes pressed the publisher for a warmer response, warning that his 'clerical friend' was discouraged. Blackwood promptly obliged, and on 22 November — Marian's thirty-seventh birthday — Lewes let the publisher know that his praise for *The Sad Fortunes of the Reverend Amos Barton* had 'greatly restored the shaken confidence of my friend, who is . . . afraid of failure though not afraid of obscurity; and by failure he would understand that which I suspect most writers would be apt to consider success — so high is his ambition.' Lewes insisted that a 'veil of anonymity' must remain over this 'shy, shrinking, ambitious' author.

While Lewes handled Blackwood, Marian wrote to Sara Hennell. For their joint birthdays — which she had forgotten — Sara had sent a photograph of herself. 'Ah how much I have to be happy and thankful for with every fresh birthday,' Marian replied — 'Life seems worth twice as much to me now as it was even last November.' Two days later she followed this with a more expansive letter, regretting that she had 'written very selfishly' on her birthday, 'all about myself and my own feelings, and no word about what, nevertheless, I *do* care for — you and *your* feelings'. Yet her mood was more elegiac than repentant, as if she could catch their old intimacy only in a backwards glance:

> We are so long in this life before we learn even a little of the sacredness and preciousness of the things that are given to us. *Now*, on looking back to the days we have passed together, and the conversations in which you have told me something of your thoughts or of your griefs, I feel what a poor, narrow cup I held out to receive all that, and how often I wounded when I might have helped you, if I had only a larger and more reverent heart. The cup would be a little larger now — for after all it was not a hard porcelain cup, but one with petals that the sun has opened a little. But now we are separated and I shall never be able to make up for past failures.

She added that she was busy with 'washing bills and literature'. She did not mention that her first work of fiction would appear in the January edition of *Blackwood's* magazine.

Lewes went to the Hampshire estate of his friend Arthur Helps for the Christmas holiday. Marian was not invited, and stayed at home alone for a fortnight. On Christmas Day she began her second tale, *Mr Gilfil's Love Story*, which also involves the untimely death of a clergyman's wife. On the last day of 1856 she opened an envelope from Blackwood — addressed to Lewes, of course. It contained a copy of January's magazine leading with *Amos Barton*, and an effusive letter: 'It is a long time since I have read anything so fresh so humorous and so touching.' There was also a cheque for £52, more than twice what she had received for any other piece of writing. In her diary she added up her literary earnings for the year: £254 and 3 shillings.

Blackwood was already talking about republishing her 'Clerical Scenes' in book form, and he invited her — not knowing, of course, who she was — to correspond with him directly. On 4 February 1857 she wrote to Blackwood and signed herself, for the first time, with her new pseudonym. She had taken the first name shared by Lewes and the daring George Sand, and a plain yet elegant English surname:

> Whatever may be the success of my stories, I shall be resolute in preserving my incognito, having observed that a *nom de plume* secures all the advantages without the disagreeables of reputation . . . Accordingly I subscribe myself, best and most sympathizing of editors,
>
> Yours very truly,
> George Eliot.

She finished *Mr Gilfil's Love Story* in the spring, and by midsummer George Eliot was halfway through a third tale of Clerical Life.

*

Nothing seems cosier than a vicar and his wife tucked away in a quiet Midlands parish — yet this seemingly inexorable fixture of English provincial life had its roots in a sixteenth-century marriage scandal that shook and splintered Europe. Clerical marriage was perhaps the most divisive issue of the Protestant reformation. The Catholic Church held that priests must be celibate, but by 1520 the rebellious monk Martin Luther was denouncing his own vow of celibacy as contrary both to scripture and to common sense. Saint Paul, no admirer of marriage, had conceded that 'it is better to marry than to burn with passion', and Luther thought the flames of desire were virtually unquenchable. Letting priests have housekeepers but not wives was, he wrote, 'just like putting straw and fire together and forbidding them to smoke or burn'. Luther wrote a series of tracts and letters on marriage, arguing that sexual desire was natural and marriage was a gift from God. Women were created for childbirth, not virginity!

During the early years of the Protestant movement several prominent reformers conspicuously defied the Church by getting married. But when in 1525 Luther suddenly married Katherine von Bora, a young nun he had helped smuggle out of her Cistercian convent, even his allies were shocked. Monastic vows were irreversible: in the eyes of the Church — and in the eyes of God — Luther was still a monk and his bride was still a nun. Spiritually speaking, they were brother and sister, committing incest. Moreover, nuns had vowed to be brides of Christ, so they were committing adultery too.

As Luther and Katherine consummated their marriage before a witness — the task fell to Justus Jonas, a reforming priest and translator

Martin and Katherine Luther in 1529, by Lucas Cranach the Elder.
Marian and Lewes visited this painting in Frankfurt, on their honeymoon.

of Luther's works, who 'could not hold back his tears' when he saw them 'lying on the marriage bed' — news of the scandal flew around Christendom. In Basle, Erasmus wrote about it to friends in Antwerp and Rome: 'All the ups and downs of comedy usually end in marriage. It looks as though the Lutheran tragedy will end in the same way. He has taken a wife who was once a vestal virgin . . . A few days after the singing of the wedding hymn, the new bride gave birth to a child,' gossiped Christendom's great scholar, adding that he had seen a picture of the bride and groom.

Luther himself declared that 'God has willed and brought about this step.' He did not cite burning desire, nor Katherine's charms, as reasons for his marriage: he had done it, he said, to please his aging father, to spite the devil and the Pope, and to give witness to his faith. But after he became a father — Katherine bore him six children — he spoke warmly of his 'God-fearing, home-loving wife': 'My Katie is in all things so obliging and pleasing to me . . . Katie, you have a good man who loves you . . . No one is so spiritual that he does not feel this natural love and affection.' Luther had rewritten the meaning of marriage, and branded it with his own sensational example.

In England, Thomas More was the most vociferous critic of Luther's marriage. Through the 1520s and into the early 1530s, as he rose in Henry VIII's court, More wrote hundreds of pages denouncing Luther's 'fylthy lyfe', his 'open lying in lechery with his lewd lover the nun'. Even after Henry VIII broke with Rome — and executed More — over his own vexed marriage question, his new Church retained the Catholic view of clerical marriage. Reforming priests with secret wives and children faced criminal charges.

The 1548 Clerical Marriage Act permitted Anglican priests to marry, but the question of clerical marriage continued to plague the Church of England even into the nineteenth century. Meanwhile, the everyday fact of married priests quietly reshaped the English way of life. Clergymen, who were supposed to teach and model Christian virtue, were no longer set apart from the laity, following different rules; the typical Anglican priest now lived in a house with his wife and children. In England, as in those regions of Europe where Lutheran and Calvinist religion held sway, marriage replaced monasticism as the most effective way to discipline sexual desire.

Even while it resisted these changes, the Catholic Church also strengthened the sanctity of marriage. Before the Reformation, canon law recognized a couple as married as long as they had both consented to become husband and wife. The Church's 1563 Council of Trent affirmed the spiritual superiority of celibacy, but also formalized the sacrament of marriage: now a priest had to officiate at Catholic weddings, and couples were not allowed to live together before they received their priest's blessing.

Under the influence of both Protestant and Catholic developments, English marriage became, in a word, more churchy. Anglican priests had a crucial role at weddings, and when they themselves married they were — at least in theory — exemplary Christian husbands. The matrimonial rite in the Book of Common Prayer expressed the sixteenth century's heightened sense of the sanctity of marriage. 'Dearly beloved friends,' the priest would begin, 'we are gathered together here in the sight of God, and in the face of his Congregation, to join together this man and this woman in holy Matrimony, which is an honourable state, instituted of God in Paradise, in the time of Man's innocence, signifying to us the mystical union that is betwixt Christ and his Church.' Marriage, the priest warned the couple, must be undertaken 'reverently, discreetly, advisedly, soberly, and in the fear of God, duly considering the Causes for which Matrimony was ordained'.

*

This history of marriage provides the backdrop to *Scenes of Clerical Life* — and all three stories call the Anglican marriage ideal into question. George Eliot's first two clerical heroes are not exactly ideal husbands. *Janet's Repentance*, her third and strongest 'Scene', takes a darker turn: its central figure is not a mediocre husband, but a desperate battered wife.

The story begins with Janet's husband, Robert Dempster, a large bombastic man dusted with snuff, holding forth in the bar of the Red Lion. The conversation has turned to religion. Dempster, a lawyer, is leading the local protest against Edgar Tryan, a recently arrived Evangelical clergyman who is planning to hold Sunday evening lectures in the parish church. Reputedly 'the cleverest man in Milby', Dempster is also admired for his ability to drink 'the best part of a bottle o' brandy' without falling over. The Red Lion is a man's world — like the world of sixteenth-century lawyers and theologians who wrangled over the marriage question and quarrelled about what God had made women's bodies for. George Eliot writes it as a comic scene, yet it seethes with hypocrisy and thinly veiled brutality. 'Tell a man he is not to be saved by his works, and you open the floodgates of immorality,' Dempster booms, before staggering home to beat his wife.

Janet has been married to this man for fifteen years. She has a sweet, playful, rather childlike disposition and is artlessly beautiful: tall and graceful, with dark eyes and a long mane of jet-black hair. But there are bruises under her clothes and her face is worn by 'heart-piercing griefs'. At night she drinks and weeps and 'wildly wishes herself dead'; each morning she is hungover and ashamed. Dempster's mother blames Janet's slapdash housekeeping for her son's temper. But the narrator knows that 'an unloving, tyrannous, brutal man needs no motive to prompt his cruelty; he needs only the perpetual presence of a woman he can call his own. A whole park full of tame or timid-eyed animals to torment at his will would not serve him so well to glut his lust for torture; they could not *feel* as one woman does.'

One cold March night Dempster, in a rage, casts Janet out of the house, and as she sits drunkenly on her doorstep she sees her whole life unfold:

> the young girl, proud in strength and beauty, dreaming that life was an easy thing, and that it was pitiful weakness to be unhappy — the bride, passing with trembling joy from the outer court to the inner sanctuary of woman's life — the wife, beginning her initiation into sorrow, wounded, resenting, yet still hoping and forgiving — the poor bruised woman, seeking through weary years the one refuge of despair, oblivion: — Janet seemed to herself all these in the same moment.

She shivers in the dark in her thin nightdress, 'the harsh wind cutting her naked feet'.

These glimpses of Janet's misery are interspersed with comic scenes surveying Milby's religious topology, with its undulating ignorance and diverse species of piety. Mr Tryan's mildly handsome features and refined, earnest nature inspire fluttering hearts as well as devout thoughts among his female followers. In her third story George Eliot became brilliant in depicting things women think and say about one another. Her dialogue reveals the elasticity of ordinary human souls: the Milby mind slides seamlessly from Miss Linnet's thick ankles and Mr Tryan's fine cambric handkerchiefs to questions of church history and doctrine. Milby is modelled on Nuneaton, the Midlands market town near Marian's childhood home where her brother Isaac Evans now lived with his wife and children. George Eliot portrays it through the eyes of a prodigal daughter — returned from a far-flung continent that has made her fluent in philosophy, theology and literature — half horrified and half amused by her old neighbours' primitive ways.

Through these characters she sketches a spiritual ideal of 'saving ignorance', in which fellow-feeling is worth more than a thousand theories. In one of his philosophical asides to the reader, her narrator scorns the Utilitarianism currently in vogue, which advises maximizing happiness and minimizing pain. 'Emotion', he argues, 'is obstinately irrational: it insists on caring for individuals; it absolutely refuses to adopt the quantitative view of human anguish.' Besides, suffering teaches people to be compassionate. Janet Dempster agrees with him, though she has never heard of Bentham or Mill: 'kindness is my religion', she tells her old friend Mrs Pettifer. Moral theories must be 'lit up by love', argues George Eliot: 'surely, surely the only true knowledge of our fellow-man is that which enables us to feel with him.'

Tryan made romantic mistakes in his youth which determined him to renounce his sensual desires, live in poverty, and pour all his passion into helping the poor and needy. His self-denial shows in his 'well-filled lips' that are 'artificially compressed', but his own experience of suffering enables him to respond wisely to Janet's despair.

Hiding from Dempster at Mrs Pettifer's house, Janet agonizes about whether to return to her violent husband. She fears she will fall into her alcoholic spiral of 'terror, and stupor, and fevered despair' if she goes home. But Dempster has control of her property, and she feels 'too crushed, too faulty, too liable to reproach' to seek legal redress. The marriage also has a moral hold on her. 'It seems a dreadful thing in life,' she says, 'when any one has been so near to one as a husband for fifteen years, to part and be nothing to each other any more. Surely that is a very strong tie, and I feel as if my duty can never lie quite away from it. It is very difficult to know what to do: what ought I to do?'

Here Janet implies that the sanctity of her marriage is rooted in sexual intimacy as much as in official vows or laws. This evokes her awe and fear — biblical passions less safe or comfortable than the sweet devotion we might more easily associate with marital piety. For modern readers, at least, Janet's belief in her marriage bond is dangerous: we want her to break free.

Neither Janet nor Mr Tryan can find a way through her dilemma. It is settled only by the author, who hurriedly contrives an accident that kills Dempster and makes Janet financially independent. Perhaps this intervention is poetic justice — but it seems more like an admission that Janet's marriage question cannot be resolved.

Janet's Repentance dramatizes the idea Marian sketched in her 1855 review of Goethe: people can be taught by 'their own struggles, by their experience of sympathy' to question the conventional dividing line between virtue and vice, sanctity and violation. While the Dempsters' outwardly respectable marriage is a ruin of all that this story holds sacred, true sanctity emerges in the unorthodox friendship between Janet and Mr Tryan, which deepens after Dempster's death. Tryan is now visibly suffering from tuberculosis, and he battles to stay alive long enough to keep Janet safe from the pull of her addiction. In return she offers him wifely devotion, making a comfortable home for him and looking after him as his health declines: 'no one could feel that she was performing anything but a sacred office.' George Eliot delicately shows them falling in love, but they share just one kiss before he dies — 'a sacred kiss of promise', as if they are betrothed for eternity.

For the rest of her long life, we are told, Janet 'walked in the presence of unseen witnesses — of the Divine love that had rescued her, of the human love that waited for its eternal repose until it had seen her endure to the end'. If marriage is a sacrament, a holy bond, then which is the truer marriage — an abusive relationship sanctioned by Church and Law, which drives a wife to despair, or the undefined intimacy that redeems her?

*

George Eliot's third Clerical Scene posed this Feuerbachian question just as Marian faced rejection from her family over her relationship with Lewes. She began writing *Janet's Repentance* in early May 1857, while preparing to leave the Scilly Isles for Jersey: they spent that spring and summer on another long seaside trip for Lewes's zoological studies. On 26 May she wrote carefully worded letters to her brother Isaac in Nuneaton, and to her half-sister Fanny Houghton, to break the 'surprising' news that she had a 'husband'. It was nearly three years since she and Lewes had first set sail.

'I have changed my name, and have someone to take care of me in the world ... My husband has been known to me for several years, and I am well acquainted with his mind and character,' she wrote to Isaac, as if stiff prose would shield her from his wrath. She added that Lewes was a scientist and scholar, and had three sons.

Her letter's second paragraph — which perhaps expressed its main purpose — focused on financial arrangements. She asked Isaac, who administered their father's estate, to pay the income from her inheritance into Lewes's London bank account, instead of her own account at the Coventry and Warwickshire Bank. She was giving Lewes control of her money, supplementing his overstretched resources with her modest income: this could now be used to help support Lewes's wife Agnes and pay his sons' school fees. In a decade which saw radical feminists — notably her friend Barbara Leigh Smith — campaign for married women to have a right to their earnings, Marian, who *was* legally entitled to her own money, voluntarily surrendered the financial independence that had made all the difference to her life. Perhaps this was Lewes's idea, and she acquiesced with mixed feelings. Perhaps she suggested it, eager to help ease his burden — and to feel more properly married, more wifely, even if it meant handing over her income to Lewes's legitimate family.

Her letter to Fanny, the daughter of her father's first marriage, was a little more forthcoming, though not exactly direct:

> Now, let me ask you to open your eyes and look surprized, for I am
> going to tell you some very unexpected news. I am sure you retain
> enough friendship and sisterly affection for me to be glad that I should
> have a kind husband to love me and take care of me. Our paths in life

lie far apart, but I, at least, shall always remember with gratitude how kind you were to me in old days, and how much pleasure it gave me to talk with you.

My husband has been well known to me for years, and marriage is a very sober and serious thing when people are as old as we are, so that the future is as little a problem to me, as it can be to any of us. He is older than I am, not at all full of wealth or beauty, but very full indeed of literature and physiology and zoology and other invisible endowments, which happily have their market value. Still better, he is a man of high honour and integrity and the kindest heart, of which, of course, I think all the better because it is devoted to me.

We shall both be hard workers, for we have three little boys to keep as well as ourselves. Two of them are in Switzerland, at a delightful school there, and the youngest is at school in England. We shall live chiefly abroad for some time, for while the boys are at school, there is no necessity for our having a fixed residence near London.

It is striking that both letters convey the kernel of Marian's news in exactly the same words: she has found someone to 'take care of me'. Over the years, in fact, she had been remarkably resourceful in finding people to protect and guide her. Through the 1840s her friendship with the Brays had this quasi-parental quality, as did several other friendships during that period. The friends she had sought in those days tended to be at least a few years older than she was; they were often much older, more experienced and established in the world, and thus equipped to take care of her in intellectual, emotional, or practical ways. Perhaps she saw her relationship with Lewes in similar terms. Her letters to Isaac and Fanny emphasize their age difference, though he was born in April 1817, just two and a half years before her.

She signed both letters 'Marian Lewes'. Fanny wrote back warmly straight away. Isaac instructed the family solicitor, Vincent Holbeche, to convey his response: 'your Brother is so much hurt at your not having previously made some communication with him as to your intentions and prospects that he cannot make up his mind to write, feeling that he could not do so in a Brotherly Spirit ... Permit me to ask when and where you were married, and what is the occupation of Mr Lewes.'

Lewes helped her draft a reply to this painful letter, which forced her to admit that 'Our marriage is not a legal one, though it is regarded by us both as a sacred bond.' She had 'withheld' this fact from her family, she explained, because 'knowing that their views of life differ in many respects' from hers, she did not want to upset them. 'I have been his wife and have borne his name for nearly three years,' she wrote, not quite accurately. She became 'Marian Lewes' in these letters to Isaac, Fanny, and Holbeche, having continued to sign herself 'Marian Evans' or 'M. E.' in letters to her friends.

Though exhausted by this correspondence, and 'intensely agitated', she carried on writing *Janet's Repentance*. There was no further response from Isaac. He now refused to communicate with her, and told their sister Chrissey, who had recently been very ill, to do the same.

She was cast out. When Janet Dempster is thrown out in her 'thin nightdress' — mentioned twice to emphasize her exposure to the bitter wind — the pain and shame of being out in the cold, improperly dressed, was Marian's inward experience. Mr Tryan's sensitivity to the 'harsh wind' of other people's judgements also expressed her own feeling:

> Every form of disapproval jarred him painfully; and, though he fronted
> his opponents manfully, and often with considerable warmth of temper,
> he had no pugnacious pleasure in the contest. It was one of the weak-
> nesses of his nature to be too keenly alive to every harsh wind of
> opinion; to wince under the frowns of the foolish; to be irritated by the
> injustice of those who could not possibly have the elements indispens-
> able for judging him rightly; and with all this acute sensibility to blame,
> this dependence on sympathy, he had for years been constrained into a
> position of antagonism.

In depicting a sensitive soul forced into battle with the world, Marian was reliving her injuries from the harsh judgements that assailed her relationship with Lewes. Yet this questionable marriage had given her new force as a critic, and was helping her to find her voice as an author. Her first two stories exposed the fallibility of a Church which presumed to legislate on the marriage question, while *Janet's Repentance* showed with unprecedented realism how the law sanctioned marital violence instead of protecting abused wives.

'He pushed her to the entrance — and thrust her out'
Frontispiece from *Scenes of Clerical Life*

Meanwhile, John Blackwood conveyed his doubts about the 'popular qualities' of *Janet's Repentance*. Though he admitted that Janet's
predicament was 'too common', the publisher advised her to '*soften
your picture as much as you can.*' Marian understood Blackwood's
objections. That island summer she read several fine marriage
novels — Charlotte Brontë's *The Professor*, Susan Ferrier's *Marriage*,
and Léonie d'Aunet's *Un Mariage en province*, as well as *Emma*, *Persuasion*, *Sense and Sensibility* and *Northanger Abbey*, which she read
aloud with Lewes — and none of these feature a violent husband or a
desperate alcoholic wife. But she refused to change her story. It was
drawn from life, she told Blackwood, and was already 'softened from
the fact, so far as art is permitted to soften and yet to remain essentially true. The real town was more vicious than my Milby; the real
Dempster was far more disgusting than mine; the real Janet alas! had
a far sadder end than mine.' More importantly, she insisted that her

creative freedom was inviolable, sacred. 'As an artist,' she declared, 'I should be utterly powerless if I departed from my own conceptions of life and character.' Perhaps, she suggested, this third Clerical Scene should not appear in *Blackwood's* magazine after all?

Lewes quickly followed this up with a letter enclosing the latest instalment of his 'Sea-side Studies', but mostly devoted to praising George Eliot's new story:

> I was in raptures with 'Janet's Repentance' when Eliot first read it to me and declared it would be the finest thing he had written. Your letter therefore considerably staggered me, as I have much confidence in your judgement; accordingly I reread the part with a critical eye to detect the objections you spoke of. In vain! Two readings have left me in the dark . . . when I think of my ignorance of clerical life and squabbles, yet find myself so interested in this story, I feel that all persons better informed must be greatly moved.

Lewes's intervention turned out to be unnecessary. A letter from Blackwood crossed his, affirming the publisher's 'great confidence' in *Janet's Repentance*, and in its author: 'In continuing to write for the Magazine I beg of all things that you will not consider yourself hampered in any way.' Blackwood hoped very much that 'many years of happy friendly and literary intercourse' lay ahead of them. And he urged her to 'write entirely from the bent of your own genius' — for, he confessed, 'I do not fall in with George Eliots every day.'

4

Vocation

Marian and Lewes spent 25 December 1857 at home. Walking in Richmond Park, the sky was so clear they could see Hampstead on its hill some miles north. It was their first Christmas together since their stay in Berlin three years earlier, when on a 'miserably wet' Christmas Day she had battled a headache to work on her translation of Spinoza. This bright day was more festive: 'We ate our turkey together in a happy "solitude à deux".'

During those winter evenings they read aloud by the fire. They took turns reading from a history of colonial India and the Christmas issue of *Household Words*, the journal edited by Charles Dickens and Wilkie Collins. Over several weeks Lewes read to her Wordsworth's 300-page poem *The Excursion* — 'which repaid us for going to the end by an occasional fine passage even to the last'. And one night she read to him the first three chapters of her new novel.

She had settled on the title *Adam Bede*, but they still spoke of it as her 'Aunt's Story'. Its plot came from her memory of a conversation with her Aunt Elizabeth, a Methodist preacher. Elizabeth Evans had visited Griff House in 1839, when twenty-year-old Mary Ann felt lonely and misunderstood by her family: 'She was loving and kind to me, and I could talk to her about my inward life, which was closely shut up from those usually around me.' Elizabeth recalled visiting a Nottinghamshire prison to counsel a young woman who was to be hanged for murdering her child; she had prayed with this woman in the cart that took her to the gallows. Her story, told 'with great feeling', affected young Mary Ann deeply: 'I never lost the impression of that afternoon and our talk together; but I believe I never mentioned it through all the intervening years, till something prompted me to tell it to George.' Lewes had remarked that the scenes between preacher and prisoner 'would make a fine element in a story'.

From those two conversations, seventeen years apart, emerged the hero and heroine of George Eliot's first full-length novel: Adam Bede, a talented carpenter resembling Marian's father, Robert Evans, and Dinah Morris, a young Methodist preacher who speaks with a 'quiet depth of conviction'. Now finding her literary voice, Marian was fascinated by the power of human voices to carry feeling across space and time.

The first pages of *Adam Bede*, which she read aloud to Lewes that December evening, find Adam in his employer's workshop, singing a hymn in his 'strong baritone' as he finishes his day's work. Adam goes off to night school while his brother Seth walks to the village green, where Dinah is preaching a rousing sermon in her 'mellow treble tones'. As Seth walks Dinah home after the preaching, he tries to persuade her to marry him — but she feels that 'our marriage is not God's will.'

Dinah Morris preaching on the common, by Edward Henry Corbould, commissioned by Queen Victoria

When Marian finished reading her chapters, Lewes suggested that Adam and Dinah should marry at the end of the novel — 'He was so delighted with the presentation of Dinah and so convinced that the reader's interest would centre in her, that he wanted her to be the principal figure at the last.' She accepted his idea 'at once', and worked on the rest of the book with this marriage plot 'constantly in view'.

If we could eavesdrop on their conversations, what would we hear? Did she read those first chapters of *Adam Bede* shyly, confidently, nervously, excitedly? Was she seeking Lewes's approval, apprehensive of his verdict, or proudly showing off her work, or defiantly proving him wrong to have doubted her talent as a novelist — or perhaps all this at once? And how did Lewes offer his response?

It is difficult to imagine unknown voices. Marian's was often described as clear and soft — 'subdued as it was, it was the voice of a strong woman,' recalled Grace Greenwood, an American writer who met 'Miss Evans' in London in the early 1850s. Herbert Spencer also noted this combination of power and restraint: 'Her voice was a contralto of rather low pitch and I believe naturally strong ... but the habit of subduing her voice was so constant, that I suspect its real power was rarely if ever heard. Its tones were always gentle, and, like her smile, sympathetic.'

George Eliot's early biographer Mathilde Blind suggests that she 'created a new voice for herself' in her youth, exchanging her family's broad Warwickshire dialect for the refined elocution of her 'ladylike' boarding-school mistress Rebecca Franklin, who laid great stress on 'the propriety of a precise and careful manner of speaking and reading'. In later life, writes Blind, 'every one who knew her was struck by the sweetness of her voice, and the finished construction of every sentence, as it fell from her lips; for by that time the acquired habit had become second nature, and blended harmoniously with her entire personality. But in those early days the artificial effort at perfect propriety of expression was still perceptible, and produced an impression of affectation.'

When Marian moved to London to edit the *Westminster Review*, almost everyone around her was of a higher social class. At parties and dinners she encountered well-dressed women, polished and cushioned by wealth extracted from far-off colonies, who spoke with clipped consonants and sugary vowels. Their voices carried that assurance of utter correctness which, like genius, can redeem the attributed sins of gender or race. Even if Marian perfectly mastered their accent, she would never acquire their complacency. These ladies could sniff out her lower-class blood, which she could not help betraying by some deep habit, like the way she stood or held her arms — and they could punish her for it swiftly, smilingly, with the sweep of an eye or an amused twitch of the mouth. No wonder she learned to subdue her voice.

We might imagine Lewes, erstwhile actor and celebrated raconteur, reading Wordsworth to her with great flair, perhaps affecting the poet's Cumbrian accent. But of course, even those who knew the couple heard only their public voices. Marian's assured literary voice — so authoritative in her *Westminster Review* essays and her letters to Blackwood — does not match the needy diffidence described by Lewes, and this hints at some elusive shift between her public and her private self.

Voice and touch are the medium of a marriage, conduits of emotional truth. And in any romantic history, voice precedes touch and usually outlasts it. Partners save for one another the softest and sharpest tones that belong only to shared life. These unguarded, unceremonious exchanges secrete intimacy: anyone who overhears them will immediately recognize the voices of a long-term couple.

In the mid-nineteenth century, before telephones and radios, speech required physical proximity. Voices, like touches, could not outlive the bodies that made them. These most vibrant elements of marriage are also the most ephemeral: they fade quickly from memory, and vanish from history. Yet those fireside conversations between Marian and Lewes, like young Mary Ann's conversation with her Aunt Elizabeth, transmitted layers of thought and feeling that sedimented like rock over the months and years — and became the foundation for George Eliot's debut novel.

*

On New Year's Eve, 1857, Marian was alone. Lewes was away in Hampshire visiting his friend Arthur Helps. She had entered the year

as Marian Evans, and was leaving it as both Mrs Lewes and George
Eliot. Since the autumn she had been signing herself 'Marian Lewes'
in letters to friends and explaining that she had 'renounced' the
name Evans. She had also, of course, been renounced by her brother
and sister.

She had recently begun a new part of her diary, written from the
back of the notebook, with a long retrospective entry titled 'How I
Came to Write Fiction'. After the slow, secretive birth of George Eliot,
this was something like a private baptism. With *Scenes of Clerical Life*
now appearing in book form and her first novel under way, she could
affirm herself as an artist by writing the story of how she came to be
one. 'September 1856 made a new era in my life, for it was then I
began to write Fiction,' she declared — and this 'I' who 'began' was
George Eliot, a new self in a 'new era'.

Her diary's odd structure expressed an emerging double life. The
back pages, devoted to her authorship, ran parallel to daily entries
written from the front. On 8 December, for example, Marian Lewes
read *Household Words*, while George Eliot received a letter from
John Blackwood offering an additional £60 for a larger print run of
Scenes of Clerical Life.

That New Year's Eve she opened her diary at the front, as Mrs
Lewes. These quiet hours at the end of a tumultuous year should not
be allowed to slip away unwritten —

> This time last year I was alone, as I am now, and dear George was at
> Vernon Hill. I was writing the introduction to Mr Gilfil's Love Story.
> What a world of thoughts and feelings since then! My life has deepened
> unspeakably during the last year: I feel a greater capacity for moral and
> intellectual enjoyment, a more acute sense of my deficiencies in the
> past, a more solemn desire to be faithful to coming duties, than I
> remember in any former period of my life. And my happiness has deep-
> ened too: the blessedness of a perfect love and union grows daily. I have
> had some severe suffering this year from anxiety about my sister and
> what will probably be a final separation from her — there has been no
> other real trouble. Few women, I fear, have had such reason as I have
> to think the long sad years of youth were worth living for the sake of
> middle age.

Our prospects are very bright, too. I am writing my new novel. G. is full of his 'Physiology of Common Life' which Blackwood has accepted with cordial satisfaction . . . And we both have encouragement to think that our books just coming out — 'Sea-side Studies' and 'Scenes of Clerical Life' will be well received.

So goodbye, dear 1857! May I be able to look back on 1858 with an equal consciousness of advancement in work and in heart.

This was not the first time she had applied the Liberal ideal of moral progress to her relationship with Lewes. 'The blessedness of a perfect love and union grows daily' — ever since their departure for Germany in 1854 she had been plotting this narrative, and now she was projecting further 'advancement in heart' into the year ahead. She closed her New Year's Eve diary entry with a tally of her earnings in 1857: the total came to £443, nearly £200 more than the previous year. Blackwood's cheques had gone straight into Lewes's bank account, but in the pages of her diary, at least, she could claim the money as her own.

Lewes returned from his trip brandishing *The Times*: inside was an appreciative review of *Scenes of Clerical Life*. She recorded this event in the George Eliot end of her diary, treasuring such 'scraps of admiration' as grounds for hoping 'that my writing may succeed and so give value to my life — as indications that I can touch the hearts of my fellow men, and so sprinkle some precious grain as a result of the long years in which I have been inert and suffering.' Her sense of achievement was fragile: 'fear and trembling still predominate over hope.' Now in her thirty-ninth year, she wondered whether she would live long enough to fulfil her ambitions.

By the end of January she had received admiring letters from Charles Dickens and Jane Carlyle, who had been sent copies of *Scenes of Clerical Life* at her request. Confessing himself 'so strongly affected' by the first two tales in the book, Dickens praised the 'exquisite truth and delicacy, both of the humour and the pathos of those stories'. He was silent about *Janet's Repentance*. Mrs Carlyle found *Scenes of Clerical Life* to be that rare thing, 'a *human* book', written from its author's heart — 'a book that makes one feel friends, at once and for always, with the man or woman who wrote it!'. These literary connoisseurs both detected feminine notes in George

Eliot's voice. Jane Carlyle, bursting with curiosity, imagined Eliot to be 'a man of middle age, with a wife from whom he has got those beautiful *feminine* touches in his book.' But Dickens felt sure this author was a woman.

'There can hardly be any climax of approbation for me after this,' Marian wrote to John Blackwood, enclosing Dickens's letter, which she wanted back as soon as possible. She hinted that she wished everyone knew that England's most acclaimed novelist admired *her* book. In these circumstances, she realized, anonymity was a mixed blessing. 'The iron mask of my incognito seems quite painful in forbidding me to tell Dickens how thoroughly his generous impulse has been appreciated,' she explained — not adding that it would also be nice to be recognized for her success.

A few weeks later Blackwood was in London, and called on Lewes and Marian. By then he was fairly sure George Eliot was Lewes's disreputable companion: in recent months Lewes's letters had shown an intimate acquaintance with the author's moods and a very keen interest in the sales of *Scenes of Clerical Life*. For Marian, however, the revelation of their secret felt momentous. She devoted a page of the George Eliot part of her diary to a detailed account of Blackwood's visit. He had talked a lot about the *Clerical Scenes*, and 'at last asked, "Well, am I to see George Eliot this time?" G. said, "Do you wish to see him?" "As he likes — I wish it to be quite spontaneous." I left the room, and G. following me a moment, I told him he might reveal me.'

Marian casts herself as a passive figure at the centre of this scene, quietly submitting to the dénouement rather as a novice might submit to a ceremonial rite. If her diary narrative about the birth of George Eliot was something like a baptism, this was her confirmation: her first reception into the literary world. Blackwood played his part by accepting her — a significant gesture towards the virtually unvisited, uninvited, unacceptable Mrs Lewes. She perceived his reaction as 'kind'. Perhaps this was a sign that her work as an author might redeem her personal life.

For the publisher, too, this first encounter with George Eliot was a satisfying occasion, thanks in part to Lewes's deft performance in the little drama. As Blackwood reported to his wife,

I drove to Richmond to see Lewes, and was introduced to George Eliot — a woman (the Mrs Lewes whom we suspected). This is to be kept a profound secret, and on all accounts it is desirable, as you can readily imagine. She is a most intelligent pleasant woman, with a face like a man, but a good expression . . . Lewes says he would do ten times the work for me that he would do for any other man, and he does not think any other editor in the world would have been able to induce George Eliot to go on. It was very flattering, as his experience of editors is very great, and he is a monstrous clever fellow.

Blackwood, knowing the less-than-respectable Mrs Lewes would be bad for business, was as keen as they were to keep George Eliot's identity secret. He visited the couple again before he returned to Edinburgh. This time she gave him the first thirteen chapters of *Adam Bede*: 'He opened it, read the first page, and smiling said, "This will do."'

After Blackwood's visit Lewes continued to correspond with him about George Eliot's work, as well as his own. For the first time he had a confidant with whom to share the trials of living with a temperamental author. 'By a strange coincidence G. E. was with me when your letter arrived with its cheque (for which thanks) and he was greatly relieved and inspirited by your approbation,' he wrote in mid-March, playfully sustaining the secret they now shared. George Eliot, Lewes continued, 'had no belief in anybody's feeling the sort of delight in his personages he feels, or in any one (I, of course, counting as nobody!) liking the story. Your hearty letter made him quite comfortable and he will doubtless write with fresh confidence — till the next desponding fit comes.' This was quite a change of tone. A year earlier, Lewes had bragged to Blackwood that his friend Eliot '(very judiciously!) looks up to my critical opinion as oracular'; now he found himself 'counting as nobody' — and Marian seemed to give more weight to Blackwood's literary judgement. Another day, Lewes addressed the publisher as his ally in handling a highly strung Pegasus, the mythical winged horse associated with poetic inspiration. Blackwood was the right sort of person to 'deal with' George Eliot, he explained, 'for you perceive his Pegasus is tender in the mouth, and is apt to lay back his ears in a restive ominous style if even the reins be shaken when he is at work.' Lewes, by contrast, was tough. He joked that his own Pegasus 'seems to have

the mouth (as well as the *pace*) of a cart horse; but your thoroughbred —
all bone and nerve — requires other treatment.'

Marian resolved to let nothing distract her from her novel. 'My heart
is in the story,' she wrote to Blackwood. She was impatient when she
'lost' two or three days' writing to illness or headaches. When her friend
Bessie Parkes asked her to contribute to the newly launched *English
Woman's Journal*, she declined: 'this is at present impossible to me,
from the complete occupation of my time . . . elsewhere.' Worried that
Bessie would take this as a slight against her journal, she confided that
'I have given up writing articles, having discovered that my vocation
lies in other paths. In fact *entre nous*, I expect to be writing *books* for
some time to come. Don't speak of that at all.'

The word 'vocation' was not chosen lightly. Marian sent this letter
to Bessie three days after finishing the eighth chapter of *Adam Bede*,
titled 'A Vocation'. Here Dinah Morris is visited by Mr Irwine, the
parish priest, who has come to inquire about her preaching — a feminine vocation forbidden in Irwine's Anglican Church, and rare among
Dinah's Methodist community. A 'vocation' — from the Latin *vocare*,
to call — is a divine summons. For Dinah, however, following her
calling means letting her own voice be heard:

> For thoughts are so great — aren't they, sir? They seem to lie upon us
> like a deep flood; and it's my besetment to forget where I am and
> everything about me, and lose myself in thoughts that I could give no
> account of, for I could neither make a beginning nor ending of them in
> words. That was my way as long as I can remember; but sometimes it
> seemed as if speech came to me without any will of my own, and
> words were given to me that came out as the tears come, because our
> hearts are full and we can't help it. And those were always times of
> great blessing, though I had never thought it could be so with me
> before a congregation of people. But, sir, we are led on, like the little
> children, by a way that we know not. I was called to preach quite sud-
> denly, and since then I have never been left in doubt about the work
> that was laid upon me . . .

> Dinah had let her work fall during this narrative, which she uttered
> in her usual simple way, but with that sincere, articulate, thrilling treble
> by which she always mastered her audience. She stooped now to gather

up her sewing, and went on with it as before. Mr Irwine was deeply interested.

Dinah, an uneducated working woman from a poor family, speaks with inexplicable refinement, as if George Eliot cannot bring herself to marry her heroine's 'thrilling treble' with the rough provincial dialect spoken by the other characters of her class. Was Dinah's vocation, with its 'deep flood' of thought and feeling, too close to her own to be coarsened by harsh vowels and lost consonants? She later adapted Dinah's words in this scene to describe how her own writing 'came from me, "as the tears come, because our heart is full and we can't help them".'

In Elizabeth Barrett Browning's epic poem *Aurora Leigh*, the poet Aurora uses the word 'vocation' to describe her art. Aurora cites this vocation as her reason for refusing her cousin Romney's marriage proposal — rather as Dinah Morris refuses Seth Bede. *Aurora Leigh* was published in 1856, and by the following summer Marian had read it three times. 'I know no book that gives me a deeper sense of communion with a large as well as beautiful mind,' she told Sara Hennell. For Aurora, an artist's path is a divine calling that means

> bursting through
> The best of your conventions with his best,
> The speakable, imaginable best
> God bids him speak, to prove what lies beyond
> Both speech and imagination.

Having imagined the artist as a male voice, Aurora asks whether she can claim this vocation — and insists that her art must not be judged by lower standards because she is a woman:

> — For me,
> Perhaps I am not worthy, as you say,
> Of work like this: perhaps a woman's soul
> Aspires, and not creates: yet we aspire,
> And yet I'll try out your perhapses, sir,
> And if I fail . . . why, burn me up my straw
> Like other false works . . .

I

Who love my art, would never wish it lower
To suit my stature. I may love my art.
You'll grant that even a woman may love art,
Seeing that to waste true love on anything
Is womanly, past question.

Writing to Bessie Parkes of her vocation, Marian was echoing Browning in daring to express — even though she must conceal it — her devotion to her art.

*

In the spring of 1858 they set off for Germany, their first journey abroad since their trip to Weimar and Berlin four years earlier. Lewes was pursuing his scientific ambitions: he was now working on a book titled *The Physiology of Common Life*, and wanted to consult pioneering physiologists in Munich. On this visit to Germany he was fêted as the author of *The Life of Goethe*. He soon befriended Karl von Siebold, Professor of Zoology and Comparative Anatomy at Munich's Maximilians-Universität. Lewes helped Siebold dissect lizards and salamanders, and conducted experiments with Siebold's grand colleague Baron Justus von Liebig, Professor of Chemistry and President of the Bavarian Academy of Sciences. While Lewes was busy turning himself into a proper scientist, Marian worked daily on *Adam Bede*, reading each new chapter aloud to her 'husband' as soon as she completed it.

'Mr Lewes is in a state of perfect bliss this morning. He is gone to the Akademie to see wonders through von Siebold's microscope and watch him dissecting,' Marian wrote to Sara Hennell from Munich. As on her honeymoon, she could move freely in German society and mixed with poets, artists and intellectuals. 'People are so kind to us that we feel already quite at home,' she reported, leaving unspoken the contrast with her English friends: Sara's sister Cara had neither visited nor invited her since she began living with Lewes in 1854. She could not help mentioning that the illustrious Professor Liebig 'seems to have taken a benevolent liking to me. We dined with him and his family yesterday.'

Towards the end of June Lewes left Munich for a week to visit his sons at Hofwyl, their boarding school in Switzerland. Marian was anxious in his absence. He returned late one evening — 'after I had suffered a great deal in thinking of the possibilities that might prevent him from coming,' she wrote in her diary, equivocating between resentment and relief; the next morning she 'read to G. all I have written during his absence, and he approves it more than I expected.' After his return she was ill for a week, as if weakened by loneliness, and she found her illness 'almost a luxury because of the love that attended me'. By then she had self-diagnosed a 'general languor and sense of depression produced by Munich air and way of life'. She was glad to leave the city in early July, when they set off for Dresden, via Vienna and Prague — 'a charming journey, right through Saxon Switzerland'.

In Dresden they found 'a whole apartment of six rooms all to ourselves for s18/- per week!'. Here they would enjoy 'six weeks quiet work, undistracted by visitors and visiting'. She was even undistracted by Lewes, who worked on his *Physiology of Common Life* 'at the far corner of the great salon', while she wrote 'in my own private room with closed doors'. Those closed doors were a highlight of her stay in Dresden. After years of cramped domesticity she rejoiced, 'happy as a prince', in having a room of her own. She made the most of it, starting work at six each morning.

During this trip she kept a travel journal and recorded the moments that most touched her. On their train journey to Munich they shared a carriage with an elderly couple 'who spoke to each other and looked so affectionately, that we said directly "Shall we be so when we are old?" It was very pretty to see them hold each other's gloved hands, like lovers.' During a stopover in Nürnberg she glimpsed charming family tableaux in first-floor balcony windows, framed by carved wood or stone: 'young fair heads of girls, or of little children, with now and then an older head surmounting them. One can fancy that these windows are the pet places for family joys.' She was moved by a hymn they happened to hear in Nürnberg's Catholic church — 'how music that stirs all one's devout emotions blends everything into harmony — makes one feel part of one whole, which one loves all alike, losing the sense of a separate self' — though her separate self returned, as soon as the singing ended, to shudder at the priests' 'hard prosaic voices'. Crossing the Danube at sunset, she watched Venus slip down through tremendous purple clouds, 'as if in a hurry to follow the sun'.

She now found herself more captivated by nature than by art. 'I feel intensely the new beauty of the sky here. The blue is so exquisitely clear, and the wide streets give one such a broad canopy of sky,' she wrote in Munich. She was thrilled to catch sight of the snow-covered Alps, 'more to me than all the art in Munich, though I love the Art nevertheless. The great wide-stretching earth and the all-embracing sky — the birth-right of us all — are what I most care to look at, after all.'

The works of art that meant most to her during these months in Germany were portraits of maternal love. She visited many paintings of the Madonna and child, which echoed and intensified the real-life mothers and infants she described in her travel journal — a baby with 'such a funny little complete face' in the Nürnberg church, held up by its mother to see the rose-decked altar; a 'charming family group' with a 'sweet baby girl' who 'cried at the sight of G. in beard and spectacles, but kept turning her eyes towards him from her mother's lap'.

When Sara Hennell wrote with news of her mother's death, Marian thought about her own mother, who had died when she was sixteen. She tentatively approached her friend's 'sacred feelings' by recalling her grief:

> I only know that it must make a deeply felt crisis in your life, and I know that the better, from having felt a great deal about my own mother and father and from having the keenest remembrance of all that experience. But for this very reason, I know that I can't measure what the event is to you, and if I were near you I should only kiss you and say nothing. I cried over your letter and felt myself with you in all you were telling me about. People talk about the feelings dying out as one gets older — but at present my experience is just the contrary.

In Dresden's art gallery Marian was overwhelmed by Raphael's great Sistine Madonna when she saw it for the first time: 'a sort of awe, as if I were suddenly in the presence of some glorious being, made my

Raphael, *Sistine Madonna*, 1512

heart swell too much for me to remain comfortably, and we hurried out of the room.' The gallery also housed Holbein's 'very exquisite' portrait of Mary as 'a divinely gentle golden-haired blond'. While this soft, placid Mary casts her eyes down, her plump body modestly shrouded in a loose black dress, Raphael's Mary gazes directly from the painting, barefoot in a see-through skirt, broad-shouldered, strong-armed, capable of all goodness.

During their month and a half in Dresden they returned to the gallery three times a week, and Marian spent the last few minutes of every visit with Raphael's 'sublimest picture' of maternal power. As the weeks went by she found it 'harder and harder to leave'. Her lost mother seems to become more vividly present during this summer — first it is 'too much' and she hurries away; later she struggles to leave, as if she has finally let herself be held, like the child in the painting.

Back in England in the autumn, she wove these multiple visions of Mary — 'unconscious easy grace' or 'very grave and sweet' or 'full of tenderness' — into her devout heroine Dinah Morris, whose serene pale face and golden hair echo the improbably fair Madonnas of Holbein and Raphael. In the Epilogue to *Adam Bede* Dinah appears radiant in the sunlight, holding her little daughter's hand, as if transfigured by marriage and motherhood: 'the rays that fall on her white borderless cap and her pale auburn hair are very dazzling.' She no longer preaches on the village green; the Methodist elders forbade women preachers in 1803, two years after her marriage. Marian's aunt Elizabeth had left the church in protest at this prohibition, and joined the more permissive New Wesleyans. But Dinah acquiesces, although as her husband points out she continues her ministry by doing 'other sorts o' teaching' in people's homes.

Adam and Dinah are married in the last chapter of the novel, titled 'Marriage Bells'. Dinah wears a wedding dress 'made all of grey, though in the usual Quaker form . . . So the lily face looked out with sweet gravity from under a grey Quaker bonnet, neither smiling nor blushing, but with lips trembling a little under the weight of solemn feelings.'

George Eliot suggests that Dinah has not abandoned her spiritual vocation, but let it take her in a new direction. Marriage and motherhood are now her vocation, carrying the necessity of a divine call that must be followed, requiring sacrifice as well as promising fulfilment. People tend to speak of vocation in the singular, as if God must want them to do only one thing, forsaking all others. Perhaps this way of thinking is inevitable in a culture so committed, at least in theory, to monotheism and monogamy. And this rather ascetic ideal of marriage, closely tied to belief in its sanctity, seems to apply particularly to the wife. It is because marriage is construed as a vocation that Dinah, like Aurora Leigh, has to wrestle with a choice between love and work, on the assumption that one must be renounced for the sake of the other. Dinah's work is eventually curtailed by her church, not by her husband, but of course the Methodists' ban on female preachers expressed

'"Dinah," he said suddenly, taking both her hands
between his' — Adam Bede proposes to Dinah

beliefs about women's proper vocation. Aurora, a strikingly modern woman, eventually finds a way to pursue her art within marriage — as did her author: Robert Browning was first drawn to Elizabeth Barrett after reading her poetry, and she wrote *Aurora Leigh* as his wife. George Eliot, however, would continue to portray heroines who struggle to reconcile artistic and romantic callings.

When Dinah finally accepts Adam's proposal after weeks of soul-searching — 'listening faithfully for the ultimate guiding voice from within' — she tells him it is God's will. 'My soul is so knit with yours that it is but a divided life I live without you. And this moment, now you are with me, and I feel that our hearts are filled with the same love, I have a fulness of strength to bear and do our heavenly Father's will, that I had lost before.' The couple kiss 'with deep joy' and promise to stay together until they die. In case the reader remains in any doubt that Dinah is doing the right thing, George Eliot gives the couple her authorial blessing: 'What greater thing is there for two human souls, than to feel that they are joined for life — to strengthen each other in all labour, to rest on each other in all sorrow, to minister to each other in all pain, to be with one another in silent unspeakable memories at the moment of the last parting?'

She wrote these closing pages of *Adam Bede* in November 1858, and sent the manuscript to her publisher that very day. Two weeks later she wrote a short essay in the back of her diary under the title 'History of "Adam Bede"'. Here she revived those other voices which had helped breathe life into her novel, recalling the conversation with her Aunt Elizabeth that was its 'germ' and noting Lewes's recommendations, all of which she had followed. 'And now,' she concluded, 'I have written this slight history of my book. I love it very much and am deeply thankful to have written it, whatever the public may say to it — a result which is still in darkness.' This was her last entry in the George Eliot end of her diary until 6 February 1859 — five days after *Adam Bede* was published.

She spent another quiet Christmas with Lewes before he went to Hampshire to stay with Arthur Helps. Once again she was alone on New Year's Eve, and once again she tallied up her earnings for the year. Adding payments for American, Dutch and German reprints of *Scenes of Clerical Life* to the copyright for her new novel produced a satisfying total of £1,745, about four times what she had earned in 1857. As she counted the blessings of a remarkably rewarding year, she reflected on Lewes's vocation as well as her own:

> 31st. The last day of the dear old year which has been full of expected and unexpected happiness. Adam Bede has been written, and the second vol. is in type. The first No. of George's 'Physiology of Common Life' — a work in which he has had much happy occupation — is published today, and both his position as a scientific writer and his satisfaction in that inward

bent of his studies have been much heightened during the past year. Our double life is more and more blessed — more and more complete.

The narrative arc of their 'double life' was still ascending: somehow, their happiness was both complete *and* increasing. While Dinah's happy ending was decided, Marian's own marriage plot must be continued into another year. And while Dinah's voice fades once she becomes a wife, her own voice was growing stronger, reaching further, sounding out new powers within her.

To my dear husband, George Henry Lewes,
I give this M.S. of a work which would
never have been written but for the
happiness which his love has conferred
on my life.

     Marian Lewes

      March 23. 1859

The first volume was written at Richmond, the second at
Munich & Dresden, the third at Richmond again. The
work was begun on the 22ⁿᵈ October 1857, & finished on
the 16th November 1858. A large portion of it was
written twice, though often scarcely at all altered in
the copying; but other parts only once, & among these
the description of Dinah & a good deal of her sermon,
the love scene between her & Seth, "Hetty's world", most
of the scene in the Two Bedchambers, the talk between Arthur
& Adam, various parts in the second volume which I can recal
less easily, & in the third, Hetty's journeys, her confession, & the cottage scenes.

Manuscript of *Adam Bede*, p. 1: To my dear husband,
George Henry Lewes, I give this M.S. of a work which would never have
been written but for the happiness which his love has conferred
on my life. Marian Lewes. March 23 1859

5

The World

One day in January, 1859, Marian went into town to research 'cases of *inundation*'. She envisioned catastrophe: torrential rain, a swelling river, bridges swept away, a flooded house, broken hearts. She saw a brother and sister drowning, hand in hand. Her next novel would be a tragedy.

She lived with her new work for just a couple of weeks before leaving it for another story, *The Lifted Veil*, a loveless tale about a young man, Latimer, who — like a novel's omniscient narrator — sees into the future and reads other people's thoughts. She constructed an improbable plot, entwining Latimer's psychological drama with the controversial sciences of phrenology and mesmerism, ending in a gory blood-transfusion scene. A strange text grew: its alienated consciousness and claustrophobic melodrama echoed Poe's science fictions, which she had noted, along with other 'eerie stories' by Wilkie Collins and Gérard de Nerval, in one of her last articles for the *Westminster Review*. This was an unexpected sequel to *Adam Bede*'s tender pastoral realism.

We meet Latimer in despair, 'longing to die, weary of incessant insight and foresight, without delusions and without hope'. He feels cursed by his clairvoyant powers. Beneath the drama and intrigue of his supernatural vision lies the common experience of depression: the pathology of 'a morbidly sensitive nature perpetually craving sympathy and support'. He inhabits a misanthropic inner world and projects its negative judgements onto others, magnifying their pettiness and egotism. Latimer describes his clairvoyance as 'double consciousness' — the name Marian gave to her own self-doubting, self-critical inner voice.

The Lifted Veil probes another kind of double consciousness too: as its title hints, it is a marriage story that explores what partners hide from one another and what they are forced to reveal.

Latimer falls passionately in love with Bertha, the only person whose thoughts he cannot see. She holds 'the fascination of an unravelled destiny'. Then he has a dreadful premonition. He sees himself married to Bertha, and the veil over her inner life is lifted: 'I shuddered — I despised this woman with the barren soul and mean thoughts; but I felt helpless before her, as if she clutched my bleeding heart, and would clutch it till the last drop of life-blood ebbed away. She was my wife, and we hated each other.' As at a wedding, lifting the veil symbolizes a loss of innocence — and beneath this veil is not a loving face or a passionate heart, but the stark truth of a 'pitiless soul'.

Latimer's vision is destined to become reality. The couple marry, and familiarity soon breeds contempt. As Bertha grows colder towards her husband, he feels 'a sort of crushing of the heart'. He suffers in his dependence on her, until one night his premonition is fulfilled:

> We were front to front with each other, and judged each other. The terrible moment of complete illumination had come to me, and I saw that the darkness had hidden no landscape from me, but only a blank prosaic wall: from that evening forth, through the sickening years which followed, I saw all round the narrow room of this woman's soul — saw repulsion and antipathy harden into cruel hatred, giving pain only for the sake of wreaking itself.
>
> For Bertha, too, after her kind, felt the bitterness of disillusion. She had believed that my wild poet's passion for her would make me her slave ... She had thought my weaknesses would put me in her power, and she found them unmanageable forces ... She found herself powerless with me, except to produce in me the chill shudder of repulsion.

Husband and wife remain deadlocked in bitter misery. Latimer loses his insight into other minds, and withdraws into solipsistic ennui. After seven years of marriage Bertha schemes with her maid to poison him. The tale ends with the dénouement of her plot — a grisly scene that seems to Latimer 'of one texture with the rest of my existence: horror was my familiar, and this new revelation was only like an old pain recurring with new circumstances.' Bertha's thwarted plan is just one more failure, and its discovery only delays the ending Latimer has long foreseen: his lonely, unmourned death.

*

At the end of April, 1859, Marian completed this 'dismal story', as she described it to John Blackwood, who reluctantly published it in *Blackwood's Magazine*. Latimer's 'double consciousness' had accompanied her through a turbulent few months.

In February the Leweses had moved to a small rented house in Wandsworth, just south of the Thames. This upheaval plunged her into 'a ridiculously desponding state'. Two weeks later a letter came from her sister Chrissey, who was very ill with consumption and regretted losing touch with her. 'It has ploughed up my heart,' Marian wrote to Cara Bray. But she hesitated to visit her sister without an invitation — and Lewes would not hear of her going away even for a couple of days, on the grounds that they had trouble with their new servant. 'It is a terrible sacrifice to me to leave home at all — quite like the prospect of a tooth-drawing,' she explained to the Brays. By 'home' she meant Lewes. 'People who have been inseparable and found *all* their happiness in each other for five years are in a sort of Siamese-twin condition that other people are not likely to regard with tolerance or even with belief,' she added, perhaps suddenly conscious that prohibiting a visit to her dying sister — whom she had not seen for three years — did not seem very reasonable. Or was she glad of an excuse to cling to her literary life, with its rhythms of writing, reading, and gratifying letters from her publisher? And was she proud to be needed by her husband?

Soon it was too late; Chrissey died in March. This loss could only deepen Marian's fury at her brother Isaac: if he had not excluded her from the family, then — Lewes and literature permitting — she might have spent time with her sister in her final months, looked after her, said goodbye.

At the same time, she had her hands full with George Eliot. *Adam Bede*, published in three volumes on 1 February, was widely acclaimed. 'A work of true genius, full of quiet power,' gushed the *Athenaeum*, while *The Times* deemed it 'a first-rate novel' and its author 'one of the masters of the art'. George Eliot was a 'man of genius', declared the *Economist*, explaining that novels by male authors 'are more in keeping with the actual world, have a wider outlook, and are more profitable than the best novels by women. *Adam Bede* is one of the best of this best class of novels.' By March a second edition was in press; Blackwood considered it a 'triumph'. Marian's feelings about her success were more complex. News of high sales and rave reviews reached her 'rather strangely' in exile from society, she told Blackwood, while Lewes reported that 'the effect upon G. E. has been almost sad, instead of joyful — but the sadness lies near joy.'

Throughout the spring they were plagued by false rumours about George Eliot's identity. *The Times* printed a letter claiming that both *Scenes of Clerical Life* and *Adam Bede* were written by a man from Nuneaton named Joseph Liggins. Lewes immediately wrote to *The Times*, in the name of George Eliot, to deny this — but literary London was now in 'a perfect fever' about the authorship of *Adam Bede*, and the Liggins rumours rumbled on.

During these painful months Marian made a new friend. Richard Congreve, a physician and scholar, and his young wife Maria — who had met Marian briefly when she was a girl — were their new neighbours in Wandsworth. Richard was a disciple of the recently deceased philosopher Auguste Comte, and had just translated Comte's *Catechism of Popular Religion*. The Congreves came to call on them in their new house, and invited them round to theirs. It was so unusual for Marian to be treated as an ordinary English wife, respectable enough to pay and receive visits, that she sent news of these low-key suburban evenings to her old friends in Coventry.

Lewes and Richard Congreve differed on matters important to them both. Lewes had embraced Comte's scientific philosophy fifteen years earlier, but was sceptical of the religious direction it had taken since then. Comte proposed a 'religion of humanity', which would involve a 'regeneration of marriage' — now intended, rather chastely, for 'the mutual improvement of both sexes, putting aside any sensual idea'. While their husbands eyed one another warily, the two women quickly became close friends. The Congreves saw that it would be impossible to enjoy Marian's company without enduring Lewes's — 'It is rather unfortunate that they are so inseparable,' Richard remarked to his wife.

Marian disliked Wandsworth, where she felt surrounded by 'houses full of eyes', and she considered Maria Congreve its 'chief charm'. Her new friend was just twenty-five, fourteen years younger than her, 'sweet, intelligent, gentle' — and adoring. When Maria went to the Continent for five months, the two women exchanged passionate letters. On her first night away Maria dreamt of Marian: 'I usually wake up so entirely mistress of the situation, but you do make such a difference to me in my rising up and lying down and in all my ways — now I actually know you, and that you will let me love you and even give me some love too,' she wrote to her the next morning — emboldened, she explained, by 'what you said to me once about your requiring to be told that people love you'. Marian confessed that she cherished 'the belief that you do really care for me across the seas there . . . Faith is not easy to me, nevertheless I believe everything you say and write.' She urged Maria to write often, and made plans to join her in Switzerland for a few days in the summer. 'Her friendship has the same date as the success of "Adam Bede",' she reflected in her journal, '— two good things in my lot that ought to have made me less sad than I have been in this house.'

That spring Marian felt doubly rejected by 'the world', denied recognition as both a writer and a wife. She did not need clairvoyant powers: she could easily imagine what people thought and said about her. She also grieved for the praise her anonymity denied her. Happiness at her success was mixed with these despondent feelings. 'I sing my "Magnificat" in a quiet way, and have a great deal of deep, silent joy,' she wrote to Blackwood,

> but few authors, I suppose, who have had a real success, have known less of the flush and the sensations of triumph that are talked of as the accompaniment of success. I think I should soon believe that 'Liggins' wrote my books — it is so difficult to believe what the world does *not* believe, so easy to believe what the world keeps repeating.

By the time she finished *The Lifted Veil* at the end of April, *Adam Bede* was ready for a third printing — but she found herself 'sadder than usual'.

In this mood, an exuberant letter from Barbara Leigh Smith — now Barbara Bodichon, married to an eminent French doctor and living in Algiers — was a burst of sunlight through the clouds. Barbara had seen an extract from *Adam Bede* and knew instantly who the author was: 'that is written by Marian Evans, there is her big head and heart and her wise wide views . . . I can't tell you, my dear George Eliot how enchanted I am. Very few things could have given me so much pleasure.' Yet even this praise highlighted Marian's disgrace along with her success. Barbara described how 'everybody' — except her husband Eugène Bodichon and their mutual friend Bessie Parkes — 'bullied' her for calling Marian her friend. She was triumphant, she wrote, not just that 'a woman' had written this great novel, but 'That YOU *that you* whom they spit at should do it!'

If Marian shared her feminist friend's defiant glee, she felt it in a minor key. Still, she was happy to be seen and known. 'God bless you, dearest Barbara, for your love and sympathy,' she wrote back gratefully:

> You are the first friend who has given any symptom of knowing me — the first heart that has recognised me in a book which has come from my heart of hearts . . . I think your letter today gave me more joy — more heart-glow, than all the letters or reviews or the other testimonies of success that have come to me since the evenings when I read aloud my manuscripts — to my dear dear husband, and he laughed and cried alternately and then rushed to kiss me. He is the prime blessing that has made all the rest possible to me — giving me a response to everything I have written, a response that I could confide in as proof that I had not mistaken my work.

She knew that Lewes would see this letter before Barbara did. After reading it, he added a postscript. 'Dear Barbara, You're a darling and I have always said so!' he began, before detailing the success of *Adam Bede*: 'over 3000 copies have been sold already and as 500 is a good success for a novel, you may estimate by that detail what my Polly has achieved.' His gloat ended with a word of warning: '— But, dear Barbara, you must not call her Marian Evans again: that individual is extinct, rolled up, mashed, absorbed in the Lewesian magnificence!' Thus in a single sentence Lewes defied his wife's conservative family

Barbara Leigh Smith Bodichon, photographed by Disdéri, *c.* 1860

and her radical friend — both of whom hesitated, for very different reasons, to call her 'Mrs Lewes'.

Reading this letter, it is striking how possessiveness seems to flare just as the seal on George Eliot's identity is broken. Lewes claims the success of 'my Polly', declares her 'absorbed' in his own greatness, and tells her friend how to name her, while Marian emphasizes that he is the one who has made her authorship possible. In this moment of breach and exposure there is vulnerability, which must be vigorously quashed by the husband, gently defended by the wife. It is a revealing moment, and also a turning point — a new direction of growth in the Leweses' marriage question. It is the first sign too of a new phase in Marian's life as an artist, now no longer confined to her relationships with her husband and her publisher. Her private self was beginning to merge with her public voice.

From now on we shall call her Eliot, continuing to reserve 'George Eliot' for her purely literary voice — though in the years to come the difference between Eliot the woman and George Eliot the author will become slighter, subtler, at times difficult to discern.

*

In late summer, 1859, Eliot and Lewes travelled across England in search of a river. They went up to north Wales, which was cold and windy; then south-east to Lichfield, not so far from Eliot's Midlands birthplace; then due south to the Dorset coast. She was looking for a setting for her tragic novel, which she had returned to at the end of April. She thought she might call it *The Tullivers*; she would eventually settle on a title suggested by Blackwood: *The Mill on the Floss*.

She needed to see the River Floss and its surrounding landscape in her mind's eye. The river would run through her novel, symbolizing both passion and memory; since its heroine will drown in the flooded Floss, it would also be a symbol of death. Her river would evoke time past and time lost, as well as the restless life-force of young Maggie Tulliver, who rushes passionately onwards seeking new knowledge, wider horizons — yet also feels herself tugged back, as if caught in an irresistible undercurrent, by her childish need for her family's love. No wonder *The Mill on the Floss* would be Proust's favourite novel.

Both her river and her novel eluded her until the autumn. In September she was 'in much anxiety and doubt about my new novel'. Then they found the Floss during a short trip to Gainsborough, a Lincolnshire market town on the River Trent, where she and Lewes hired a boat and rowed a few miles to its junction with the smaller River Idle. Along this river was a sleepy hamlet amidst flat fields and a wide, open sky. Further upstream would be the Mill, Maggie's obscure birthplace. On their return Eliot reported in her diary that 'certain new ideas have occurred to me in relation to my new novel and I am in better hope of it.'

Her search was also an inward journey, into childhood memories. She recalled an untidy little girl, the youngest of three siblings: her brother was their mother's favourite, and her sister 'always neat and tidy'. For as long as she could remember, she had been 'easily moved to smiles or tears . . . capable of the keenest enjoyment and the keenest suffering . . . affectionate, proud and sensitive in the highest degree'.

She saw herself in the family scene, 'an old-fashioned child, already living in a world of her own imagination':

> The child turns over the book with pictures that she wishes her father
> to explain to her — or that perhaps she prefers explaining to him.
> Her rebellious hair is all over her eyes, much vexing the pale, ener-
> getic mother who sits on the opposite side of the fire . . . The father
> is already very proud of the astonishing and growing intelligence of
> his little girl.

This little girl 'could not be satisfied' with her limited world: 'I was constantly living in a world of my own creation.' Eliot still felt within her this child's 'absolute need of some one person who should be all in all to her, and to whom she should be all in all'. Her desire for exclusive love made her 'very jealous in her affections'.

Neither of her parents had fulfilled this desire. Her father worked long hours, and her mother had withdrawn into illness very early in her life. When she was eighteen months old, Christiana Evans gave birth to twin boys who died within a few days. Even before Mary Anne learned to talk, she had sensed her mother's suffering. 'Child-hood is only the beautiful and happy time in contemplation and retrospect — to the child it is full of deep sorrow, the meaning of which is unknown,' she wrote to Sara Hennell when she was twenty-four. She thought that 'the sorrows of older persons which children see but cannot understand are worse than all.'

Eliot's mother is as elusive as she is influential, a figure delineated more by her absence than her presence. This maternal silhouette casts a long shadow, stretching through her daughter's life in the shape of a longing for love, a deep pool of grief, and a keen sense of the joys and pains of emotional attachment. Eliot would eventually explore this legacy in a poem that stages a dialogue between 'Self' and 'Life':

LIFE.
I was thy warmth upon thy mother's knee
When light and love within her eyes were one
. . .
It was bliss and it was I:
Bliss was what thou knew'st me by.

SELF.

Soon I knew thee more by Fear
And sense of what was not,
Haunting all I held most dear;
I had a double lot:
Ardour, cheated with alloy
Wept the more for dreams of joy.

Chrissey, the eldest child of their parents' marriage, went to boarding school at a very young age, while Isaac and Mary Anne were sent away daily to a neighbour. The jealous little girl clung to her brother, the only person who was always there. When she was five, she and Isaac had to go to different boarding schools. Whenever they came home for the holidays they became 'inseparable playfellows' again. Aged about seven, 'a deeply felt crisis occurred in her life': her brother was given a pony 'to which he became passionate attached ... he cared less and less to play with his sister.'

In *The Mill on the Floss* Eliot entered, for the first time, into a child's experience. Penetrating the easy nostalgia of 'contemplation and retrospect', she submerged herself in deeper currents of memory, with renewed fury at Isaac sharpening her vision. Her novel's opening scene moves on a 'mighty tide', following the River Floss inland, past the market town of St Ogg's; moving from the river to its banks to a small stone bridge, the narrator's gaze rests on a little girl standing at the edge of the water.

Maggie Tulliver will grow up to be a tall gypsyish beauty rather than a failed English rose. But she shares her author's ardent clinging nature, her intelligence, her love of books and music, her powerful imagination, her disapproving mother, her childish devotion to her brother. Maggie feels herself a little sister more than a daughter: 'the first thing I ever remember in my life is standing with Tom by the side of the Floss while he held my hand,' she says when she is seventeen. Eliot, too, despite her rift with Isaac, remained a 'little sister' in her imagination.

When Eliot was a young woman Charles Bray had used phrenology to diagnose her possessive need for love. Examining a cast of her head, he noted her 'adhesiveness' and pronounced her 'not fitted to stand alone ... always requiring someone to lean upon'. Now we might be

Maggie Tulliver with her brother Tom

more inclined to think of her withdrawn mother, and the feelings of anxiety and rejection — that uneasy 'sense of what was not' — a mother's absence induces in a small child.

Maggie Tulliver is not sent away from home at a young age; her parents are more present than Mary Anne's were. Her hungry heart is simply her nature. Perhaps Eliot believed that a human being's need for love requires no diagnosis or explanation. But to such a heart, cast out of an unremembered paradise of maternal warmth, the ideal of marriage — two people vowing 'to have and to hold' one another for ever — seems like heaven.

Eventually Maggie is forced to choose between keeping her brother's love and fulfilling her grown-up needs in marriage. Eliot had been forced into the same choice; she had gained a future, while Maggie must perish, only because she chose differently. Her novel seems to say that survival comes at the cost of the past, an ambiguous anchor that might hold you steady or drag you down. Maggie drowns united with her brother Tom; Eliot lives, and all the ties to her childhood loves are cut. She cried as she wrote the novel's final scenes.

*

The Mill on the Floss depicts two worlds, one nested within the other. A cosmopolitan narrator — versed in Aristotle's *Poetics* and Sappho's poetry, Dante and Shakespeare, Bossuet and Gibbon, Faraday and the *Bridgewater Treatises* — conjures Maggie Tulliver's unenlightened provincial milieu, even more restricted than the 'walled-in world' Eliot had sought to escape as a young woman. The narrow world of St Ogg's is one of the novel's chief protagonists, silent but powerful, with a hand in everybody's fate.

Readers must move back and forth between these two worlds. The grand culture discovered by Eliot over years of study, and enlarged further through her conversations and travels with Lewes, is very distant from St Ogg's. But like the small tributary of the Floss that leads to the Mill, a tiny stream flows from this wider life into Maggie's world. As a child, Maggie is conscious of immense vistas of far-away knowledge. She earnestly teaches the local gypsies about geography ('that's about the world we live in') and Christopher Columbus ('a very wonderful man, who found out half the world'). Objects that wash up in St Ogg's are fragments of an intellectual richness that lies beyond it, out of reach. When one of Walter Scott's *Waverley* novels finds its way into Maggie's hands, it is a token of the Romanticism that pervades the narrator's milieu.

Eliot herself had moved from one world to the other — from life in the Evans family to life with Lewes — and now found herself unable to return. As her own horizons expanded, she saw more clearly how her century's physical and moral landscapes were being refashioned by ideas, industry, ambition. The very concept of the world was changing, with a new notion — 'the environment' — emerging from pioneering research in natural history, biology and zoology. European explorers and colonizers had discovered exotic natural habitats in other continents, and brought home numerous specimens of flora and fauna that flourished there.

In 1816 the French naturalist Georges Cuvier published *Le règne*

animal, a four-volume opus examining animal life in its complex relations to surrounding 'conditions of existence'. Eliot had read Cuvier in
1848, and returned to him during her short trip to Switzerland in the
summer of 1859. When she and Lewes read *On the Origin of Species*
the day it was published, at the end of that year, they found Cuvier's
notion of 'conditions of existence' at work in Darwin's theory that each
species 'becomes adapted to the conditions of life of its own region'.

In the hands of philosophers, this rather indefinite sense of myriad
conditions of life was shaped into a new concept: *le milieu*, the
'medium' or 'environment'. The concept of *milieu*, crystallized by
Comte in the 1830s, encompasses social as well as natural conditions
of life. It became a cornerstone of the ambitious new science of 'sociology' that Comte sketched in his later works. 'The world within is
essentially at all times under the regulating power of the world without, from which also it draws its nourishment and stimulus,' wrote
Comte in his *Catechism of Popular Religion*. Eliot read Richard Congreve's translation of this book in the autumn of 1859, while she was
working intensively on *The Mill on the Floss*.

Lewes had introduced Comte's ideas to English readers in his *Biographical History of Philosophy*, completed in 1846, and it was here
that Eliot's old flame, Herbert Spencer, first encountered Comte. Eliot
herself had persuaded Spencer to read Comte's *Cours de philosophie
positive* during their ambiguous courtship in 1852. Drawing on
Comte's notion of *milieu*, Spencer proposed 'environment' as a single
term that could name biological, physical and social circumstances.
His *Principles of Psychology* set out to analyse the mental and bodily
aspects of relations 'between every living organism and the external
world', according to the principle that 'the state of an organism is
constantly affected by the state of its environment.' Anticipating Darwin's theory of adaptation, Spencer here announced that 'the broadest
and most complete definition of life will be — *The continuous adjustment of internal relations to external relations.*' Eliot and Lewes had,
of course, acquired a copy of Spencer's *Principles of Psychology* as
soon as it came out in the summer of 1855: 'Mr Lewes is *nailed* to the
book by his interest in it,' she told Sara Hennell.

By the end of the 1850s, then, the combined efforts of Cuvier,
Comte, Spencer and Darwin had conceptualized a world that could

be studied by the natural and social sciences. They all agreed that the relationship between an organism — whether plant, animal or human — and its surroundings was fundamental to life and growth. Lewes and Eliot were at the centre of these intellectual developments and understood them better than anyone. Eliot also knew how remote from all this were the market towns of middle England: such ideas did not so much as trickle into ordinary provincial life. As she channelled the latest philosophical and scientific methods into her new novel, she found a literary form that could vividly reveal the interactions between self and world. Instead of pursuing this theme across the vast terrain of 'nature' or 'society', she approached it as a marriage question, staged in an intimate domestic setting.

*

The inhabitants of St Ogg's know nothing about grand theories of *milieu*, environment, or 'conditions of life'. Their worldview — a virtually unfathomable mix of myth, ritual, and common sense — is formed by centuries of Christianity, tightly woven with occult codes and folk traditions passed down from untraceable ancestors.

Nineteenth-century Christian culture remained deeply ambivalent towards 'the world'. A new Anglican hymn proclaimed it full of 'all things bright and beautiful' — signs of God's good and providential design — yet it was frequently envisaged as a fallen realm beset by dangers, a dark shadowy valley between paradise lost and redemption promised. Once Adam and Eve are expelled from the Garden of Eden, human beings are no longer at ease in the world: men have to toil on thorny ground to feed themselves, women must endure the 'painful labour' of childbirth. Over the centuries, theologians emphasized more inward aspects of this Fall. It was a descent into freedom, shameful self-consciousness, and dark desires — and thus into spiritual struggles that mirror the earthy physical hardships described in Genesis.

The Mill on the Floss borrows from biblical myth to tell a tale of vanished childhood innocence, entwined with a respectable family's financial 'downfall'. Tom Tulliver, Maggie's brother, must work hard and joylessly to pay off his father's debts. Maggie also has to work for a living, but her most significant labour is internal — the 'labour of choice' — and she is punished by expulsion from her brother's affections as well as from her family home. The narrator looks back wistfully to the prelapsarian comforts of childhood: 'There is no sense of ease like the ease we felt in those scenes where we were born, where objects became dear to us before we had known the labour of choice, and where the outer world seemed only an extension of our own personality.'

The novel portrays a family: four people thrown into the world together. 'Character is destiny,' declares George Eliot, quoting the Romantic poet Novalis, then immediately corrects him: 'But not the whole of our destiny.' It is the fraught negotiation between self and world that shapes our lives — as Herbert Spencer put it, *the continuous adjustment of internal relations to external relations.*

Each member of the Tulliver family inhabits the world differently. Rash, honest, hapless Mr Tulliver is baffled by 'this puzzlin' world'. Like a biblical prophet transplanted to Middle England, he laments its serpentine deceptions:

> if the world had been left as God made it, I could ha' seen my way, and held my own wi' the best of 'em; but things have got so twisted round and wrapped up i' unreasonable words, as aren't a bit like 'em, as I'm clean at fault, often an' often. Everything winds about so — the more straightforward you are, the more you're puzzled.

Eventually the world crushes him, and his fragmented last words are a fitting epitaph: 'This world's . . . too many . . . honest man . . . puzzling.'

His small-minded wife Bessy shrinks her world to a manageable size, and populates it with 'household gods' — her cherished linen, her silver sugar-tongs, her patterned china cups. Her fixation on these trivial things gives her a pattern to live by. When the family loses everything, she is reduced to 'helpless imbecility':

> the objects among which her mind had moved complacently were all gone — all the little hopes, and schemes and speculations, all the pleasant little cares about her treasures which had made this world quite comprehensible to her for a quarter of a century, since she had made her first purchase of the sugar-tongs, had been suddenly snatched away from her, and she remained bewildered in this empty life.

Tom Tulliver sets out to conquer the world that has defeated his father and impoverished his mother. Dutiful and disciplined, conventional and pragmatic, he promises to be 'a man who will make his way in the world'.

Tom resembles his mother's side of the family. Bessy Tulliver's three sisters have secured their place in the world by making good marriages. Amidst the novel's sweeping destructive forces these marriages provide life-rafts, as well as comic relief. The eldest sister, Mrs Glegg, a hilarious battle-axe in mouldy clothes, is locked in combat with long-suffering Mr Glegg, while her pill-popping sister Mrs Pullet is kept in her spectacularly selfish comfort zone by a docile husband. In these passionless, childless relationships, questions of love and happiness do not arise. The houses of Glegg and Pullet have very different atmospheres — one is hard, contrary, miserly, puritanical; the other soft, harmonious, cosseted, indulgent — but both are unimpeachable shared worlds, tightly sealed and thoroughly solid. They are creaturely adaptations, not so unlike those observed by Darwin in the Galapagos islands. 'To render the world habitable: that is the great object,' Spencer had explained in his 1851 book *Social Statics: Or, the Conditions Essential to Human Happiness* — and these comic marriages accomplish precisely this. They are habits, acquired habitats, that ensure safe passage between individual and social worlds.

Maggie is different from the rest of her family. While her mother's life is absorbed in petty particulars, she inhabits a 'triple world of reality, books and waking dreams'. While Tom's unimaginative nature adapts readily to their provincial milieu, Maggie's 'excessive feeling' drives her to push beyond its limits. First her aesthetic longings struggle against its hard-nosed materialism, then her sexual desires threaten to break its moral codes. Her transgressive quality finds symbolic expression when the River Floss bursts its banks and floods the surrounding fields — and at moments the novel itself threatens to overflow its literary form.

Just as the Glegg and Pullet marriages are ways of making a home in the world, so marriage seems to offer Maggie the chance to contain her passions within conventional bounds. Two wealthy suitors want to marry her. Sensitive Philip Wakem, a hunchbacked artist, offers her

Maggie and Philip (left); Maggie and Stephen (right)

intellectual and aesthetic fulfilment, while handsome Stephen Guest, her cousin Lucy's unofficial fiancé, offers sexual fulfilment.

It is sometimes said that Stephen Guest is an unworthy object of Maggie's love, but this underestimates the physical attraction between them — their intense consciousness of one another's presence, and a young woman's pleasure in being desired for the first time. Stephen is tall, good-looking, clever, attentive, charming and rich. To dismiss his appeal for Maggie is to confuse her world for the reader's: against George Eliot's wide horizon he may cut an inconsequential figure, but within Maggie's small-town milieu this eligible young man *is* the horizon, the very limit of what might be hoped for. Her longing for him is so strong that it tempts her to betray her dearest friends.

As a little girl, Maggie's imagination busied itself with 'refashioning her little world into just what she should like it to be'. When this continues into adolescence, it meets more resistance:

> everybody in the world seemed so hard and unkind to Maggie: there was no indulgence, no fondness, such as she imagined when she fashioned the world afresh in her own thoughts. In books there were people

who were always agreeable or tender, and delighted to do things that made one happy, and who did not show their kindness by finding fault. The world outside the books was not a happy one, Maggie felt: it seemed to be a world where people behaved the best to those they did not pretend to love, and that did not belong to them. And if life had no love in it, what else was there for Maggie?

Mr Deane, Tom and Maggie's prosperous uncle, crushes this longing for a bookish life: 'The world isn't made of pen, ink and paper, and if you're to get on in the world, you must know what the world's made of.'

There is of course irony here, which George Eliot — with her materials of pen, ink and paper very much in view — seems to be enjoying. Mr Deane's daughter Lucy is just the sort of character Maggie likes to find in books: sweet, agreeable, and delighted to do things that make Maggie happy. Indeed, Lucy Deane seems to have stepped out of a Jane Austen novel. As she looks forward to marrying Stephen Guest, she plots her cousin's own 'pretty ending' in marriage to Philip Wakem. 'There is something romantic in it — out of the common way — just what everything that happens to you ought to be,' Lucy tells Maggie — 'And Philip will adore you like a husband in a fairy tale.'

Later, when Maggie and Stephen fall in love, their marriage is envisaged as an alternative happy ending. Public opinion — a gossipy chorus that George Eliot christens 'the world's wife' — gives its approval to this plot: 'What a wonderful marriage for a girl like Miss Tulliver — quite romantic!'. The local vicar, whose compassionate voice carries real moral authority, decides that a marriage between Stephen and Maggie would be the best outcome of a difficult situation.

But *The Mill on the Floss* is a tragedy: Destiny will not permit this ending. It seems as if the ink-and-paper world of St Ogg's cannot be ordered according to the desires of its characters, its readers, or even its author. Maggie unwittingly predicts her own fate when Philip gives her Walter Scott's marriage novel *The Pirate*, which she once started and didn't finish: 'I went on with it in my own head, and I made several endings; but they were all unhappy. I could never make a happy ending out of that beginning.'

*

Should Maggie subdue her passionate nature, or express it? She is continually drawn into this dilemma, and pulled in both directions. 'I was never satisfied with a *little* of anything. That is why it is better for me to do without earthly happiness altogether,' she tells Philip — echoing Eliot's youthful confession to Maria Lewis that she found 'total abstinence much easier than moderation'. Through Maggie's 'labour of choice' the novel explores two ways of responding to a world where human passions cannot find a happy home.

In the midst of her family's troubles Maggie finds relief in reading Thomas à Kempis's *Imitation of Christ*, a fifteen-century devotional work counselling self-sacrifice. Eliot had procured a quaint illustrated copy of this book ten years earlier, and enjoyed its 'cool air as of cloisters': having long left behind her adolescent piety, she wrote breezily to Sara Hennell that 'it makes one long to be a saint for a few months.' She reread it while writing *The Mill on the Floss*.

Thomas à Kempis was an Augustinian monk who sought the kingdom of heaven through 'contempt of the world'. Maggie clutches at this philosophy of renunciation, yet she cannot resist reading *The Pirate* when Philip lends it to her. These two books — a manual of Christian asceticism and a Romantic novel of passion and adventure — are slices of a vast European tradition of religion, philosophy and art, as if George Eliot has opened the curtains of Maggie's world an inch or so, letting in shafts of light from her own wide horizons. Ascetic renunciation and Romantic creativity were a kind of double movement, current and counter-current, shaping the intellectual history that Eliot had embraced as her milieu. And she herself had lived through both of them intensely, as phases of her personal formation.

Medieval asceticism, institutionalized in monasteries, sought to purify bodily desires by withdrawing from worldly temptations. After Luther's break with his monastic vows put marriage at the heart of Christian life, pre-Reformation works such as *Imitation of Christ* were drawn back into Lutheran culture by Pietism, a popular spiritual movement that flourished in northern Europe for over two centuries. In this Protestant context, the virtues of sacrifice, obedience and humility extolled by Thomas à Kempis could be cultivated outside the cloister, and particularly in married life.

Pietism infused the liberal Protestantism of Strauss and Feuerbach, which Eliot's translations had brought to English readers. It was a religion of the heart, emphasizing inward experience and stirring holy feelings through devotional music, books and images. The movement included radical, counter-cultural strands that challenged church hierarchies and experimented with new forms of communal living. It sowed seeds that flowered in Romanticism: several early German Romantics were sons of Pietist leaders. Like their fathers, these philosophers and poets wanted to feel reverence and awe — but they sought these feelings in nature and art and sex, rejecting the narrower Christian moralism they had been schooled in. Some Romantics challenged the institution of marriage, in a spirit contrary to ascetic self-denial, yet still aspiring to a higher life: they thought bourgeois marriage a mere social convention that suppressed free love and natural desire. Others saw marriage as a vehicle for Romantic ideals: thus a new notion, marrying for love, was born. Friedrich Schlegel's experimental (and semi-autobiographical) novel *Lucinde*, published in 1799, depicts a love affair both before and after marriage, playing with traditional gender roles and insisting on its heroine's sexual fulfilment.

When Maggie Tulliver tries to 'fashion the world afresh' in her imagination, George Eliot is depicting the creative impulses of Romantic art within an ordinary woman's life. The alternative marriage plots imagined for Maggie would carry her along the contrary currents of asceticism and Romanticism — towards either a self-sacrificial marriage to Philip, whom Maggie is not in love with, or a passionate, transgressive marriage to Stephen.

*

While writing this novel Eliot brought together two parts of herself. She was unveiled to the world as the author of *Adam Bede* in the summer of 1859, when she was about halfway through *The Mill on the Floss*. The writer and the wife were finally united — though the little sister was still lost.

There were other losses, too. Just before they made George Eliot's identity public, Eliot and Lewes shared the secret with Sara Hennell and the Brays while they were visiting London. Sara had brought along the manuscript of a theological treatise she had been working on for several years. She was looking forward to discussing it with her old friend — who suddenly transformed into a celebrated novelist before her eyes. To make matters worse, Lewes informed her of 'our decided disapprobation' of her treatise. She had not asked for *his* opinion, and there is something awful in this marital 'we' issuing joint judgement on her cherished manuscript. Sara went home in tears and wrote Eliot a sonnet, beginning —

> Dear Friend, when all thy greatness suddenly
> Burst out, and thou wert other than I thought,
> At first I wept — for Marian, whom I sought,
> Now passed beyond herself, seemed lost to me.

Eliot also felt the 'after-sadness' of their meeting. She admitted she had 'blundered' and treated her friend with 'too much egoism and too little sympathy'.

By this time, the rumour mill was spinning: the world's wife was in full flow. On the train back to Coventry, Sara bumped into an acquaintance who reported that Eliot's brother had guessed the secret: 'Mr Evans of Griff has been heard to say, after reading Adam Bede — "No one but his Sister could write the book" — "there are things in it about his Father that she must have written."' Barbara Bodichon, who spent her summers in London, sent Eliot a detailed account of drawing-room gossip. Everyone was speculating that 'Mrs Lewes' was George Eliot. 'From their way of talking it was evident they thought you would do the book more harm than the book would do you good in public opinion,' Barbara wrote, not very tactfully.

These rumours defeated the Leweses, though of course they did not put it that way. Eliot's cross reply to Barbara contained two post-scripts by Lewes. The first announced that 'we have come to the resolution of no longer concealing the authorship.' Lewes affirmed both their defiance of the world and the impossibility of ignoring its judgements:

> It makes me angry to think that people should say that the secret has been kept because there was any *fear* of the effect of the author's name. You may tell it openly to all who care to hear it that the object of

anonymity was to get the book judged on its own merits, and not pre-judged as the work of a woman, or of a particular woman.

Lewes kept his second postscript secret from Eliot: 'P.P.S. *Entre nous*. Please don't write or tell Marian anything *unpleasant* that you hear unless it is important for her to hear it. She is so very sensitive, and has such a tendency to dwell on and believe in unpleasant ideas that I always keep them from her ... She knows nothing of this second postscript, of course.'

As for Eliot — she confessed to Barbara that it would be nice to retreat from 'this hard noisy world'. She was fortunate, she wrote bravely, to have the consolations of friendship and love: 'Thank God there is an abundance of pure human feeling that makes no noise, else we might sink into the belief that it is but a devil's world.' She was also grateful for Maria Congreve's loyal devotion. 'The other day', she wrote to her, 'I said to Mr Lewes, "Every now and then it comes across me, like the re-collection of some precious little store laid by, that there is Mrs Congreve in the world."' Maria, however, was still far away in Switzerland.

That summer, she found another devoted friend — a puppy, Pug, which John Blackwood had procured from Bethnal Green to cheer her up. Pug did not mind whether she was George Eliot, or Mrs Lewes, or plain Marian Evans. He was resolutely on her side. Pug couldn't manage a bark, she informed her publisher, 'but *en revanche** he sneezes powerfully and has speaking eyes ... He sneezes at the world in general, and he looks affectionately at *me*.'

*

When *The Mill on the Floss* was published in the spring of 1860, with George Eliot's identity now public, it was received as the work of a female author. It was also received as a novel of passion, revolving around the kind of romantic marriage hard-won in *Jane Eyre* and longed for in *Villette*. One critic drew out this comparison, while lamenting George Eliot's lapse of moral seriousness in deciding to 'exhibit ascetic religion as a temporary phase in a young woman's

* On the other hand

George Lewes with the dog, *c.* 1864

career.' This reviewer recognized that 'passion, and especially the passion of love, is so avowedly the chief subject of the modern novel that we can scarcely quarrel with a novelist because the passion she chooses to describe is of a very intense kind.' 'But,' he continued squeamishly,

> there is a kind of love-making which seems to possess a strange fascination for the modern female novelist. Charlotte Brontë and George Eliot, and we may add George Sand, all like to dwell on love as an

overmastering force, which, through the senses, captivates and enthrals the soul. They linger on the description of the physical sensations that accompany the meeting of hearts in love ... Perhaps we may go further, and say that the whole delineation of passionate love, as painted by modern female novelists, is open to very serious criticism. There are emotions over which we ought to throw a veil.

Lifting the veil of conventional moralism was a Romantic gesture, and this critic was right to perceive that George Eliot, like Brontë and Sand, delighted in it. But in the end Maggie Tulliver chooses sacrifice, not passion. She renounces marriage to Stephen to be faithful to her friends Lucy and Philip, and she renounces marriage to Philip to be faithful to her brother Tom.

The inward tragedy of *The Mill on the Floss* is that Maggie's heart remains fragmented, dispersed in different directions. Duty, renunciation, intellectual discovery, aesthetic pleasure, sexual desire: these are the elements of marriage, and Maggie's passion runs through them all, but they never concur. She never finds herself whole. According to Herbert Spencer's theory, a flourishing life requires harmony in the organism's 'internal relations' as well as in its 'external relations' with the world. Perhaps it is Maggie's failure to cohere with herself that prevents her marriage question from being resolved.

Manuscript of *The Mill on the Floss*, p. 1: To my beloved Husband,
George Henry Lewes, I give this M.S. of my third book, written,
in the sixth year of our life together, at Holly Lodge, South Fields,
Wandsworth, & finished March 21st, 1860.

6

Motherhood

On the first day of 1860 Lewes presented Eliot with an extravagant New Year's gift: a forty-eight-volume set of Walter Scott's *Waverley* novels, bound in Morocco leather with ornate gilded spines. He had inscribed the flyleaf of the first volume:

To Marian Evans Lewes,
The best of Novelists and Wives,
These works of her longest-venerated and best-loved Romancist are given

> by her grateful Husband.
> 1 January 1860.

It was the beginning of a new decade, as well as a new year — and besides, Lewes could afford to be generous. His own earnings in 1859 had been modest, around £350, much of which went to support his wife Agnes and their children, but his bank account was swelled by £2,000 from Eliot's writing. *Adam Bede* was still selling fast, and John Blackwood had offered a further £2,000 for *The Mill on the Floss*. Their new prosperity gave Lewes freedom to pursue his scientific research. In the first weeks of 1860 he splashed out on a microscope, and they planned a long-awaited trip to Italy.

That spring Eliot finished *The Mill on the Floss*, had the folios bound, and dedicated to Lewes 'this MS. of my third book, written in the sixth year of our life together.' Three books in six years: this was the issue of their marriage. With Lewes's help she had conceived and nurtured each book until it was ready to go out into the world. She felt especially protective towards *Scenes of Clerical Life*, her first-born work.

They both embraced the analogy between authorship and mother-hood. George Eliot would now 'rock the cradle of the new "little stranger" with fresh maternal vigour,' Lewes had promised Blackwood when she resumed *The Mill on the Floss* after a trip to Switzerland. And on the day she finished the novel she wrote in her diary 'Magnificat anima mea!' — the words of rejoicing and gratitude sung by Mary in Luke's gospel as she expects the birth of her miraculous baby. When it was published Eliot described it as 'my youngest child'.

They had planned to set off for Italy as soon as the new novel was done, keen to leave England before it reached the critics in early April. Lewes also had a book on the way: Blackwood was about to publish the second volume of *The Physiology of Common Life*, his foray into serious science writing. Their trip to Italy would be, for once, a 'real holiday, which we have never had since we were married', Lewes explained to Barbara Bodichon. They would follow the well-trodden route of the 'grand tour' through Paris, Rome, Florence and Venice, which gave young English aristocrats a dose of high culture before they settled down — a privilege that now, in middle age, lay within the Leweses' reach.

Eliot saw this as their last chance to travel before their life together changed indefinitely. That summer, Lewes's eldest son Charles would leave Hofwyl, his Swiss boarding school, and return to London to live with them. She was going to be a stepmother.

She had not yet met Lewes's three sons — Charles, Thornton (named after Thornton Hunt, who had fathered Agnes's four younger children) and Herbert, known as Bertie. Lewes was an affectionate father: in one typical letter to Charles he signed himself 'Ancient Bear', and said how much he longed to 'have a hug of my three cubs'. For Eliot, though, these sons had been out of sight and more or less out of mind in Switzerland, and when Lewes made his annual visits to Hofwyl he went alone. The boys only learned of her existence in the summer of 1859, when the unveiling of George Eliot had enabled Lewes to tell them not only that he was separated from their mother and living with another woman, but that this woman was the celebrated author of *Adam Bede*. This exciting fact conveniently eclipsed the more disconcerting aspects of their situation. Since then, Eliot and seventeen-year-old Charles had embarked on a careful correspondence, in preparation for their first meeting.

During this period of gestation Lewes breezily filled letters to his sons with references to 'your mother' — meaning Eliot — while referring to their actual mother as 'Agnes'. Eliot was more sensitive to her ambiguous position in the family. While she claimed the role of wife, she knew she did not have the same right to be called a mother. Even 'stepmother' was disputable, in her circumstances, and in any case stepmothers were so often associated with wickedness and strife that this seemed best avoided.

So who was she to these unfamiliar children? This question turned correspondence with a schoolboy into a significant literary challenge, even for George Eliot. Charles had made a great effort with his first letter, composed in his best handwriting on pretty decorated paper, and bravely beginning 'Dear Mother'. At the end of her reply to this letter, Eliot tried out 'your loving mother', which felt so awkward that she found herself placing a full stop, rather than her usual comma, between this closing salutation and her signature:

> You are an excellent correspondent, so I do not fear you will flag in writing to me; and remember you are always giving a pleasure when you write to your loving mother.
>
> > Marian Lewes.

That full stop, the tiniest mark on a page, swells with meaning. Eliot cannot quite connect her own name with this loving mother — and that name, too, suddenly looms large under the imagined gaze of a young man who bore irrefutable witness to the first Mrs Lewes.

In her next letter to Charles her punctuation again betrays some uneasiness, this time by shrouding 'Mother' in quotation marks:

> Good by, dear Charles. Kisses "over the water to Charlie!" from
> > His affectionate "Mother"
> > Marian Lewes.

Her third letter — which touched briefly on the subject of German literature — solved the problem by translating the troublesome word into German: 'Your loving Mutter'. This probably came as a relief to everyone, and the Lewes boys followed her lead. Now she was

'Mutter', as well as Marian Lewes (or Marian Evans Lewes) and George Eliot.

*

If only the question of motherhood itself were so easily resolved. This role comes heavy-laden with centuries of expectation, and Eliot was not capable of taking it lightly. While she had the intellectual resources to challenge conventional ideals of marriage, her Feuerbachian sense of the sacredness of human ties combined with her own need for love — and her pride — made being a good mother part of what it meant to be, as Lewes put it, the 'best of Wives'.

In November 1859, a few weeks after writing her third letter to Charles Lewes, she had turned forty. She was still young enough to have a child of her own. When she was a very young woman she had loved holding her sister Chrissey's baby daughter, Mary Louisa, whom she would rock to sleep, 'feeling a sort of rapture in the mere presence, even though she might want the time for reading'. For many years, though, she had rocked only metaphorical cradles, and had little contact with children or adolescents. There were clear reasons not to have a baby with Lewes: the child would be conspicuously illegitimate; it would disrupt her writing; in the first years of their relationship they could not afford another dependant, though this was changing now.

At that time Eliot did not write about these reasons, nor about wanting a child — and perhaps she did not speak about any of this either. Nor did she write about the monthly tides that came carrying waves of despair, along with a reminder of the possibility of motherhood and a premonition of the pain and danger of childbirth. She asterisked her periods in her journal, but these 'turns' or 'monthlies' were seldom discussed in Victorian England. Menstruating women washed their blood-soaked napkins furtively, whether with relief or disappointment. Even if the question of pregnancy passed monthly through Eliot's body without much rumination, it could not have been entirely detached from thoughts of her own mother, for whom childcare seemed to have been an intolerable burden, and her sister Chrissey, weakened by at least three childbirths and dead at forty-four.

Such thoughts would fit with Lewes's opinion that motherhood was an almost insurmountable obstacle to literary success. In 1852, just before they began their affair, he had contributed an article on 'The Lady Novelists' to the *Westminster Review*, under Eliot's editorship. It was no coincidence that Jane Austen and Charlotte Brontë were both childless: Lewes reflected that 'for twenty of the best years of their lives, women are mainly occupied by the cares, the duties, the enjoyments, and the sufferings of maternity. During large parts of those years, too, their bodily health is so broken as to incapacitate them for any strenuous exertion.'

Having arrived in her stepsons' lives too late for the daily work of motherhood — feeding, clothing, washing, teaching, scolding, drying tears, bedtime stories — Eliot immediately assumed the parental role of fretting about their futures and offering unsolicited moral guidance. 'Your father and I', she wrote in that first letter to Charles, 'with our grave old heads, cannot help talking very often of the need our boys will have for all sorts of good qualities and habits in making their way through this difficult life.' She could offer financial support, too: her first motherly act was to buy Charles a watch, and she would soon be providing him with a London home. In return, the prospect of this son's entrance into her life with Lewes offered an initiation in maternal ambivalence.

From the start she saw clearly what was at stake in her new role: love, time, freedom. The very first sentence she wrote to Charles expressed the fundamental issues: 'I look forward to playing duets with you as one of my future pleasures, and if I am able to go on working, I hope we shall afford to have a fine grand piano.' Within this pleasant vision of prosperous domestic harmony lies a worry — that unsettling 'if' — about how motherhood will affect her writing. Her second letter to Charles, written half a year before his expected arrival, emphasized her finite resources and pre-emptively protected her working hours. She must write to him late at night, she explained, because she had 'no time' to do so 'by daylight', and could offer him only 'the fag end of my wits'. The brevity of her third letter, written 'very tired' one night at the end of 1859 when she was immersed in *The Mill on the Floss*, underscored the point. Here she warned that she was 'likely to be a poor correspondent' for the next few months,

'having my head and hands full'. She inquired about Charles's progress in algebra, and — echoing young Maggie Tulliver's longing to
join in her brother's schoolwork — wished she could study it with
him, 'if I could possibly find time to rub up my knowledge'.

Eliot's next message to Charles, scribbled at the bottom of one of
Lewes's letters in the first days of the new decade, reflected that the
time of his leaving school — still a few months away — was 'now ...
so near'. She expressed a mixture of aspiration and anxiety: 'Let us
hope that we shall all — father and mother and sons — help one
another with love.' More pointedly, as she confided to a friend,
Charles's arrival would 'make a new epoch in our domestic life, for
hitherto we have lived alone. I hope my heart will be large enough for
all the love that is required of me.' And what about Lewes's heart:
might her place in it shrink when she was sharing it with his eldest
son? Would there be enough love to go around? Their hard-won 'solitude à deux' was coming to an end.

She also contemplated the loss of their freedom. Their holiday in
Italy would be their 'last bit of vagrancy for a long, long while', she
wrote to Sara Hennell — and then they would 'return through Switzerland and bring Charlie home with us'. Perhaps the prospect
brought to mind her old life in Warwickshire, when she was not much
older than Charles, looking after her father and 'walled in' by domesticity. 'We want to get away to Italy, if possible, to feed my mind with
fresh thoughts,' she explained to Blackwood in January 1860 — and
they must go 'before the boys are about us, making it difficult for us
to leave home'.

Lewes, as usual, seemed more optimistic. On the brink of their
departure he wrote to Charles full of news of their two new books,
and the latest success of *Adam Bede*, which would be 'translated
into Hungarian, Dutch, German, and French'; his *Life of Goethe*
was coming out in France, and his *Biographical History of Philosophy* in Germany — 'so you see we are becoming quite European
celebrities.' 'All England', too, was 'on tiptoe with expectation for
The Mill on the Floss'. On the mother question, Lewes was typically commanding. 'Her genius is nothing to her tenderness and
goodness, and you will all love her,' he decreed, 'nearly as much as
I do, when you come to know her.' The boys should expect them

Charles Lewes

to turn up in Switzerland 'some time in June'. Meanwhile, Charles must let his hair grow 'nice and long, so that when your mother embraces you, she may embrace a good-looking chap!' Even Lewes felt a twitch of anxiety about his reconfigured family: he was stage-managing that first encounter between 'mother' and son three months ahead of time.

*

Two days after dispatching the last pages of *The Mill on the Floss* to Blackwood they set off for Paris, their 'hearts set on Italy and Italian skies'. They planned to arrive in Rome in time for Holy Week in early April. After two nights at the grand Hôtel du Louvre an overnight train took them south-east to the end of the railway line at St Jean de Maurienne. There they squeezed into a diligence carriage to Mont Cenis. Close to midnight, they drank hot coffee at a roadside inn, then boarded a sledge to cross the Alps into Italy. This snowy passage unveiled a Romantic landscape of pristine 'Nature', white and pure and uninhabitable, more celestial than worldly. For Eliot,

> The human bustle and confusion made a poetic contrast with the sublime stillness of the starlit heavens spread over the snowy tableland and surrounding heights. The keenness of the air contributed strongly to the sense of novelty: we had left our everyday conventional world quite behind us and were on a visit to Nature in her private home.
>
> Once closely packed in our sledge, congratulating ourselves that, after all, we were no more squeezed than in our diligence, I gave myself up to as many naps as chose to take possession of me, and actually slept without very considerable interruption till we were near the summit of the mighty pass. Already there was a faint hint of the morning in the starlight which showed us the vast sloping snowfields as we commenced the descent. I got a few glimpses of the pure far-stretching whiteness before the sharpening edge of cold forced us to close the window.

They travelled by train through Turin and Genoa, then by overnight boat to Livorno, and on to Pisa — then back to Livorno, and another night sea-crossing to Civita Vecchia. During those days they climbed church towers, visited palazzo gardens, went to the opera, evaluated frescoes, and caught the end of Sabbath prayers in a synagogue, which Eliot found 'not unlike a dissenting chapel'. Amidst all this she observed 'what gives beauty to every corner of the inhabited world — the groups of children squatting against walls or trotting about by the sides of their elders, or grinning together over their play'.

She had always imagined Rome as a mixture of ruined grandeur and vibrant modern life. But when they first caught sight of the city from their train window, 'there was nothing imposing to be seen'. The sky was grey. They scrambled for a small expensive room in a tourist hotel, then trudged through dirty streets, dejected at 'the probable relations our "Rome visited" was to bear to our "Rome unvisited"'. Things began to improve the next day, when they found cheaper lodgings and moved in for a month.

On their fourth morning in Rome the clouds turned to rain, and Eliot began a long letter to Maria Congreve. She described her gradual rise 'from the depth of disappointment to an intoxication of delight', then broke off mid-sentence because, she hurriedly explained, 'the rain has left off, and my husband commands me to put on my bonnet.' When she resumed her letter in the afternoon, she gossiped about Lewes's poor health — horrible headaches and hearing loss that made her anxious, though otherwise things were 'perfect' — and the volatile political situation in Italy, which she did not take very seriously. She seemed more affected by local mothers and children:

> Oh, the beautiful men and women and children here! Such wonderful babies with wise eyes! — such grand-featured mothers nursing them! As one drives along the streets sometimes, one sees a Madonna and child at every third or fourth upper window; and on Monday a little crippled girl seated at the door of a church looked up at us with a face full of such pathetic sweetness and beauty, that I think it can hardly leave me again.

Halfway through this letter to Maria, they submerged themselves in the Easter crowds at St Peter's. Their Anglican prejudices, radicalized by Lewes's atheism, made them suspicious of popery, and with its throngs of tourists and hoards of gold the Vatican was possibly the worldliest place in Rome. On Maundy Thursday they were, for once, separated, and had no way of finding one another in the vast piazza; the Pope came past Eliot and she knelt to receive his blessing. 'Altogether, these ceremonies are a melancholy, hollow business', she wrote to Maria on Good Friday, 'and we regret bitterly that the Holy Week has taken up our time from better things. I have a cold and headache this morning, and in other ways am not conscious of improvement from the Pope's blessing.' The following day, a young priest came to bless their lodgings. As Lewes put it, he 'sprinkled holy water and gabbled out some phrases with indifference and haste that were shocking. He then went into the bedroom and blessed the conjugal bed in the same style.' Thus their disreputable union was unwittingly sanctified by the Roman Catholic Church.

They stayed in Rome for almost the whole of April. Once free of the Easter ceremonies, they devoured the city's art and architecture — marble temples, mosaic altarpieces, dark catacombs, and of course all the galleries and museums.

From Rome they travelled south to Naples, which they loved more than anywhere they had seen before, and on to Salerno, Paestum, Amalfi and Sorrento. In the middle of May they arrived in Florence, where they settled for two weeks and began a new itinerary of hectic sightseeing. Hoping to avoid the 'perpetual noisy pic-nic' of English and American tourists, they stayed in the *Pension Suisse*, the quietest hotel in the city — or at least in their guidebook.

Early in their stay in Florence, Eliot sent John Blackwood a rather fretful letter, anxious for news of the *Mill on the Floss* and uncertain of her future as an artist:

> As for me, I am thrown into a state of humiliating passivity by the sight of the great things done in the far past — it seems as if life were not long enough to learn, and as if my own activity were so completely dwarfed by comparison that I should never have courage for more creation of my own. There is only one thing that has an opposite and stimulating effect: it is the comparative rarity even here of great and truthful art, and the abundance of wretched imitation and falsity. Every hand is wanted in the world that can do a little genuine, sincere work.

Perhaps in response to this fidgety mood — a sign of her re-emerging creative ambition, two months after completing her second novel — Lewes suggested a new project. Reading about Savonarola one morning, it occurred to him that she could write 'an historical romance' about this firebrand Dominican friar, who became the scourge of Renaissance Florence. 'Polly at once caught the idea with enthusiasm,' Lewes wrote in his journal that night.

The next morning, 22 May, they visited the Dominican convent of San Marco, where Fra Savonarola had lived in the 1490s, his apocalyptic sermons drawing huge crowds that spilled out of the convent's church and garden. After lunch they browsed old bookshops until they found a copy of Savonarola's poems, then went to the Uffizi gallery and bought a new French biography of the controversial friar.

*

During their visit to Florence, Eliot fell in love with Fra Angelico — also a Dominican friar, though in some ways the antithesis of Savonarola. Fra Angelico spent years decorating the San Marco convent after Medici patrons acquired it for his community in the middle of the fifteenth century. The Dominicans were the Order of Preachers, a vocation that encompassed writing and illustration as well as oral preaching. Their great theologian, Thomas Aquinas, exemplified the Dominican motto: *Contemplata aliis tradere.** The Order's silent rule made urban convents like San Marco havens of meditation and study, directed to their mission of teaching Christian faith to as many people as possible.

While Thomas Aquinas pursued this mission in immense scholastic treatises, Fra Angelico did so as an artist. He sought to manifest truth in painting. In his work Eliot found exquisite images of human forms filled with spiritual meaning, and traces of an artist's hand not entirely unlike her own — for her mission was to manifest truth in fiction. Whenever they visited the Uffizi gallery she 'always paused with longing' by a Fra Angelico triptych of the Madonna and child, surrounded by 'unspeakably lovely angels'.

The Dominicans, like the Cistercians, were devoted to the Virgin Mary and wore white habits to symbolize her purity. In the fourteenth century Mary was embraced by a new culture of chivalry, as well as by the monastic and mendicant orders that saw her as their spiritual patron and muse. She began to be called 'Our Lady' — 'Notre Dame' in France, 'La Madonna' in Italy — and Dante's *Paradiso* glorified her as the 'Mystic Rose' and 'Queen of Heaven', circled by crowds of adoring angels. Fra Angelico painted some of the most beautiful Madonnas ever seen, achieving a delicate equilibrium between Mary's

---

* To pass on to others things contemplated

spiritual, mythical and human presence. During his lifetime, though, powerful Florentine families, emboldened by Renaissance ideals, were commissioning other artists to make more humanist images of Mary, dressed alluringly in fine clothes, to commemorate their wealth and power. By the end of the fifteenth century Fra Savonarola was thundering against these worldly vanities, and burning some of them in spectacular bonfires in Florence's central piazza — before being burned himself on gallows in the same square.

＊

San Marco housed these layers of history, along with Mary herself, enthroned at the centre of a great altarpiece in the inner sanctum of its church. Women were not allowed into the corridors and dormitories, so Lewes went in to take notes for Eliot on Fra Angelico's graceful figures, many of them Mary, that still float on the convent's cool stone walls. As

One of Fra Angelico's San Marco frescoes, which Lewes described to
Eliot during their visit to the convent in 1860

she waited for him in the cloisters, she contemplated two huge Crucifixions, the only frescoes visible to female visitors.

In her pursuit of Fra Angelico's inaccessible Madonnas, Eliot was following in the footsteps of another literary traveller, Anna Jameson, a prolific author and a good friend of Barbara Bodichon. Mrs Jameson, as she was often known, had started to write books in the 1830s, after marrying a barrister — probably to escape her job as a governess — and separating from him four years later. Among her early works were *The Relative Social Position of Mothers and Governesses* and a collection of essays on Shakespeare's female characters. She then turned to the medieval period, and produced a series of erudite books collectively titled *Sacred and Legendary Art*. Third in the series was *Legends of the Madonna*, published in 1852 — two years before the Immaculate Conception became official Catholic doctrine. This book combined Jameson's chief interests: the history of fine art and the contemporary 'Woman Question'. She eventually gained special access to the forbidden frescoes at San Marco, during her last Continental trip in 1858. She had died in London about a week before Eliot and Lewes set off for Italy.

Jameson, an Anglo-Irish Protestant, was wary of the Catholics' veneration of Mary, yet fascinated by the multiple meanings and enduring power of her image. Iconographies of Mary connected her with the sun, the moon, the star of the sea — *Stella Maris*, one interpretation of her Jewish name, Miriam. Mary was both the lily, symbol of purity, and the rose, symbol of love and beauty. She might be a garden or a temple, a well or a fountain; a cedar tree, exalted for its deep perfume and healing powers, or an olive tree, the sign of peace, hope and abundance.

Seen through the critical gaze of liberal Protestants like Jameson, Mary could represent the duality of fallen woman and blessed virgin. As a mythical figure she resembled Eve, the first woman, mother of the human race, and also the original sinner. As an historical figure she was morally ambiguous. Drawing out her scandalous side, Søren Kierkegaard emphasized that Mary was shameful in the eyes of her neighbours: unmarried, pregnant and betrothed to a poor man who was not the father of her child. 'Has any woman in the world been so infringed upon as was Mary, and is it not true that the one whom God blesses, he curses in the same breath?' wrote Kierkegaard in 1843. He concluded that Mary's inner life was paradoxical, full of fear and trembling — 'no one could understand her.'

Mary also embodied wisdom and philosophy. Medieval paintings of the Annunciation often depict her with a book, open at the seventh chapter of the Book of Wisdom. In this Greek text from the Jewish scriptures, Wisdom is personified as a female figure. After the birth of Jesus, the book on Mary's knee is replaced by a child — not because she now has no time to read, but because her son is Wisdom itself, nurtured inside her womb.

In *Legends of the Madonna* Jameson traced Mary's ancient roots to ideas of 'a mother-goddess' found across different cultures. She explained how Mary merged with Diana, the Greek goddess of both fertility and chastity, to become 'the impersonation of motherhood, all beauty, bounty, and graciousness; and at the same time, by virtue of her perpetual virginity, the patroness of single and ascetic life'. Many early worshippers of Mary were women. Her title of 'Theotokos', the Mother of God, was disputed until the fifth century, when the Council of Ephesus confirmed it. Only then did images of Mary with her holy child become emblems of orthodox faith.

Jameson herself saw a 'great hope' in the 'perpetual iteration' of Mary's image — 'hope in a higher as well as a gentler power than that of the strong hand and the might that makes the right'. Her favourite painting was Raphael's Sistine Madonna, which had so affected Eliot in Dresden:

> there she stands — the transfigured woman, at once completely human and completely divine, an abstraction of power, purity, and love, poised on the empurpled air, and requiring no other support; looking out . . . quite through the universe, to the end and consummation of all things . . . I have stood before it and confessed that there is more in that form and face than I had ever yet conceived. I cannot here talk the language of critics, and speak of this picture merely as a picture, for to me it was a revelation.

This Madonna, more than any other, expressed 'the union of the divine and human in the feminine form' — the visionary power of an independent woman.

Perhaps guided by Jameson, Eliot was similarly moved by paintings of Mary. Though she had to rely on Lewes's descriptions of Fra Angelico's San Marco frescoes, she visited his Madonna of the Stars in the Church of Santa Maria Novella, as well as the Linaioli Tabernacle in the Uffizi. The 'iteration' of Mary's image across Europe, east and west, was especially concentrated in Florence and Rome; it is no wonder Eliot saw Madonnas in windows and on street corners during her Italian tour. In Florence she admired more of Raphael's paintings of the Madonna and Child, and many treatments of the subject by other artists. But it was Fra Angelico's work she wanted to take back to London with her. They bought engravings of his pictures from a Florentine print shop, and Lewes commissioned a local artist to copy one of the San Marco frescoes, to hang above Eliot's writing desk at home. She would contemplate it while she made her own art.

At this moment in her life Eliot was beginning to identify herself as a mother, as well as an author, and reflecting with some anxiety on how these roles might go together. In Fra Angelico's paintings she could glimpse an ideal of motherhood — encompassing profound wisdom as well as perfect love — fused with the creative genius and patient craft of a devout artist. Perhaps this fusion would be impossible to achieve back home, in their unholy ménage à trois. Yet Mary, her namesake, had also taken an unconventional path through maternity and marriage; she had believed in something impossible, and it had come to be.

As Anna Jameson recognized, images of the Madonna and child possess immense emotional power. Deeper than doctrine, this can cut through social norms and institutional structures. It is difficult to look at one of those Fra Angelico Madonnas and not feel like a child again — maybe because the loveliness of her face is an echo of our own mother's face, always beautiful to a young child. This experience might kindle the 'feeling of absolute dependence' that Schleiermacher, the great Romantic theologian, found to be the essence of religion. Or it might inspire longing for what Mary offers: infallible gentleness, infinite peace, undivided attention, perfect understanding, unconditional acceptance, powers of protection reaching across space and time — the fantasy, in short, of a wholly unambivalent mother.

*

Eliot and Lewes ended their Italian tour with a week in Venice. She fell in love again: 'What stillness! What beauty! Looking out from the high window of our hotel on the Grand Canal, I felt that it was a pity to go to bed.' They visited more paintings and churches; shopped for lace, glass and jewellery; enjoyed the 'dreamy delight' of gliding on the canals serenaded by gondoliers. They liked to stroll around the Piazza di San Marco 'as the stars were brightening, and look at the grand dim buildings, and the flocks of pigeons flitting about them, or to walk on to the Bridge of La Paglia and look along the dark canal that runs under the Bridge of Sighs — its blackness lit up by a gas light here and there, and the plash of the oar of blackest gondola slowly advancing.' One evening they were out on the lagoon as the sun was setting, 'and the wide waters were flushed with the reddened light: I should have liked it to last for hours; it is the sort of scene in which I could most readily forget my own existence and feel melted into the general life.'

After Venice they made their way to Switzerland, and arrived at Berne, five miles from Lewes's sons' boarding school, on 23 June. As Charles Lewes was dutifully growing his hair in preparation for this day, all three brothers were feeling apprehensive. One of their school-friends had met Agnes; how should they explain things when Lewes turned up with a different 'Mother'? It was also unclear whether Agnes was aware of their new relationship with Eliot: did *she* know that *they* knew about the new Mrs Lewes? Thornton, the most assert-ive of the three, had written to Lewes seeking answers to these questions. He had also asked Eliot, rather optimistically, to persuade Lewes to let him and his brothers join them on holiday in Italy.

Lewes and Eliot spent two days with the boys before they left Berne, bringing Charles home with them. This was the beginning of a gradual integration into one another's family. Of course, Eliot's parents and sister were dead, and her brother was not speaking to her. But on their way home they stopped in Geneva to visit the D'Alberts, a middle-aged couple who had become substitute parents when she lodged with them for a winter ten years earlier, just after her father died. 'It was a great delight to me to see how truly they loved and prized Polly,' Lewes wrote in his journal. Rather like the Brays in Coventry, François D'Albert-Durade and his wife had adopted young Mary Ann — or Marianne, as they called her — during her months in their home. She had enjoyed being 'indulged' like 'a spoiled child': she called Madame D'Albert 'Maman', and loved to 'lean on' her. François D'Albert was an artist, and had painted her portrait.

Until George Eliot's identity was revealed in the summer of 1859, she had been out of touch with this couple for some years. Just as the lifting of her pseudonymous veil emboldened Lewes to tell his sons about her, so it had prompted her to write to François D'Albert:

Does it ever happen to you now to think of a certain Englishwoman, née Marian Evans? . . . In these last three years, a great change has come over my life — a change in which I cannot help believing that both you and Madame D'Albert will rejoice. Under the influence of the intense happiness I have enjoyed in my married life from thorough moral and intellectual sympathy, I have at last found out my true vocation, after which my nature had always been feeling and striving uneasily without finding it. What do you think that vocation is? I pause for you to guess.

I have turned out to be an artist — not, as you are, with the pencil and the pallet, but with words. I have written a novel which people say has stirred them very deeply — and not a *few* people, but almost all reading England. It was published in February last, and already 14,000 copies have been sold. The title is 'Adam Bede'; and 'George Eliot', the name on the title page, is my *nom de plume*.

François D'Albert had responded warmly to this news of marital and literary success. He had perceived that she was someone for whom marriage would be either 'hell or paradise' — '*Tant que je vous connaissais, le mariage devait être pour vous l'enfer ou le paradis.*' He understood that a marriage might crush her free spirit, or fulfil her longing for exclusive love. It might, indeed, do both at once.

Drawing-room gossip had predicted that revealing George Eliot to be the dubious Mrs Lewes would harm her books. Though this was not entirely inaccurate, it turned out to be the other way around.

Widespread acclaim for *Adam Bede* and *The Mill on the Floss* led more people to accept Eliot's domestic situation. When Elizabeth Gaskell wrote with warm appreciation for her work, she expressed tolerance, if not wholehearted acceptance: 'I wish you *were* Mrs Lewes . . . still, it can't be helped.' After they returned from Italy, Lewes's mother, who had previously refused to meet Eliot, began to call on them. Even Queen Victoria was rereading *Adam Bede*, and telling her daughter to read it too.

Eliot saw that her new role as 'mother' to Lewes's sons would also strengthen her claim to be his wife. Even before she met Charles, Thornton and Bertie, she was describing them to friends as 'our boys'; Charles soon became 'our eldest boy'. She set out her case in a sharp letter to her friend Clementia Taylor, a suffragist and anti-slavery campaigner, who had made the mistake of addressing her as 'Miss Evans':

> For the last six years I have ceased to be 'Miss Evans' for any one who has personal relations with me — having held myself under all the responsibilities of a married woman. I wish this to be distinctly understood; and when I tell you that we have a great boy of eighteen at home who calls me 'mother,' as well as two other boys, almost as tall, who write to me under the same name, you will understand that the point is not one of mere egoism or personal dignity, when I request that any one who has regard for me will cease to speak of me by my maiden name.

Yet while motherly duties gave her a claim to the moral high ground, the day-to-day burden of those duties laid her rather low. The summer and autumn months of 1860 were largely filled with preparing Charles for exams to qualify him for a job in the General Post Office, and with moving to central London so that he could easily get to work. She wrote relatively little. Even her journal entries were sparse, and those she did manage to write reported 'anxiety and trembling', 'want of health and strength', 'physical weakness accompanied by mental depression', 'self-dissatisfaction and fear that I may not be able to do anything more that is well worth doing'.

During those months she sat several times for her portrait by Samuel Laurence, an old friend of Lewes. He painted sadness as well as intelligence in her eyes, and anger around the mouth. The slight incline of her head suggested resistance. She looked fed up. Lewes, not surprisingly, rejected the finished painting, and refused to let Laurence exhibit it in public. It was a sensitive, even beautiful portrait of a writer, wife and mother — but very far from a beatific Madonna.

Eliot attributed her depression to 'the loss of the country': like many Victorians, she found city life taxing on her health and spirits, and took remedial 'tonics' to counter its effects. But even before they left Wandsworth's green fields for Marylebone, she had felt oppressed.

George Eliot by Samuel Laurence, 1860

Within a week of returning from Italy she had confessed to Madame D'Albert, her 'dear Maman', that despite 'many blessings' she was 'weighed down' by anxiety, and found life 'toilsome' — 'I have always to struggle against a selfish longing for repose.' At the end of the year she was still in a sulky frame of mind. The past nine months had 'not been fruitful in work'; too many 'distractions' gobbled up her days. She was already longing for the time, hopefully no more than three years hence, when they would 'have so far done our duty by the boys as to be free to live where we list'.

Surely part of the problem was that she was angry, and had no one to blame. Charles himself was irreproachable: amiable, conscientious, quiet and helpful around the house; they did indeed play duets on the piano in the evenings. They became very fond of one another. Nor could she fairly blame Lewes for having three children, whom she had known about when she chose to live with him. Caught in a double bind of resentment and guilt, she twisted her dissatisfaction inward.

*

These circumstances were not at all conducive to beginning a big historical novel about Savonarola's Florence. Transferring George Eliot's distinctive 'realism' from the remembered past of provincial England to a remote place and time would require detailed research. Though she had experienced Italy's streets, voices and faces — and glimpsed their fifteenth-century ancestors in Renaissance paintings — she would have to master a large cast of characters, with unfamiliar costumes and customs, and a web of complex political events. While she was 'meditating' this daunting project, two other stories emerged: 'Brother Jacob' and *Silas Marner*. The first was a short story, the second a short novel which seemed to thrust itself upon her: it 'came *across* my other plans by a sudden inspiration'. In their literary form these works offered relief from the weight of her unwritten novel; both have a fairy-tale quality, eschewing historical and geographical specificity. They were forgiving, uncluttered channels through which her creative life could flow.

These stories also provided release for the emotional knots she had tied herself in. Both feature a theft of gold sovereigns that is symbolically linked to parenthood. The plot of 'Brother Jacob' turns on a son stealing his mother's saved-up gold. Silas Marner, 'the weaver of Raveloe', has his treasured hoard stolen from him, and replaced by the golden curls of a baby girl. At the beginning of the story, his gold is his most treasured companion; since he has earned it by weaving, it is closely associated with his work.

Silas Marner bears strong thematic resemblances to Eliot, despite their superficial differences. His weaving and her writing are solitary occupations that stand as mutual metaphors: Silas weaves 'a tale of linen'. He has been excluded from his previous life in a religious community, essentially his adopted family, which falsely accused him of theft and cast him out. Now he lives on the margins of Raveloe, and is fearful of the villagers, who in turn regard him with suspicion. Like Eliot, he becomes a parent by taking on someone else's child.

The thefts which recur in these stories provided a rationale for the anger and injustice that Eliot felt, but could not articulate directly. Twenty years earlier, when she was just nineteen, she had written a poem that likened books to 'chests of gold' which she secretly hoarded, 'miser like'. Now that she was a writer as well as a reader, the link between gold and productivity established at the beginning of *Silas Marner* made this simile all the more pertinent to her literary life. Moreover, the idea of stolen gold resonates uncannily with letters written the previous autumn, when she was working out her relationship to Charles Lewes, contemplating his arrival in London, and anticipating the loss of her precious writing time. That year the trees had been stripped bare by storms. 'What an Autumn!' she wrote to Charles Bray: 'There never was such a dead robbery committed on one's gold — one's autumn gold.' Her third letter to Charles Lewes, written the same week, echoed this theme: 'I have no memory of an autumn so disappointing as this. It is my favourite season. I delight especially in the golden and red tints under the purple clouds. But this year the trees were almost stripped of their leaves before they had changed colour — dashed off by the wind and rain. We have had *no* autumnal beauty.' Every other paragraph in this brief letter warns Charles that she is short of time, and cannot spare much for him. This chain of associations links the 'robbery' of her autumn gold to her fear that Charles will take away her writing.

In *Silas Marner* George Eliot dwells on the connection between Silas's lost gold and golden-haired Eppie, the little girl who takes its place. This exchange cannot be explained: Silas is 'so confused' by it that 'he could only have said that the child was come instead of the gold — that the gold has turned into the child.' The story's explicit moral is that this warm, soft, human treasure is far greater than his hard coins, which have only an illusory value. As he becomes a parent, Silas gains infinitely more than he lost: not just a beloved daughter, but the respect of his neighbours. However, like the logic of a dream, this moral pattern lays the ground for its inversion. What if the stolen treasure is something deeper, more inward than money — like an artist's vocation? In this case, gold is not her reward for work, but the work itself. Her gold is her power, her voice, her chance for beauty.

At the same time, the miracle of Eppie — an ideal child who needs no discipline, and grows up to be a sweet-tempered, devoted daughter — allowed Eliot to explore a childless woman's longing for a baby. She portrays with great tenderness a motherless young woman, Nancy Lammeter, who achieves her desired marriage against the odds, yet cannot have a child and misses the chance to adopt Eppie. When a girl loses her mother, as Mary Ann Evans did at sixteen — and perhaps in an emotional sense long before that — she might yearn for a daughter to restore the relationship she has lost. She might also fear this restoration of a love that brought both mother and child too much suffering.

Besides an adoptive parent and a childless couple, *Silas Marner* depicts two alternative natural mothers. Kind, patient, comforting Dolly Winthrop teaches Silas how to look after Eppie, whereas the child's real mother, Molly, is a feckless barmaid and opium addict — a lower-class girl who must be sacrificed to advance the story's plot. Dolly is an obscure Midlands Madonna, thoroughly domesticated into conventional life, while Molly is a failed mother and a fallen woman: her husband is so ashamed of her that he pretends she does not exist. She dies in the cold on the outskirts of the village, close to Silas Marner's house. These two opposing archetypes dramatize a duality entrenched in Christian culture; they also embody both the remarkable resources and the fallibility of ordinary mothers. In the space between them lies the rich and varied field of maternal ambivalence.

At the beginning of the novel Silas, like Molly, is a spurned, marginal, fallen figure. In the absence of human warmth, he is barely human himself, merely a creature of mechanical habit. He is addicted to money, as Molly is addicted to opium. Through parenthood, he becomes Dolly's closest friend; at the story's fairy-tale ending they are joined through their children's marriage in a kind of holy family.

Thus Silas too comes to resemble Mary. His perfect child came to him unbidden, miraculously, almost supernaturally, and transformed

Silas Marner and Eppie by Hugh Thomson, 1907

him into someone blessed. This new Silas is humble, full of gratitude, innocent — almost sexless, probably a virgin. Like Dolly, he is a healer, whose peculiar wisdom is called upon by others in times of need. His patience is endless and his parental love is pure.

Perhaps Eliot hoped for a similar transfiguration — or perhaps she just wanted her gold back. Both motherhood and authorship were, she knew, routes to rehabilitation in society. They were even routes to love, and curiously intertwined within her. When she finished *Silas Marner* in the spring of 1861, she once again wrote in her diary 'Magnificat anima mea!'

Manuscript of *Silas Marner*, p. 1: To my beloved Husband George Henry Lewes I give this M.S. of my fourth book written in London, 1861

7

Disillusion

By 1861 they were settled in a smart rented townhouse in north-west London, tucked into the slice of genteel streets and squares between Baker Street and the Edgware Road. The house was one of several 'middle-class residences' on Blandford Square, a few doors down from Barbara Bodichon's London home. Blandford square also contained the Convent of the Sisters of Mercy and a House of Mercy recently established for 'the protection of young women of good character, who are intended for service, or who may be for a time out of employment'. From this haven of rectitude Eliot and Lewes often walked north-east across Regent's Park to its Zoological Gardens, or south-east through Marylebone to Piccadilly for concerts at St James's Hall. When Barbara was in town she called on Eliot several times a week, occasionally with her husband. On Sundays the two women tried out services at various London churches while Lewes, the confirmed atheist, stayed at home.

Their household included Charles Lewes and two live-in servants, Amelia and Grace, who shopped, cooked, cleaned, and sent clothes to the laundry. On weekdays Charles went out to work at the General Post Office, and the Leweses' 'double solitude' fell into its customary routine: quiet working hours after breakfast, lunch at half past one, an afternoon walk, dinner at five when Charles came home. Eliot became a little less reclusive. They began to have more visitors at home, though when she received invitations she always declined them. They bought a grand piano, and on Saturdays hosted small gatherings of friends for music and conversation. Attending these soirées still carried a frisson of scandal, especially for female guests — and some found excuses to stay away — but the Leweses' domestic life had acquired some semblance of respectability.

Eliot did not like living in the city. She found it 'ugly' and alienating: in the spring she confessed to Barbara 'a sort of sick longing at the faintest sketch suggesting a broad sky and a distance, this London life oppresses and *de*presses me so terribly'; during the winter she complained of 'a constant depression of vitality from this foggy air of London. The yearning for the blue sky and the fields haunts me constantly.' Even her enjoyment of concerts was 'much diminished by the gas and bad air'. She and Lewes dosed themselves with quinine, and with sea air and spa cures when they could get away. Lewes's physical health was particularly bad, and he grew alarmingly worn and thin.

For all the 'privileges' it conferred, London demanded 'sacrifices' of both body and mind. Eliot explained to several friends that these sacrifices were for Charles's sake, 'to make a home for him' — and he was 'a dear, precious boy, worth a great deal of sacrifice for the sake of preserving the purity and beauty of his mind'. They had leased the house in Blandford Square for three years, and after that, she hoped, this delicate parental duty would be done.

Apart from the afflictions of urban life, she conceded that 'we have all the blessings that are worth desiring' — most of all, 'a life of perfect love and a union that every year makes closer'. Lewes also expressed gratitude for 'such domestic happiness as can be given to a few'. He wrote proudly of Eliot's 'perfect love for the children'.

In the spring of 1861, after *Silas Marner* was published, they returned to Florence to spend a month researching her Italian novel: again Lewes roamed San Marco and took notes for her on the cells and frescoes. He thought that she was doing too much research, that she was too daunted by the prospect of writing about a place and time beyond her experience. 'As I often tell her,' he wrote to John Blackwood from Italy, 'most of the scenes and characters of her books are quite as *historical* to her direct personal experience, as the 15th century of Florence.' Lewes believed that his wife knew 'infinitely more of Savonarola than she knew of Silas, besides having deep personal sympathies with the old reforming priest which she had not with the miser'.

Back in London, Eliot told Blackwood that she struggled to hear Savonarola talking, as she had heard the voices of her English characters, though she 'could not tell how the feeling and knowledge came to her'. She also wrestled with the familiar 'demon' of despair, which returned 'whenever an old work is dismissed and a new one is being meditated'. Dreading failure, she accused herself of being 'too egoistic' and resolved to conquer her emotions. Yet through the summer she found herself 'much afflicted with hopelessness and melancholy', 'struggling constantly with depression'.

Instead of writing her novel she devoured a history of Renaissance philosophy, a four-volume history of religious orders, a sixteen-volume history of medieval Italian republics, a six-volume work on Florentine architecture, and several biographies of Savonarola. She researched art history, medical superstitions, ecclesiastical vestments, Roman law; she read Machiavelli, Politian, Cicero, Petrarch, Epictetus, Juvenal. She disliked going into town, and Lewes became her literary hunter-gatherer, scouring the city's second-hand shops and stalls for the books she needed, or borrowing them from the British Museum in Bloomsbury. Eliot found this bustling public library 'a painful way of getting knowledge': its new circular Reading Room was a microcosm of city life, with nowhere to hide from judging eyes. She preferred the private London Library, established twenty years earlier by Carlyle in the exclusive homely style of a gentleman's club, but its collection was limited and eventually she had to brave the 'sneezes and wheezes' in the British Museum. She spent several afternoons there, always with Lewes, researching fifteenth-century costumes and 'table equipage', studying the letters and biographies of forgotten Florentines.

Lewes was impatient for her to start writing, and reported glumly to Blackwood that she was 'buried' in old books. Autumn came and went, while her 'desponding' and 'brooding' continued — 'trying to write, trying to construct, and unable'. One day in November she felt so 'utterly dejected' during their afternoon walk in Regent's Park that she nearly decided to give up the Italian novel.

'Polly is still deep in her researches,' Lewes wrote to Blackwood in December:

> At present she remains immoveable in the conviction that she *can't* write the romance because she has not knowledge enough. Now as a matter of fact I know that she has immensely more knowledge of the particular period than any other writer who has touched it; but her distressing diffidence paralyses her.

This is between ourselves. When you see her, mind your care is to discountenance the idea of a Romance being the product of an Encyclopaedia.

Eliot was, in fact, making progress. She had by now a clearer sense of her story. Unrelenting darkness gave way to 'flashes of hope succeeded by long intervals of dim distrust'. Just before Christmas, Blackwood visited and brought along his wife — a great concession — and he and Lewes 'reproached' Eliot for procrastinating. She promised to make a fresh start on New Year's Day, and on 1 January 1862 she recorded in her diary: '*I began my Novel of Romola.*' This would be the first George Eliot work since *Janet's Repentance* to be named after its female heroine.

*

The difficulty of beginning *Romola* was proportionate to its immense ambition. In both its theme and its form, this work took several new directions at once. Written during the only period of Eliot's life with Lewes spent in central London, it was her first — and only — urban novel. While *Adam Bede* exudes 'the breath of cows and the scent of hay', *Romola* unfolds in rooms stuffed with books and dusty antiquities, in crowded streets and noisy squares. Even its outdoor spaces are enclosed: the heroine paces back and forth across her roofed loggia, and Florence itself is contained within its walls, the countryside beyond merely a vague promise of freedom that will never be fulfilled.

During its slow gestation, the story about 'the life and times of Savonarola' proposed by Lewes had mutated into a dark psychological marriage drama, its oppressive interiority mirroring its urban setting. The popular 'historical romance' he had envisaged became a devastating chronicle of deceit, disappointment and despair. Readers would find themselves drawn inside this treacherous marriage, moving between the experiences of husband and wife as their shared subjectivity is constructed and ruined, while they remain inseparably tied.

Romola was also George Eliot's most philosophical novel yet. Its Renaissance setting provides an eclectic intellectual milieu in which

'The Young Wife' — Romola walled-in in Florence.
Illustration by Frederic Leighton, 1862

Christianity jostles with ancient Greek and Roman philosophies —
stoicism, Platonism, hedonism, scepticism — and with new kinds of
humanism and satire. The novel dramatizes these diverse ethics and
probes their limitations on the testing ground of marriage. More
profoundly still, it is preoccupied with the unsettling distinction
between appearance and reality, revived by the scholars of Renaissance Florence when they turned to the works of Plato, whose
famous parable of the cave enacts the primal scene of European
philosophy. Plato invited his readers to imagine a group of prisoners chained inside an underground cave, watching a play of shadows

on the wall. The prisoners are oblivious to the actors and puppets parading behind them, producing these shadows; their necks are shackled and they cannot turn their heads. Because they have no concept of the difference between shadows and solid objects, between surface and depth, between illusion and reality, they simply believe whatever they see.

Plato's parable evokes a desire for truth: no one wants to be a deluded prisoner. At the same time, it suggests that we are all like these prisoners. Thus the reader is cast into double consciousness — an ambiguous state of belief and disbelief that renders everything questionable. Whether we call this state wonder or anxiety, it is the beginning of philosophy. It may lead to a passionate pursuit of wisdom, as for Plato's teacher Socrates. But it can also harbour scepticism. Some ancient philosophers saw the gap between appearance and reality as a chasm that can never be bridged; they argued that we should concentrate on reconciling ourselves to uncertainty, instead of chasing truths.

Although Plato thought the work of philosophy was reserved for exceptional men, his cave conjures questions that every child awakens to, sooner or later. And we live these questions over and over again, each time we wonder how someone is really feeling, if a person meant what they said, whether a rumour is true. Since such questions can arise whenever we encounter something that has interiority or depth, they are omnipresent in our dealings with other human beings. One lesson of Plato's cave is that we rarely live in the clear light of knowledge; our usual condition is a chiaroscuro of faith and doubt in appearances that may or may not be warranted. The truth of some things might never see the light of day.

Yet Plato's cave possesses a revelatory power. It is a literary construction that allows us at once to imaginatively inhabit the cave, and to watch ourselves doing so, as if from the outside, bringing our ignorance into view — a miraculous mirror that reflects our own blind spots. In George Eliot's hands, the novel permits a similar disclosure. With the help of an omniscient narrator, readers are simultaneously drawn inside a character's consciousness and shown its limits, errors and delusions.

THE FIRST KISS.

'The First Kiss' — Tito and Romola before their marriage.
Illustration by Frederic Leighton, 1862

Romola turns this philosophical mirror on marriage, revealing a delicate structure assembled from a shifting configuration of desires and appearances, sustained by trust, and haunted by the question of truthfulness. When Romola de' Bardi marries handsome, hedonistic Tito Melema she plunges into the condition dramatized in Plato's cave. Their shared life becomes a shadowy prison of half-truths and outright deceptions, her husband himself a play of charming surfaces that conceal manipulation and betrayal. Even when she discovers his true nature and tries to escape, she is turned back to this dark marriage chamber — just as Plato's philosopher, who climbs out of the cave into the sunlight, must descend again into its shadows and find a way to live among them.

Romola, the motherless daughter of a humanist scholar, has been schooled in ancient Greek and Roman philosophy, but she is unprepared for life beyond her father's library. Marriage proves more arduous than metaphysics: its promises more seductive, its disclosures more catastrophic. A wife, like a philosopher, does not want to live under illusions — yet her disillusionment must be an agonizing process, like dying by a thousand cuts. Romola's hopeful heart will flinch at each tiny tear in the veil that covers the 'dissidence between inward reality and outward seeming'.

Tito promises to bring Romola perfect happiness, and to help her carry on her father's scholarly work. Before their wedding he presents her with a small cabinet decorated with a painting of themselves as Bacchus, god of pleasure and intoxication, and Ariadne, whom Bacchus rescues from grief. Romola's brother Dino has betrayed their father's humanist ideals by joining the San Marco friars and becoming a disciple of Savonarola. On his deathbed, Dino describes a terrifying vision of his sister's imminent marriage and gives her his crucifix, which Tito locks inside the painted cabinet. He pockets the key. 'Romola, you will look only at the images of our happiness now,' Tito tells her, 'I have locked all sadness away from you.' 'But it is still there — it is only hidden,' she replies.

As a young wife, Romola becomes adept at concealing the truth from herself. Though she is conscious of 'a little heartache in the midst of her love', her imagination busily makes excuses and compensations, 'trying to see how Tito could be as good as she had thought he was':

> It was clear that their natures differed widely; but perhaps it was no more than the inherent difference between man and woman, that made her affections more absorbing. If there were any other difference she tried to persuade herself that the inferiority was on her side. Tito was really kinder than she was, better tempered, less proud and resentful; he had no angry retorts, he met all complaints with perfect sweetness; he only escaped as quietly as he could from things that were unpleasant.

It belongs to every large nature, when it is not under the immediate power of some strong unquestioning emotion, to suspect itself, and to doubt the truth of its own impressions, conscious of possibilities beyond its own horizon. And Romola was urged to doubt herself the more by the necessity of interpreting her disappointment in her life with Tito so as to satisfy at once her love and her pride. Disappointment? Yes, there was no other milder word that would tell the truth. Perhaps all women had to suffer the disappointment of ignorant hopes, if only she knew their experience.

In such passages, the narrator's voice hovers indistinctly inside and outside Romola's mind, colluding in her self-deception. Her marriage has become the ground beneath her feet, and the part of her that knows it rests on shifting sands is scrambling to secure it. 'She felt equal to any self-infliction that would save her from ceasing to love. That would have been like the hideous nightmare in which the world had seemed to break away all round her, and leave her feet overhanging the darkness.'

Just as Tito tries to lock away suffering beneath a façade of happy images, so Romola hides the true character of their relationship from other people. George Eliot's commentary here is ambivalent:

Poor Romola! There was one thing that would have made the pang of disappointment harder to bear; it was, that any one should know he gave her cause for disappointment. This might be a woman's weakness, but it is closely allied to a woman's nobleness. She who willingly lifts up the veil of her married life has profaned it from a sanctuary into a vulgar place.

The uncertainties that arise within the gap between 'inward reality and outward seeming' haunt any effort to know the truth of a marriage, whether from the inside or from the outside. Tito presents his deceptively beautiful face to Romola, while she presents the perfect surface of their marriage to the world. George Eliot attributes this partly to Romola's pride, cast as both a strength and a weakness of her character, but she also suggests that keeping up appearances is a wife's duty. It would be 'vulgar' to expose a marriage's secret sufferings — yet Romola's efforts at concealment deserve both pity and critique. Does the sanctity of marriage need to be sustained by illusion? This question seems to trouble George Eliot, and brings her narrative voice into conflict with itself.

*

On 23 May 1862 Eliot recorded in her diary that 'very important decisions have been made.' She had accepted £7,000 — an unprecedented sum — to publish *Romola* in twelve monthly instalments in the *Cornhill* magazine. John Blackwood had been informed of George Eliot's 'defection', as the publisher put it in an angry letter to his colleague: 'The going over to the enemy without giving me any warning and with a story on which they both said I was fully intitled to calculate upon, sticks in my throat but I shall not quarrel — quarrels especially literary ones are vulgar.' Blackwood pronounced himself 'sorry for and disappointed in her', and attributed the decision to 'the voracity of Lewes'.

Blackwood's assessment was at least partly correct. Eliot's carefully worded diary entry noting that 'decisions have been made' — rather than that she, or Lewes, or both of them together, had decided — sidestepped the question of how she had come to leave her loyal publisher and break her new novel into parts. In fact George Smith, proprietor of the *Cornhill* and an old friend of Lewes, had called one day in January and asked if she were open to a 'magnificent' offer. 'This made me think about money,' she wrote in her diary that evening, 'but it is better for me not to be rich.' In February, with just a few chapters of *Romola* written, Smith offered £10,000 for it — close to one million pounds today. Lewes was excited — this was 'the most magnificent offer ever yet made for a novel' — but to his 'disgust' she declined, for various reasons. Smith proposed to publish *Romola* in sixteen instalments, which seemed to her too many; he wanted to begin serialization in May, which was too soon; and she would 'regret' leaving Blackwood.

Three years earlier she had managed to resist Lewes's wish to publish *The Mill on the Floss* as a lucrative series of one-shilling instalments. This 'Nightmare of the Serial' would, she felt, be stressful for her and detrimental to the novel, but it had taken 'much talking' to make Lewes let go of the idea. Now she found herself fighting a similar battle for *Romola*. 'I cannot consent to begin publication until I have seen nearly to the end of the work,' she wrote in her diary on 1 March. As far as she was concerned, the idea of *Romola* appearing in the *Cornhill* was 'given up'.

Lewes, however, was still negotiating with Smith. The two men privately agreed that other forms of publication would be considered, and a new proposal made. Smith knew that to lure George Eliot he must first win over her husband. In April Lewes was offered the editorship of the *Cornhill*, which Thackeray had just resigned, but he did not want such a large responsibility. On 8 May he accepted the position of 'chief Literary Adviser' at the 'pleasant salary' of £600 per year, for which he would do no more than read a few articles. Lewes was flattered and delighted by this 'very handsome' arrangement. He avoided telling Eliot that his influence in procuring *Romola* was central to his new role at the *Cornhill*: 'If I join you my first thought naturally will be the strength of the Magazine & therefore I should endeavour to persuade Mrs Lewes to publish her new work in it,' he had written to Smith on 3 May, without her knowledge. 'She is, as you know, reluctant and diffident; but she will I am pretty sure be guided by my wishes, even against her own preference for the other form of publication.'

The following week Smith called again to Blandford Square, and Eliot read him several chapters of *Romola*. The publisher was charmed by her voice, 'one of the softest and most agreeable voices' he had 'ever known'. Smith later recalled that 'Lewes and I did all we possibly could to persuade her' to accept the £10,000 offer: 'Lewes himself by no means shared George Eliot's artistic scruples. He seconded me heart and soul.' After a long walk with Lewes — who no doubt kept up the persuasion all the way to Hampstead and back — Eliot agreed to receive £7,000 for publication in longer instalments, beginning in July. She had so far written less than a quarter of the novel. Having resolved not to publish any part of it before the whole work was nearly finished, she now faced a year of monthly deadlines.

More immediately, she had to face John Blackwood. Under some strain, she wrote him a passive-aggressive letter suggesting that her work, and her decision to publish elsewhere, did not matter much to him. Blackwood concealed his annoyance in a generous reply, written, to her relief, 'in the perfect spirit of gentlemanliness and good feeling'.

A month later Blackwood was in London, and went to see her. As he was leaving Blandford Square, Lewes felt unwell, and Eliot seized her few moments alone with her publisher to explain that 'under all the circumstances she had felt that she must accept the enormous offer that had been made — that she could never feel to another publisher as she felt towards him — that pleasure to her was gone in the matter and she did not feel sure that she had acted right.' Blackwood could not tell whether she meant that she may have acted wrongly towards him, or unwisely for herself. Either way, it seemed impossible to voice these doubts in front of Lewes.

*

As Romola's disillusion with Tito grows, she turns her doubts on herself. The narrator notes that she 'quiets' her stubborn questioning by 'that subjection to her husband's mind which is felt by every wife who loves her husband with passionate devotedness and full reliance'. George Eliot's reader sees by now that this trust is misplaced: Tito is unworthy of reverence, and entirely unreliable. Yet Romola perseveres in 'suppressing' herself. She labours, 'as a loving woman must, to subdue her nature to her husband's. The great need of her heart compelled her to strangle, with desperate resolution, every rising impulse of suspicion, pride, and resentment.'

The abuse endured by Janet Dempster in *Scenes of Clerical Life* is pushed beneath the surface of this novel, though in strong words like 'strangle' the scattered clues to violence become unmistakeable. Romola's inward habits of checking herself, doubting herself, are 'self-inflictions' that carry out, behind closed doors, the brutality of patriarchal power. George Eliot perceives that this brutality is the human cost of a refined civilization built by great men, fearful of death and anxious to preserve their names.

Romola is the daughter of such a man, and she grew up learning to placate him. She submitted entirely to her father's will and helped him with his scholarly labours, while he complained about her inferior feminine intellect. One day before her marriage he rages about his lost son Dino, with whom he might have shared in 'the triumphs of this century' — 'the names of the Bardi, father and son, might have been held reverently on the lips of scholars in the ages to come.' When Romola puts a comforting hand on her father's knee, he lets his left hand, weighted with massive rings, 'fall a little too heavily on the delicate blue-veined back of the girl's right, so that she bit her lip to prevent herself from starting.'

She married Tito, who seemed so gentle and light-hearted, to fulfil her father's ambition to preserve his library for posterity — but also to escape his brooding anger, and her own grief for her lost mother. Yet after eighteen months of marriage Romola's love is 'bruised,

THE BLIND SCHOLAR AND HIS DAUGHTER.

'The Blind Scholar and His Daughter'
Illustration by Frederic Leighton, 1862

despairing'. Her father is now dead, but she has been 'subdued' once again by her husband. As she waits up for him late one night, and finally hears him come home, her mouth is 'quivering' and her glance is timid. Tito, meanwhile, feels 'all that sense of power over a wife which makes a husband risk betrayals that a lover never ventures on'. In fact, he has a secret second wife.

Romola's suppressed distrust of Tito is confirmed when she learns that he has sold her father's library. She sinks into a depression that fills the air with demons: when the bells ring out from the Palazzo Vecchio's tower, she hears a peal of triumph at 'the desolation of her life'. She has 'lost her belief in the happiness she once thirsted for'. This happiness, like the husband who promised it, has turned out to be 'a hateful, smiling, soft-handed thing, with a narrow, selfish heart'.

Like Janet Dempster — though in very different circumstances — Romola wrestles with the question of whether to leave a destructive marriage. Eventually she makes a daring plan to escape not just the marriage, but also the patriarchal power that has formed and corrupted it. She prepares to go to Venice and apprentice herself to Cassandra Fedele, an orator and philosopher and 'the most learned woman in the world'. But this new dream is still 'childish', still shaped by her father's will: Romola hopes to become 'wise enough to write something which would rescue her father's name from oblivion'.

Early the next morning she leaves Florence in disguise, seeking a 'new life'. She climbs the steep path out of the city's 'accustomed walls and streets' and as the sun rises she feels 'free and alone'. For the first time in her life there are no walls, 'no human presence interposing and making a law for her.'

This feeling lasts only a moment before she encounters a new father figure. It is Savonarola, who immediately turns her into a 'wife' and 'daughter' again:

> You are Romola de' Bardi, the wife of Tito Melema . . . You wish your true name and your true place in life to be hidden, that you may choose for yourself a new name and a new place, and have no rule but your own will. And I have a command to call you back. My daughter, you must return to your place . . . You are a wife . . . Come, my daughter, come back to your place!

Savonarola's 'innate need to dominate' echoes Tito's 'masculine pre-
dominance'. Romola makes her conditioned response: she is 'subdued',
and 'almost unconsciously' falls to her knees — 'Father, I will be
guided. Teach me! I will go back.' She returns to Florence, and to the
marriage that seems to be her 'inexorable external identity'.

Tito will never know she tried to leave him, and they live together in
estrangement. One night they argue in the street, and when she threatens
to defy her husband he 'seizes her wrists with all his masculine force', and
tells her 'I am master of you.' Passers-by approach them, and Romola's
'habitual sense of personal dignity' prevents her from asking for help;
instead she 'yields' to Tito's assault and conceals it. Indignation rises
within her, but quickly gives way to 'more complicated feelings'. In
another scene, husband and wife silently confront one another:

> She looked up at him with that submission in her glance which belonged
> to her state of self-reproof; but the subtle change in his face and

Left: 'Escaped' — Romola leaves the city, and her marriage.
Right: 'Father, I Will Be Guided' — Romola submits to Savonarola's
command to 'return to her place'. Illustrations by Frederic Leighton, 1863.

manner arrested her speech. For a few moments they remained silent, looking at each other.

Tito himself felt that a crisis was come in his married life. The husband's determination to mastery, which lay deep below all blandness and beseechingness, had risen permanently to the surface now, and seemed to alter his face, as a face is altered by a hidden muscular tension with which a man is secretly throttling or stamping out the life from something feeble, yet dangerous.

This tableau of surreptitious violence erupts into another argument. Romola feels 'as if her mind was held in a vice by Tito's', and she yields to him again. 'Marriage must be a relation either of sympathy or of conquest,' remarks George Eliot.

Romola's submission to Savonarola has 'utterly bruised' her will, just as her husband bruised her wrists and her father bruised her hand. Now she feels in 'need of direction even in small things'. She becomes Savonarola's disciple, and her trust in this new spiritual father becomes her anchor in a treacherous world — 'something like a rope suspended securely by her path' — which saves her 'from staggering, or perhaps from falling'.

The heroine of *Romola* thus binds herself to a chain of father figures: her father, her husband, her priest. All three tell her she is irrational, too much swayed by her feelings. George Eliot sometimes reinforces this view, while also showing how these men are driven by their own desires and fears.

Eventually Romola will lose her faith in Savonarola. She will be freed from her marriage by authorial fiat, when Tito — like all the novel's father figures — meets his death. This is an ambiguous liberation, because in the narrator's eyes there is no compensation for a failed marriage, 'no compensation for the woman who feels that the chief relation of her life has been no more than a mistake . . . The deepest secret of human blessedness has half whispered itself to her, and then for ever passed her by.' Likewise, the loss of Savonarola's authority cuts Romola adrift. Without purpose, without faith in goodness or love, she is 'orphaned', thirsty, empty, longing to die.

*

George Eliot wrote her fiction with a painterly hand, and *Romola*'s densely layered themes took her far beyond the realism of *Clerical Scenes* and *Adam Bede*, which she had compared to seventeenth-century Dutch paintings of humble interiors. This historical novel is hyper-realist, with its detailed descriptions of Florentine clothes, buildings, festivals and figures of speech, and its portraits of real people: Niccolò Machiavelli, Bernardo del Nero, Piero di Cosimo, as well as Girolamo Savonarola. At the same time it is a symbolist work, rich in images drawn from allegory and myth, prophecy and dreams, elaborately woven with allusions and analogies and metamorphoses — all the forms native to unconscious life.

Romola morphs from Antigone to Ariadne as she passes from her father to her new husband, and changes again into a lonely Madonna — in one scene carrying a dark-skinned, black-eyed Jewish baby boy — in the final phase of her story. Those closing chapters conjure a dreamy matriarchal vision that breaks free of realist constraints of time and place: Romola herself becomes the stuff of legend, as if George Eliot cannot envisage a future for this heroine within her own milieu.

Romola's epilogue constructs a domestic tableau that is, once again, ambiguous. Women and children are assembled in a peaceful fatherless family, finally free of the violence seething through the novel. But Romola herself seems to be elsewhere. Instead of attending to the children, she gazes 'absently on the distant mountains ... evidently unconscious of anything around her'. The yearning that sent her from her father to Tito, and from Tito to Savonarola, remains unfulfilled. Is she longing for something divine — 'the Great Mother' or 'the Kingdom of God' — or simply for the wide skies and clear air beyond the city walls? Is her very presence in this scene a stoical acquiescence to the fate her author has devised for her, just as she previously submitted to her father, her husband, her priest? Has Romola found a resting place where, free to mourn at last, she can sink into memories of her lost loves? Or is she looking towards her future, reminding readers that her life is not yet finished?

If George Eliot's debut novel resembles a homely Dutch painting, this challenging middle work is more in the style of Piero di Cosimo, a 'strange freakish painter' who produced remarkably lifelike portraits

THE VISIBLE MADONNA.

'The Visible Madonna' — Romola as Mary.
Illustration by Frederic Leighton, 1863

as well as fantastical allegories and vivid devotional works. Eliot and
Lewes probably visited his *Mary Magdalene Reading* in Rome in
1860, a few weeks before *Romola*'s seed was sown — and it is tempt-
ing to see Piero's transformation of the passionate saint into a serene,
studious Florentine as a prototype for the novel's pre-Raphaelite red-
haired heroine. Like other high-Renaissance painters, Piero di Cosimo
combined his period's new naturalism with the symbolist vocabulary
of medieval art.

Romola is self-conscious about its own painterly form. Piero di
Cosimo is the novel's most important minor character, drawn from

Vasari's *Lives of the Artists*. He portrays its fictional protagonists in a series of mythical scenes — Romola and her father as Antigone and Oedipus; Romola and Tito as Ariadne and Bacchus; Tito as Virgil's Sinon, the treacherous Greek spy who recurs as an emblem of falsehood in the works of Dante and Shakespeare.

Plato was suspicious of artists as the creators of illusions — copies of the appearances of this world, which are themselves mere shadows of the truth. George Eliot's portrait of Piero di Cosimo complicates this view. Piero certainly produces appearances: he creates carnival masks as well as paintings, and he makes the allegorical triptych of Romola and

THE PAINTED RECORD.

'The Painted Record' — Romola with Piero di Cosimo.
Illustration by Frederic Leighton, 1863

Tito that 'locks away' the truth of their marriage. Yet of all the novel's characters, he sees the truth most clearly. When he paints Tito, he draws the young man's hidden fear onto his handsome face. The disparity between Piero's own appearance and his inward life is the reverse of Tito's insincere charm: his grouchy exterior hides a kind heart, and his apparent cynicism masks devotion to the goodness he perceives in Romola.

A prophetic figure as well as an illusionist, this artist holds the key to shameful things — a frightened man, a disappointing marriage — that others try to lock away. At the same time, he avoids 'betraying' his own feelings — and how interesting that betrayal can mean either hiding or revealing something. When Romola visits Piero's house and sees his portraits of her father and husband, the scene between them is a complex dance of disclosure and concealment, pretence and half-truths. While Romola shares some of her characteristics with Eliot the woman — her early loss of her mother and devotion to her father, her intelligence and studiousness, her pride and perhaps also her submissiveness — Piero di Cosimo is an avatar of Eliot the artist.

*

While she was working on *Romola*, Eliot discussed with Barbara Bodichon 'the spiritual blight that comes with No-faith'. In returning to Renaissance Christendom from the vantage point of the 1860s, she redoubled the juxtaposition of eras and cultures that had created a new world in fifteenth-century Florence, folding that many-layered past within the present. Romola's turn as the Madonna, for example, condenses biblical and medieval traditions, their re-imaginings by humanist artists, and the maternal archetype at the centre of Comte's new 'religion of humanity'. Just as scholars like Romola's father had retrieved an ancient civilization, so George Eliot's historical novel helped to retrieve the Renaissance for the Victorian age. The story of Romola and Savonarola was a faux-antique mirror reflecting modern themes of faith and credulity, doubt and despair, illusion and disillusion.

The novel's first instalment in the *Cornhill* opened with a 'Proem', which emphasized the 'broad sameness' of human life across 'more than three centuries and a half' — from 1492 to 1862 — and found parallels between Renaissance Florence and contemporary London. Both cities were animated by 'the unrest of a new growth'. Their inhabitants lived within a 'strange web of belief and unbelief', a tangle of superstition and Enlightenment, faith and reason. The fifteenth century, like the nineteenth, was an age of scientific and spiritual uncertainty: 'Who knew — who was sure . . . ?' For Eliot's generation, God was not yet dead, but 'His' authority was challenged by some of the most cultured minds in Europe.

Romola's 'Proem' prepared the *Cornhill*'s readers to see a young wife's struggle with questions of trust and fidelity as a microcosm of their own crisis of faith. Marriage and religious belief were already entwined in complex ways for those readers. When the early German Romantics had challenged Christian doctrine and morality in the heady aftermath of the French Revolution, they had also challenged the institution of marriage and experimented with sexual freedom. Yet for many mid-century thinkers grappling with the consequences of new scientific and political theories, the domestic pieties of marriage not only endured the decline of religious belief, but provided consolation for it.

Matthew Arnold's poem 'Dover Beach', written during this period, suggested that romantic fidelity — true love — could fill the emptiness left by a retreating 'Sea of Faith':

> Ah, love, let us be true
> To one another! for the world, which seems
> To lie before us like a land of dreams,
> So various, so beautiful, so new,
> Hath really neither joy, nor love, nor light,
> Nor certitude, nor peace, nor help for pain;
> And we are here as on a darkling plain
> Swept with confused alarms of struggle and flight,
> Where ignorant armies clash by night.

Romola evokes a similar mood of spiritual desolation. For George Eliot, however, marriage is not a reliable refuge from the confusions and conflicts of the modern world. Finding truth in love seems no easier than finding it in science or history or religion. Faith in another person can be as liable to illusion — and disillusion — as faith in God.

Nevertheless, *Romola* equivocates on its marriage questions, and sometimes seems to echo Arnold's insistence on fidelity. In one scene, as Romola takes off her betrothal ring, George Eliot reflects that this ring possesses 'that force of outward symbols by which our active life is knit together so as to make an inexorable external identity with us'. In removing it, Romola feels she is 'somehow violently rending her life in two'. If violence and violation have fractured this marriage, there also seems to be violence and violation in leaving it. What if there is 'something in human bonds which must prevent them from being broken with the breaking of illusions'? This question hangs in the air unanswered — one of those many untold truths that illuminate nothing, and 'only haunt us' as we fumble in the dark.

Romola's soul passes a dark night in the shadow of this question; 'no radiant angel comes across the gloom with a clear message' for her. Likewise, George Eliot refuses to be this angel for her readers:

> In those times, as now, there were human beings who never saw angels or heard perfectly clear messages. Such truth as came to them was brought confusedly in the voices and deeds of men not at all like the seraphs of unfailing wing and piercing vision — men who believed falsities as well as truths, and did the wrong as well as the right. The helping hands stretched out to them were the hands of men who stumbled and often saw dimly, so that these beings unvisited by angels had no other choice than to grasp the stumbling guidance along the path of reliance and action which is the path of life, or else to pause in loneliness and disbelief.

Passages like this one require us to share Romola's uncertainty, to decipher mixed messages, to shoulder the 'burden of choice' that the heroine of this novel — and perhaps its author too — seems eager to relinquish.

*

Romola's intricate symbolic and philosophical schemes, as much as its painstaking realism, were the fruit of Eliot's year of preparation. During 1861 she had been 'meditating' her unwritten novel as well as researching it, and despite Lewes's impatience it is astonishing that it took her only three years to make a work of such imaginative and intellectual density. The process of construction almost defeated her. She continually lapsed into 'depression and incapacity', compounded by recurrent anxiety about falling behind. This 'malaise' continued until the last pages were written. One laconic diary entry from the summer of 1863, when she was writing the novel's final part, sums up the mood of those months: 'Heavy and good for nothing. Only at p. 18.'

Though publishing serially in the *Cornhill* made writing *Romola* even more difficult than it would otherwise have been, it brought one significant compensation. Frederic Leighton, a painter influenced by the pre-Raphaelites, was commissioned to illustrate the novel's monthly instalments; he 'knew Florence by heart', having lived there as an art student, and Lewes thought him 'by far the *best* man to be had in England'. During his first visit to Blandford Square the handsome young artist cast a painterly eye on the 'curious mixture' in George Eliot's face:

> Miss Evans (or Mrs Lewes) has a very striking countenance. Her face is large, her eyes deep set, her nose aquiline, her mouth large, the under jaw projecting, rather like Charles Quint; her voice and manner are grave, simple, and gentle. There is a curious mixture in her look; she either is or seems very short-sighted. Lewes is clever. Both were extremely polite to me; her I shall like much.

Eliot and Leighton entered into a frequent correspondence as they exchanged chapters and drawings. For the first time since the early years with Sara Hennell, she had a creative partnership unencumbered by money or marriage. Her letters to and from Leighton were not mediated by Lewes; they expressed admiration for one another's work while discussing fine details of Florentine costume and speech. 'I am more gratified, I think, by your liking these opening chapters than I have yet been by anything in these nervous anxious weeks of decision about publication,' she wrote to him in May 1861, as he prepared his drawings for *Romola*'s first instalment. By the autumn their collaboration had deepened her thinking about artistic freedom and truthfulness, and caused her to reflect on the limits of fidelity between visual and literary art. She described to Leighton the 'misery' of knowing her work 'must often be in error', and her pleasure in having his 'hand and mind to work with'.

The *Cornhill* also changed her relationship to her readers. She could not write this book in peace and then leave the country before it was published to escape the reviews. Though she had feared that her stepson Charles would prevent her from travelling, it was serialization, not motherhood, that kept her at home until the novel was finished in June 1863. Meanwhile, readers followed the fortunes of Romola, Tito and Savonarola through successive issues of the *Cornhill*, and some shared their responses with her as she continued to write the story.

One of those readers was Sara Hennell, who told Eliot that she found Romola 'very, very beautiful' — an ideal figure 'so outside of, so altogether above my own experience' because she is 'so loved . . . so wanted'. Sara was disobeying Lewes by offering these melancholy thoughts. He had warned her not to write to Eliot about *Romola*: 'No one speaks about her books to her, but me; she sees no criticisms.' Eliot knew that Lewes had 'snatched up' at least one letter from Sara that contained something he did not want her to see. This 'unlucky snatch' was one of several 'magical disappearances', she explained to her old friend, with an irony pitched perfectly between indulgence and frustration, acquiescence and protest. 'Very slight things make epochs in married life', observes the narrator of *Romola*, and delicate little scenes like this one — a wife pretends not to notice her husband's 'sleight of hand' at the breakfast table — quietly register choices about how much truthfulness a relationship permits, and how much duplicity it requires.

Despite Lewes's protectiveness, Eliot seemed quite willing to discuss her novel with discerning readers. She told Sara that she did not intend *Romola* to be 'popular': she was ready to defy the public's expectations and claim her freedom to write out of her 'own varying unfolding self, and not to be a machine always grinding out the same material or spinning the same sort of web'. She also entered into a correspondence with Richard Holt Hutton, who reviewed the completed novel in the *Spectator*. Hutton was a gifted young critic steeped in philosophy and theology, and he at least partially understood the intellectual drama of Christian faith and liberal culture played out in *Romola*. His review hailed the novel as George Eliot's greatest yet. Hutton thought Tito the most 'wonderful piece of painting in English romance', and found 'the portrait of Savonarola . . . almost impossible not to feel as faithful as history, as it is great as romance.' Romola herself, however, seemed to him only 'half-revealed, and more suggested than fully painted', and he deplored the novel's 'feeble and womanish' ending.

Eliot responded warmly to Hutton's efforts to interpret what he called *Romola*'s 'great artistic purpose', although like most authors she could not help thinking of all the things her critic missed — 'of course if I had been called on to expound my own book, there are other things that I should want to say.' She also accepted his critique of Romola:

> I am not surprised at your dissatisfaction with Romola herself. I can well believe that the many difficulties belonging to the treatment of such a character have not been overcome, and that I have failed to bring out my conception with adequate fullness. I am sorry she has attracted you so little; for the great problem of her life, which essentially coincides with a chief problem in Savonarola's, is one that readers need helping to understand. But with regard to that and to my whole book, my predominant thinking is — not that I have achieved anything, but — that great, great facts have struggled to find a voice through me, and have only been able to speak brokenly.

Romola's narrator twice explains this 'great problem' that Romola and Savonarola share. Both characters wrestle with the question of 'where the duty of obedience ends, and the duty of resistance begins'; 'where the sacredness of obedience ended, and where the sacredness of rebellion began'.

If this was a political and spiritual question, it must also be a marriage question. It was still an audacious question for any wife to ask. Female submission was an enduring ideal: in the same year J. S. Mill published *The Subjection of Women*, the anti-feminist author Sarah Ann Sewell insisted that 'it is a man's place to rule, and a woman's to yield.' When a woman made her marriage vows — in the nineteenth century as in the fifteenth — she stood before a priest and promised to obey her husband; this obedience became her sacred duty. With what right did she place limits on that duty? Could she simply decide to resist, to rebel? To whom might resistance be a duty — in whose eyes is rebellion sacred?

Eliot had not vowed to obey Lewes, but their marriage was sacred to her and she saw herself as a dutiful wife. So she, too, wrestled with Romola's question, behind closed doors in Blandford Square.

To the Husband
whose perfect Love has been
the best source of her insight & strength,
This manuscript is given by
his devoted Wife, the writer.

—

The manuscript was begun on the 1st of January, 1862
& finished June the 9th 1863.

Manuscript of *Romola*, p. 1: To the Husband whose perfect Love has been the best source of her insight and strength, this manuscript is given by his devoted Wife, the writer. The manuscript was begun on the 1st of January, 1862 & finished June the 9th 1863.

8

Success

During the 1860s the curtain was raised on the Leweses' married life. When they entered this decade their relationship was conspicuous but virtually unseen: the scandalous circumstances which drew attention to them had also made Eliot reclusive. Only their closest acquaintances — Barbara Bodichon, John Blackwood, the Congreves, Herbert Spencer, occasionally Sara Hennell and the Brays — spent any time with them as a couple. After they moved to Marylebone this small circle expanded to include Charles Lewes and the few trusted friends who joined them on Saturday evenings in Blandford Square. Through the middle years of the 1860s, George Eliot's success exposed the interior of their marriage to many more curious eyes and ears. As the intrigue of celebrity mingled with the intrigue of scandal, people were eager to meet them and swap opinions about them. No longer only an intimate drama, their marriage also became, at times, a social performance.

Romola paid for a suitable stage. In 1863, ten years into their relationship, they bought a house in St John's Wood, half a mile north-west of Blandford Square, between Regent's Park and Lisson Grove. Here the 'roar of London' was just a 'faint murmur', but they could still walk into town. The house was a Regency villa named The Priory, situated on the north bank of the canal in a pretty garden, where roses bloomed in the summer. Eliot's writing room looked onto this garden: it was up on the first floor, secluded from the clatter and thrum of the basement kitchen. Lewes had the ground-floor study.

Sparing no expense, they had The Priory decorated by Owen Jones, the pioneering architect who elevated interior design to a fine art. Jones designed their wallpaper, chose their curtains, hung their pictures on the walls. He also styled Eliot to match her elegant surroundings. For

the housewarming party she wore a new grey silk dress — 'the consequence', she told Maria Congreve, of a 'severe lecture' from Jones on
her 'general neglect of personal adornment'.

In this unimpeachably tasteful home, with its wide light drawing
room, they could host gatherings of 'men and women of rank and reputation': successful people like themselves. Every Sunday afternoon they
were 'at home' to painters and poets, scholars and reformers, cultured
aristocrats and wealthy patrons of the arts. Illustrious visitors came
from America and the Continent — Emerson and Longfellow, Wagner
and Turgenev — to pay homage to the great George Eliot.

In they all came and there they both were, so very much themselves:
Lewes cheery, voluble, imperious, weaving through the crowded
drawing room; Eliot quiet, inward, omniscient, enthroned on her Vol-
taire chair. He was all surface and she was all depth. Visitors were
fascinated by the contrast:

> Lewes paced the floor the whole time, going from one guest to another,
> gesticulating, speaking with pleasure and interest to each one, his whole
> face radiating delight when he saw that conversation flowed vividly
> and the guests were enjoying themselves. George Eliot never aban-
> doned her customary composure. In the usual place, lost in the large
> Voltaire armchair, protected from the light by a dark lampshade, she
> usually devoted herself to one guest at a time, as if oblivious to the fact
> that she was hostess of the salon.

Many guests reported a similar sequence of impressions on meeting
her. They were struck first by what Henry James called her 'vast ugliness', then by her beautiful voice. Within a few minutes they would
fall under the spell of some profound inner beauty, in spite of the large
head and nose, the bad 'English' teeth, the offensively long chin. Literary young women were especially drawn to her: Octavia Hill
admired 'a nervous intensity of expressive power in her hands'; Julia
Wedgewood discerned a 'great consciousness of power' beneath her
quiet manner. The artist Georgiana Burne-Jones thought her grey eyes
looked as though they had been 'washed by many waters'.

At The Priory, Lewes's role in supporting his wife's career expanded
from praising her work and negotiating with publishers to stage-
managing a salon dedicated to her genius. As she sheltered in a dimly

The drawing room at The Priory

lit corner of the drawing room, he organized the guests, making sure they all had their turn to speak to her and preventing anyone from spending too long by her side. Perhaps there was some personal compensation in this: Eliot had paid a high social price for their first years together, and now Lewes brought the great and the good to her feet. Of course, it was her writing that drew them all to The Priory, but he orchestrated these 'religious services', as he came to call them, and his bossy directions allowed her to be gracious and serene.

While most visitors were enchanted by George Eliot, opinions of Lewes were mixed. Women tended to find him charming and funny, his ugliness 'redeemed' by his good humour; men were often more critical. People used words like 'worship', 'adoration' and 'devotion' to describe his attitude to his wife. Some guests were taken to an inner sanctum — Lewes's study — to see Frederic Burton's portrait of Eliot on the wall, and beneath it her bound manuscripts, carefully covered by a curtain, each one dedicated to her husband. One visitor thought

Frederic Burton's 1865 portrait of George Eliot, which hung in Lewes's study

the drawing room itself was like a shrine. 'She was his chief topic of conversation, the pride and joy of his life, and it was quite evident that she returned his ardent devotion with a true love,' recalled an American pilgrim.

But Lewes's blend of extroversion and insecurity made his faults more visible than Eliot's. The playwright Steele MacKaye, who wanted to adapt *Silas Marner* for the stage, compared the couple to 'the

Princess and the Dragon': he found Lewes 'outrageously egotistical, and so void of good taste as to even bully the woman — who has sacrificed everything for him — in front of me.' Charles Eliot Norton, an art critic and Harvard professor, also thought him tactless, vain and a little vulgar. Lewes loved to feel that he was among important people and, lacking his wife's self-censorship, enjoyed bragging about his high connections. He began one of these boasts by joking that his head was 'where his tail ought to be'.

By encouraging these Sunday visitors to revere George Eliot, Lewes made them even more inclined to deem him unworthy of her. At times she also suffered on her pedestal, which exposed as well as elevated her. People who were envious or simply unkind wanted to bring her down — they sniffed out her 'peasant' roots and whispered that she was affected; they scrutinized her comportment, then criticized her for being self-conscious. In those years, as the Second Reform Bill was debated in Parliament and the press, at working men's clubs and gentlemen's clubs, fine distinctions of social class were reshaping England's political landscape — and even Owen Jones's impeccable drawing room could not insulate the Leweses from snobbery.

*

By the time they moved to The Priory, Eliot could claim to be the most successful woman in England. Lewes's career was also flourishing, despite his poor health and his attentiveness to Eliot's work. In the early 1860s he published two books with George Smith's press, *Studies in Animal Life* and *Aristotle: A Chapter from the History of Science.* The first collected a series of articles that had already appeared in the *Cornhill* magazine, and introduced readers to a new science: 'Biology — the science of Life is now becoming generally adopted in England, as in Germany. It embraces all the separate sciences of Botany, Zoology, Comparative Anatomy, and Physiology.' The second book also explored the science of life, giving particular attention to Aristotle's *De Anima,** from which Lewes drew deep and current questions about the relations between 'life and mind', and between science and

* *On the Soul*

metaphysics. He surveyed definitions of life offered by modern philosophers, from Kant to Herbert Spencer, before venturing his own: 'Life is
the dynamical condition of the organism.' He explained that Aristotle's
concept of *dunamis*, meaning potential or potency as well as motion,
named a 'dark' and 'solemn' mystery at the heart of nature. New biological research would illuminate at least some of this mystery.

The intellectual ambition of *Aristotle* was nothing new for Lewes,
but unlike his previous books this was a scholarly monograph, full of
long footnotes. It would strengthen his reputation as a serious scientist
and philosopher. In 1865 he was persuaded to become the first editor
of the *Fortnightly Review*, a highbrow journal of 'Politics, Literature,
Philosophy, Science, and Art' funded by some of his eminent friends. Its
inaugural issue carried Part I of Walter Bagehot's *The English Constitu-
tion*, the opening of Anthony Trollope's latest novel, an article on atoms
by Sir John Herschel, an essay on rationalism and witchcraft by George
Eliot, and pieces on both science and literature by Lewes himself.

Their success did not bring contentment. They had worked for everything they had, taught themselves everything they knew, yet England's
collective class consciousness imposed, as a kind of levy on their
achievements, a sense of not being good enough for those whose prosperity had been assured since birth. And failure — the thought of it, the
threat of it — is the shadow side of success; the greater the success, the
larger the shadow. Eliot's doubts about her literary ability had deepened with *Romola*, which was, in Lewes's words, 'flatly received by the
general public' though praised by 'almost all the elite'. Now expectations were even higher, the scrutiny more intense. Even in purely
financial terms, her success was tempered by some disappointment. She
had earned 'an abundant independence', but she knew that her gain
was George Smith's loss: the *Cornhill* had not made money on *Romola*
and sales of the book, which followed magazine publication, were
slow. Was *Romola* a failure? Whether the criteria were commercial or
literary, she could not be sure of the answer to this question.

They were also anxious about Lewes's sons, now young men who
must make their way in the world. Charles seemed safely established
as an administrator at the General Post Office, but after a year in the
job he was not promoted with his peers. Eliot and Lewes both recorded
this 'painful disappointment' in their journals — 'more painful than

almost anything that has occurred to us for years'. This was the pain of failure, sharpened by embarrassment. Their friend Anthony Trollope had helped place Charles in the Post Office, and they had to hear from him that their boy was 'careless, slow and inefficient'. Dutiful Charles did improve, and advance, and in 1865, aged twenty-three, he moved out of The Priory to marry Gertrude Hill, a satisfyingly suitable young woman from Hampstead. The news of their engagement 'made Polly happy, and me rather melancholy', wrote Lewes: 'the thought of marriage is always a solemn and melancholy thought to me.' Eliot liked her new daughter-in-law. 'Sometimes', she told Sara Hennell, 'it requires an effort to feel affectionately towards those who are bound to us by ties of family, but it is as easy to me to love Gertrude as it is to love the clear air.'

Thornton, the second son, was much more troubling. In some ways he was the most promising of the three boys — he had Lewes's literary flair, his bright inquiring intelligence and his great optimism — but he was also strong-willed and rebellious. Unlike Charles he was a disruptive, demanding presence in the home; Eliot found him 'at once amiable and troublesome, easy and difficult to manage'. Thornton liked being outdoors, and saw himself as a man of action. His vivid imagination, fed by schoolboy novels about colonial adventure and conquest, conjured fantasies of military glory. He had spent his boarding-school years dreaming of joining anti-imperialist freedom fighters abroad — the Sardinian-French alliance against the Hapsburgs in Austria, Garibaldi's troops against the Bourbons in Sicily.

Following his brother to a bureaucratic position at the Post Office was out of the question for Thornton. In any case, he was too unruly to have at home for long enough to launch him on a London career: this difficult middle child threatened their domestic harmony and distracted Eliot from her writing. During the 1860s the challenge of guiding Thornton to financial independence while keeping him at a safe distance caused the Leweses much anxiety. Like many other Victorian middle-class parents — lacking the land and property resources of the aristocracy, but unable to contemplate any kind of trade or manual work for their educated sons — they turned to the colonies.

British India was the most desirable outpost, so when Thornton left school he was sent to Edinburgh to spend a year preparing for the

Indian civil service examinations. Lewes looked forward to him earning an annual salary of £1,200 by the age of twenty-five — '*That* isn't
to be made by Aristotle or Reviewing!' But in 1863 Thornton failed
his final exams, and refused to try again. He wanted to go to Poland
and join the uprising against the Russian empire. Lewes and Eliot
were aghast at the thought of 'coarse men engaged in guerrilla warfare', who would no doubt 'demoralise' their boy — 'to say nothing',
she added archly, 'of Thornie's utter unfitness for military subordina-
tion'. Just as they were preparing to move into The Priory, they were
plunged into a 'nightmare of uncertainty' about his future.

By this time Lewes's third son Bertie was also staying with them —
'Conceive us, please, with three boys at home, all bigger than their
father!' This 'congestion of youthfulness' was too much for Eliot. Her
letters to friends conveyed a sense of crisis. She was fortunate, she conceded, to have 'a dear companion who is a perpetual fountain of courage
and cheerfulness and of considerate tenderness for my lack of those
virtues' — though of course it was the sons of this dear companion who
were causing all the trouble. Even after these anxious weeks had passed,
she could barely hide her scorn at Thornton's failure: 'He failed, and we
found that he had expected to fail; and this for a time was a great grief
and disappointment to us.' Meanwhile Lewes, ever practical, set about
finding another colonial destination for his wayward son.

Thornton might go east or west: this was the time when Englishmen could boast that the sun never set on their Queen's empire. In the
autumn of 1863 — when Thornton's future was being decided — Eliot's friend Cara Bray published a large textbook on the history and
geography of the British Empire, detailing 'possessions' in Europe,
Asia, Africa, America and Australasia. In the wake of the violent
Indian Mutiny and its brutal suppression by the British East India
Company, Bray expressed some ambivalence towards imperial rule.
Her book promised to describe 'the relations of England with her
colonies and dependences, unbiassed by mere conventional option or
exaggerated national sentiment' — but she certainly saw the Empire
through English eyes, and her overarching narrative was triumphant:

> although the dispersion of the English race among these widely differing
> tribes has not been an unmixed good — oppression, corruption, and even

destruction having been in many cases the consequence to the savage races of the approach of the whites, and the selfish policy of the dominant power towards the dependent nations having been the great drawback to the advantages of civilisation: yet still the great aggregate influence from the progress of England's dominion has been sun-like; fertilising and productive to the earth itself, and diffusing the light of a higher intelligence, and the glow of a truer humanity to its inhabitants.

Moreover, Bray argued, the Empire brought moral advantages not only to colonized peoples but to British migrants too. England's fast-growing industrial towns and cities had wrenched people from the land, resulting in 'a serious deterioration of the race'. Emigration to the colonies gave these dislocated urban workers a chance to get back to nature — 'to be thrown upon their mother earth for the renewal of their strength'.

Middle-class parents considering colonial careers for their sons were not inclined to dwell on the ethical questions raised by Cara Bray. These families tended to see the Empire less as an opportunity for moral improvement — and still less as a political problem — than as an expedient for young men whose prospects in England did not seem bright. At that time the colonies were perceived as lands of opportunity. They seemed reassuringly British, but with lower standards of competence than might be required at home — ideal for respectable boys of middling ability. Charles Dickens, for example, sent four of his six sons (as well as several fictional characters) to the colonies. One of those sons, Frank Dickens, had failed his exams for the British civil service and proved himself useless in the office of his father's journal *All the Year Round* before becoming a police superintendent in Bengal.

Lewes thought about sending Thornton to Canada, but his friend Edward Bulwer-Lytton — who had recently served as Secretary of State for the Colonies under Lord Derby — advised against it. Eventually they settled on Natal, now the east region of South Africa. This was Barbara Bodichon's idea; she knew English settlers who could help Thornton establish himself there. Cara Bray's textbook informed Victorian readers that Natal was first colonized by Dutch migrants from Cape Colony in the 1830s, then subjected to British rule 'by proclamation' in 1845. About a third of its population were white settlers and the natives were Zulus and other 'Kafir' nations: the

Amakosa, Amatimba and Amaponda. 'Much of their allegiance they seem to have transferred to the British Governor, whom they regard as their sovereign protector; and to the whites they make excellent servants,' explained Bray, with the complacent racism typical of this time. 'The climate is healthy and pleasant, and less liable to drought than that of the Cape; and the soil is generally more fertile.' Apart from the risk of meeting 'hyenas of a particularly ferocious aspect', it all sounded very promising.

In October 1863 nineteen-year-old Thornton was, as both Lewes and Eliot put it, 'at last' shipped off to Natal. They prepared him for his journey to Africa in much the same way they would prepare themselves for a trip to Berlin or Rome: by brushing up on the local language, and connecting with a few friends of friends who lived there. 'He went in excellent spirits', Eliot assured Sara Hennell, 'with a large packet of recommendatory letters to all sorts of people, and with what he cares much more for — a first-rate rifle and revolver — and already with a smattering of Dutch and Zulu picked up from his grammars and dictionaries.' Bertie, who had been 'backward' at school, was sent to a Scottish farm to learn agriculture. He would later go out to join his brother in Natal. A great relief descended on the newly decorated Priory. 'At last,' wrote Eliot, 'we have gained our quiet domesticity with no interruption in our tête à tête beyond the occasional presence of our eldest boy.'

In *Romola* she had set the marriage question within an extended historical period, stretching back through the fifteenth century to the ancient cultures rebirthed at that time. This long history became the milieu of her own life's story. Now that story unfolded in wider geographical horizons. Being English, and in London, during those years made people imagine themselves at the centre of the globe, with the curious mixture of parochialism and expansiveness this entailed. The fact of having a son, and then two sons, in Africa brought this imperial experience home to Eliot and Lewes. And while he glowed with pride at moving in the highest social circles, her fiction became preoccupied with the thick tangle of class, property, inheritance and struggle for nationhood that was shaping Britain's experiments in Empire and Reform.

*

Though they never visited the colonies, Eliot and Lewes travelled frequently around the British Isles and on the Continent during the 1860s. Lewes's health worsened — after many years of damaging his body 'by overwork and over-confidence' — and they chased restorative cures at fashionable English and German spa resorts. They continued to devour high culture, touring the cities of France, Belgium, Holland, Italy, Germany and, in 1867, Spain, where they went as far south as Granada, saw the Alhambra under 'transcendent' skies, and befriended a 'captain of the gypsies'. In their first years together they had been delighted by how cheaply they could live abroad; now their travels were eased by first-class trains, private carriages and comfortable hotels. They avoided other tourists and enjoyed the luxury of dining alone in their rooms.

In 1864 they spent a few weeks in Italy with one of their new friends, the artist Frederic Burton, who would paint Eliot's portrait and become Director of the National Gallery. At the Scuola di San Rocco in Venice he pointed out a small *Annunciation* by Titian, which they had not noticed on their previous visits. Eliot had long been drawn to this biblical scene and had, of course, seen many other paintings of it, but Titian's *Annunciation* 'brought a new train of thought'. To her it revealed the tragic situation of a young woman who is called to 'renounce the expectation of marriage':

> A young maiden, believing herself to be on the eve of the chief event of her life — marriage — about to share in the ordinary lot of womanhood, full of young hope, has suddenly announced to her that she is chosen to fulfil a great destiny, entailing a terribly different experience from that of ordinary womanhood. She is chosen, not by any momentary arbitrariness, but as a result of foregoing hereditary conditions: she obeys. 'Behold, the handmaid of the Lord.' Here, I thought, is a subject grander than that of Iphigenia, and it has never been used.

Biblical tradition suggests that Mary passes miraculously, effortlessly, from ordinariness to greatness when she is visited by the angel Gabriel. But Eliot saw in this painting a woman wrestling with the 'terrible difficulty' of adjusting her own need for love to the 'dire necessities' bestowed by society or Fate. Her Mary bore the weight of an unchosen inheritance.

This burden of a past that must be carried into the future was, she thought, the tragedy of every human life. She linked it particularly to female experience. She seemed to see herself in Titian's Mary, and to see something universal in herself. We do not choose, but are 'chosen': this is how women have learned to think about marriage. Being chosen for greatness — 'favoured among women', as Mary was — might well be a blessing, bringing fame and glory and other trappings of success. But by now Eliot knew that this was a variation on life's tragic theme, and not an exemption from it.

Inspired by her encounter with Titian's *Annunciation*, she planned a tragedy in five acts. It would be set in fifteenth-century Spain under the Inquisition — the same period as *Romola* — and she would write it in blank verse. By turning to poetry, then seen as the highest literary art, she was reaching for the greatness of Wordsworth, Milton, Shakespeare, Dante, even of Euripides and Sophocles. She was excited about this new work, which 'made an epoch' in her career: 'for the first time in my serious authorship I have written verse, and George declares it to be triumphantly successful.'

She wrote three acts of the Spanish drama, but as she struggled over Act Four she became so despondent that Lewes took the manuscript away from her. He had lost patience with the lengthening poem, and found it tedious. In the spring of 1865 she was 'in deep depression feeling powerless'. Lewes was just then beginning his editorship at the *Fortnightly Review*, and she worried that it was too much for him. But in the midst of her unhappiness she wrote admiringly of his generosity and dedication: 'Dear George is all activity, yet is in very frail health. How I worship his good humour, his good sense, his affectionate care for everyone who has claims on him! That worship is my best life.'

By the end of that year, things were looking up a bit: she was now, as Lewes put it, 'miserable over a new novel'. This would be *Felix Holt: The Radical*, which stages a complex inheritance plot in England's unsettled political landscape following the 1832 Reform Act. While *Romola* had folded a fifteenth-century story into nineteenth-century concerns, *Felix Holt* made a narrower historical pleat from the 1830s to the 1860s. The first Reform Act had changed England's electoral system and cautiously extended voting rights, while keeping the aristocracy in power; the second Reform Act, being debated as Eliot wrote the novel, would extend the franchise further to many working men.

Eliot was no admirer of the old system, nor was she optimistic about new reforms. She feared that an uneducated electorate would be swayed by demagoguery — and for the same reason she felt ambivalent towards proposals, supported by her feminist friends, to allow women to vote. In *Felix Holt* she probed the pitfalls of populism, advocating education and self-discipline for the working classes. But the novel's most compelling character is bitter Mrs Transome, who remains aloof from the political plot. Mrs Transome married for money and now, in late middle age, rattles around her mansion and bullies her feeble husband. Like Romola's marriage, this is a relation of conquest rather than sympathy, but here the roles are reversed: Mr Transome shrinks in fear from an adulterous wife.

While Victorians were divided on the question of whether male adultery ought to be condemned as a sin or tolerated as inevitable, female adultery was much more widely censured. This double standard, embodied in the ancient archetype of the fallen woman, had been reaffirmed in English law when a new Divorce and Matrimonial Causes Act was passed in 1857, resulting in a leap in the annual divorce rate from a mere handful to several hundred. This Act of Parliament — which changed the process for obtaining divorces rather than the legal grounds for granting them — decreed that a wife could divorce her husband only if he was 'guilty of incestuous Adultery, or of Bigamy with Adultery, or of Rape, or of Sodomy or Bestiality, or of Adultery coupled with Cruelty, or of Adultery coupled with Desertion, without reasonable Excuse, for Two Years or upwards'. A man, however, was entitled to divorce his wife on the grounds of adultery alone. Female infidelity was considered unnatural, unseemly, and shameful for all concerned. A husband could claim financial compensation from the man who had taken his wife: the law regarded her as akin to property that had been stolen or trespassed upon. Most dangerously of all, the illegitimate children of adulterous wives threatened the system of patrilineal inheritance that ordered English society.

The stigma of female adultery sours Mrs Transome's soul and

shapes the plot of *Felix Holt* — and it probably also explains why Lewes never sought the divorce that would free him to marry Eliot. Though the 1857 Divorce and Matrimonial Causes Act made divorce procedures simpler and much more affordable, there remained the problem that according to the law Agnes and Eliot were both women 'guilty of Adultery', as the Act put it — a specifically sexual guilt that must be proved in court if either Lewes or Agnes petitioned for divorce. And the greater Eliot's fame grew, the more people would relish scandalous details of her personal affairs.

*

Eliot battled through 'dreadful nervousness and depression' to finish *Felix Holt*. Lewes rightly thought it inferior to *Adam Bede*, and wrongly predicted that it would be more popular than *The Mill on the Floss*. George Smith turned it down, having been burned by *Romola*. John Blackwood took it for £5,000, so delighted to have George Eliot back — and unaware that Lewes had offered it to Smith first — that for once he let his head be commanded by his heart. Renewing this relationship was a joy to both author and publisher, and their correspondence blossomed again.

Before and after publication Blackwood kept up a campaign of superlative praise for *Felix Holt*. Sales, however, were disappointing. Behind the scenes at the publishers' office on Paternoster Row, Blackwood's colleagues assessed the book's prospects bluntly. The story was too weak for a bestseller, and *Romola*'s mixed reception did not help. *The Mill on the Floss*, their last big George Eliot novel, had been carried along by the great success of *Adam Bede*, whereas this new book, they said, followed after 'a failure'.

Blackwood lost a lot of money on *Felix Holt*, but he remained committed to Eliot. When she retrieved her dramatic poem from Lewes's study and set to work on its fourth and fifth acts, he agreed to publish it despite the genre's limited appeal. They settled on the title *The Spanish Gypsy*. The poem pursued the themes of feminine submission and renunciation explored through Maggie Tulliver and Romola: 'I will take this yearning self of mine and strangle it,' vows Fedalma, the Spanish gypsy, another passionate woman who subdues her strong will to a duty she did not choose. While those earlier tragic heroines feel bound to obey the commands of a father or a family code, Fedalma must submit to a racial identity — an inheritance she feels in her blood rather than in her social conditioning. She discovers that she is a gypsy — 'a race more outcast and despised than Moor or Jew' — only after falling in love with a Spanish duke who has persecuted her race. The stakes of this conflict are raised by the duke's religious devotion to Fedalma, and by his 'worship' of Love itself.

Fedalma is no ordinary gypsy, but the daughter of a gypsy king; her task is 'to be the angel of a homeless tribe'. At first she resists this destiny, still determined to marry her duke:

> I belong to him who loves me — whom I love —
> Who chose me — whom I chose — to whom I pledged
> A woman's truth. And that is nature too,
> Issuing a fresher law than laws of birth.

The poem's tragic logic refutes this Romantic argument, and dictates that the lovers must be separated for ever:

> He would not go away
> Till she was gone; he would not turn his face
> Away from her at parting: but the sea
> Should widen slowly 'twixt their seeking eyes.

This ending fulfils a fate dictated by the loss that haunts all love. Fedalma and her duke glimpsed it in the first act of their drama, as they leapt together into their unknown future:

> All love fears loss, and most that loss supreme,
> Its own perfection — seeing, feeling change
> From higher to lower, dearer to less dear.
> Can love be careless? If we lose our love
> What should we find? — with this sweet Past torn off,
> Our lives deep scarred just where their beauty lay.

The Spanish Gypsy takes almost 400 pages to reach its sad climax, in which a 'sweet Past' is indeed torn away. Blackwood, usually so eloquent in appreciation and reassurance, was not sure what to say about it. 'There is no question as to its being good, but how good is the question,' he wrote to William Blackwood, his nephew and colleague, as he struggled to feel interested in the story. He gallantly read and re-read it, praising the beauty of its 'language and thoughts'.

When it was published in 1868, 'fit for a Drawing-Room Table' in its bright-blue cloth binding and gold lettering, *The Spanish Gypsy* received mixed reviews and sold about as well as Blackwood expected. Eliot was paid in hundreds rather than thousands. Lewes seemed to overcome his misgivings, and professed delight in her poem. Perhaps conscious of his grasping reputation, Eliot invited Cara Bray 'to admire what my husband is, compared with many possible husbands — I mean, in urging me to produce a poem rather than anything in a worldly sense more profitable'.

Her submission to the strict discipline of poetry had honed her artistic powers. 'My poem has been a great source of added happiness to me,' she reflected on her forty-ninth birthday — 'all the more, or rather principally because it has been a deeper joy to Mr Lewes than any work I have done before. I seem to have gained a new organ, a new medium that my nature had languished for.'

Now she awaited new inspiration in her creative life, which she called her 'higher life — a life that is young and grows, though in my other life I am getting old and decaying.' She might begin a second long poem; perhaps she would never write another novel. She was entering the menopause and imagined herself an old woman, with limited time for work ahead. With Lewes's health so frail, she could not help contemplating the loss of love. The bittersweet sadness of Fedalma's final parting from her duke, across the widening ocean, hung over her own horizon. She sympathized with Queen Victoria, still in mourning after the death of Prince Albert in 1861: 'I am a woman of about the same age, and also have my personal happiness bound up in a dear husband.' But Eliot was, in her own way, happy. At the end of 1868 she reflected gratefully that this year had been 'as rich in blessings as any preceding year of our double life'. She also noted some moral improvement in herself: 'I enjoy a more and more even cheerfulness, and continually increasing power of dwelling on the good that is given to me.'

*

While Eliot deepened her art and Lewes pursued his science, Thornton was struggling in Natal. He sent regular letters home, though they took months to arrive. By the summer of 1865 he was bankrupt after spending six months trying to make a living as a trader. 'Times are still so bad here', he wrote to Lewes, 'I can't get credit to start on another trip, to redeem the failure of the first.' Like most of his letters from Africa, this one did not inspire confidence. He was living in the unpromisingly named Tent Hotel, reduced to working there as a 'general bottle-washer' — but even this was precarious, because the hotel was up for auction. He had sold his guns for oxen, which had died. He was 'half eaten up by lice'. Basuto tribesmen, who lived across the colony's western border, had invaded his town, killed his Boer neighbours and stolen his cattle. Thornton now planned to join the Natal Frontier Guard and 'wreck vengeance' on the Basutos. He could not help comparing his dream of being an anti-imperial freedom fighter to his present situation, which struck him as equally dangerous yet less noble: 'Who would have thought, that by my coming out here, instead of going to Poland, I should have fallen from the frying pan into the fire, and instead of fighting an enemy I hate, I should have to fight one I despise.'

Thornton's subsequent dispatches confirmed that it was difficult to survive in south Africa, let alone flourish: 'This country is so fearfully unsettled, that it is hard enough for the present inhabitants to get anything to do . . . the state of disturbance here is so uncomfortable.' He seized the only opportunity that presented itself, volunteering as a soldier for the Free State Boers — Dutch settlers who had claimed territory beyond the north-west border of Natal and were waging war against the native Basutos. The plan was to capture more Basuto land and seize their cattle and horses. Meanwhile, Thornton was camped in an abandoned house in a deserted village, 'almost eaten up by flies'. He was proud of his home-made bread and beef pies, though the last pie he had eaten was full of maggots. Letters from his father, which brought news of Charles's honeymoon in Italy and copies of the *Fortnightly Review*, must have arrived like missives from another world.

By the summer of 1866 Thornton was back in Natal, having sold his watch and chain to repay debts. The good news was that the

Basutos had 'given up the best fourth of their country' to the coloniz-ers. As a volunteer soldier, Thornton was entitled to a farm 'along the new boundary line' between the Orange Free State and Basuto terri-tory. These frontier farms were intended to protect the Free State from 'future wars', and white settlers had to agree to occupy them 'on mili-tary tenure'. Thornton did not yet have the title deeds to his farm, he explained, but Lewes should send Bertie out with £400, enough to build them a house, buy a waggon and guns and stock the farm. Lewes at once shipped his youngest son off to Natal.

Poor Bertie, arriving in Cape Town before sailing on to Durban, found George Eliot's novels and that impressive first issue of the *Fort-nightly Review* in the city library. It soon became clear that Thornton would not receive a farm. 'The Free State Govt. has broken its prom-ises, and done all the Volunteers out of the farms,' he wrote to Lewes in December 1866. The brothers spent a quarter of Bertie's money on a remote, uncultivated plot of land in the Boer-settled region north of Natal known as the Transvaal. They cut bricks out of dry mud to build themselves a house. Six months later their 'magnificent mud mansion' burned to the ground.

By the end of 1867 Thornton was seriously ill — 'in agony' at night, and 'so weak' during the day that he couldn't work. His next letter told of failed crops and kidney stones, which he treated with a 'homeo-pathic cure'. Ever optimistic, he hoped he would soon regain 'the use of my loins & legs'. Bertie also tried to look on the bright side: 'There is still war in the Free State. I am very glad Thornton did not get a farm there for we should not have been able to stop on the farm for fear of being killed by the Basutos.' Lewes and Eliot might have pieced this together from Thornton's plan to live on the frontier of stolen territory.

At the beginning of 1868 Eliot assured her Swiss friend François D'Albert-Durade that 'our family is very prosperous.' Charles, she was pleased to say, 'has just been promoted in his office and has dou-ble his former salary with a constant increase yearly, and the prospect of further promotion as the years go on'. They had not yet received the most alarming letters from Natal, and she reported that 'our two boys there, in partnership of the farm they have bought, agree admi-rably and are very happy in their occupation.'

In October, Thornton wrote to his father asking to borrow £200 to get through the next year, and more money to return home for a short time to consult an English doctor. 'I am gradually wasting away . . . I can hardly stoop to touch the ground, I can't sit up for half an hour, all I can do is lie down . . . It is my last chance in life,' he explained, rather apologetically. As if destined to be disruptive, Thornton arrived in London weeks earlier than expected, in the spring of 1869. Eliot and Lewes had just returned from another trip to Italy. The following day was a Sunday, with guests expected at The Priory. When Henry James turned up that Sunday afternoon, he found himself in the midst of a family crisis. Thornton was writhing on the floor in agony, Lewes had

Thornton Lewes, aged about seventeen

gone out for morphine, and Eliot was flustered. They called Sir James Paget, the surgeon who attended Queen Victoria.

The cause of Thornton's illness, which affected his glands and spine, remained mysterious. His pain could be so excruciating that it made him hysterical; at other times he was calm and cheerful. One day in May, Paget pronounced his case 'very serious' and Agnes Lewes was called to The Priory to see her son. Lewes and Eliot hired a full-time nurse, and spent much of May and June in and out of Thornton's sick room — 'our days have been broken into small fragments', she wrote to Cara Bray. By July, though, their life had resumed much of its usual routine: prodigious reading, writing, afternoon walks, visits to the British Museum, guests on Sunday afternoons, some weekends away in the country. Lewes had started an ambitious new book, *Problems of Life and Mind*, and Eliot was writing poetry and working on 'A Novel called Middlemarch'. Her progress was slowed by 'interruptions' from Thornton and her own ailments, but by the autumn she had written three chapters.

On 11 October Paget confirmed that Thornton was 'drifting away'. He died on 19 October. That night Eliot wrote a short eulogy in her diary: 'Through the six months of his illness, his frank impulsive mind disclosed no trace of evil feeling. He was a sweet-natured boy — still a boy though he had lived for 25 years and a half . . . This death seems to me the beginning of our own.'

*

Bertie Lewes struggled on in Africa after his brother left. He spent a few lonely months 'buried alive' on the failed farm, then moved to Natal and got married. Regretting that he had never learned a trade, he scraped by driving waggons and raising sheep. He never returned to England, and died in 1875 from a disease similar to Thornton's.

The fate of Lewes's younger sons confirms the naïvety of Cara Bray's idea that young Englishmen might gain spiritual strength by being 'thrown upon their mother earth' in distant colonies. And of course when colonial prospectors did manage to extract wealth from African soil and people, these dubious successes had terrible human costs.

When Bertie fell ill in the 1870s he was not encouraged to come home. Lewes and Eliot would quietly provide for his young widow and two children, and were reticent about his death in letters to their friends. It is hard to avoid the thought that this unfortunate son's obscure life in South Africa had no place in the story of family prosperity that Lewes and Eliot had worked so hard to construct.

At times marriages, like nations and churches, survive by policing their borders against threats to their stability. These hostile alien forces might be inconvenient relatives, former partners, disturbingly attractive new friends, or dissenters who refuse to believe in the relationship. Agnes Lewes was virtually erased from the family narrative so that Eliot could claim the role of mother to her sons, as well as wife to her husband. Sara Hennell was treated rather like a threatening ex-partner who had to be put down and kept in her place, especially in Lewes's presence. Moreover, Sara was a heretic: a marriage resister herself, she always regarded Eliot's relationship with Lewes as 'a calamity', brought about by her old friend's 'defective self-esteem and self-reliance, and her sufferings from loneliness'. Perhaps Sara held too tightly to her image of the friend she used to have; she, in return, was cast as a thing of the past — less a friend than a memorial of the friendship they once shared.

It is not at all obvious that we are entitled to make moral judgements about these people, whose inner lives we only glimpse from afar. But if we were to seize that right, we would have to conclude that Eliot was not to blame for the untimely deaths of her two stepsons. Complicated social and political factors led Lewes to choose colonial careers for these hapless young men, and perhaps they were genetically disposed to the illnesses that killed them. Still it seems that her marriage, and the creative life that was inseparable from it, could not sustain the presence of Thornton and Bertie. She knew this, and it was not a comfortable thought. In light of their misadventures in Natal, we might detect a confessional tone when satirical Mrs Cadwallader, *Middlemarch*'s most astute gossip, suggests sending a certain young man to the colonies: 'That is how families get rid of troublesome sprigs.' After Bertie died, Eliot raised and then refuted the idea that she should reproach herself, as if struggling to keep guilty feelings at bay. Her stepson's fate could not have been foreseen, she reasoned, and 'must be borne with resignation — is in no case a ground for self-reproach, and in this case, I imagine, would hardly have been favourably altered by a choice of life in the old country'.

The religious language used by Eliot and Lewes to describe their double life — and the atmosphere at The Priory that prompted visitors to speak of worship, shrines, devotion, reverence — conjures a cosy domestic piety, but also hints at something more savage and ruthless. Religion, we know, is often far from peaceful. The sacrifice demanded by things held as sacred has never been confined to the self-denying renunciations that George Eliot required of her heroines — and that Eliot herself felt so conscious of performing when she moved to London for Charles's sake. Sometimes others are sacrificed instead: calves, lambs and children have all been laid on altars. Years later, Eliot would reflect that her life with Lewes had been a 'dual egotism'. Aided by greater hindsight, we can see more clearly how the success of this marriage — like the success of Victoria's Empire — was bound up with failures, losses, and some brutal choices.

From George Eliot (otherwise Polly) to her dear Husband, this thirteenth year of their united life, in which the deepening sense of her own imperfections has the consolation of their deepening love.

August 4. 1866.

Manuscript of *Felix Holt*, p. 1: From George Eliot (otherwise Polly)
to her dear Husband, this thirteenth year of their united life,
in which the deepening sense of her own imperfections has
the consolation of their deepening love. August 4, 1866.

9

Philosophy

In 1869 Barbara Bodichon and her friend Emily Davies established a 'College for Women' in a rented house in a sleepy Cambridgeshire village, with an initial intake of five students: this would eventually become Girton College, Cambridge. Eliot donated £50 to the cause, 'From the Author of *Romola*'. The same year, nine women were allowed to sit a specially designed examination at the University of London. The six who passed received a Certificate of Proficiency instead of a degree. Their alma mater could claim to be the first university in the world to admit female students.

These few women had ventured onto masculine territory, and many of its natives thought they were trespassing there. Until the 1860s, Oxford and Cambridge colleges did not permit fellows to have wives: scholars, like monks, were expected to sacrifice marriage for their vocation. Decades would pass before women could work in England's universities as teachers and researchers, eighty years before Cambridge allowed women to receive degrees. Most men of learning thought it entirely natural that wives belonged to a domestic sphere, separate from the domain of intellectual work and occupied instead by that daily battle with inconveniences which must be waged in order to make a comfortable home. How could marriage be a site for philosophy, even a path towards knowledge?

Eliot would pursue this question in *Middlemarch*, which simmered unwritten through most of 1870. After Thornton's death she had set it aside and returned to poetry. 'She lavished almost a mother's love on the dear boy, and suffered a mother's grief in the bereavement,' Lewes wrote to their friend Tom Trollope on her fiftieth birthday, in

November 1869. She was still 'very sad' — 'But she will get to work, and *that* will aid her.'

Life now felt short. 'The number of our birthdays to come shrinks fast', she wrote to Sara Hennell, and to Barbara Bodichon she described 'a deep sense of change within, and of a permanently closer relationship with death'. That winter she wrote 'The Legend of Jubal', a long mythical poem which begins with a dawning consciousness of mortality. This brings 'new terrors', but also intensifies the value of life:

> It seemed the light was never loved before,
> Now each man said, ''Twill go and come no more.'
> No budding branch, no pebbles from the brook,
> No form, no shadow, but new dearness took
> From the one thought that life must have an end;
> And the last parting now began to send
> Diffusive dread through love and wedded bliss,
> Thrilling them into finer tenderness.

The poem finds in this sense of life's fragility a spur to work harder. Knowing they will die, human beings feel 'the stings of new ambition'. For some people, death awakens a philosophical passion — 'A yearning for some hidden soul of things'.

Throughout 1870 Eliot explored her own experience of mortality. In some moods, her shrinking life appeared to be losing value, not gaining it. 'I think too much, too continually of death now, almost to the partial eclipse of life — as if life were so narrow a strip as hardly to be taken much reckoning of,' she wrote to her stepson Charles. Disavowing the stinging ambition she had acknowledged in her poem, her letters to several younger friends played with the possibility of settling for a modest influence on the world she must prepare to leave behind. The most important thing, she told Oscar Browning — a flamboyant Eton schoolmaster who had become her devoted friend — was to 'make a few lives near to us better than they would have been without our presence in the world'. When unhappily married Jane Senior confided her longing 'for a wider existence', Eliot advised her to see 'how diffusive your one little life can be'. She told Maria Congreve that the 'hungry ambition' and 'strong egoism' of her younger days was now waning. It was a relief, she wrote, to find that getting older brought 'comparative quietude of personal cravings'.

Eliot explained how she tried to reconcile herself to death in a letter of condolence to another young friend, Edith Bulwer-Lytton, who had just lost her uncle. This letter, written from Harrogate during one of Lewes's spa cures, prescribes a mixture of emotional and intellectual life:

At present the thought of you is all the more with me, because your trouble has been brought by death; and for nearly a year death seems to me my most intimate daily companion. I mingle the thought of it with every other, not sadly, but as one mingles the thought of some one who is nearest in love and duty with all one's motives. I try to delight in the sunshine that will be when I shall never see it any more. And I think it is possible for this sort of impersonal life to attain greater intensity — possible for us to gain much more independence, than is usually believed, of the small bundle of facts that make our own personality.

I don't know why I should say this to you, except that my pen is chatting as my tongue would if you were here. We women are always in danger of living too exclusively in the affections; and though our affections are perhaps the best gifts we have, we ought also to have our share of the more independent life — some joy in things for their own sake. It is piteous to see the helplessness of some sweet women when their affections are disappointed — because all their teaching has been, that they can only delight in study of any kind for the sake of a personal love. They have never contemplated an independent delight in ideas as an experience which they could confess without being laughed at. Yet surely women need this sort of defence against passionate affliction even more than men.

Here Eliot returns to the question of thought and feeling — how to bring them together — that lies at the heart of her philosophy. Envisaging a happiness that transcends 'personal' attachments, she sees this 'more independent life' as typically male. Yet she claims her right to it, and invites her friend to share the 'independent delight in ideas' she has experienced first-hand. These few sentences reach for an intellectual life which does not deny or even resist the pull of emotions, yet provides a kind of ballast for love, passion, grief, without explaining them away.

Her letter's shift from the thought of death to this ideal of independence echoed the Spinozist ethics she had absorbed during her unofficial honeymoon. Spinoza replaced the Christian doctrine of personal immortality with an expansion of the human mind: as we understand more and more, we enlarge our share of God's eternal knowledge. He argued that this communion with truth is the highest human happiness. Of course our bodies die, along with all the memories that make up our personal identity — but the more we share in truth, the greater the part of us that is eternal. When she practised enjoying the sunlight that would outlast her, Eliot was trying to cultivate this Spinozist detachment. And when she wrote that she thought it possible to intensify 'this sort of impersonal life', to gain 'much more independence, than is usually believed, of the small bundle of facts that make our own personality', she was confessing her faith in the philosopher's peculiar blessedness. Yet while Spinoza found no place in wisdom for sadness, Eliot's feminine stoicism made a home for suffering. She did not believe in consolation, she told Edith: in the midst of grief, 'sorrow must be sorrow.' Sadness is not just permitted, but inevitable.

That summer, as Eliot and Lewes devoured news of France and Prussia invading each other — a war that would soon bind the German states into a nation — they were entering a particularly philosophical phase of their shared life. In May they had visited Oxford for the first time and befriended Benjamin Jowett, Professor of Greek and Master of Balliol College. Jowett was preparing to publish his landmark translation of Plato's dialogues, many years in the making, and in August he sent Eliot and Lewes part of the manuscript. As the season turned, they moved on from Plato to Hegel: Lewes began revising his *Biographical History of Philosophy* for a fourth edition, and over the autumn months he expanded his original chapter on Hegel from twenty to sixty pages — no doubt under the influence of Jowett, who fostered a growing interest in Hegelian thought at Oxford.

Hegel was the nineteenth century's great heir to both Plato and Spinoza, the two European philosophers who had achieved the deepest integration of metaphysics and ethics. From these thinkers Hegel inherited a confidence that the world responds to our desire to understand it: our rational minds, like the rest of us, are already part of nature, and so capable of knowing it from the inside. He added to this Spinozist legacy his century's obsession with 'development', which would underpin evolutionary theory as well as his progressive view of history. Hegel's ambitious philosophical system promised to make sense of relations between living, changing human beings, as well as between binary concepts such as freedom and necessity, subject and object, being and non-being. As Lewes put it in his revised *History of Philosophy*, Hegel's works disclosed 'a world of relations'.

With his physiologist's devotion to observable facts, Lewes was instinctively critical of Hegel's 'Absolute Idealism', and previous editions of his book had dismissed and ridiculed it. Although his 'entirely rewritten' chapter took Hegel more seriously, Lewes remained a committed empiricist — a scientist at heart, rather than a philosopher. Noting that Hegel thought empiricism 'trivial', he argued that Hegel's system 'leaves all the questions for which Science is useful just as much in the dark as ever, and is therefore unworthy of the attention of earnest men working for the benefit of mankind'. Lewes, like so many Victorians, weighed the value of knowledge on a utilitarian scale: what mattered was its usefulness. He insisted that philosophy should cohere with the latest science, and illuminate its findings. 'In Astronomy, Physics, Chemistry, Biology, Psychology,' Lewes declared, Hegel's system 'is utterly useless'. What was the point of dwelling on non-being when there were so many beings to observe, so many facts to discover?

On their afternoon walks that autumn, Lewes and Eliot discussed Hegel, as they had discussed Spinoza fifteen years earlier. Despite her efforts to pursue philosophical joy, Eliot had relapsed into depression. Transfusing her emotions into art, she wrote 'Armgart', a dramatic poem about an ageing female singer — a subject that allowed her to explore artistic ambition. 'I triumph or I fail,' says Armgart: 'I never strove for any second prize.' Some believe that 'too much ambition has unwomaned her', while she 'often wonders what her life had been / Without that voice as channel to her soul'.

Eliot was uncertain how long her own literary voice would hold out. In October, after finishing 'Armgart', she sunk again into 'almost total despair of future work'. These feelings so enveloped her that she had to look back through all the other gloomy entries in her diary to remember that previous bouts of despair had not, in fact, presaged creative decline. On the contrary, they were labour pains — signs that a new life, still hidden, was nearly ready to be born.

*

Just two months later, on the last day of 1870, Eliot recorded in her diary that she had written 'only 100 pages' of a new story. Its title was 'Miss Brooke', and she would soon see a way to merge it with the novel she had planned, started, and abandoned the previous year, during Thornton's last months. Those hundred pages became the opening of *Middlemarch*. Full of ease, they read as if their author has emerged from the valley of the shadow of death to bright green pastures rolling beneath a glorious sky. George Eliot's earlier novels are tragedies with comic scenes breaking through like patches of light in a clouded landscape; their humour, as in Shakespeare's tragedies, is often concentrated in minor characters. Their openings, in particular, tend to be thickety. By contrast, 'Miss Brooke' is sun-filled comedy that carries an immense weight lightly and draws the reader, apparently without effort, into its earnestness.

Dorothea Brooke — another motherless heroine — is a wealthy, refined young woman thirsty for knowledge, passionately seeking a purposeful life. Her mind and heart are 'open, ardent', shining through large eyes. She is disturbed by her own privilege: 'I think we deserve to be beaten out of our beautiful houses with a scourge of small cords,' she says — words that, written in a beautiful house, were themselves a small scourge upon their author. 'What are we doing with our money?' asks Dorothea, as she pours her spiritual fervour into plans to improve housing for the poor. Like Plato, she has high ideals, and stubbornly persists in the radical belief that truth is inseparable from justice.

No one in Middlemarch takes Dorothea's ideals seriously. Her younger sister Celia teases her about her 'notions'. Celia Brooke, placid and sensible, would never imagine herself a philosopher, but she is

Aristotle to her sister's Plato: while Dorothea yearns for 'some lofty conception of the world', Celia keeps her dainty feet firmly on the ground. She is a keen observer of slight things, and distrusts any ideas that float free of common sense. Mr Brooke, the sisters' uncle and guardian, is an amateur intellectual of chronically trivial mind, who waffles amiably while letting his tenant farmers live in squalor.

Thus ensconced in a provincial life which seems 'nothing but a labyrinth of petty courses, a walled-in maze of small paths that led no whither', Dorothea longs for higher ground. She finds a route for her philosophical ambitions in Edward Casaubon, a clergyman and scholar twice her age with a local reputation for 'profound learning'. He is writing a clever-sounding book titled *The Key to All Mythologies*. 'Dorothea, with all her eagerness to know the truths of life, retained very childlike ideas about marriage'; ironically, she is most foolish in her pursuit of wisdom. Imagining that it must be a 'glorious piety' to endure the odd habits of a great man, she looks dreamily at Mr Casaubon and sees 'a living Bossuet', 'a modern Augustine':

> Here was a man who could understand the higher inward life, and with whom there could be some spiritual communion; nay, who could illuminate principle with the widest knowledge: a man whose learning almost amounted to a proof of whatever he believed!
>
> ...'He thinks with me,' said Dorothea to herself, 'or rather, he thinks a whole world of which my thought is but a poor twopenny mirror. And his feelings too, his whole experience — what a lake compared with my little pool!'

While Dorothea constructs her ideal Casaubon, Celia, the thorough empiricist, is closely observing the man himself. She notices his 'two white moles with hairs on them', how he scrapes his spoon when eating soup, the way he always blinks before he says anything. Dorothea is disgusted by Celia's petty turn of mind. She tells herself that she will 'learn everything' if she becomes Casaubon's wife:

> 'It would be my duty to study that I might help him the better in his great works. There would be nothing trivial about our lives. Everyday-things with us would mean the greatest things. It would be like marrying Pascal. I should learn to see the truth by the same light as great men have seen it

by. And then I should know what to do, when I got older: I should see how it was possible to live a grand life here — now — in England . . .'

When Dorothea receives a letter from Casaubon proposing marriage in high academic style, she accepts, feeling 'the glow of proud delight — the joyous maiden surprise that she was chosen by the man whom her admiration had chosen'.

Celia, however, senses 'something funereal' in her sister's engagement. Mr Brooke tells Dorothea to take her time, but she rushes into it. He warns her that marriage is 'a noose' and a husband 'likes to be master', and sure enough she soon falls into a Romola-like habit of suppressing her thoughts and feelings. On her honeymoon she is dismayed to find her mind 'continually sliding into inward fits of anger and repulsion, or else into forlorn weariness'. Her husband's 'measured official tone' of voice begins to 'affect her with a sort of mental shiver'.

And now Celia's crass remarks about Casaubon's dry sallow face

Dorothea Brooke and Mr Casaubon

and those two white moles strike us afresh as a wise prophecy of sexual doom. Dorothea's new husband keeps her at arm's length when she kisses him, hinting 'by politely reaching a chair for her' that he finds her bursts of affection 'rather crude and startling'. This man, confides the narrator, cannot respond to his wife's desire: 'he was prepared only for those amenities of life which were suited to the well-adjusted stiff cravat of the period.'

Casaubon remains scrupulously buttoned-up, and his warm-blooded young wife feels 'humiliated' by this rejection. Worst of all, his intellect is not the great 'lake' Dorothea had imagined it to be. Casaubon's mind is turning out to be an exact replica of the 'walled-in maze of paths that led no whither' she had sought to escape by marrying him:

> How was it that in the weeks since her marriage, Dorothea had not distinctly observed but felt with a stifling depression, that the large vistas and wide fresh air which she had dreamed of finding in her husband's mind were replaced by anterooms and winding passages which seemed to lead nowhither? I suppose it was that in courtship everything is regarded as provisional and preliminary, and the smallest sample of virtue or accomplishment is taken to guarantee delightful stores which the broad leisure of marriage will reveal. But the door-sill of marriage once crossed, expectation is concentrated on the present. Having once embarked on your marital voyage, it is impossible not to be aware that you make no way and that the sea is not within sight — that, in fact, you are exploring an enclosed basin.

Poor Casaubon, meanwhile, is lost and floundering. In his marriage, as in his scholarship, he steadies himself by his habitual correctness. The pedantry of his pamphlets is translated into fastidious 'propriety' towards his wife; his unfailing politeness allows him to believe himself an 'irreproachable husband'. Casaubon's correctness parodies the wisdom Dorothea once attributed to him.

In love as in philosophy, correctness is not merely a poor substitute for wisdom, but an obstacle to it. Socrates was the wisest man in Athens precisely because he knew that he knew nothing — and he could therefore long passionately for wisdom, and spend his life pursuing it. And the best lovers are willing to be in the wrong, to feel confused or uncertain or curious about their partner and about themselves — and can therefore seek to know hidden things, explore unchartered territory.

*

Eliot's decision to merge 'Miss Brooke' with the plot she had planned for *Middlemarch* allowed her to set Dorothea and Casaubon in parallel with another couple, Lydgate and Rosamond. Like Dorothea, Lydgate has a passion for knowledge: he is an ambitious young doctor who hopes to advance medical science. Because he is a man, he has exactly the opposite view about how marriage relates to his pursuit of truth. Lydgate sees marriage as a hindrance and distraction, and intends to avoid or at least defer it. But Rosamond Vincy, the prettiest girl in town, proves too clever for him.

When Lydgate finds himself engaged to Rosamond, he adjusts his expectations of marriage: his charming docile wife will make a pleasant background for his work. If Lydgate is wrong to want this, he is all the more mistaken to expect life with Rosamond to provide it. This fair, flower-like young woman seems a far cry from dried-up Casaubon, but she shares his defining trait of utter correctness. Just as Casaubon transfers this attitude from his scholarly work to his marriage, so Rosamond transfers it from her finishing-school knowledge of etiquette, taste, dress, comportment. And the result is the same. She feels 'quite sure that no one could justly find fault with her'. Her assurance of being an irreproachable wife is the hard, unyielding core of her power to control her husband. Over time, this marriage creates a finely woven 'noose' or 'yoke' for both partners.

The story of Lydgate and Rosamond dramatizes ideas Eliot had discussed fifteen years earlier in a short essay on Mary Wollstonecraft, written for Lewes's journal the *Leader* during their honeymoon trip to Germany. This essay concentrates on Wollstonecraft's ingenious argument that allowing women equal access to proper education will make life easier for men. Ignorant wives, Wollstonecraft observed, tend to cultivate a petty vanity that 'makes them value accomplishments more than virtues'; such women are 'slavish', but their very weakness gives them 'too much power' over their husbands. Glossing this thought, Eliot had identified 'a notion commonly entertained

among men' — that 'an instructed woman, capable of having opinions, is likely to prove an impracticable yoke-fellow, always pulling
one way while her husband wants to go the other, oracular in tone,
and prone to give curtain lectures on metaphysics.' ('Curtain' here
refers to the canopied four-poster beds of the time: this wife is keeping
her unlucky man awake with philosophical arguments.) But surely,
Eliot argued, 'so far as obstinacy is concerned, your unreasoning animal is the most unmanageable of creatures.' This challenge to received
opinion precisely captures Lydgate's mistake in choosing Rosamond,
whose graceful accomplishments are, in the words of Eliot's *Leader*
essay, 'mere acquisitions carried about, and not knowledge thoroughly assimilated so as to enter into the growth of her character'. In
light of Wollstonecraft's belief that the feminine heart would 'expand
as the understanding gained strength, if women were not depressed
from their cradles', Rosamond's selfish intransigence can be traced to
a shallow education that provided little scope for growth — a circle
of causes which ends up oppressing her husband too.

Eliot's analysis of these relationship dynamics also seems indebted
to her discussions of Hegel with Lewes — and in particular their study
of Hegel's *Phenomenology of Spirit*, which explores 'Lordship and
Bondage'. *Middlemarch* transforms this rather abstract account of the
evolving, unstable dance of Self and Other — their mutual attraction,
and their continual reaching for freedom and recognition — into a
moving human story. The scene in which Lydgate accidentally becomes
engaged to Rosamond plays ironically with Hegelian themes of mastery and dependence, strength and weakness:

> Lydgate, forgetting everything else, completely mastered by the outrush
> of tenderness at the sudden belief that this sweet young creature
> depended on him for her joy, actually put his arms round her, folding
> her gently and protectively — he was used to being gentle with the
> weak and suffering — and kissed each of the two large tears. This was
> a strange way of arriving at an understanding, but it was a short way.
> Rosamond was not angry, but she moved backward a little in timid
> happiness, and Lydgate could now sit near her and speak less incom-
> pletely. Rosamond had to make her little confession, and he poured out
> words of gratitude and tenderness with impulsive lavishment. In half

an hour he left the house an engaged man, whose soul was not his own, but the woman's to whom he had bound himself.

The marital violence that took physical expression in *Janet's Repentance* and *Romola* is spiritualized in *Middlemarch*. It becomes less gendered, and even more intense — not only brutal, but murderous. The novel's wives wield at least as much soul-crushing power as their husbands: Dorothea, for all her wifely submissiveness, threatens Casaubon's fragile ego with her questions about his work, and he cowers under her scrutiny before retaliating with tighter control. And in the recent past lurks the story of Lydgate's first love Laure, an actress who literally murdered her husband.

Analysing how human self-consciousness is formed in relation to others, who meet our desires with their own, Hegel described a 'life-and-death struggle' in which 'each seeks the death of the other'. He argued that this struggle tends ultimately to reconciliation, a balance among equals who recognize one another in mutual dependence. But the process might get stuck in its destructive phase, which then reiterates itself unto death.

This unhappy possibility gives a dark meaning to a couple's wedding promise to stay together 'till death do us part', which hangs like a Hegelian oracle over *Middlemarch*, while the Hebrew marriage prayer quoted at the head of one chapter takes on a bitter irony: 'Mercifully grant that we may grow aged together.' In a section of the novel titled 'Waiting for Death', Dorothea's marriage becomes a death sentence.

Middlemarch thus confirms Hegel's insistence — and anticipates the discovery of psychoanalysis — that desire and destruction are thoroughly entwined. George Eliot examines the interplay of philosophical and erotic passions, and asks whether they tend to life or to death. Who would Dorothea have been without her ideals, her notions, her yearnings for what is not reducible to the here and now — and without the terrible mistake those passions led her to?

The novel suggests several possible answers to this question, but one answer is enacted before our eyes: she might have had the contented life of her sister Celia. She could have married her other eligible neighbour, Sir James Chettam, the 'amiable baronet' who pursues Dorothea before he is thwarted by Casaubon and settles for her

Lydgate and Rosamond, moments before their engagement.
Illustration for *Middlemarch* by Charles Brock, 1908

younger sister. And who wouldn't want to marry an amiable baronet? Yet something is lost on that steadier, more complacent path — a deeper inwardness, better self-understanding, knowledge of pain and weakness and sheer limitation that blossoms in Dorothea's compassion for human suffering beyond her own personal attachments. Her hard-earned emotional intelligence transforms past mistakes into wisdom. Late in the novel, in a moment of crisis, Dorothea finds that all her 'vivid sympathetic experience returned to her now as a power', and this illuminates the path ahead, 'as acquired knowledge asserts itself and will not let us see as we saw in the day of our ignorance'.

*

We all inhabit an 'imagined otherwise', suggests George Eliot, as she weaves through the plot of *Middlemarch* alternative possibilities, things that might have been. The novel's negations and questions — its numerous 'nots' and 'what ifs' — channel a flow of hidden desires. Here the marriage question grows metaphysical. Within the quotidian experience of married life a series of possible worlds arise, as silent pangs of regret or jealousy or longing, barely discernible to an observer, flare with inward intensity. In these moments George Eliot reveals to her readers the nature of human consciousness, even the nature of reality itself.

The idea that negations and questions may be a powerful element of reality was nothing new. Saint Augustine believed that sin is non-being, an absence of goodness — and that the world is full of it. The biblical myth about the origin of sin begins with a prohibition: God tells Adam and Eve not to eat from the tree of knowledge of good and evil, because if they do so they will die. God's 'not' carves a little empty space for desire to grow into. A serpent slides through this space with a question, insinuating an alternative version of events: 'Did God really say you should not eat from any tree in the garden?' Then a contradiction: 'You will not die.' Tempted, Eve notices that the fruit from the prohibited tree is 'desirable for gaining wisdom'; when she and Adam eat it, their eyes are opened. The story of Adam and Eve contains the first question in the Hebrew Bible — and all of a sudden there is a rich tangle of meaning: doubt, desire, disobedience, death, and the discovery of philosophy.

While Eliot, Lewes and others in their century questioned the beliefs about human sinfulness that still shaped Christian culture, new patterns of nothingness were emerging. Hegel made negation the driving force of logic, metaphysics, psychology, nature and history, arguing that in all these domains being is inseparable from non-being, just as life is haunted by death. For Hegel, Goethe's archetypal plant — a 'ceaseless activity' of form in flux, growing, branching, transforming — expressed this truth: blossom negates bud, and fruit negates blossom. The evolutionary theories pioneered by Darwin and Spencer stretched the scientific imagination to consider new dimensions of existence: in addition to a dizzying array of actual species were countless forms of life which did *not* survive, and innumerable beings that might have been. In those middle decades of the nineteenth century, anyone with a speculative turn of mind had a vast terrain of non-being to explore.

Lewes was averse to such speculations. What does not exist cannot be observed or measured; absences, possibilities, counterfactuals and other varieties of nothingness lie beyond the reach of evidence. Lewes was a positivist as well as an empiricist: he believed not just that scientific method is the only reliable source of knowledge, but also, more radically, that reality consists solely in what can be known by this method — solely in 'facts', which are empirically verifiable. This philosophical position is aptly called positivism, because it expels all negativity, even all possibility, from existence.

When he rewrote his chapter on Hegel, as *Middlemarch* was gestating, Lewes tightened his critique of Hegel's more speculative metaphysics. He described the arguments he was having on this subject: 'A friend, to whose revision this chapter is much indebted, urges, in defence of Hegel, "that it is not the business of Philosophy to discover particular empirical facts, but to investigate the general relation between the Cosmos and the thinking mind."' Lewes countered that this 'general relation' must be drawn from facts — otherwise it would have no truth. Facts, for Lewes, were the bedrock of reality, and philosophy must conform to them.

The 'friend' Lewes mentions here could be Professor Jowett, or one of the other Oxford Hegelians whom he consulted in 1870. But he might as well be referring to Eliot, who was studying Hegel alongside him and beginning to conceive how *Middlemarch* might investigate the 'relation between the Cosmos and the thinking mind'. Her novel would be full of negations, paths not taken, things that might have been. It would be one vast consciousness teeming with possibilities, humming with desire.

She wove this vibrant negativity into the very sentence structure of *Middlemarch*, letting non-being jostle with authorial assertion. When the puritanical banker Nicholas Bulstrode is introduced, for example, one possible image is summoned and dismissed before we hear what he actually looks like: 'Do not imagine his sickly aspect to have been of the yellow, black-haired sort: he had a pale blond skin, thin grey-sprinkled brown hair, light-grey eyes, and a large forehead.' A yellow-skinned, black-haired Bulstrode appears on the page even as he is rejected, and his ghostly presence haunts the sentence. 'I will not even refer to Dido or Zenobia,' declares satirical

Mrs Cadwallader, when she makes the case for a widow's second marriage.

The novel ends with a tangle of negation that almost parodies this semantic pattern. Echoing Eliot's own professed hope to 'make a few lives near to us better than they would have been without our presence in the world', the narrator concludes that 'the growing good of the world is partly dependent on unhistoric acts; and that things are not so ill with you and me as they might have been, is half owing to the number who lived faithfully a hidden life, and rest in unvisited tombs.' Here Eliot leaves us with a vision of a world where acts are *un*historic and tombs *un*visited, assuring us that it is 'not so ill' as it 'might have been'. This is not merely the fictional world of *Middlemarch*: it is our world too. And by suggesting that its incomplete ('growing') goodness is only *partly* dependent on, *half* owing to, those hidden lives that the novel has brought to light, she gestures off-stage — or off-page — to some other possible source of goodness. This closing sentence is dense with nothingness, as if all the unfactual presences that haunted the preceding eighty-six chapters have gathered here to wave us off.

The novel's marriage plots unfold in this mesh of possibility, threaded with fact and feeling while letting in the light of alternative worlds. It is not unusual, of course, for the heroine of a nineteenth-century novel to navigate a choice between two or more potential suitors, before realizing one of those possibilities in marriage. This happens early in *Middlemarch*, as Dorothea chooses Casaubon and rejects Sir James Chettam, and Rosamond chooses Lydgate and rejects every other young man in Middlemarch. What follows is an initiation into possibilities that lie on the far side of marriage.

Within both the Casaubon and Lydgate marriages grows an 'imagined otherwise' in the shape of Will Ladislaw, Mr Casaubon's artistic young cousin. Discovering that she can continue to court suitors as a married woman, Rosamond pursues a flirtation with Ladislaw that slides towards infidelity. In a story pulsing with the power of the negative, Ladislaw's attempt to persuade himself that he is *not* wooing Dorothea is evidently disingenuous: 'but still — it could not be fairly called wooing a woman to tell her that he would never woo her. It must be admitted to be a ghostly kind of wooing.' Other romantic paths shimmer into view then disappear: Rosamond finds a brief diversion in Captain Lydgate, her husband's flashier cousin; philanthropic Lord Triton would be perfect for Dorothea.

Mary Garth, the novel's third heroine, must contemplate two very different husbands. She resolves that the man she does not choose will 'never tempt her deliberate thought'. The word 'deliberate' is carefully placed: Mary cannot help having 'visions of another kind of life'. All three young wives must figure out how to live with their fantasies — how to reconcile their choice of one man with their desire for others — and they each respond to this question differently.

Creating a fictional world so alive with possibility enabled George Eliot to explore sexual jealousy and regret. Or perhaps it was the other way around: did her need to understand how jealousy or disappointment spin from desire produce the shimmering, tangled web of *Middlemarch*, stretching the fabric of the novel to encompass imagined possibilities? Whereas Romola apparently feels no anger towards the woman who slept with her husband and bore his children, *Middlemarch*'s characters seethe with jealousy at the mere thought of extra-marital attraction. Dorothea is jealous of Rosamond, and Rosamond is jealous of Dorothea. Casaubon, 'jealous as a fiend', seeks to curtail his wife's freedom from beyond the grave. Jealousy also rages where there is no question of betrayal: Mary Garth's two admirers are jealous of one another; Sir James Chettam feels jealous when Dorothea accepts Casaubon, and he is still jealous of her suitors when he is happily married to her sister.

As Eliot and Lewes knew very well, infidelity and second marriages are two ways in which an alternative love might pass from possibility to actuality. *Middlemarch* poses moral questions about both kinds of second love. We hear sharply diverging opinions on widows who marry again, before Dorothea is rewarded with a happy second marriage. When Rosamond makes space for 'another presence' within her married life, George Eliot summons Dorothea's passionate moral voice to warn her against temptation:

'Marriage is so unlike everything else. There is something even awful in the nearness it brings. Even if we loved someone else better than — than those we were married to, it would be no use' — poor Dorothea, in her palpitating anxiety, could only seize her language brokenly — 'I

Dorothea interrupts Will Ladislaw and Rosamond Lydgate

mean, marriage drinks up all our power of giving or getting any bless-edness in that sort of love. I know it may be very dear — but it murders our marriage — and then the marriage stays with us like a murder — and everything else is gone. And then our husband — if he loved and trusted us, and we have not helped him, but made a curse in his life . . . '

With these unfinished thoughts Dorothea vividly invokes the awfulness of adultery, yet offers no practical means to avoid it. Her impassioned argument is completed by Mary Garth's loyalty to her flawed first love: 'When a tender affection has been storing itself in us through many of our years, the idea that we could accept an exchange for it seems to be a cheapening of our lives. And we can set a watch over our affections and our constancy as we can over other treasures.'

While Casaubon's 'imagined otherwise' is entirely consumed by his jealous fears, Lydgate's becomes a realm of regret. His soul cannot grow or flourish in his marriage. Thoughts of what 'might have been' crystallize this commonplace tragedy — 'I meant everything to be different with me. I thought I had more strength and mastery'; 'She married me without knowing what she was going into, and it might have been better for her if she had not married me.' Here he is talking to Dorothea, who perpetually feels that 'there was always something better which she might have done, if she had only been better and known better.'

Although no one in Middlemarch voices the possibility of a marriage between Dorothea and Lydgate, this spectre breaks into Lydgate's fleeting comparisons between Dorothea and his wife, and in Rosamond's jealousy. If only Dorothea had not accepted Casaubon so hastily — then she and Lydgate might have been united in their ardour for new knowledge and social reform, and she would be the perfect wife he hoped for: beautiful, submissive, comfortably rich, sensible with money. The suggestive negations coursing through the novel, lighting up its fantasy-life, nudge us to intuit and inhabit such possibilities.

The novel also contains a voice of dissent from all these speculations. Dorothea's sister Celia, whose staunch empiricism has been carefully established in early chapters, refuses to imagine her life otherwise. She can stretch her thoughts to the idea that Dorothea might have become a mother, like her. But when Sir James regrets that Dorothea 'was not a queen', she protests: '"But what should we have been then? We must have been something else," said Celia, objecting to so laborious a flight of imagination. "I like her better as she is."' Celia's disavowal of possibility is surely connected to her remarkable lack of jealousy, even though her husband is still half in love with her sister. She seems unconcerned with Sir James's hidden thoughts or desires; only his palpably faithful conduct is real for her.

There is an echo here of Lewes's positivist, commonsensical resistance to Hegel's idealism. And there are further echoes of Lewes in Celia's practical kindness, astute observations, teasing humour, and acceptance of things as they are. Perhaps his finest quality as a husband was his ability to love Eliot as she was, just as Celia prefers Dorothea as she is. This inner resemblance might explain why Celia is so fondly drawn, so companionable, so easy to love — and she is, it must be said, devoid of Lewes's more glaring faults. The relationship between the Brooke sisters seems to dramatize something of Eliot's marriage: a deep philosophical difference between idealism and empiricism, between ambiguity and certainty, between yearning for truth and devotion to fact, coupled with a deeper affection and mutual love. Both pairings combine turbulent, self-critical sensitivity and steady cheerful good sense.

George Eliot the author, however, overcomes the rift between idealism and empiricism, even as she explores this difference through her characters. She brings the scientist's eye to *Middlemarch*, as well as the artist's hand and the philosopher's soul. With observations as fine as its conception is large, this novel accomplished, for the first time in English fiction, a synthesis of universal and particular, of inner truth and outer world, of spirit and matter, of theme and form — a synthesis far more complete than Hegelian philosophy could achieve, despite its encyclopaedic ambition.

*

As she worked on *Middlemarch* through 1871 and 1872, Eliot was living Dorothea's dream of marital collaboration. She and Lewes spent the summer of 1871 deep in the Hampshire countryside 'like two secluded owls'. During the long light evenings she read 'books of German science, and other gravities' aloud to him. Each morning Lewes 'sifted' her post, selected letters to read to her at lunchtime and wrote replies on her behalf. This left her free to write in solitude through the first hours of the day. When she fell ill, he was 'housekeeper, secretary and Nurse all in one'.

As usual, she read her novel to Lewes as it grew; he suggested changes to the structure of 'Miss Brooke', which she followed. He negotiated simultaneous publication in Britain and America, and proposed to Blackwood a new publishing strategy. *Middlemarch* would first come out in eight parts, each comprising about a dozen chapters — half the usual length of a single volume of a novel — and published two months apart. Part I appeared in December 1871, bound in green paper covers. When the complete four-volume novel was published the following year, *The Times* declared it a 'perfect' work of art.

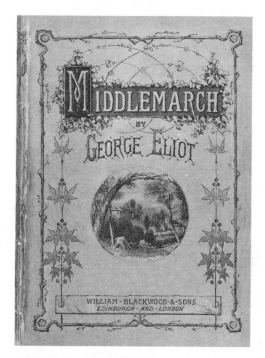

Middlemarch, first edition. Owen Jones advised on the cover design.

In those first years of the new decade, a small cast of particularly devoted admirers emerged within Eliot's growing circle of visitors and correspondents. There was Alexander Main, a young Scotsman who liked to read her novels aloud on the rugged beach at Arbroath — 'It is a mercy he was not drowned,' Blackwood remarked drily when he heard about this Romantic extravagance. Main sent Eliot long, ardent and rather intimate letters praising her work, which she received with a mixture of appreciation and embarrassment. He wanted to edit an anthology of short passages from the novels and poems; Lewes took up this idea, and pushed it to Blackwood.

Main's preface to *Wise, Witty and Tender Sayings . . . of George Eliot* — which Blackwood did publish, very lucratively, in 1872 — declared that 'what Shakespeare did for the Drama, George Eliot has been, and still is, doing for the Novel.' Still conscious of his prize author's 'peculiar' marital situation, Blackwood winced at the dedication Main wrote for the book:

TO

GEORGE ELIOT

IN RECOGNITION OF

A GENIUS AS ORIGINAL AS IT IS PROFOUND

AND

A MORALITY AS PURE AS IT IS

IMPASSIONED

'I would take out the allusion to morality,' the publisher wrote confidentially to William Blackwood, 'as it might raise vulgar discussion.' Main, however, belonged to a different generation — and a lower social class — and for him George Eliot was not a sinner but a saint. She had 'for ever sanctified the Novel by making it the vehicle for the grandest and most uncompromising moral truth'.

Meanwhile, parcels started to arrive from another admirer, Elma Stuart, a young widow with a talent for woodwork. Effusive letters accompanied handmade gifts: an oak book slide, a walnut mirror frame, a little table, a writing board, all elaborately carved and inscribed with George Eliot's name. Elma then began to make her items of underwear, lovingly knitted from the softest wool — which Eliot, who always felt the cold, gladly received.

And then there was John Cross, a handsome young banker who had done well enough to retire from the family business at the age of thirty. He was tall and rather distinguished-looking, with wavy red hair and bright blue eyes. Cross and his mother became friends with the Leweses in the late 1860s, and Cross grew close to Eliot. They wrote one another letters; she called him 'Nephew' and 'Johnny'. He helped her to invest her large earnings in banks and railways in Africa, Australia, Canada and South America, colonial speculations which doubled her annual income.

As these devotees anthologized, carved, knitted and invested for Eliot, an intense young writer and activist named Edith Simcox was reading *Middlemarch*. Edith came from a wealthy London family and her brothers were fellows at Oxford, but in other respects she resembled Eliot as she had been twenty-five years earlier: an ambitious yet self-questioning woman with a powerful literary voice, dedicated to the life of the mind — and born too early in her century to have access to a university education. Also like Eliot, Edith had educated herself prodigiously, then found a channel for her talents in journalism, writing reviews under the genderless pseudonym 'H. Lawrenny'. She had been boyish as a child, and felt herself to be 'half a man'.

Edith Simcox reviewed *Middlemarch* in the Oxford journal *The Academy* in January 1873, shortly after the novel was published in full. While Blackwood had tempered his delight in *Middlemarch* with grumbles about its lack of narrative 'interest', Edith recognized that it marked a new 'epoch' in literature by taking all its drama 'from the inner life'. This novel was innovative, she observed, in making material circumstances serve 'the artistic presentation of a definite passage of mental experience'. She thought it George Eliot's greatest work — and to say this was to say that 'it has scarcely a superior and very few equals in the whole wide range of English fiction'.

Perhaps Edith was already in love with George Eliot by the time she finished reading *Middlemarch*. While working on her review she met Eliot for the first time, and in the years to come would pursue a despairing, one-sided love affair with her. Edith found Eliot very beautiful, and longed for her obsessively. And with the heightened consciousness of a jealous lover, she perceived John Cross as her romantic rival — 'the fatal Johnny', she once called him, arriving early at The Priory one afternoon to find that Cross had got there first.

All these admirers were born around 1840: they belonged to the same generation as Eliot's stepsons, and as the children she might have had if her life had taken a different path. They worshipped her not only as a great artist and moral teacher, but also as a figure in whom erotic and maternal fantasies could be ambiguously merged. Surrounded by love and admiration, her position was now very different from what it had been when she first met Lewes two decades earlier, bruised and insecure after a series of romantic rejections.

Surely all this passionate attention suggested the possibility of other loves — and then there was the thought, whether or not she allowed herself to think it, that another love might one day be more than a possibility. She was herself Lewes's second wife; if she died before him, would he find a third? If she survived him, would she have a second chance? Eliot could not dwell on the idea of her own death without also being aware of Lewes's mortality. 'What is better than to love and live with the loved?' she wrote to Edith Bulwer-Lytton — the young woman with whom she had shared those thoughts about intellectual independence before she began writing 'Miss Brooke' — 'But that must sometimes bring us to live with the dead.'

'Miss Brooke', a story that turns on the question of a woman's second marriage, came into being as one of those unbidden works which thrust itself upon Eliot, cutting across another project she had planned. In this respect it was like *The Lifted Veil* and *Silas Marner*, fantasy-tales of marriage and motherhood that gave form to half-hidden fears and desires.

From this phase of her inner life, wrestling with thoughts of death — and of what might lie beyond it — emerged a work of art that invokes our 'imagined otherwise', and responds to it with a vigorous defence of sexual fidelity. As Eliot entered her last decade with Lewes, she had new reasons to practise the ethic of vigilance — that resolve to 'set a watch over our affections and our constancy' — which she urged in *Middlemarch*.

When Blackwood read the manuscript he was struck by the thought that 'we never know who are to influence our lives.' While nineteen-year-old Dorothea Brooke stood wide-eyed at the beginning of her journey, Eliot, in her sixth decade, felt herself drawing to the close of her life and her marriage. Yet it was possible that an unknown future, perhaps even another love, might still lie ahead. Who knew how the cast of characters now gathered around her, drawing her to the centre of their own life-stories, might alter her imagined ending? As the narrator of *Middlemarch* puts it, 'any one watching keenly the stealthy convergence of human lots, sees a slow preparation of effects from one life on another.' Meanwhile, 'Destiny stands by sarcastic with our *dramatis personae* folded in her hand.'

To my dear Husband George Henry Lewes,
in this nineteenth year of our blessed union
                              December, 1872.

Manuscript of *Middlemarch*, p. 1: To my dear Husband George Henry Lewes, in this nineteenth year of our blessed union. December, 1872.

IO

Destiny

'Was she beautiful or not beautiful?' This is Daniel Deronda's first question when he notices a striking young woman playing roulette in a German casino. It becomes our question too as we watch her through Daniel's eyes. Our curiosity is soon drawn to her inner life. First she is winning at roulette, then she stakes everything, and loses. Gambling turns out to be a metaphor for marriage: a few weeks later, back in England, this woman will stake her soul on marriage to a wealthy man — and we will watch her lose it.

Gwendolen Harleth, George Eliot's last and most compelling heroine, does not want to fall in love. She dislikes romantic attention, shrinks from sexual intimacy, and feels no longing to become a wife. On the other hand, her family have just lost their money in a stock-market

Gwendolen Harleth playing roulette

crash. Gwendolen is spoilt, proud, and childishly devoted to her mother: marrying her neighbour Henleigh Grandcourt will avert the indignity of taking a job as a governess, and make her mother financially secure. As for Grandcourt himself, Gwendolen knows little about him. She finds him handsome enough, and he shares her disdain for commonplace people. He is rich, courteous and appealingly self-contained: an archetypal English gentleman.

Daniel Deronda brings together the different aspects of the marriage question — political, metaphysical, moral, emotional, spiritual — which had taken shape in Eliot's previous works. The novel explores Jewish emancipation, recently analysed by Karl Marx as 'the Jewish question', and draws on mystical teachings about the destiny of human souls amidst a cosmic struggle between good and evil. Gwendolen's marriage drama will be enacted across continents swept by tides of world history, and beneath stars and planets that evoke both ancient gods and the marvels of modern physics. Under such vast skies a bourgeois marriage plot seems so trivial. 'What in the midst of that mighty drama are girls and their blind visions?' asks George Eliot — 'Could there be a slenderer, more insignificant thread in human history than this consciousness of a girl, busy with her small inferences of the way in which she could make her life pleasant?' Yet her answer hints that the soul of this naïve, self-absorbed young woman is a 'vessel' for everything her novel contains. Girls like Gwendolen, on the brink of marriage, 'are the Yea or Nay of that good for which men are enduring and fighting. In these delicate vessels is borne onward through the ages the treasure of human affections.'

A fragile feminine vessel, carrying treasure to be passed through generations, sounds like a metaphor for childbearing, evoking expectant mothers' physical vulnerability and their task of shaping the hearts of children who will hold the future in their hands. But *Daniel Deronda* resists the idea that women should only be maternal vessels. They might carry other kinds of treasure, in particular the power to make art. They contain voices which can sing and vibrate inside other people. Whether they become mothers or artists, or both, or something else, their souls — like all human souls — are microcosms of the struggle between good and evil that continually creates the world.

Daniel's question about Gwendolen's beauty quickly alights on this idea: 'Was she beautiful or not beautiful? and what was the secret of form or expression which gave the dynamic quality to her glance? Was the good or the evil genius dominant in those beams?' These first thoughts begin to link a marriage plot and a cosmic drama, and near the end of the novel George Eliot completes the circle with an old Jewish joke. '"The Omnipresent," said a Rabbi, "is occupied in making marriages." The levity of the saying lies in the ear of him who hears it; for by marriages the speaker meant all the wondrous combinations of the universe whose issue makes our good and evil.'

*

Unlike George Eliot's other novels, *Daniel Deronda* is set in the very recent past — virtually the present — and opens to an unknown future. Its heroes and heroines, born around 1840, belong to the same middle-class generation as Eliot's stepsons and devoted younger friends — Edith Simcox, Elma Stuart, John Cross. Living at the centre of a sprawling, dubious empire, this generation was bereft of the old moral certainties. They were searching for their voices, or just drifting without purpose. Unsure of their vocation, let alone their destiny, perhaps they even doubted the meaning of these words.

Seeds for *Daniel Deronda* were scattered in the early 1870s, while Eliot was still completing *Middlemarch* and Lewes was working on his 'Key to All Psychologies', as he jokingly named the first volume of *Problems of Life and Mind*. One seed was watching Geraldine Leigh, Byron's granddaughter, lose £500 at the roulette table in a German spa resort; both Eliot and Lewes found this a 'painful sight'. Another came from the science of starlight: reading John Tyndall's popular lectures on physics, they learned that the tail of a comet is one hundred million miles long, yet its compressed matter could fit in a horse-drawn cart. 'A sky as vast as ours', Eliot copied into her notebook, 'could be formed from a quantity of matter which might be held in the hollow of the hand.' A third seed was their friend Emanuel Deutsch's journey to Palestine. Deutsch, a Jewish philologist and Talmud scholar who worked as a librarian at the British Museum, used to visit The Priory every week to tutor Eliot in Hebrew. In 1872 they said their last goodbyes to him: he was terminally ill and set off for Jerusalem, hoping to be buried in his Holy Land.

Over the next few years these disparate seeds would be nourished by wide reading and gathered into a single work of art. Everything is connected, from the entire cosmos to a single human soul, from ancient stars to a fleeting game of chance: this was the grand vision — at once scientific, aesthetic and spiritual — of George Eliot's final novel.

The idea of a Jewish story crystallized during 1873. When Eliot and Lewes returned to Germany that year they visited synagogues in Frankfurt and Mainz. They contemplated a trip to Palestine, but decided it was too far to travel, with their fluctuating health. North America, where George Eliot had many devoted readers, likewise seemed out of reach. Lewes's work on *Problems of Life and Mind* kept being stalled by bouts of illness, and Eliot began to suffer from painful kidney stones as well as her usual headaches, colds and depressions.

By 1874 they had been together for twenty years. Instead of venturing further east or west, beyond the continent they had visited so often during those two decades, they remained in England and looked for a second home in the rural counties south of London. This English countryside felt like Eliot's homeland, from which city life, despite the comforts of The Priory, still seemed a kind of exile. 'Town, with its necessity of receiving numerous visitors, soon becomes a weariness to my country-bred nature, and with the first hour of stillness among the fields and lanes and commons I get a delicious sense of repose and refreshment,' she wrote in the spring of 1874.

So they hoped to buy a country house where they could spend the summers, and eventually retire permanently — perhaps in the area around Weybridge in Surrey, where John Cross lived with his mother and sisters. The Crosses had become a sort of adopted family, and they spent several Christmases with them in Weybridge. 'Johnnie' was instructed to find them 'a house with undeniable charms, on high ground in a strictly rural neighbourhood (water and gas laid on nevertheless)'; it must have 'at once seclusion and convenience of position', and be 'neither of the suburban villa style nor of the grand Hall and Castle dimensions'. Johnnie searched in vain throughout 1874.

Meanwhile they rented a cottage in Surrey from June to September, and worked quietly on their books in their customary dual solitude:

writing or studying in the mornings, walking in the afternoons, reading together in the evenings. Usually she read aloud to him; occasionally he read to her. Eliot spent that summer absorbed in what Lewes called 'her Hebrew and Oriental studies'. By then she had been 'brewing' and 'simmering' *Daniel Deronda* for several months. This involved research on the daunting scale she had undertaken for *Romola*, but with a much wider scope. She copied out Auguste Comte's entire Positivist Calendar, with its thirteen solar months named after Moses, Aristotle, Dante, Shakespeare and other great men — a new pantheon of religion, poetry, drama, philosophy, science, industry and politics, from ancient to modern times. Her novel would encompass all of this.

She read about Islamic history, the life of the Buddha, ancient Egyptian religion, Norse mythology. Reaching deep into Britain's past, she researched old English heraldry and Celtic folklore, and compiled a 'Topography of Arthurian Legend'. Gwendolen, she discovered, was a renowned beauty of King Arthur's court, as well as a Welsh Venus and an ancient moon goddess — like Artemis and Diana, she carried a bow and arrow, and symbolized both chastity and childbirth. Here was Goethe's 'eternal feminine' archetype, expressed in a form native to the British Isles: the Welsh 'gwen' and Saxon 'cwen' meant white, woman, wife and queen.

Most of all, though, Eliot studied Judaism. She immersed herself in towers of books on Jewish history and philosophy, which Lewes had hunted down for her in bookshops or borrowed from the London Library. She learned about the Tanakh, or Hebrew Bible, and the ancient rabbinic traditions of Mishnah and Talmud. She made detailed notes on the Kabbalah, an esoteric tradition of Jewish mysticism based on Neo-Platonic philosophy which emerged during the Middle Ages, and was revived in the sixteenth century.

The Kabbalah teaches that the source of all things is an unknowable, indescribable God, named in Hebrew *En-Soph*, meaning no end, or *Ohr En Soph*, endless light. Like an infinite sun, the En-Soph 'rays out' a spiritual force, through ten widening circles, each one emanating from the last. These emanations create countless worlds: our world of finite things is one among many. 'Individuals in the lower world', noted Eliot, 'have their types in the higher, so that nothing here is trivial, but all has a higher significance.' Another day, she jotted down a Talmudic saying: 'Man's life like the shadow of a bird that flies.'

These images of cosmic connections between higher and lower, greater and smaller, a soaring bird and its shadow on the earth, echoed the thought that an unfathomably vast comet-tail could be squeezed into a horse cart. And the Kabbalistic idea that nothing is trivial, everything has a higher significance, responded to a peculiarly modern crisis of meaning. Since the Copernican revolution, Europeans had wondered about their place in an unbounded universe that no longer centred on themselves. Alongside her notes on Judaism, Eliot copied a few passages from Fontenelle's *Entretiens sur la pluralité des mondes*, where the seventeenth-century poet describes his evening walks with a beautiful woman. Looking up at the starry sky, this philosophical couple consider the idea that 'every fixed star is a sun, which diffuses light to its surrounding worlds.' Eliot picked out a part where Fontenelle's companion feels lost in infinite space: 'Is every fixed star the centre of a vortex, as large perhaps as ours? The amazing space comprehending our sun and planets is but a little portion of the universe?' she wonders one night. 'Surely,' she muses, 'the very idea of ourselves is as nothing, when we are thus lost amongst millions of worlds . . . the earth begins to diminish into such a speck, that in future I shall hardly consider any object worthy of eager pursuit.'

Two hundred years later, this bewilderment and ennui had only increased. With new sciences challenging theological doctrines of creation, the meaning and purpose of human life seemed more precarious than ever. Comte's positivist calendar, beginning with the month of Moses and ending with the month of Bichat, the pioneer of modern biology, suggested a progression from religion to science — although Comte built a new humanist religion on scientific foundations. When John Tyndall was elected President of the British Association for the Advancement of Science in 1874, he used his inaugural lecture to endorse the evolutionary theories of Darwin and Spencer, and to urge that 'all religious theories, schemes and systems, which embrace notions of cosmogony, must submit to the control of science.' Lewes and Eliot read Tyndall's lecture in the journal *Nature* a few days after it was delivered. Lewes, of course, was already convinced that modern science made religious metaphysics redundant.

But Eliot knew that an artist does not need to choose between religion and science. Art stretches across human history, intersecting with myth and experiment and philosophy in every century. To her, the Kabbalah's mystical teachings suggested a way to make a marriage plot — concentrated on the slender thread of a silly girl's consciousness — reflect larger things: the century, the Empire, even the whole universe. 'Nothing here is trivial, but all has a higher significance' became, in George Eliot's hands, an artistic principle. She could create a fictional cosmos governed by this law. In its literary form, *Daniel Deronda* would be a Kabbalistic novel.

*

Eliot also discovered in the Kabbalah a mystical vision of human souls joining together and helping one another. All souls were born from the En-Soph and seek to return to their divine source, but sometimes a soul becomes isolated, too weak to travel alone. So it 'chooses a companion soul of better fortune and more strength. The stronger of the two then becomes as it were the mother; she carries the sickly one in her bosom and nurses her as a woman her child.' Fragile souls long to be coupled, to grow strong enough to pursue their spiritual destiny.

This ideal of dependence raises some tricky practical questions. How does a lost, lonely soul know which companion to choose? Should it wait to be chosen, trusting in the gods or the stars? What if the stronger soul crushes or overwhelms the weaker one, instead of helping it to grow?

These questions elude religious dogma as well as scientific proof. They are existential questions, which arise in the middle of life — and often in the middle of the night — as we struggle to understand ourselves. How do you know that you are travelling on the right path, with the right person, towards your true destiny? Might you have taken a wrong turn? Have you lost yourself in the wrong person? Of course, the questions can also be turned around. Can you be certain that you are good for your partner — that their life with you is better than it would otherwise have been?

When John Cross's sister Emily announced her engagement, Eliot confronted this last question and tried to answer it reassuringly. 'That is really the highest good of a wife,' she advised her younger friend, 'to be quite certain in the midst of the dimness and doubt which this difficult world surrounds us with, that there is one close to her whose life is every day the better for her.' Then she crossed out 'certain', and wrote 'sure' instead. Certainty belongs to objective knowledge, to things that can be proved true or false, whereas being sure is a feeling, closer to trust than to knowledge. 'The very possibility of a constantly growing blessedness in marriage is to me the very basis of good in our mortal life,' she wrote to Emily's fiancé. In an uncertain world, this 'possibility' was something to hold on to, something to believe in, something to hope for.

*

At the beginning of *Daniel Deronda*, Gwendolen Harleth is a long way from this marital piety: she just wants to be free to do as she likes. She hopes at most for status and power as the wife of a wealthy man. Instead she finds herself helpless and humiliated in Grandcourt's hands, and haunted by the thought of those hands tightening around her neck. 'Pinched' and 'crushed' by her husband's tyrannical will, she feels that her soul is dying. This slow spiritual smothering provokes a recurring fear of strangulation: 'That white hand of his which was touching his whisker was capable, she fancied, of clinging round her neck and threatening to throttle her.' Grandcourt's own death seems her only hope for release — but this fantasy keeps turning 'as with a dream-change into the terror that she should die with his throttling fingers on her neck avenging that thought'.

Gwendolen is held captive by her husband's eyes as well as by his hands. He keeps her under 'surveillance' and compels her to perform her wifely role according to his wishes: 'Constantly she had to be on the scene as Mrs Grandcourt, and to feel herself watched in that part by the exacting eyes of a husband who had found a motive to exercise his tenacity — that of making his marriage answer all the ends he chose, and with the more completeness the more he discerned any opposing will in her.' When she goes to visit her mother, Grandcourt waits outside on his horse, or in his carriage. She is always afraid of being observed, and later 'rebuked' or 'punished' for her behaviour.

George Eliot hints at sexual domination behind closed doors. In one scene Gwendolen sits in her fine evening clothes 'like a white image of helplessness', and her husband seems to 'gratify himself with looking at her'. During an argument Grandcourt is turned on by her resistance and submission. She tries to leave the room, he bars the door; she retreats, he advances — 'It followed that he turned her chin and kissed her, while she still kept her eyelids down, and she did not move until he was on the other side of the door.' This coercive kiss is an emblem of their sexual relationship, its aggression echoed in frequent 'shocks of humiliation' that leave Gwendolen feeling used and ashamed, struggling to 'adjust herself'. She resorts to various coping strategies: 'proud concealment, trust in new excitements that would make life go by without much thinking; trust in some deed of reparation to nullify her self-blame and shield her from a vague, ever-visiting dread of some horrible calamity; trust in the hardening effect of use and wont that would make her indifferent to her miseries'.

The Grandcourts' awful marriage, concealed behind its polished, privileged exterior, plays out a specifically English political drama. When they travel abroad, 'this handsome, fair-skinned English couple manifested the usual eccentricity of their nation, both of them proud, pale, and calm, without a smile on their faces, moving like creatures who were fulfilling a supernatural destiny.' George Eliot makes the narrative gaze linger on Grandcourt's pale skin, and highlights its racial significance by transplanting his 'white hand', which Gwendolen imagines tightening around her throat, to some colonized territory: 'If this white-handed man with the perpendicular profile had been sent to govern a difficult colony, he might have won reputation among his contemporaries. He had certain ability, would have understood that it was safer to exterminate than to cajole superseded proprietors, and would not have flinched from making things safe in that way.' Forced to go sailing with her cruel husband, Gwendolen becomes his 'galley-slave'. Marital and colonial 'despotism' merge; both resemble 'those fatal meshes which are woven within more closely than without, and often make the inward torture disproportionate to what is discernible as outward cause'.

Of all George Eliot's marriage plots, this one is the most pathological. Gwendolen's relationship with Grandcourt elicits symptoms of various nervous disorders which were receiving scientific attention at this time: hysteria, neurosis, frigidity, anorexia nervosa. Before her marriage Gwendolen was already liable to 'fits of spiritual dread', 'ashamed and frightened, as at what might happen again'. When alone, she would experience 'an undefined feeling of immeasurable existence aloof from her, in the midst of which she was helplessly incapable of asserting herself' — the way a child feels when a power-ful man looms over her. Perhaps this man is her mother's second husband, a shadowy figure who came and went during her childhood; Gwendolen did not like him to come home, and longed to escape from him. The image of this stepfather suddenly returns in the darkest hour of her marriage, when she is stuck in a boat with Grandcourt on an open sea: 'It came over me that when I was a child I used to fancy sailing away into a world where people were not forced to live with any one they did not like.'

These clues point to an undisclosed trauma, which has made Gwen-dolen cling to her mother. Until she leaves home to get married, she sleeps in her mother's bedroom like a little girl. She likes to be admired, but feels 'a sort of physical repulsion' if anyone comes too close. When Grandcourt kisses her neck during their engagement, her heart beats faster 'with a vague fear', and after her wedding her heart races for rea-sons she does not quite understand — 'was it some dim forecast, the insistent penetration of suppressed experience, mixing the expectation of a triumph with the dread of a crisis?' This 'insistent penetration' of buried memories foreshadows the sexual aggression that lies just beneath Grandcourt's gentlemanly veneer. From the way this man treats his dogs, we know he enjoys humiliating weaker creatures. When Gwendolen is finally alone with him on their wedding night, she collapses in hysterical screams — and we are left to imagine how the evening ends.

Ten years before Charcot taught Freud to hypnotize his patients, and twenty years before Freud and Breuer published their *Studies of Hysteria, Daniel Deronda* dramatized the 'momentous discovery', as Freud called it, that hysterical symptoms 'are determined by certain experiences of the patient's which have operated in a traumatic fash-ion and which are being reproduced in his psychical life in the form of mnemic symbols'. The novel's innovative chronology — begin-ning in the midst of adult life, then flashing back to childhood scenes — gives literary form to the idea that the secrets of human destiny are ordained not by a God or a planetary alignment, but by 'suppressed experience'. Though Gwendolen's dark fantasies seem like premonitions, they are really 'ghosts' of the past. And the novel stages this inward drama, which Gwendolen cannot see. We watch the ghosts moving within her, 'making no break in her more acknowledged consciousness: dark rays doing their work invisibly in the broad light'.

All this makes Gwendolen a singularly fascinating character. Yet George Eliot links her sexual and emotional vulnerabilities to a destiny shared by all women. Alone in her bedroom on her wedding night — before her husband comes in — Gwendolen sees herself repeated ad infinitum in glass panels, 'like so many women petrified white'. This vivid image evokes the psychic energy of repetition generating her neurosis, but it also places her in a long procession of

Gwendolen's hysteria: illustration by H. Winthrop Pierce, 1888

virgin brides who have gone before her, and will follow after her, across the marital threshold.

Gwendolen's half-conscious sense of this shared legacy is revealed in a sudden impulse of generosity towards her younger sisters, whom she had previously despised. Now she feels a tender solidarity with these innocent girls, also destined to be wives. Initiated into married life and forced to guard its secrets, she has, the narrator remarks, become even more beautiful. Her soul has acquired 'the nameless something which often makes a woman more interesting after marriage than before, less confident that all things are according to her opinion, and yet with less of deer-like shyness — more fully a human being'.

*

During their travels Eliot and Lewes had watched at close quarters as European nations came into being: Italy in the 1860s, the *Romola* years, and Germany in the early 1870s. Could the Jewish people dispersed across the continent become a nation too? There seemed to be a growing consciousness of 'the wonderful union of Religion and Nationality in Judaism', as one nineteenth-century rabbi put it — and this consciousness was often concentrated on Palestine, a site of Jewish memory and longing. Emanuel Deutsch had talked many times about his hopes for a Jewish homeland. After his first brief visit to Jerusalem in 1869, his eyes would fill with tears when he recalled standing at the Wailing Wall 'among his own people'.

Daniel Deronda stages a debate on the future of Judaism in a fictional pub named the Hand and Banner in London's Holborn district, where a 'philosophical club' of working men meets once a week. Here idealistic Mordecai envisions 'a land and a polity' where his people may 'share the dignity of a national life'. Pragmatic Gideon, who sees himself as a 'rational Jew', argues that 'a man's country is where he is well off': he wants to abandon all 'superstitions and exclusiveness' and 'melt into the populations we live among'.

This scene was inspired by Lewes's distant memories of the smoke-filled room in Holborn's Red Lion Inn where, in his bohemian youth, he had learned about Spinoza from 'a German Jew . . . a calm meditative amiable man, very poor, with weak eyes and chest; grave and gentle in demeanour'. These recollections fused with Eliot's recent memories of Emanuel Deutsch to form the fragile physique of Mordecai, and his intense longing for 'our own better future and the better future of the world'.

Daniel Deronda unfolds in the mid-1860s, when successive reforms were making it easier for Jewish citizens to vote in elections and to hold public office. At the Hand and Banner, Gideon argues that Jews in England now have political equality and no longer need to feign Christian beliefs. As if fulfilling Gideon's vision of prosperous assimilation, Benjamin Disraeli — whose family had joined the Church of England when he was a child — became Leader of the Conservative Party and Britain's first Jewish-born prime minister in 1868.

Disraeli had stayed in Downing Street just a few months before losing the next general election to Gladstone's Liberals. But early in 1874 he led his party to their first majority in more than thirty years. 'Do you mind about the Conservative majority? I don't,' Eliot wrote to Barbara Bodichon a few days after the election. She reminded John Blackwood — who was delighted by the prospect of a 'quiet steady government' — that she was 'no believer in Salvation by Ballot'.

Disraeli was a novelist as well as a politician, and his fiction was unusual for its sympathetic Jewish characters. More common were caricatures of grasping, untrustworthy Jews, from Dickens's child-snatcher Fagin to Joseph Emilius, the unctuous social climber in Anthony Trollope's *The Eustace Diamonds*, which had been serialized in the *Fortnightly Review* at the same time as *Middlemarch* was published in its monthly parts. Eliot now had a policy of 'fasting' from contemporary fiction, but she made an exception for Trollope, her old friend. She read *The Eustace Diamonds* as well as *The Way We Live Now*, novels depicting a cynical and decadent late-Victorian society. By the 1870s the goodness which pure-hearted heroines like Dinah Morris and Dorothea Brooke diffused through the early decades of the century seemed to have evaporated. Trollope portrayed Jewish characters and their easy infiltration into high society as a symptom, if not the cause, of this moral decline.

Eliot was plotting a different diagnosis of modern England, and the place of Judaism within it. Her new novel would play with

Jewish stereotypes and challenge readers to rethink them. Resisting the prevailing tendencies of assimilation and anti-Semitism — which, as Trollope's latest novels showed, were often intertwined — she created sweet-faced, diminutive Mirah Cohen and her long-lost brother Mordecai: virtuous characters who embrace their distinctive Jewishness.

The moral and spiritual currents of *Daniel Deronda* flow through these Jewish characters, while the Christian establishment fails to protect or nurture human goodness. Gwendolen's uncle, a thoroughly worldly Anglican vicar, has some inkling of Grandcourt's shady past but urges his niece to marry him anyway, for the sake of increasing her 'rank and wealth'. By dramatizing the moral bankruptcy of her native religion, George Eliot casts a retrospective shadow over the wiser, kinder Christians in her previous novels, set in an earlier time. *Daniel Deronda*'s turn to Judaism suggests that the spiritual possibilities of Christianity belong only to the past, to nostalgia rather than to hope.

During the autumn of 1874 Eliot read her first chapters to Lewes. One November afternoon they walked to Blackfriars Bridge, the setting for one of Mordecai's prophetic scenes, and stood together above the rushing river, watching the sunset. She told John Blackwood that her new novel had now passed from 'the simmering' to 'the irrevocable'. She pushed on through the winter, through doubt and despair, to finish Volume One.

In April 1875 William Blackwood called at The Priory, eager for news of the book. Eliot 'hung her head low' and told him it was 'detestable'. Lewes assured the publisher that it was 'perfectly charming and all about English Ladies and Gentlemen and a scene laid in Wiltshire'. He probably thought it best not to mention its Jewish sympathies or its critiques of Church and Empire — after all, John Blackwood had declined to publish *Problems of Life and Mind* because he disliked its treatment of religion. Lewes suggested letting their guest take the first volume of *Daniel Deronda* up to Edinburgh, so that his uncle could read it and offer encouragement. William Blackwood was struck by Eliot's 'face of horror and fright and meek expression . . . She seemed just to tremble at the idea of the M.S. being taken from her as if it were her baby.'

'Here I have listened to the messages of earth and sky':
Mordecai on Blackfriars Bridge at sunset, *Daniel Deronda*

*

George Eliot crams themes from her previous novels into *Daniel Deronda*. She returns to questions of voice and vocation first posed in *Adam Bede*; Daniel's mother Alcharisi, like the heroine of 'Armgart', is an ageing singer who faces the loss of her voice. Both Gwendolen and Mordecai possess uncanny clairvoyant powers that resemble Latimer's second sight in *The Lifted Veil*. The novel's plot turns on financial inheritance as in *Felix Holt* and *Middlemarch*, and on ethnic inheritance as in *The Spanish Gypsy*. Daniel, Mirah and Gwendolen all share Romola's longing for a lost mother, and Alcharisi shares her struggle to escape patriarchal power. Like *Middlemarch*, *Daniel Deronda* is vibrant with possibilities, darkened by fantasy, rife with sexual jealousy, and haunted by ghostly presences. From the first page we cannot help hoping that Daniel and Gwendolen will get together, and their story unfolds in the shadow of this 'imagined otherwise'.

Yet *Daniel Deronda* is very different from anything that came before — and not just because it ends with a Jewish wedding. 'Whether it will rival *Middlemarch* is a question — at any rate it breaks new ground. I shall be curious to see the effect it will produce on you,' Lewes wrote to Blackwood, unusually tentative, while the novel was still in progress. Its bold experiments in literary form, inspired by the Kabbalah, achieve a new density of meaning. Blending the realist and symbolist techniques developed in her earlier works, George Eliot creates a heroine who is at once an individual and an archetype, both psychologically truthful and a cipher for colonial oppression, for Jewish rootlessness, for a cosmic struggle between good and evil. Gwendolen is also a mirror reflecting experiences dispersed through the novel: Mordecai's second sight, Daniel's need for a mother, Grandcourt's cruelty, Mirah's degrading exploitation by her father. She is a shattered mirror, composed of all the painful shards lodged in the hearts of these other characters. Nevertheless, she is always entirely herself.

And in this novel, for the first time, George Eliot makes her heroine marry for money. Her opening scene in a decadent casino places money centre-stage, and parallels are soon drawn between gambling and commerce. The age-old mixture of money and vice is clotted around the sinister figure of Lapidoth, Mirah's father, a gambling addict, pimp and thief. Lapidoth is an anti-Semitic caricature, but his stereotyped Jewish vice radiates through an upper-class British milieu of colonial slave-owners and stock-market speculators, as well as through the Grandcourts' archetypally English marriage. So many scenes — the parties, the clothes, the horses, the prawns Mrs Grandcourt pushes around her plate at breakfast-time — are furnished by an invisible flow of money from distant colonies. These winnings of rich men's games accumulate in grand London houses and tranquil country estates through a rinsing mechanism of trade, investment, and inheritance.

Gwendolen, a delicate flower cultivated in this milieu, metamorphoses from gambler to prostitute, in spite of her 'fierce' chastity. A few months into her marriage she realizes that she has 'sold herself' to her husband — 'sold her truthfulness and sense of justice, so that he held them throttled into silence, collared and dragged behind him to witness what he would, without remonstrance'. This horrible image echoes the 'yoke' and 'noose' that symbolize marriage in *Middle-march*, but here yoke and money merge in the valuable jewels placed on Gwendolen's neck and fingers. As in *The Eustace Diamonds*, these supposed love tokens are entirely transactional. After she agrees to marry Grandcourt, he sends her a magnificent diamond ring and a £500 cheque with the instructions, 'Pray wear this ring when I come at twelve in sign of our betrothal. I enclose a cheque . . . for immediate expenses.' She is forced to wear his 'poisoned' diamond necklace when she becomes his wife. Soon we are watching a tormented Gwendolen 'hurting herself with the jewels that glittered on her tightly-clasped fingers pressed against her heart'. At the end of the novel she resembles a penitent, sorrowing Mary Magdalene.

Daniel Deronda's kabbalistic composition, with its emanations of meaning across different spheres, allows George Eliot to portray prostitution as a pathology of art as well as of marriage. Gwendolen, a wife who has sold herself and must act a part, mirrors Mirah, who was 'taken up and used by strangers' when her father forced her to act and sing in theatres as a child. Acting is not simply an art or a trade, but a social performance — and Gwendolen, like Mirah, 'must learn her part, must go to rehearsal, must act and sing in the evening, must hide her feelings'. Later, when Mirah works as a respectable singer in upper-class homes, she still risks becoming a 'commodity disdainfully paid for by the fashionable public'.

This theme surely touched Eliot's own experience — and it had taken her years to confront it through her art. She had, of course, been branded a fallen woman when she assumed the role of Lewes's wife, and she grew as an author under that shadow. Yet when she transformed herself into George Eliot and Mrs Lewes in the 1850s, she believed that art, like marriage, was something sacred. Twenty years on she still believed this. Now she also knew that the sanctity of art is as fragile as the sanctity of love, similarly liable to violations and corruptions. England's bestselling novelist could not ignore the fact that people write for money, just as they marry for money. And the success of authorship, like the success of a marriage, is often measured by financial gain.

When her creativity collided with commerce, Eliot tended to feel anxious, as if the sacred were touching the profane. Dividing the labour of authorship between herself and Lewes — she made the art, and he sold it — was, in a way, a solution to this problem. Lewes certainly embraced the myth of her purity: in the 1870s he began to refer to her as 'Madonna', at first to acknowledged acolytes like Elma Stuart, Alexander Main and John Cross, and later to other friends, including Barbara Bodichon and John Blackwood.

But this meant that lines between sacred and profane were drawn inside their marriage, and tensions between artistic and financial motives were sewn into the structure of their relationship. Unsurprisingly the anxieties did not go away, and erupted in their painful wrangling over the sale of *Romola*. In 1874, as tremendous sales of *Middlemarch* made the Leweses wealthier than ever, Eliot agonized about the price of her new poetry collection — should this slender pocket-sized volume be sold at five shillings (Blackwood's suggestion) or six shillings (Lewes's preferred price)?

Although it was a relief to let Lewes be the intermediary between herself and Blackwood on all business matters, this cast his role in an uncomfortable light. If she was selling herself, what part was he playing in the transaction? Eliot's earnings were still sent to Lewes, and deposited in his bank account. Questions about how much her publisher or her readers should pay for her works touched on sensitive points: not just the collision between art and commerce, but also the fact that her professional success so conspicuously eclipsed her husband's. Did this compromise his masculinity — for him, or for her, or in other people's eyes? And if so, could his control over her authorship — and its proceeds — redress the balance? Lewes was sometimes perceived as greedy and grasping. He was heard to boast that 'she does not write unless I make her do it', and gossips whispered that George Eliot was 'worked harder than any carthorse'.

These perceptions did not need to be factually true to have some influence, conscious or unconscious, on the imaginative work of *Daniel Deronda*, which insistently links prostitution with the roles of both artist and wife. When seedy Lapidoth appears in person at the end of the novel — an 'eager and gesticulating man' with 'an ineffaceable jauntiness of air, perhaps due to the bushy curls of his grizzled hair, the smallness of his hands and feet, and his light walk' — he looks and moves like Lewes, and echoes his easy, vivacious talk. Lapidoth, who made his daughter perform and profited from her talent, has returned to take her money. There is something dream-like about his fleeting appearance in the story, as if a shadowy presence — maybe a dangerous thought — has suddenly materialized. One night he slips away as quietly as he arrived.

If the loving, good-humoured friendship of Dorothea and Celia Brooke expressed a sunny aspect of the Leweses' marriage, the sordid relation between Mirah and her father, with its uneasy power dynamic and air of shame, could have emerged from its shadow side. Lapidoth is not a portrait of Lewes, but he may be a vessel for deep-held resentments on both sides — a means of expressing them, while keeping them contained. Their marriage was now, after all, twenty years old: the same age as Gwendolen Harleth, and perhaps just as complicated.

*

Daniel Deronda is supposed to be the person who rescues Gwendolen's soul, after her 'last great gambling loss' — her marriage to Grandcourt — plunges her into terror and despair. Here lies the novel's great ambiguity: George Eliot imposes this narrative arc, yet gives us reasons to distrust it. From their first encounter in the casino, Daniel's effect on Gwendolen is questionable. As soon as he sees her he begins to judge her: is she beautiful or not beautiful? Watching her at the roulette table, his 'evil eye' jinxes her play, makes her feel ashamed, and foreshadows Grandcourt's creepy surveillance. Daniel's aura of superiority repeatedly casts her in a subordinate role. After she gambles away all her money and pawns her necklace, he redeems it for her, forcing her into his debt and, she feels, entangling her 'in helpless humiliation'. That necklace prefigures the one she receives from Grandcourt, which becomes a slave's yoke and an emblem of spiritual strangulation.

For all her fragility, Gwendolen is full of 'fire and will', overflowing with energy and wit and intelligence. Daniel's earnest moralizing conspires with her brutal marriage to make her meeker, more submissive. We might even say that Daniel's conspicuous virtue, like Grandcourt's choking hands, threatens to squeeze the life out of this brave, spirited young woman.

'I am cruel,' Daniel admits, before he leaves her for the last time. Devastated and abandoned, Gwendolen clutches at their shared narrative of moral improvement: 'I said . . . I said . . . it should be better . . . better with me . . . for having known you.' She is left crying hysterically in the night to her mother. 'I am going to live . . . I shall live. I shall be better,' she says again and again. Perhaps she finally has a chance now that Grandcourt is dead, and Daniel, at last married to Mirah, is sailing off to the Holy Land with his perfect little wife.

But there is a beautiful moment in Gwendolen and Daniel's final scene together, when they weep and dry one another's tears. Their souls, like their hands and eyes, mirror one another; their tears are a great release for two people who have laboured for a long time, with immense effort, to press down their sadness. Gwendolen finally finds her own maternal power, and Daniel is at last allowed to be a child. In this moment of parting, both souls are at once child and mother, reflecting one another's sorrow and responding with solace and love. This is an image of what their marriage might have been, if destiny had not intervened.

*

After *Daniel Deronda*, Lewes was asked if George Eliot would write another novel. 'Never again,' he said, 'it takes too much out of her.' In 1876, when Eliot was completing the book, she was frequently unwell with kidney problems, toothaches, headaches, fatigue, 'nervous wear'. John Blackwood thought she looked worn out, and suspected that Lewes 'fidgets her in his anxiety both about her and her work and himself'. Yet as she wrote the last chapters of *Daniel Deronda* that spring, she lived in 'the passion of the moment', caught up in the 'the excitement of writing'. She was absorbed in the lives of her 'spiritual children' — Gwendolen, Daniel, Mirah and Mordecai — as she sent them into their futures.

Lewes and Blackwood agreed to publish *Daniel Deronda* in the same lucrative format they had devised for *Middlemarch*: first in substantial paper-bound monthly parts, and then as a four-volume novel. It was advertised as a tale of modern English life. Monthly publication began in February 1876 and ran until September. Eliot finished the last chapter in the middle of this period, in early June. Lewes declared it her greatest work.

Once again he shielded Eliot from reviews, armed with his paper scissors. 'Mr Lewes carefully protects me from reading about myself, and as soon as I know that there is an article on me in any periodical, I wait till it is cut out before I take up the print for other reading. But Mr Lewes reads everything about me that comes his way,' Eliot explained to Elma Stuart shortly after Part I of *Daniel Deronda* was published.

She soon gleaned enough, however, to know that her Jewish characters were not well received. Mirah was too good, Mordecai was too weird — and Gwendolen, alas, was just too fascinating. This 'mermaid witch' had beguiled John Blackwood from the start, and as usual his instincts were confirmed by the reading public, for whom Gwendolen's marriage plot eclipsed the novel's grand themes of Jewish longing and belonging. By now Eliot's literary art was so fine that her most eminent critics, skilled only in the mechanics of character and plot, did not perceive the patterns of image and metaphor that give *Daniel Deronda* its kaleidoscopic form, producing reflections of Mirah and Mordecai in Gwendolen's inner life. Eliot was consoled by appreciative letters from Jewish readers, and by news that a Hebrew translation of the Hand and Banner scene had appeared in a German-Jewish newspaper. 'This is better than the laudation of readers who cut the book into scraps and talk of nothing but Gwendolen. I meant everything in the book to be related to everything else there,' she wrote to Barbara Bodichon.

In the autumn of 1876, after a long holiday in Switzerland, Lewes negotiated with Blackwood a new edition of George Eliot's complete works. Lewes insisted on a royalty scheme that gave him 'free command over editions and prices'. This agreement followed several days of marital debate at The Priory, during which Lewes probably raised the possibility of offering the rights to a different publisher.

He may or may not have seen a letter Eliot had sent to Blackwood a couple of weeks earlier. She had, she told her publisher, been looking over their old correspondence, which now stretched back twenty years to Blackwood's letter praising *The Sad Fortunes of the Reverend*

Amos Barton in the autumn of 1856. She told him how much she owed him, that she could not have written her novels without him — 'you may conceive this in her language,' Blackwood wrote delightedly to his nephew, describing this 'most charming letter from George Eliot'. To Eliot, he confessed that

> Tears came into my eyes, and I read the passage at once to my wife who was sitting beside me when I received the letter. I look upon such expressions coming from you, as the very highest compliment that a man holding the position I do could receive, and I shall keep the letter for my children as a memorial that their father was good for something in his day. You are too good about my poor letters which I always felt to be too meagre and too few but I do look back upon our correspondence with pride and pleasure.

With his usual discretion, Blackwood did not tell her that his tears were also prompted by 'the context about herself'. He meant, surely, the peculiar vulnerability of her unconventional marriage situation,

John Blackwood, publisher

and perhaps also her vulnerability in relation to Lewes. Her dependence on Blackwood — a loyal editor who had always recognized her talent, and valued her art above its market price — made her grateful letter all the more touching. And why not be moved to tears by this quiet love between publisher and author — a conservative family man and a fallen woman, bound into a deep friendship, indeed a shared destiny, by their devotion to George Eliot's art.

At the end of that year, just after Eliot's fifty-seventh birthday, John Cross finally found their country house. It was in Witley, a Surrey village about an hour by train from London Waterloo, on the same railway line as Weybridge. Their friend Alfred Tennyson, the Poet Laureate, lived nearby. The house, called The Heights, stood on 'a gentle hill, overlooking a characteristic bit of English scenery' — a lawn, large gardens, trees and green fields.

They bought The Heights and moved in the following summer. After a decade of long journeys to European alps and forests, seeking respite from city life, this English hillside offered permanent sanctuary. Their promised land turned out to be a little disappointing: inside, the house was not quite right, but its surroundings were idyllic — 'a land of pine-woods and copses, village greens and heather-coloured hills, with the most delicious old red or grey brick, timbered cottages nestling among creeping roses'. Lewes told friends that Witley was 'paradise'; it felt very satisfying to walk in his own woods, serenaded by thrushes and blackbirds and cooing pigeons.

John Cross, who was a natural sportsman — tall and athletic, fond of rowing — urged his beloved 'aunt' to take daily exercise for the sake of her health. He set up a tennis net on their lawn, brought them racquets and balls, and taught them how to play. By the autumn Eliot found herself 'quite renovated', 'in more bodily comfort than I have known for years', and 'at last in love with our Surrey house'.

When Blackwood visited The Heights, he said to Eliot, 'Something should be born here.' She seemed to agree with him. She was drawn to many possible subjects for a new novel, each one bringing an 'enlarging vista' to her mind. The difficulty was — as she wrote on the last day of 1877, and the last page of the diary she had kept for sixteen years — 'to decide how far resolution should set in the direction of activity rather than in the acceptance of a more negative state.

The Heights, Witley

Many conceptions of works to be carried out present themselves, but confidence in my own fitness to complete them worthily is all the more wanting because it is reasonable to argue that I must have already done my best.'

Curiously, she did not here mention Lewes's opinion, nor their perfect love and growing happiness, usually a fixture of these end-of-year diary entries. But one rainy day at The Priory, she posed the question of her future to John Cross, who had just given her an expensive badminton set. Rather coquettishly — touched by the youthful spirit of Gwendolen, perhaps — she invited her 'dearest Nephew' to tell her what to do:

> Which would you choose? An aunt who lost headaches and gained flesh by spending her time on tennis and Badminton, or an aunt who remained sickly and beckoned death by writing more books? Behold yourself in a dilemma! If you choose the plump and idle aunt, she will declare that you don't mind about her writing. If you choose the pallid and productive aunt she will declare that you have no real affection for her. It is impossible to satisfy an author.

Manuscript of *Daniel Deronda*, p. 1: To my dear Husband,
George Henry Lewes. October, 1876.

Wishing me like to one more rich in hope,
Desiring this man's art & that man's scope,
With what I most enjoy contented least;
Yet in these thoughts myself almost despising
Haply I think on Thee — & then my state,
Like to the lark at break of day arising
From sullen earth, sings hymns at heaven's gate;
For thy sweet love remember'd such wealth brings,
That then I scorn to change my state with kings.

[Shakespeare, Sonnet 29]

11

The Other Shore

'For God's sake, tell her not to have the photograph reproduced!' cried Lewes, rushing up the stairs to her study. He had just seen a letter from Cara Bray, which mentioned her fading copy of Eliot's photograph. This picture had been taken at a Regent Street studio two decades earlier, in 1858, just after *Scenes of Clerical Life* was published, when George Eliot's identity was still unknown even to John Blackwood. It had given her 'rather a horror of photography'. The camera captured features that all her portraits softened: a long face, crooked protruding teeth, and that magnificent nose which drew comparisons with the physiognomy of John Locke, Dante, and Savonarola himself. At the centre of the picture, though, is a beautiful feminine hand — her writing hand, here employed, rather ineffectually, to conceal the size of her chin. Eliot was already replying to Cara. 'It needs the friendly eyes that regret to see it fade, and must not be recalled into emphatic black and white for indifferent gazers,' she explained, after conveying Lewes's message word for word. 'Pray let it finally vanish,' she added, optimistically. The photograph was soon being printed on postcards labelled 'George Eliot', and several reproductions are now in London's National Portrait Gallery.

During the 1870s Eliot's thoughts often turned to the question of biography — some lasting portrait of herself that would be for ever associated with her work. As John Blackwood said, she had 'risen so high' that people were inevitably curious about her. She found this troubling. One shard of personal experience in *Daniel Deronda* is Gwendolen's ambivalence about being looked at: she craves attention and admiration, but finds herself painfully judged and controlled by other people's eyes. Eliot shirked inquiries about the details of her life,

George Eliot. London Stereoscopic & Photographic Company,
after John Mayall (1858), copied in the 1870s

had a 'horror of being interviewed and written about'. Although it
was many years since the connection between George Eliot and the
scandalous 'Mrs Lewes' had been kept secret, the fear that judgements
about her life might somehow contaminate her authorship still lingered. Indeed, this worry became more acute: now it was not the sales
of her books that were at stake, but her enduring reputation as an
artist.

The Leweses had almost everything: a loving marriage, two homes,
as many servants as they needed, a carriage, grandchildren — Charles
Lewes and his wife Gertrude had three little daughters — devoted
friends, and an enviable social life. Eliot was 'sated with praise'. Her
desire for recognition now leapt further into the future, beyond her own
death, and expressed itself in anxieties about 'the stability of her
fame'. She had once feared she could not write her books; now that
they were written and acclaimed, she was afraid of 'spoiling' them.

Her eyes were on posterity, and rather than triumphing in her 'influence' she dwelt on its fragility.

As she and Lewes devoured biographies of great writers — Blake, Scott, Wordsworth, Keats, Byron — they could not help thinking about the biography of George Eliot. This prospect came into sharper focus after the death of Dickens, a writer of their own generation whom Lewes had known well. A three-volume *Life of Charles Dickens* soon appeared, written by his friend John Forster, prompting Lewes to publish his own assessment of Dickens in the *Fortnightly Review*. Without mentioning George Eliot, Lewes argued that Dickens's novels lacked the intellectual power and philosophical insight that distinguished his wife's writing: 'The world of thought and passion lay beyond his horizon . . . I do not suppose a single thoughtful remark on life or character could be found throughout the twenty volumes . . . he never seems interested in general relations of things.' Dickens was not even well read. Having been to his house and examined his unimpressive bookshelves, Lewes could pronounce him 'completely outside philosophy, science and the higher literature'. Dickens was merely a popular author, his vivid imagination perfectly suited to a mass readership 'occupied with sensations rather than ideas'. More 'cultivated minds', of course, perceived the 'pervading commonness' of books that were 'wholly without glimpses of the nobler life'. Between the lines, Lewes was instructing the critics on how to assess George Eliot's genius.

For Eliot, Forster's *Life of Charles Dickens* conjured unsettling visions of some future biographer prying into her personal affairs, and diverting attention from her art. 'Is it not odious that as soon as a man is dead his desk is raked, and every insignificant memorandum which he never meant for the public, is printed for the gossiping amusement of people too idle to re-read his books?' she wrote to Blackwood. This 'fashion' for literary biography was 'a disgrace to us all. It is something like the uncovering of the dead Byron's club foot.' The intense ambition that had churned within her as a girl was still there, shifting its shape, generating fresh anxieties. Perhaps this ambition was Eliot's club foot — a shameful and unseemly secret, as incongruous in an ageing woman as a deformed limb in a virile young poet. Her gentle demeanour, her thoughtfulness for others, her reticence about herself, and the idea of artistic purity all helped to cover it up.

When an admiring reader of *Daniel Deronda* wanted to publish her reply to one of his letters in the *Jewish Chronicle*, she spelled out her fear: 'any influence I have as an author would be injured by the presentation of myself in print through any other medium than that of my books.' And when Elma Stuart asked permission to mention her in an autobiographical essay, she replied: 'My writings are public property: it is only myself apart from my writings that I hold private, and claim a veto about as a topic.' In other words, Elma could refer only to George Eliot's writing, and not to their friendship. Eliot refused to read what Elma wrote about her until the essay was published — and she especially insisted that Lewes should not be involved either. While she tended to retreat from public view, he was more inclined to curate her image.

As the Leweses felt their lives fading, George Eliot was becoming immortal. 'Hardly anything could have happened to me which I could regard as a greater blessing than this growth of my spiritual existence while my bodily existence is decaying,' she wrote in her journal after *Middlemarch* was published. *Daniel Deronda* crowned an artistic legacy that critics and scholars would take more than a century to reckon with.

She worried that if she wrote more, or revealed her personal life, or tethered her 'spiritual existence' as an author to any specific political cause, she might diminish George Eliot's legacy. At times she hesitated even to state her own opinions, as if she had created something so exquisite that she dared not breathe on it. She found herself becoming 'more and more timid — with less daring to adopt any formula which does not get itself clothed ... in some human figure and individual experience'. Yet this reticence was not merely a symptom of anxiety about her reputation. It was also a 'sign' of her moral destiny: 'if I help others to see at all it must be through that medium of art.' Here Eliot seems to sense that what she ascribes to timidity, as if it were a personal quirk, could be a philosophical imperative. Her need to keep thought clothed in human form was a need to integrate intellect and emotion, ideas and experience — to inhabit and convey feeling, not simply analyse it.

*

On her birthday in 1870 Lewes had given her 'a Lock-up book for her Autobiography'. Eliot contemplated writing her own life, with mixed feelings and a sense of complexity. She told Emily Davies that it was 'impossible for her to write an autobiography, but she wished that someone else could do it, it might be useful — or, that she could do it herself.'

That was in 1869, on the verge of writing *Middlemarch*; perhaps an autobiography seemed impossible just because her time and energies were needed for the next novel. Did she hope that Lewes would write it for her? No one was better qualified: his biography of Goethe was his most successful work, and of course he had privileged access to her life story. But she seemed to have some qualms about this, which made her determined to prevent Lewes from influencing Elma Stuart's essay about her. An autobiography of George Eliot should, she believed, be edifying; it should augment the influence of her art. She could write her history 'better than anyone else,' she told Emily Davies, 'because she could do it impartially, judging herself and showing how wrong *she* was.' She was thinking especially of her youthful rebellion against her father, and what she now considered to be her misplaced sense of moral superiority over him. It is difficult to imagine Lewes, high priest of her shrine, dwelling on her faults and mistakes.

He got into the habit of recording her daily reading in his own diary; perhaps these notes would be useful if either of them came to write her life. They began to hear that old acquaintances — John Stuart Mill, Harriet Martineau, Herbert Spencer — were writing autobiographies. Martineau's was published posthumously in 1877, and they read it together. The book provoked Eliot's ambivalence: she recommended it to Cara Bray, but told Sara Hennell that it deepened her 'repugnance to autobiography, unless it can be so written as to involve neither self-glorification nor impeachment of others'. Martineau's own narrative had been supplemented by a biographical account of her feud with her brother, James Martineau, and this touched on a painful part of Eliot's life story. Likewise, when she cringed at Martineau's willingness to discuss reviews of her books, she was thinking about herself — wishing she had never 'said a word to anybody about either compliments or injuries in relation to my own doings'. She would certainly not be writing 'such things down' to be published after her death.

Other questions, more difficult to articulate, seem to lurk beneath these thoughts about the pitfalls of life-writing. If she wrote an autobiography, who would be named as its author? Having come into being in 1857, George Eliot could not claim to have been born in Warwickshire in 1819, nor could this masculine voice narrate first-hand her experiences as a daughter, sister, wife and mother — yet Mary Anne Evans was long lost, and if she wrote as Marian Lewes people would accuse her of falsehood before they opened the book. How should she write about her relationship with Lewes — might it somehow be framed penitentially as a regretted rebellion, like her breach with her father, yet also defended as a moral choice? And was her existence sufficiently solid and distinct to be the subject of an autobiography? This is a philosophical question arising from George Eliot's fiction: *Middlemarch* treats character as fluid, 'a process and an unfolding', and *Daniel Deronda* is composed of an ensemble of interconnected selves. It is also a particular, personal question. Eliot and Lewes were so closely woven: their marriage was, she felt, a shared life, a double life. Even its inwardness was a solitude *à deux*.

'The beings closest to us,' she wrote in her last novel, 'are often virtually our interpreters of the world.' For so long now she and Lewes had looked out through one another's eyes. Back in 1859, he had warned Barbara Bodichon that her old friend Marian Evans was 'extinct, rolled up, mashed, absorbed in the Lewesian magnificence!'. Since then his own life had been changed, perhaps eclipsed, by George Eliot's magnificence. It was during her writing hours that she lived most apart from Lewes — upstairs in a room of her own, while he was downstairs in his study — but this writing self, diffused into its art, was perhaps the most elusive of all.

*

Eliot expressed these uncertainties about life-writing in a new semi-fictional, knowingly genre-bending work, neither a novel nor an autobiography. For the first time since *The Lifted Veil* she wrote in the first person. Her narrator, Theophrastus Such, is an uncanny mixture of features identical to and different from her own — like a photographic negative, a likeness in which certain elements are inverted. He was born in the rural Midlands to a Tory father who, like Robert Evans, was a contemporary of Scott and Wordsworth — men born around 1770, just over a hundred years previously. Theophrastus is, in other words, a child of both Romanticism and conservative Middle England. Now he lives in London, and his 'consciousness is chiefly of the busy, anxious metropolitan sort'. He is bookish and an author, with a special interest in moral philosophy. He feels 'a permanent longing for approbation, sympathy, and love'. Yet he is a man, lives alone, has remained a bachelor, and has failed as an author, having written only one book, which 'nobody is likely to have read'. He is 'not rich', and has 'no very high connections'. Perhaps he resembles the person Marian Evans might have become, if she had not met Lewes.

The new work, initially titled *Characters and Characteristics of Theophrastus Such*, was a series of short satirical essays. They explored various aspects of authorship — research, originality, plagiarism, productivity, reputation, self-importance — as well as the intertwined themes of moral character and national character, returning to questions about Jewishness and Englishness investigated in *Daniel Deronda*. The first essay, 'Looking Inward', muses on the problems of autobiography, which Theophrastus finds to be fraught with the twin perils of 'self-ignorance' and 'self-betrayal'. He is a keen observer of the 'characters' he meets — but can he give a true account of his own character? While he harbours 'secrets unguessed by others', other people can perceive secrets unguessed by him. 'Is it then possible,' he asks, 'to describe oneself at once faithfully and fully?' It seems not. Any autobiography, like any biography, must be incomplete, studded with secrets, and even somewhat untrue.

Theophrastus Such is named after the ancient Greek philosopher Theophrastus, Aristotle's pupil, friend and collaborator: together they studied ethics and metaphysics, plants and animals, logic and poetry, stars and stones. In his most enduring work, the *Characters*, Theophrastus applied Aristotle's method of close observation to social life. His humorous character sketches embody vices in human types — the Flatterer, the Complacent Man, the Surly Man, the Coward, and so on.

Theophrastus's *Characters* created a new genre for moral philosophy.

Rather than considering abstract definitions of right and wrong, or formulating rules and maxims, or constructing theories of utilitarianism and deontology, Theophrastus put the question of what kind of people we want to be — and what kind of people we want to be with — at the heart of ethical thinking. Eliot had followed his lead when she refused to adopt any philosophical formula that was not 'clothed in some human figure and individual experience'. Through the seventeenth-century *salonistes* they inspired, Theophrastus's character sketches shaped a literary tradition which she had drawn on as she experimented with fiction-writing during her honeymoon months with Lewes. As George Eliot she, too, had pioneered a new genre for moral philosophy.

The *Theophrastus Such* essays are less an account of an individual life than an expression of Eliot's milieu, in which life and art, history and fiction and philosophy, were thoroughly entangled. It was Isaac Casaubon's Greek and Latin edition of Theophrastus's *Characters*, published at the end of the sixteenth century, that made the work influential in the modern period. The Leweses' good friend Mark Pattison, Rector of Lincoln College in Oxford, completed a biography of Isaac Casaubon in 1875, and this — together with *Middlemarch*'s fictional philologist, Edward Casaubon — brought both Casaubon and Theophrastus to the attention of Victorian readers. Another friend, the eminent Cambridge classicist R. C. Jebb, had just published an English translation of the *Characters*. Pattison and Jebb and their wives were regular Sunday guests at The Priory, and hosted the Leweses in Oxford and Cambridge. By inhabiting the persona of a modern-day Theophrastus, Eliot invoked the interlaced intellectual and social worlds which she and Lewes had entered and explored together — woven out of ancient texts, Victorian biographies, erudite talk over heavy dinners in panelled College dining halls, and the thrum of machines as a new century beckoned.

*

Eliot worked steadily on her *Theophrastus* essays through 1878. 'Life is very sweet to us though verging near to the valley of the shadow — or perhaps because it is so verging, and the time together is so precious,' she wrote to Elma Stuart at the beginning of that year. 'Madonna is very "jolly" in spite of the London fogs & rain, enjoying the concerts & seeing her friends, & adding to her encyclopaedic stores of knowledge,' Lewes told John Blackwood — adding in parentheses that jolly was '*her* word, but a "jolly" Madonna I have never seen, though I have known her joyous & brilliant.'

In May they moved to Witley to spend their second summer in their country house, now altered, decorated, and filled with expensive new furniture. They went to Oxford for a few days in June, visiting Jowett at Balliol College and the Pattisons at Lincoln College. Back at The Heights, they took turns being unwell. 'My Little Man is sadly out of health, racked with cramps from suppressed gout and feeling his inward economy all wrong,' Eliot told Elma at the end of June. 'Madonna I grieve to say is and has been much out of sorts, but nothing serious,' Lewes reported a few days later. 'I get up at 6, and before breakfast take a solitary ramble, which I greatly enjoy but which I can't get Madonna to share. Instead of this, she sits up in bed and buries herself in Dante or Homer. When the weather is cooler I hope to get her into regular practice of lawn tennis, but at present except our drives in the afternoon she gets but little of the sunshine and breezes to put colour into her cheeks.'

By August, Eliot was feeling better and Lewes had relapsed. 'I wish I could tell you better news of my Little Man,' she wrote to Elma: 'Morally he is as good as this summer weather and the lovely country, but physically he is below the mark — suffering still from nightly cramp, and often so wanting in his usual spirit and mental energy that he is unable to have his morning's study. But he fights resolutely against these ills, walking before breakfast, and having mild games of tennis.' John Blackwood received a more dire report from Lewes — 'I can't work at all, and can't read for more than an hour . . . even listening to Mrs Lewes reading soon wearies me' — though this might have been embellished to excuse them from a planned visit to Blackwood on the Fife coast that summer. 'We look forward eagerly to better luck next year,' added Lewes, ever optimistic. Eliot felt 'great anxiety' about him, but by the end of August he seemed better — 'and I as usual have taken his place as invalid,' she wrote to Cara Bray.

Amidst these bouts of illness they managed to receive visits from

Maria Congreve and her husband, Thomas Trollope and his wife, Tennyson, and Edith Simcox, who had been pining daily for her beloved Eliot ever since they left London, and was thrilled to be allowed to make the pilgrimage to Witley. Sometimes John Cross came over from Weybridge, occasionally with one of his sisters but usually alone, and joined them for tennis and afternoon drives through the local countryside. His mother was dying. 'The shadow of trouble was on both our houses,' Cross later recalled, echoing Eliot's thought that 'love is never without its shadow of anxiety.' Their shared sense that life was passing and sorrow was to come made their friendship 'much more intimate'.

They stayed on at Witley into the autumn, watching the colours of their woods and gardens change. 'This place is getting lovelier and more loved every week,' Lewes wrote to his son Charles. The sun shone through September and October, and once more Eliot relished her autumn gold — glorious, transient, bittersweet, filled with the aching beauty of human love. In this season of remembrance she thought of old friends. 'Do you remember once giving me a little water-colour of your own, because of my fondness for autumn, and propping it up on my mantelpiece at Foleshill?' she wrote to Sara Hennell on 15 October — 'O, how long ago! And you wore a bronze-coloured dress at that time.' She also wrote to Barbara Bodichon that day: 'I miss so much the hope I used always to have of seeing you in London and talking over everything just as we used to do — in the way that will never exactly come with any one else. How unspeakably the lengthening of memories in common endears our old friends!' Lewes was still gouty, but 'joyous as ever, and we are intensely happy in our bit of country.'

They returned to The Priory in mid-November. *Theophrastus Such* was now finished, and on 21 November — the day before Eliot's fifty-ninth birthday — Lewes summoned himself from sickness to send the manuscript to John Blackwood. That afternoon he 'imprudently drove out . . . with his usual eagerness to get through numerous details of business', and returned home exhausted. Over the next few days Eliot sent brief notes to Sara and Barbara, writing of 'deep trouble' and 'a deep sense of change within'. Doctors came and went; Lewes seemed better, then worse. Edith Simcox waited outside The Priory in the rain, anxious for news.

As Lewes lay in bed and Eliot sat beside him, they talked about her new book: how it should be printed, how it should be advertised. Blackwood sent a specimen page, and they looked at it together on 28 November. 'O how nice!' said Lewes, after examining it closely. The next day seemed like it might be his last; Charles Lewes and John Cross were called to the house. Lewes died at dusk the following evening.

*

Suddenly their double life had been transfigured into awful grief. It was never Eliot's way to flee from suffering, and now she stayed close to its source. Grief is a mode of love; she withdrew into it and felt its pain intensely. Often sadness and fear overwhelmed her: when she was a girl she had hysterical fits, especially at night, and these returned now. She did not attend Lewes's funeral at Highgate Cemetery. For weeks she did not go outside or see anyone except the servants and Charles. She could talk only about Lewes. As soon as he died she resolved to 'carry out his wishes' by finishing his last book — the third series of *Problems of Life and Mind*. She immersed herself in his manuscript, his published work, his letters and journals. She also set up a Cambridge studentship in science in his name, endowed with £5,000, a huge sum. When she was not working on Lewes's book she read poetry about death and loss, and copied out fragments that spoke of being merged with sorrow, possessed by grief.

For a few months after Lewes's death Eliot seems to disappear, not only from her friends' lives but also from the pages of her diary. The word 'I' vanishes, along with the 'we' that constantly recurred through the entries written during their years together. Now verbs stand alone without a subject, brave and bleak, fending for themselves. Each day is distilled to one or two bare phrases, each week a litany of blank tasks — 'Finished second reading of M.S.', 'Reread discussion on the position of Psychology', 'Worked at M.S.', 'Revised Introduction', 'Sent cheque' — interspersed here and there with a laconic lament: head miserable, heart bruised. It is as if Lewes has taken her soul with him.

But though her literary voice had faded to a whisper, it was still alive. At first it rose between the lines of other people's writing. On 1 January 1879 she copied a couplet by William Browne, and re-wrote the second verse:

> Some little happiness have thou and I
> For thou has died ere thou didst wish to die.

Then she wrote out a few lines from Shakespeare's *King John* —

> Kneeling before this ruin of sweet life,
> And breathing to his breathless excellence
> The incense of a vow, a holy vow,
> Never to taste the pleasures of the world,
> Never to be infected with delight,
> Nor conversant with ease and idleness,
> Till —

And completed them with four lines of her own:

> Death
> Shall give thy will divineness, make it strong
> With the beseechings of a mighty soul
> That left its work unfinished.

Reading and writing was the fabric of their shared life, and now this literary communion offered a way to 'live with' Lewes. She wrote memories of their years together; like the letters they exchanged, these memories would not be revealed to posterity. Reading through his diaries, she stumbled on precious remnants of his love: 'Wrote verses to Polly', he had written one day in 1874. A couple of times she was visited by 'his presence'.

Eliot's relationship with Lewes did not end when he died. It is difficult to specify when relationships end; after all, they can persist at long distances, even the distance between the living and the dead. Death or another kind of separation is often felt as a change rather than a cessation. Like most widows, Eliot continued to live imaginatively with her husband after his death, and this was possible only because imagination was an element of their shared life all along. Moving on would mean shifting her place within the world they had made and inhabited together — a world made strange by his absence, and darkened by her grief.

Their intellectual collaboration had always been devotional, and continuing Lewes's unfinished work kept this core of their marriage alive for a few more months. Lewes had struggled through illness to write his last book, *Problems of Life and Mind: Third Series*, and the manuscript was nowhere near publishable. Eliot edited, revised and rearranged the text. She clarified, tightened and developed Lewes's arguments, and added some entirely new material.

Mostly she revised the style rather than the substance of the book, but in a section on 'The Logic of Feeling' she made significant changes. Here Lewes, the positivist, was trying to make sense of human emotions. He considered anger to be the fundamental egoistic emotion, expressed in 'aggressive and defensive impulses'. He argued that sexual and parental relationships, as well as War, Trade and Commerce, are shaped by 'the organised tendency to domineer, which arises from the desire to make others afraid of and subservient to us'. Eliot changed all this: she saw fear, not anger, as the primal emotion. In place of Lewes's emphasis on domination, she described a 'sense of dependence on individual beings or other-selves which lies implicitly in the sexual and parental relations'. This feeling of dependence transforms our self-centred desires and emotions into sympathy for others:

> the consciousness of dependence is the continual check on the egoistic desires, and the continual source of that interest in the experience of others which is the wakener of sympathy; till we finally see in many highly wrought natures a complete submergence (or, if you will, a transference) of egoistic desire, and an habitual outrush of the emotional force in sympathetic channels . . . Appetite is the ancestor of tyranny, but it is also the ancestor of love.

Here, writing under Lewes's name, she provides the kind of direct theoretical statement she had refused to make as George Eliot. Love and dependence are inseparable. From birth to death a human being is never independent, and should not strive to be. On the contrary, a deeper awareness of dependence nurtures emotional growth.

*

It was a harsh winter, with snow and bitter east winds. The days slowly grew lighter and longer, and beneath the frozen ground new life was being prepared. Eventually Eliot came downstairs, went into the garden, walked beyond The Priory's grounds, and drove out in her carriage. In January she began to write letters. The first friend she saw, in February, was John Cross, who was also in mourning: his mother had died a few days after Lewes. During the spring Eliot saw her grandchildren, and many friends — Maria Congreve, Georgina Burne-Jones, Elma Stuart, Herbert Spencer ('asking advice about his autobiography'), Clementia Taylor, Edith Simcox, Anthony Trollope.

By early March she had corrected the proofs of her *Theophrastus Such* essays and returned them to John Blackwood. Anxious as ever that judgements about her moral character might injure her influence as an artist, she did not want people to think she had written the book while Lewes was dying, or during her first weeks of mourning. She asked Blackwood to add a note to the published edition explaining that the manuscript had been completed in the autumn, but held back from printing because of Lewes's death. Blackwood fretted about the wording: how to avoid using contentious words like 'husband' or 'widow', without specifying more precisely the relationship between George Eliot and G. H. Lewes? In the end, the publisher's note referred to 'the domestic afflictions of the author'.

Eliot had contemplated a sequel to her Theophrastus essays, if the first series was well received. *Impressions of Theophrastus Such*, as it was finally titled, sold out soon after it was published in the summer of 1879, but she wrote nothing more. George Eliot's writing life coincided with her collaboration with Lewes — and this now came to a close as she corrected the proofs of the last volumes of *Problems of Life and Mind* and sent them off to press. John Blackwood died later that year, sealing the end of an era.

There was, however, one more marriage plot to write. Eliot and Cross were now seeing one another frequently. Things had shifted in April, when he mentioned that he wanted to read Dante's *Divine Comedy* and she offered to read it with him. Reading together was something she had done with Lewes — and Dante's great work was one of George Eliot's chief literary influences. Cross was stepping into the world Eliot and Lewes had shared, yet in that world she had a new role. Without Lewes she was no longer Madonna, the part he had devised for her. Now she might be Beatrice, the voice of experience, Dante's poetic muse and spiritual guide — teacher and lover combined.

Eliot returned to Witley for the summer and Cross, nearby at Weybridge, was 'backwards and forwards continually'. She often played the piano for him. Back in London in the autumn, they visited galleries and exhibitions together. A few cryptic entries in her 1879 journal suggest that they were questioning what they meant to one another. Some 'crisis' occurred in the spring; a 'decisive conversation' took place in August; and choices were made in the autumn. October was 'a solemn time', perhaps 'a painful time'.

Most striking during these months is Eliot's silence. Just as she had not confided in Sara Hennell or Cara Bray about her romance with Lewes in 1854, so now she did not talk to her closest friends about her growing intimacy with John Cross. Barbara Bodichon had proved herself consistently open-minded and accepting throughout their long friendship, and Eliot's devoted younger friends would no doubt have felt honoured to be taken into her confidence. Yet she did not share with anyone her hopes, doubts and questions about Cross, nor discuss the decision that was gradually taking shape between them. Her diary, like her letters, tells us nothing about their relationship: throughout 1879 his name is barely mentioned.

One of her few surviving letters to Cross from this period, written in a lover's idiom on black-edged mourning paper, gives a glimpse into the complexity of their relationship. She compares him to Lewes — 'Thou dost not know anything of . . . the histories of metaphysics or the position of Kepler in science, but thou knowest best things of another sort, such as belong to the manly heart — secrets of lovingness and rectitude. O I am flattering.' Here the old epistolary dance she had practised forty years earlier with Maria Lewis is in full flow, taking back with one hand what was offered with the other. Eliot's meaning is impossible to pin down. Refusing to commit to selfless love and steadfast faithfulness, she signs herself 'at this particular moment thy tender Beatrice'.

On the anniversary of Lewes's death she spent the day in his room.

She reread his letters, then packed them away 'to be buried with me'. Soon after that, in mid-December, she copied Emily Brontë's poem 'Remembrance' into her diary. Rather like putting away Lewes's letters, this poem expresses thoughts of moving on as much as looking back — and poses questions about forgetting:

> Cold in the earth — and the deep snow piled above thee
> Far, far removed, cold in the dreary grave!
> Have I forgot, my only love, to love thee,
> Severed at last by Time's all-severing wave?
>
> . . .
>
> Sweet love of youth, forgive, if I forget thee
> While the world's tide is bearing me along;
> Other desires and other hopes beset me,
> Hopes which obscure but cannot do thee wrong!

While Brontë looks back half her lifetime, through 'fifteen wild Decembers' to the death of her lover, it was not yet fifteen months since Lewes had passed away.

To complicate things still further, the pressure of Edith Simcox's affections intensified during these months. Lewes's presence had kept the boundaries clear; now Edith grew bolder. 'I kissed her again and again and murmured broken words of love,' Edith wrote in her diary after one particularly fraught evening in March 1880. Eliot held these advances at bay by advising her friend to marry and insisting that heterosexual love was 'more and better' than any other love. Not surprisingly, Edith found these remarks hurtful. 'Will you never say anything kind to me?' she retorted, then persuaded Eliot to kiss her and 'returned the kiss to the lips that gave it'. Of course Edith was both thrilled and frustrated by this exchange, which could only fuel her passion. It is impossible to say how Eliot felt about it — whether she pitied or feared Edith's desire, whether she was excited or repelled by those kisses, or perhaps all this at once. A few days later she confessed herself 'much oppressed with difficulties and trials in my own inward life'.

Was some kind of shared life with this younger woman an 'imagined otherwise' which came briefly into being that evening? This is a tantalizing possibility: what if Eliot's sexual choices had been even more scandalous, rather than less so, in her later life? And might Edith — an accomplished writer and literary critic as well as a devoted admirer — become Eliot's first biographer? She was certainly eager to take on the task.

In early April, one month after that intense scene with Edith, Eliot and Cross made their decision. They would marry in four weeks, on 6 May, in an Anglican ceremony at St George's in Mayfair, a grand Regency church favoured for society weddings. They would sign new wills before setting off, that afternoon, on a honeymoon journey to Italy. Cross told Charles Lewes about their marriage plans just a week before the wedding. He tasked Charles with telling Maria Congreve, Elma Stuart and Edith Simcox — the friends who loved Eliot most intensely.

*

The newly formed marriage question that brought Eliot to choose John Cross had deep roots, reaching into her shared life with Lewes. It had grown in a tangle of desires and fears, weaving through her ambitions and anxieties for George Eliot's legacy. Charles Dickens's status as a great English writer had been secured by his burial in Westminster Abbey, close to the graves of Chaucer and Spenser and watched over by statues of Shakespeare and Milton. Eliot wished to be buried there too; this was, after all, no more than she deserved. Dickens's personal life — his extramarital affairs and cruel separation from his wife — had not excluded him from Poets' Corner, but she knew that her own case might well be treated differently.

Although she had gained more than she could have hoped during her years with Lewes, respectability had stayed just beyond her reach. It was not just that they were legally unmarried; there was also his rumoured free-loving past, his illegitimate birth and sketchy upbringing, his atheism, the whiff of vulgarity about him. Their relationship had opened her path to becoming George Eliot, yet it also tainted her public image in ways that now threatened her legacy.

She evidently valued Cross's companionship and affection, and had every reason to feel physically attracted to him. She already enjoyed a sense of comfortable belonging in his family, as she had previously belonged with the Brays in Coventry, and the Albert-Durades in Geneva. And Cross offered even more than this. A proper marriage to a thoroughly proper man — tall, handsome, wealthy, Rugby-educated, well-bred, charming, confident yet appropriately reserved at dinner parties — might restore her to the solid ground she had lost, all those years ago, when she set sail with Lewes. By marrying Cross she was embracing the Anglican establishment, and hoping it would embrace her in return. For this purpose St George's Church was the perfect choice of wedding venue, symbolizing the three pillars of Victorian respectability: class, religion, marriage.

There was also the chance that Cross could produce the seemingly impossible life story she had hoped for: an autobiography, written by

John Walter Cross aged thirty (far right) in 1870,
with his brother Richard James (far left) and two businessmen

someone else. And as her husband, he could make it the story of a wife — something Lewes, for all his biographical skill, could never have accomplished. Of course we cannot simply infer motives from results, but in this case the results do seem to fulfil Eliot's acknowledged wishes. After her death Cross produced the first 'Life' of George Eliot; he described it as her autobiography, and it was published by William Blackwood and Sons in a format to match the Cabinet edition of her works. Its title page displayed her married status: *George Eliot's Life, As Related in Her Letters and Journals, Arranged and Edited by Her Husband, J. W. Cross.*

If Eliot did not directly ask Cross to write her autobiography, she certainly nudged him towards it. During their short marriage she told him many details about her early life. One day she suggested that he should 'do some one work — a contribution to the world's possessions'. He replied, not very seriously, that the only thing he could think of was writing her life, if he survived her. She 'smiled and did not answer — did not protest'.

*

When he reaches this part of the book, my editor is shocked. He has been filled with admiration for Eliot — so gifted, so brave, so thoughtful and profound — and now I am suggesting that she married John Cross so that he would write her biography and have her buried in Westminster Abbey. He does not like it at all. Why must we ascribe to her such mercenary motives? 'No!' I cry — it comes out louder than I meant it to — and explain that of course her reasons were mixed: she liked Cross, genuinely cared for him, probably fancied him too. My editor is still frowning. Usually I am rather in awe of him, but now I launch into a vehement speech. Why does *anyone* get married? — people don't choose a partner just for their intrinsic qualities, but for the whole world they bring. Very often marriage promises some change for the better: an end to loneliness, alleviation of hardship, escape from parental control, the kudos of an attractive or successful spouse, a nicer home, a new social circle, the prospect of children, help with life's practicalities, creative inspiration . . . When a relationship seems to be reduced to such extrinsic motives, we are quick to judge it harshly. But this is not how I see Eliot's marriage to Cross at all! I pause for breath. 'So *say all that*!' he says with a sweep of the hand, and of course I follow his advice.

While Romanticism bursts through conventional moral codes, it carries a moralism of its own — an urge to purify marriage of its self-interest, its worldliness, its pragmatism. I am sure that ambition, mixed with love and loneliness, provided Eliot with a motive for marrying Cross — just as a similar mixture had led her to choose Lewes. Like my editor, she disapproved of this particular motive, and devised a marriage plot that carefully concealed it.

'A great momentous change is taking place in my life — a sort of miracle in which I could never have believed, and under which I still sit amazed,' she wrote to Georgiana Burne-Jones on the eve of her wedding. During her honeymoon she developed this narrative in letters to other friends, who had heard the news from Charles Lewes or read an announcement in *The Times*. These letters remain vague about details, while implying she has been taken by surprise to find her 'friendship' with Cross suddenly turning into marriage. Channelling the artlessness of Dorothea Brooke or Silas Marner, she spins the story as a romantic fable: this astonishing thing has happened all of a sudden, without her choosing, planning, or even hoping for it. She had never imagined herself marrying Cross — just as Dorothea had never imagined marrying Will Ladislaw. Even Barbara received a version of this story. 'All this is a wonderful blessing falling to me beyond my share after I had thought that my life was ended,' Eliot wrote to her old friend, as if her marriage had dropped out of the sky. The whole thing, she told Maria Congreve, was 'something like a miracle-legend'.

While she represented the marriage as Cross's noble act, his own account echoes her sense of being swept away. Perhaps he was imitating her language; perhaps — and this seems plausible — he really felt like this about marrying George Eliot. 'The great event that has happened in my life seems to have taken away from me all power of doing, or thinking of, anything except how marvellously blessed is my lot — to be united for life with her who has so long been my ideal,' he wrote to Elma Stuart from a Paris hotel, after 'a delicious six days' happiness' of married life. Eliot was now, he added, 'at rest in my care'.

Her honeymoon letters do not mention what seemed to Cross

obvious: she had been suffering from 'heart-loneliness', and did not want to live alone. To the extent that she assumed any agency — and she could not exempt herself entirely from the decision, since she had, after all, accepted Cross's proposal — she offered a moral explanation. Marriage would improve her character, revive her sympathy. 'I shall be a better, more loving creature than I could have been in solitude,' she told Barbara. Writing to Charles, she emphasized her loyalty to Lewes — 'I would still give up my own life willingly if he could have the happiness instead of me.' She implied that marrying Cross had saved her from moral decline: 'But marriage has seemed to restore me to my old self. I was getting hard, and if I had decided differently I think I should have become very selfish. To feel daily the loveliness of such a nature close to me, and to be grateful to it, is the fountain of tenderness and strength to endure.'

This reasoning echoes the passage on dependence and sympathy she had added to *Problems of Life and Mind*. In Lewes's name she had argued that dependence on a partner (or a parent) generates selfless love, and Cross later wrote of the 'mutual dependence' that had grown between them after the deaths of Lewes and Mrs Cross. This was such a natural growth that we might wonder how it could have been otherwise: here were two close friends, both bereft of the companions they had loved, lived with and depended on, stumbling through an altered world.

Omitting any reference to her own happiness or her hopes for posterity, Eliot's moral fairy tale effaced a longer, messier story of deliberations, crises and anxious soul-searchings between the spring of 1879 and the spring of 1880, when their marriage was, as Cross put it, 'finally decided'.

Indeed, this marriage may have taken shape as an 'imagined otherwise' while Lewes was still alive. In the summer of 1877, when Eliot had just moved to Witley and saw a lot of Cross dashing about in shirtsleeves on their tennis lawn, she seized an opportunity to reflect on marriage between an older woman and a younger man. The novelist Anne Thackeray had just married her twenty-three-year-old cousin, and Eliot — rounding up their seventeen-year age gap to 'nearly 20 years' difference' — remarked to Barbara that this was 'one of several instances that I have known of lately, showing that young men with even brilliant advantages will often choose as their life's companion a woman whose attractions are wholly of the spiritual order'. Anne Thackeray was, in fact, an attractive woman of forty. Eliot's description is a closer fit for a fantasy of marrying Cross.

Edith Simcox was not surprised to learn that Eliot and Cross were married. The idea had already crossed her mind 'in some dim form'. This thought, dim or otherwise, seems to have hovered around the Leweses' marriage in its last years; by 1877, and maybe earlier, both Eliot and Lewes were teasing Edith about her romantic rivalry with 'the fatal Johnny'. It might have occurred to Cross too. Perhaps Lewes spoke of it when he summoned him to The Priory the day before he died.

It is quite possible that Eliot really did find her marriage to Cross surprising, even if it was also in some way anticipated. We do not expect our dreams to come true, or our buried fantasies to spring into being in the world.

*

Like Gwendolen Harleth, Eliot was consciously gambling on her marriage. She knew there was a risk it might damage her reputation rather than enhance it. Many Victorians disapproved of second marriages. The step would undoubtedly bring her personal life into the public eye, which could not be trusted to look upon her kindly. Charles Lewes later learned that she 'had twice broken it off as impossible — had thought of all the difficulties — the effect upon her influence and all the rest'.

She may or may not have thought that she was gambling on Cross himself. She had known him for years, much longer than she had known Lewes before she committed to him. Cross shared her nervous disposition, which he managed with regular exercise, just as she had learned to keep her 'violent emotions' in check with hard work. They were both very anxious in the weeks leading up to the wedding, when the veil that had been drawn over their relationship would be suddenly and dramatically lifted. Their plan to leave immediately for the Continent on the day of their wedding followed a well-established line of flight — first to escape gossip about the Leweses' scandalous liaison, and later to escape reviews of George Eliot's novels. Cross had lost weight, a visible sign of the worry and stress they were trying to conceal. The pressure of expectation was intense — and while Lewes's brash confidence had provided the antidote to Eliot's disquiet, Cross's anxious eagerness to please mirrored and doubled it. None of these troubles were mentioned in the 'chronicle of our happy married life' which Eliot began compiling on their honeymoon for family and friends back home.

On her first day as Mrs Cross her diary burst into an exuberant first-person plural: 'We crossed the Channel delightfully in a private cabin on deck, and then went on to Amiens, where we were made very comfortable at the Hotel du Rhin. We went to see the Cathedral before dinner and looked at the wondrous woodcarving in the choir. In the morning we repeated our visit and had a view of the façade.' This busy, happy 'We' seems to revive the woman who had toured Europe as Mrs Lewes. Cross was surprised to see her looking 'many years younger' in the bright, dry air of the Continent, full of an energy he had never seen before — 'almost a magical effect'. She devised a curriculum of shared reading that returned to old loves. They would read Goethe's great poem *Hermann und Dorothea*, and philosophical works she and Lewes had studied together — Comte's *Discours pre-liminaire* on Positivism, Herbert Spencer's *Principles of Sociology* — as well as Shakespeare and Milton, Wordsworth and Scott.

Temperatures rose as they travelled south and east, and late spring tipped towards midsummer. In her role as Beatrice, Eliot led her new husband around the Italian galleries and museums she had visited with Lewes. Cross did his best to follow her. 'Looking at pictures or sculpture' was, he found, 'always fatiguing work'; reading and writing 'filled in all the interstices of time'.

'Johnnie has entered with great interest into the art of all the won-drous towns from Milan to Venice, and to me the journey has been a precious revival of memories fifteen or sixteen years old,' she wrote to his sisters from Venice, five weeks into their marriage. It was exactly twenty years since the Leweses had first visited the island city and stayed up late to watch its dark waters rippling under the stars.

Now she described visiting the lido and 'sitting to watch' the sea under a merciless June sun. Poor Cross, struggling to enjoy a rather confined existence — shuffling between hotel room and gondola, or from one painting to the next — longed to go swimming in the lido, but Eliot's own ideas about what was healthy prohibited a cold swim. A couple of days later Cross suffered some kind of breakdown, and jumped from their hotel balcony into the Grand Canal. Police were called, and recorded the incident as a suicide attempt; local newspapers reported on the story. Eliot could not cope, and summoned Cross's brother by telegram — replaying, with dreadful irony, the black comedy of Casaubon inviting Dorothea's sister to join them on their Italian honeymoon.

Cross's mental health seemed to improve over the next few days. As soon as he was well enough to travel, the newlyweds made a hasty departure from Venice and sought refuge in a German spa.

Her fairy tale had turned into a horror story — as fairy tales sometimes do. It is difficult to imagine that she did not feel some inward fury at this nightmarish twist in her marriage plot. Cross was supposed to 'watch over' her, not the other way around, and jumping out of the bedroom window on their honeymoon would hardly dignify her reputation. Rumours reached London that George Eliot's new husband had 'tried to drown himself'. As on her first honeymoon, lascivious gossip flew around town; once again not-quite-spoken questions about her sex life fluttered through respectable drawing rooms.

Marrying Cross also risked more predictable humiliations. Some people muttered that she had moved on quickly from Lewes, while others laughed or sneered at the spectacle of a sixty-year-old bride and her handsome groom, two decades younger. The 'old story' of Eliot's first improper marriage was revived, not laid to rest. Well-to-do women gleefully swapped reports of seeing George Eliot at London's most fashionable milliners and dressmakers, 'choosing her trousseau'.

One of those women was Caroline Jebb, the pretty wife of R. C. Jebb, who had translated the original Theophrastus's *Characters*. Back in England at the end of that turbulent summer, she met Mr and Mrs Cross at the home of mutual friends near Witley. She found him 'fine-looking, a good talker, altogether an exceptionally interesting man,' and sensed that Eliot felt jealous when he talked 'so much' to her, a woman his own age. From this little drama of mutual attraction, Mrs Jebb constructed a narrative about their entire married life:

'He may forget the twenty years difference between them, but she never can ... Such a marriage is against nature. She will constantly realize that no power on earth can make her a suitable wife for him.' Whether or not such speculations matched what Eliot thought and felt, she could not help being drawn into these stories, which competed with her own narrative.

It is not surprising that her marriage to Cross was complicated and difficult to explain to other people, nor is it surprising that she chose it. It offered a second chance in a double sense — pulling in two different directions. On the one hand, she sought to repair the damage done to her reputation when she embarked on her life with Lewes. Her late marriage might even be configured as repentance and redemption. It did indeed bring a reconciliation with her brother Isaac, who broke his twenty-three-year silence with a note of congratulation.

On the other hand, the marriage was an attempt to regain the shared life she had lost when Lewes died. And what a heart-rending labour of conjoined hope and sadness, that great effort to restore the world they had built together, stone by stone. It is possible that Eliot's second — or first — marriage really did retrieve lost time, for a short while. Yet her journal entries quickly relapse into the terse phrases and widowed verbs of the previous year and a half. Perhaps there was loneliness in this transfigured double life.

Her rejuvenated health did not last either. She suffered from her old kidney troubles in the autumn of 1880, when they were at Witley and preparing to move into a new London home — a grand town house on Cheyne Walk in Chelsea, facing south across the Thames and the meadows on the other side. One of her last letters, to Cara Bray, struck a note of melancholy gratitude: 'It is difficult to give you materials for imagining my "world." Think of me as surrounded and cherished by family love ... If it is any good for me that my life has been prolonged till now, I believe it is owing to this miraculous affection that has chosen to watch over me.'

At the end of that year she died quite suddenly, three days before Christmas, eight months into her marriage, and two years after losing Lewes. She had just turned sixty-one. The Crosses had lived in their Chelsea house for less than three weeks — 'this new House we meant to be so happy in,' he wrote to Elma Stuart the day after her death. In

George Eliot's last home: 4 Cheyne Walk, Chelsea, by Walter William Burgess

his wife's beautifully furnished study Cross found a few pages in George Eliot's hand: the beginning of some story. And he found himself alone with thousands of books that had been moved from The Priory, and arranged on new shelves in the same order as before.

Last Words

Why are we so intensely curious about other people's relationships? Does the hope of uncovering their secrets lure us because this might unlock the mystery of our own attachments — so close, so familiar, yet riddled with depths and intricacies that resist our comprehension?

Curiosity, the desire to know, is a philosophical passion, and can be awakened by the sheer contingency of marriage. What if I had never met my partner, or if the timing had been even slightly different? Each life contains so many moments of encounter — seeds light enough to be lifted by a breeze, yet potentially a great love, a lifelong partnership, a profound tenet of faith. These seeds are scattered daily, tiny tokens of the baffling coincidence of destiny and chance that seems to make us who we are. How does one of them become the root of a double life, the origin of an entire world? And then — does living in this world with me make my partner more or less happy than he or she might have been, in some other possible world?

Eliot's life, as well as her art, has taught me that when philosophy directs its desire to such questions, its habitual modes of rationalism and empiricism will not do. Marriage resists these lines of inquiry not because we have failed to think clearly or to gather sufficient evidence, but because of the complexity and aliveness of the human heart. Certain things seem inclined to hide in the heart's darker reaches, and perhaps some of them should remain hidden there. It is this element of mystery that makes it feel right to speak of marriage as an initiation and a sacrament, even outside a religious context.

On this uncertain terrain we have to find a different path, pursue some other kind of wisdom that yields both less and more than explanation. This is partly a matter of uncovering emotional truth. It also means inhabiting our own mystery, living our questions as they arise and change, contending with life's 'imagined otherwise' — the happiness or fulfilment that might have been if we had chosen to be single, or chosen someone else, or stayed with an ex-partner, or avoided the wrong turns we made in our relationships, whether those were awful betrayals or simply careless words. When we are lucky in love, thinking about how things might be otherwise makes way for gratitude, not regret: where would I be without you?

All this is a work of imagination — even a work of art — which must marry thought and feeling, as Eliot marries them in her fiction. I say 'marry' because it is a daily work. Elated during her honeymoon in Weimar, Eliot pictured a 'lovely rainbow' that could 'blend all the hues of thought and feeling', which sounds so easy and spontaneous — but usually it is more difficult than this, especially for philosophers. Herbert Spencer, for example, seemed to take refuge from perplexing emotions in intellectual work, while Spinoza was determined to explain the nuances of human feeling with geometrical precision. Though their achievements were impressive, it may be even harder to learn to think feelingly, to feel thoughtfully. At the end of *Middlemarch*, Celia is naturally curious about her sister's relationship with Ladislaw — 'I cannot think how it all came about.' And Dorothea cannot explain it: 'you would have to feel with me, else you would never know.' These words — the last words we hear between the sisters — are also George Eliot's message to her readers. Even in her sixth decade she saw herself not as a teacher, but as 'a companion in the struggle for thought'.

Eliot understood that emotional truths are more layered than linear, with deep interior dimensions. These truths provoke political questions, spiritual questions, cosmic questions. Intense, subtle, tender, they must be handled with great care. This is what is so exciting about Eliot's philosophy. She searched for truths not in order to form crisp definitions or moral judgements, but to make space for souls to grow, to stay curious, to feel alive.

Nevertheless, the urge to judge keeps pulling us back, and that is something to be curious about too. Beneath the superficial pleasure of gossip and the fleeting sensations of power felt in passing judgement on another person, lies some grasp of the moral stakes of marriage.

These stakes are so high precisely because they concern the growth of our souls. It can be quite literally a matter of life and death, as Janet, Maggie, Romola, Dorothea, Lydgate and Gwendolen all discover.

In some religious traditions there is a belief that at the end of their life each person is judged by God, and rewarded or punished accordingly. This can sound like a threat, but perhaps it is good to believe that judgement must be withheld until a life is whole, and that only an omniscient being is able to judge truly. If we imagine how much God would see of a single life — every thought, every feeling, every experience, every word that is heard and spoken — it becomes clear that our own judgements are based on very partial knowledge of a tiny fraction of another person's life. God would examine how a life is entwined with the lives growing around it. He would look at the whole milieu that formed it, and at tangled roots reaching deep underground. His judgement would not be cluttered and confused, as ours is, by a strange mixture of ideas about how human beings are supposed to behave.

In the days after Eliot died, a handful of men representing the Church of England pronounced their verdict on her life. Cross did his best to persuade them to bury her in Poets' Corner in Westminster Abbey, as she had wished, but they decided that the author of *Middlemarch* did not belong there. They cited her 'notorious antagonism to Christian practice in regard to marriage'. At some point their Church had ceased to be a refuge for sinners and become a palace of propriety — and Eliot's late Anglican marriage was not enough to gain entry to it.

'She cannot eat her cake and have it too,' opined Thomas Huxley, one of the Victorian luminaries who refused to support Cross's efforts to have his wife buried in the Abbey. This implies that Eliot had reaped rewards from her scandalous relationship with Lewes, and could not expect to reap the rewards of respectability as well. Of course, her marriage to Lewes was extremely rewarding, but not because it was unconventional: if the new Divorce Act had been passed ten years earlier, or if Agnes had died in one of her many childbirths, Lewes might have been her legal husband *and* helped her to become George Eliot. She had suffered rather than benefited from the scandal of her life with Lewes. So Huxley's remark was not logical — nor was it fair, considering that Dickens had been deemed acceptable.

But it expressed something more emotive, more visceral. George Eliot was greedy, she wanted too much, and this was not how a woman was supposed to be. Though her heart railed against it, Eliot probably shared this belief: from her youth to her last years she felt ashamed of her ambition.

She was buried in the unconsecrated part of Highgate Cemetery, next to Lewes's grave. This now strikes many of her readers as romantic, though it was not what she had hoped for. The large obelisk above the grave seems to have been chosen, presumably by Cross, to make up for its obscure location. It bears two of her names, George Eliot and Mary Ann Cross, while hidden below ground are all those words written to, from and about Lewes. Her grave is not alongside his but touches it obliquely, reminding us that she had not planned to be buried here. It is a plot both suitable and unsuitable for George Eliot: an appropriately ambiguous resting place.

The graves of George Eliot (above, centre), and
G. H. Lewes (below, centre), Highgate Cemetery

In 1980, one hundred years after her death, George Eliot was finally admitted to Westminster Abbey. A stone was laid for her in Poets' Corner, squeezed between memorials to Dylan Thomas and W. H. Auden. Here she is remembered as Mary Ann Evans, as well as George Eliot — a choice of names that represents a greater portion of her sixty-one years while setting aside both her marriages.

The Church of England's change of heart about receiving George Eliot testifies to its own larger tolerance, and to history's confirmation of her literary greatness. Did it also reflect changed perceptions of marriage? Perhaps not. The Church was — and is — still insisting that only one shape of love, between a man and a woman, can be sanctified as marriage. Its doctrines had certainly become less influential within wider culture, but here too the marriage ideal was thriving, despite the radical politics of the sixties and seventies. In the summer of 1981, one year after George Eliot was honoured in Westminster Abbey, 750 million people watched as Diana Spencer married Prince Charles in St Paul's Cathedral. There is something of Gwendolen Harleth in Diana — a statuesque English goddess, for ever young, mythical and archetypal as well as ordinary, at once tragic and triumphant, compelling yet helpless, secretly desperate in her fine clothes, destined to be trapped in a pathologically English marriage.

I was four years old that summer. Any memories of the wedding day are submerged by photographs and replayed TV footage: my generation grew up with the image of Diana's ivory silk dress, and that flock of enviable blonde bridesmaids dressed as miniature brides. The princess's own marriage fantasy had survived her parents' bitter divorce, in which her mother lost custody of her children. Shy Diana in navy eyeliner and a high-collared blouse, showing off her sapphire engagement ring; demure Diana on the edge of a polo field, watching her prince gallop around — she still rises effortlessly to mind. She was the chosen one. And that is the essence of the fairy tale: to be chosen as a wife. Many of us watched this fantasy darken as our parents divorced, and as Diana lived out her fate; yet it stayed strong, and seems to keep recurring. Just recently I was teaching a small third-year philosophy class and one of my students mentioned that she had got married that weekend. As we questioned her excitedly — did she wear a white dress, had she taken her husband's name, did their relationship feel different now? — I noticed another student wiping tears from her eyes. They were not unhappy tears. Her mother, she said, had also married young.

I think this is something to be conscious of as we make our own judgements about George Eliot — how we ourselves have inhabited the marriage questions we grew up with, how difficult it is to think them through while we are tangled up inside them. Having searched for the meaning of Eliot's life, I am struck — sometimes overwhelmed — by how complex and ambiguous it was. Are all human lives like this, if you look at them closely enough? For her, at least, life was complicated by a marriage question weighted by family expectations and cultural norms, bound up with ideas of success, and inseparable from a woman's self-image. This made it difficult for her to speak truthfully about marriage, even to her closest friends.

And the stakes of Eliot's marriages were especially high. Neither of these relationships could fail. With Lewes, ever-growing happiness and perfect love were the only way to justify her decision to break the rules of propriety. By the time she married Cross, she was — partly through Lewes's efforts — a celebrity and a sage, propped on a pedestal and expected to 'vent wisdom', as she once remarked gloomily. Cross seemed stunned by their marriage, dazzled by the radiance of its ideal. 'It is almost too great happiness to have got the best,' he wrote in the first week of their honeymoon, struggling to make sense of his anxiety. 'The great object of my life now will be to justify her trust and to fulfil worthily the high calling which I have undertaken.'

I will not try to weigh up these shared lives according to some scale of good and bad, right and wrong. The questions and contradictions and mysteries of Eliot's life, along with her faults and mistakes, have been laid out in these pages. We have noticed her moments of ruthlessness and duplicity, as well as her immense fortitude. At times we might have wished she was a better friend, and a better feminist — more supportive of women's suffrage, for example, or as generous in donating to Girton College as in endowing a studentship in Lewes's name. We may have felt disappointed to find that when this brave, brilliant woman was finally, properly married, she represented this as being chosen rather than as choosing. But we should remember that women, just as much as men, censured and shunned her when she settled down with Lewes. On the question of choice, Eliot's biographer Rosemarie Bodenheimer seems right to see her decision to be with Lewes as a traumatic experience, severing her from friends and family, permanently wounding her intense pride, and losing the respected place in the world she had earned as editor of the *Westminster Review*. It is no wonder she shrank from choosing again — or at least from being seen to choose.

Near the end of her life she told Charles Lewes that she could not have written her books if she 'hadn't been human with feelings and failings like other people'. Cherishing those books while expecting her heart to be purer than my own, her decisions tidier and less ambiguous, would be like trying to have my cake and eat it too.

Something else that strikes me, reflecting on George Eliot's marriage question, is the quality of devotion that cuts through all this complexity. Devotion is not a passing feeling. It is attention given, work done, tasks shared, disappointments borne, anger endured, quarrels forgiven, loss grieved. Lewes was devoted to George Eliot with a vigour and stamina that seem remarkable. He was steadfastly cheerful through her recurrent depressions, relentlessly encouraging through her self-doubt. 'The secret of his lovableness,' Edith Simcox wrote of Lewes, 'was that he was happy in being kind.' As we know, he was not a religious man, but putting her work before his own — answering her letters to give her time to write, poring over reviews of her books — became a daily practice of devotion.

John Cross, similarly, gave her years of practical service, before their marriage as well as during it. His three-volume 'autobiography' of George Eliot occupied him for four years after her death. It was a great devotional labour: interviewing people who knew her, reading all those letters, cutting bits out — editing his wife as he imagined she would have wished. Few things seem less romantic than compiling an index, but in Cross's case even this became a work of love. Ironically, his biography would be much maligned for making George Eliot *too* respectable — in a new century, with new values, this pious portrait damaged her reputation instead of redeeming it.

I hesitate to insist that Eliot was as devoted to her husbands as they were to her: this question is difficult to judge. I think she loved Lewes through his bursts of temper, his showing off, his strenuous efforts to stay in control. She supported him financially as he pursued his scientific work. She also supported several members of his family, including his wife, for many years; her payments to Agnes continued after Lewes's death. Much of her penultimate year was spent finishing his last book. She accompanied Cross through his devastating mental breakdown. It is devotion to her art, however, that shines most constantly through the pages of her diaries and letters.

Cross concludes his *Life of George Eliot* by expressing faith in that art: 'The place that may belong to her in the minds and in the hearts of future generations will be finally adjudged on the merits of her works. We who write and we who read to-day will never know that final verdict, but I think that those of us who loved her may trust to it with confidence.' These are touching and generous last words. Finally reaching the end of his self-effacing task, her husband thought it important to say that George Eliot had not belonged only to him. She was loved by different people, and in different ways. Cross knew that 'those of us who loved her' included not just Lewes, but also the women who 'loved her lover-wise' — Edith Simcox, Maria Congreve, perhaps Sara Hennell — and other close friends.

It was something of a Victorian custom for widows to write biographies of their eminent husbands. Perhaps a biographer's devotion is a little like the devotion of a spouse. Writing a person's life means living with them intimately, struggling to understand them, wondering how far they can be trusted, dealing with the ways they resist, annoy, disappoint, challenge and elude you. It means staying with them for their whole life, if not for your own — though such a close encounter with another person is bound to leave you changed, even as you move on.

Acknowledgements

My thanks to King's College London for supporting my research, and to the British Library, the Senate House Library, the London Library, the Beinecke Rare Book and Manuscript Library, the New York Public Library, the Morgan Library, the Nuneaton Museum and Art Gallery, and the Herbert Art Gallery and Museum.

The Marriage Question is indebted to many previous biographies of George Eliot, especially those by Nancy Henry, Gordon Haight, Rosemary Ashton and Rosemarie Bodenheimer. The George Eliot Archive, edited by Beverley Rilett, has been an invaluable source of texts and images.

Stuart Proffitt and Alice Skinner at Penguin, Eric Chinski at FSG, and Sarah Chalfant at the Wiley Agency have all helped to bring this book into the world. I am so grateful for their thoughtful reading and wise counsel.

For reading drafts along the way, huge thanks to John Tresch, Nancy Henry, Juliette Atkinson, Saffya Alaoui, John Cottingham, Stephen Grosz, Louisa Watson, Cal Flyn. And for conversations about *The Marriage Question* (and the marriage question) thanks to Rose Gibbs, Tamara Barnett-Herrin, Sheila Heti, Karen Kilby, Simon Oliver, Chris Insole, Lara Feigel, Alice Albinia, Kathy O'Shaughnessy, and John Tresch, again, above all.

This book is dedicated to my mother, Susan Carlisle (1950–1995) and to her mother, Cynthia Carlisle (1922–2018).

List of Illustrations

1. Griff House. Engraving from John Cross's *Life of George Eliot*, 1885. Image provided by the George Eliot Archive, edited by Beverley Park Rilett.
2. Sara Sophia Hennell. Self-portrait, 1830-1850. Reproduced by kind permission of the Herbert Art Gallery and Museum, Coventry.
3. A young woman believed to be Mary Ann Evans. Portrait attributed to George Barker, c. 1845.
   Image provided by Andrew Sim, reproduced by kind permission of the George Eliot Fellowship.
4. Agnes Lewes, George Lewes and Thornton Hunt. Sketch by William Thackeray, c. 1850. © National Portrait Gallery, London
5. Madame de Staël. Portrait by Marie-Éléonore Godefroid, 1813. © Alamy.
6. Madeleine de Souvré, Marquise de Sablé. Artist and date unknown. © Alamy.
7. George Henry Lewes. Photograph by John and Charles Watkins, 1864. © National Portrait Gallery, London.
8. Caroline Bray. Watercolour portrait by Sara Hennell, 1835. Reproduced by kind permission of the Herbert Art Gallery and Museum, Coventry.
9. Martin and Katherine Luther. Double portrait by Lucas Cranach the Elder, 1529. © Uffizi Gallery, Florence.
10. Janet Dempster is cast out. Illustration for 'Janet's Repentance', *Scenes of Clerical Life*, by W. Hatherell, 1900-1909. Image provided by the George Eliot Archive, edited by Beverley Park Rilett.

11. Dinah Morris preaching on the common. Painting by Edward Henry Corbould, 1861. Reproduced by kind permission of the Royal Collection Trust.

12. Sistine Madonna. Painting by Raphael, 1512. © Staatliche Kunstsammlungen Dresden. Elke Estel/Hans-Peter Klut.

13. Adam Bede proposes to Dinah. Illustration for *Adam Bede* by William Small, c. 1885. © Alamy.

14. Dedication to *Adam Bede*, Add MS 34020, p. 1r., 1859. © British Library Board / Bridgeman Images.

15. Barbara Leigh Smith Bodichon. Photograph by Disdéri, c. 1860. © National Portrait Gallery, London

16. Maggie and Tom Tulliver. Illustration for *The Mill on the Floss* by G. Demain Hammond, 1911. Image provided by the George Eliot Archive, edited by Beverley Park Rilett.

17. Maggie Tulliver and Philip Wakem. Illustration for *The Mill on the Floss* by G. Demain Hammond, 1911. Image provided by the George Eliot Archive, edited by Beverley Park Rilett.

18. Maggie Tulliver and Stephen Guest. Illustration for *The Mill on the Floss* by W. L. Taylor, 1888. Image provided by the George Eliot Archive, edited by Beverley Park Rilett.

19. George Lewes with the dog. Photograph by John and Charles Watkins, 1865. © National Portrait Gallery, London.

20. Dedication to *The Mill on the Floss*, Add MS 34023, p. 1r., 1860. © British Library Board / Bridgeman Images.

21. Charles Lewes. Albumen carte-de-visite, photographer unknown, 1862. © National Portrait Gallery, London.

22. The Annunciation, Convento di San Marco. Fresco by Fra Angelico, 1440s. © Alamy.

23. Marian Evans Lewes. Portrait by Samuel Laurence, 1860. Reproduced by kind permission of the Mistress and Fellows of Girton College, Cambridge.

24. Silas and Eppie. Illustration for *Romola* by Hugh Thomson, 1907. Image provided by the George Eliot Archive, edited by Beverley Park Rilett.

25. Dedication to *Silas Marner*, Add MS 34026, p. 1r., 1861. © British Library Board / Bridgeman Images.

Notes

Abbreviations

GEL   *George Eliot's Letters*, ed. Gordon S. Haight (Oxford: Oxford University Press, 1954–1978), vols. I to X

Journals   *The Journals of George Eliot*, ed. Margaret Harris and Judith Johnston (Cambridge: Cambridge University Press, 1998)

LGHL   William Baker (ed.), *The Letters of George Henry Lewes* (Victoria, BC: University of Victoria, 1995–1998), vols. I to III

Cross   *George Eliot's Life, As Related in Her Letters and Journals*, arranged and edited by John Walter Cross (Cambridge: Cambridge University Press, 2010), vols. I to III

PREFACE

p. x *'this double life . . .'*: LGHL III, p. 38 (letter to Cara Bray, Richmond, October 1856).

p. xi *'All around us, the intellectual lightships . . .'*: J. A. Froude, *Thomas Carlyle: A History of His Life in London* (London: Longmans, Green, and Co., 1884), vol. I, p. 291; *'Ah love, let us be true . . .'*: Matthew Arnold, 'Dover Beach'; *'I don't consider myself a teacher . . .'*: LGHL III, p. 83 (letter to Mary Ponsonby, The Priory, 11 February 1875).

pp. xi–xii *an 'inadequate endowment of emotion . . .'*: LGHL III, p. 83 (ibid.). Eliot made her assessment of Spencer in this letter: 'I have known him for more than twenty years & have the greatest respect for him, but in studying his works you should bear in mind that his share of human fallibility depends in a high degree on an inadequate endowment of emotion. (I except the emotions which sustain an energetic antagonism.) Hence in spite of his eminent powers, his integrity, & his elevation of purpose, there is a vast amount of human experience to which he is as good as dead. Few men seek more than he does after the things that make for truth and rigid justice, few are freer from any stain. But his theorizing, & his mode of pursuing arguments, are often injuriously affected by the negation I have mentioned, & to a certain extent he himself would acknowledge this.' Spencer never married.

p. xiii *'we are now all bent on tracing the phases of development . . .'*: G. H. Lewes, *The Life and Works of Goethe* (London: David Nutt, 1855), vol. II, p. 150; *a plant is not merely a physical thing*: see J. W. von Goethe, *The Metamorphosis of Plants*, ed. Gordon L. Miller (Cambridge, MA: Massachusetts Institute of Technology Press: 2009), pp. xviii–xix; *Goethe's Botanical Writings*, trans. Bertha Mueller (Honolulu: University Press of Hawaii, 1952), pp. 6, 14, 162; Astrida Orle Tantillo, *The Will to Create: Goethe's Philosophy of Nature* (Pittsburgh, PA: University of Pittsburgh Press, 2002), pp. 65–6; Stephen Jay Gould, *The Structure of Evolutionary Theory* (Cambridge, MA: Harvard University Press, 2002), pp. 283–91; G. H. Lewes, *The Life and Works of Goethe*, vol. II, pp. 139–47 (where Lewes discusses Goethe's 'doctrine of Morphology').

Goethe wrote a poem, originally for his wife, to explain the scientific theory developed in *The Metamorphosis of Plants*. The poem ends as follows:

> Ah, think thou also how from sweet acquaintance
> The power of friendship grew within our hearts,
> To ripen at long last to fruitful love!
> Think how our tender sentiments, unfolding,
> Took now this form, now that, in swift succession!
> Rejoice the light of day! Love sanctified,
> Strives for the highest fruit — to look at life
> In the same light, that lovers may together
> In harmony seek out the higher world!

– see *The Metamorphosis of Plants*, pp. xxiv, 3.

p. xiii *the 'process and unfolding' of human character*: see George Eliot, *Middlemarch* (London: Penguin Books, 1994), p. 149 (Chapter 15).

p. xv *she liked 'to feel free'*: GEL II, p. 158 (letter to Charles Bray, 21 Cambridge Street, London, 27 May 1854); *'in a mental greenhouse'*: *The Autobiography of Margaret Oliphant*, ed. Elisabeth Jay (Oxford: Oxford University Press, 1990), p. 15. 'Though her marriage, so called, is not one that most of us would have ventured on, still it seems to have secured her a caretaker and worshipper unrivalled — nasty little body though he looked,' continues Oliphant, with some bitterness (p. 17); *'We mortals, men and women, devour many a disappointment between breakfast and dinner-time'*: *Middlemarch*, p. 62 (Chapter 6); *'nothing but a humiliation . . .'*: George Eliot, *Daniel Deronda* (London: Penguin Books, 1995), p. 425 (Chapter 35).

p. xvi *birth control and sexual satisfaction*: Rosemary Ashton reports that in 1856 Eliot told her friend Barbara Leigh Smith 'that she and Lewes were sexually happy and that they practised some form of birth control, not thinking it right, in their circumstances, to have children'; Barbara conveyed this in a letter to her friend Bessie Parkes, and Ashton's source is Bessie's daughter, Marie Lowndes, who recalled seeing the letter — see Rosemary Ashton,

George Eliot, A Life (London: Penguin Books, 1997), pp. 161, 402–3. The visitor who saw Lewes kiss Eliot's hand was Edith Simcox: see *A Monument to the Memory of George Eliot: Edith Simcox's Autobiography of a Shirt-maker*, eds. Constance M. Fulmer and Margaret E. Barfield (New York, NY: Garland Press, 1998), p. 33 (2 June 1878). Kathryn Hughes emphasizes the couple's 'emotional and sexual compatibility' and concludes that 'Marian's marriage with Lewes had been fully sexual' — see *George Eliot: The Last Victorian* (London: Fourth Estate, 1998), pp. 220, 479. On the basis of Marie Lowndes's recollection of letters from Barbara Leigh Smith to her mother, Gordon Haight reports that 'in their intimate marital relationship [Lewes was] unsensual, extremely considerate', which suggests restraint more than passion — see *George Eliot: A Biography* (London: Penguin Books, 1992), p. 205.

p. xvii **wider, less traditional ideas of married life**: see, for example, Elizabeth Brake's critique of 'amatonormativity' in *Minimising Marriage* (Oxford: Oxford University Press, 2012), and Ronald Den Otter, *In Defense of Plural Marriage* (Cambridge: Cambridge University Press, 2015). In 1980 Adrienne Rich, a feminist poet and academic, proposed the concept of 'compulsory heterosexuality' or 'prescriptive homosexuality' — a precursor to the more recent notion of 'heteronormativity' — to name 'the covert socialisations and the overt forces which have channelled women into marriage and heterosexual romance' — see Rich, 'Compulsory Heterosexuality and Lesbian Existence', *Signs*, vol. 4, no. 5 (1980), pp. 631–60. This analysis could be applied to Eliot's personal marriage question, as we see her resisting the pull of a series of erotic female friendships.

I. SETTING SAIL

p. 1 **A secret elopement on borrowed funds**: in Susan Ferrier's comic novel *Marriage* (1818), Lady Juliana, a naïve young bride, runs off to marry in Gretna Green, with disastrous consequences. Marian read this novel in Jersey in 1857: see *Journals*, p. 281.

pp. 1–2 **'I said a last farewell to Cambridge Street this morning . . .'**: *Journals*, p. 14. 'We' had already crept into a few of her letters: in June 1853, for example, she told Cara Bray and Sara Hennell that 'We went to see Rachel [in the play *Adrienne Lecouvreur*] again', and 'We are going to have a party tonight' — GEL II, p. 104.

p. 2 **'like some region of the unconscious'**: see Kathy O'Shaughnessy, *In Love with George Eliot* (London: Scribe, 2019), p. 77; **'I am preparing to go to Labasse-cour'**: GEL II, p. 165 (letter to Sara Hennell, London, 10 July 1854). Lewes had referred to Belgium as 'Labassecour' in the spring of 1853, just after *Villette* was published: see LGHL I, p. 227 (George Lewes to Frederick Ward, London, Spring 1853). Perhaps Lewes and Marian read *Villette* together; they certainly discussed it: 'I want to know what *you* think of Villette. Lewes was describing Currer Bell [Charlotte Brontë] to me yesterday as a little, plain, provincial, sickly-looking old maid. Yet what passion, what fire in her! Quite as much as in George Sand, only the clothing is less voluptuous.' — GEL II, p. 91 (letter to Charles and Cara Bray, London, 5 March 1853); *In 1852 she read Jane Austen's Sense and Sensibility*: see GEL II, p. 31.

pp. 2–3 *'The Miss Dashwoods were young, pretty and unaffected . . .'*: Jane Austen, *Sense and Sensibility* (Oxford: Oxford University Press, 1970), pp. 32, 40 (vol. I, chapters VIII and X).

p. 3 *the brief, heady period in a young woman's life*: see Claire Tomalin, *Jane Austen: A Life* (New York: Vintage Books, 1997), p. 242: 'the short period of power, excitement and adventure that might come to a young woman when she was thinking of choosing a husband'; *'I sometimes regretted that I was not hand-somer . . .'*: Charlotte Bronte, *Jane Eyre* (London: Penguin Books, 2006), Chapter XI, p. 117.

pp. 3–4 *'A woman's body belongs to her husband . . .'* Barbara Leigh Smith, *A Brief Summary, in Plain Language, of the Most Important Laws Concerning Women, together with a Few Observations Thereon* (London: John Chapman, 1854), p. 6.

p. 4 *'courted and wedded as an angel . . .'*: Smith, *A Brief Summary of the Most Important Laws Concerning Women*, p. 13. Smith quotes from an 1845 essay on the 'The Rights of Woman' by the reforming American judge E. P. Hurlbut, who argued that 'woman is to be regarded not only as the companion and equal of man, but as the same intellectual being as himself, possessed of the same senti-ments and affections — the same emotions and wants, and consequently of the same natural rights' — see Hurlbut, *Essays on Human Rights and their Political Guarantees* (New York: Greeley and McElrath, 1845), pp. 144–6. Smith's pamph-let stands in a history of feminist critique of marriage reaching back to Mary Wollstonecraft's *Vindication of the Rights of Woman* (1792), and carried for-ward by John Stuart Mill (see below) and in twentieth-century works such as Simone de Beauvoir's *The Second Sex* (1949), Betty Friedan's *The Feminine Mys-tique* (1963), Juliet Mitchell's *Woman's Estate* (1971), Kate Millett's *Sexual Politics* (1972), Shulamith Firestone's *The Dialectic of Sex* (1979), Lenore Weitz-man's *The Marriage Contract* (1983) and Carole Pateman's *The Sexual Contract* (1988). In recent years several feminist philosophers have published books call-ing for the abolition of state-recognized marriage: see Tamara Metz, *Untying the Knot: Marriage, the State, and the Case for their Divorce* (Princeton, NJ: Prince-ton University Press, 2010), Elizabeth Brake, *Minimizing Marriage* (Oxford: Oxford University Press, 2012) and Clare Chambers, *Against Marriage* (Oxford: Oxford University Press, 2017). Chambers argues that marriage not only oppresses both married and unmarried people through its legal status, but also enacts 'symbolic violence' by teaching women that 'they are flawed and failing if unmarried' — see *Against Marriage*, pp. 22–7; *'to put on record a formal pro-test . . .'*: *The Letters of John Stuart Mill*, ed. Hugh S. R. Eliot, vol. I (London: Longmans, Green and Co., 1910), pp. 158–9. Mill's statement is dated 6 March

1851; he married Harriet Taylor the following month. In July 1851 Harriet Taylor Mill's long article 'The Enfranchisement of Women' appeared anonymously in the *Westminster Review*: it argues that women have been 'taught to regard their degradation as their honour [and] to think, that to repel actively even an admitted injustice done to themselves, is somewhat unfeminine, and had better be left to some male friend or protector'. Taylor Mill singled out for criticism 'the literary class of women, especially in England', whom she found to be 'ostentatious in disclaiming the desire for equality or citizenship' because they were anxious not to provoke men to say 'that learning makes women unfeminine, and that literary ladies are likely to be bad wives' — Harriet Taylor Mill, *Enfranchisement of Women* (London: Trübner and Co., 1968), pp. 20–21. J. S. Mill would later argue, in *The Subjection of Women* (1869), that marriage was a form of 'slavery' and that a woman's duty to submit to sex with her husband was 'the lowest degradation of a human being'. In 1870 the Married Woman's Property Act allowed wives to keep property they had acquired after marriage, and in 1882 a further Act gave them legal rights to property they had owned before marriage. Only in 1991 did it become possible for a man to be charged with raping his wife; until then, forced sex between a married couple did not legally count as rape — see Chambers, *Against Marriage*, p. 14; *'their precocious selfishness'*: Sarah Stickney Ellis, *The Wives of England: Their Relative Duties, Domestic Influence, and Social Obligations* (London: Fisher, Son and Co., 1843), p. 68; *'It is perhaps when ill . . .that men are impressed with a sense of their own importance . . .'*: Ellis, *The Wives of England*, p. 79' *'not yet crossed the Rubicon . . .'*: Ellis, *The Wives of England*, pp. 1–2; *'daily and hourly trials . . .'*: Ellis, *The Wives of England*, pp. 166–205; *'But why then all the fine talk we hear about marriage?'*: Ellis, *The Wives of England*, pp. 3–4; *'evasive' grey-blue eyes*: Grace Greenwood, in K. K. Collins (ed.), *George Eliot: Interviews and Recollections* (London: Palgrave Macmillan, 2010), p. 39.

p. 5 *'temperament of genius'*: Collins, *George Eliot: Interviews and Recollections*, p. 15 (from Charles Bray, *Phases of Opinion and Experience during a Long Life: An Autobiography* (London: Longmans, Green and Co., 1884); others who knew her similarly described her 'artistic' temperament: see pp. 73, 117 (George Smith, Eliza Lynn Linton). As a young woman Marian described her 'wrought up sensitiveness' — GEL I, p. 75 (letter to Maria Lewis, Griff House, 5 December 1840); *'felt a depression . . .'*: GEL II, p. 102 (letter to Maria Lewis, Foleshill, Coventry, 12 August 1841); *Lewes had 'a wife still living' and could not divorce her*: Nancy Henry's *Life of George Eliot: A Critical Biography* (Hoboken, NJ: Wiley-Blackwell, 2012) surveys different accounts of the obstacles to Lewes's divorce, noting that 'prior to the 1857 Matrimonial Causes Act, divorce would have been impossible for financial reasons' (p. 100). Before 1857, a divorce cost around £1,000, equivalent to about £90,000 today: see Margaret K. Woodhouse, 'The Marriage and Divorce Bill of 1857', *The American Journal of Legal History*, vol. 3, no. 3 (1959), pp. 260–75. Evidence suggests that Agnes Lewes would have been happy for Lewes and Eliot to marry: see Haight, *George Eliot: A Biography*, p. 179.

p. 6 *'a desire insatiable for the esteem of my fellow creatures'*: GEL I, p, 19 (letter to Elizabeth Evans, Griff House, 5 March 1839); *'Life as a whole is throughout of a divine nature . . .'*: Ludwig Feuerbach, *The Essence of Christianity*, trans. George Eliot (Cambridge: Cambridge University Press, 2012), p. 268; *'With the ideas of Feuerbach I everywhere agree'*: GEL II, p. 153 (letter to Sarah Hennell, 21 Cambridge Street, London, 29 April 1854); *The book was published a couple of weeks before she set sail with Lewes*: see Haight, *George Eliot: A Biography*, p. 143. This is the only publication to appear under her own name: the title page reads 'Translated from the Second German Edition [of 1843] by Marian Evans, translator of Strauss's "Life of Jesus"' — Feuerbach, *The Essence of Christianity*, p. iii.

p. 7 *her mother Christiana died after a long illness*: see David Paterson, *Fair Seed-Time: Robert Evans, Francis Newdigate and the Making of George Eliot* (Market Harborough: Troubadour Publishing, 2019), p. 184; *Mary Anne and Isaac wept together*: see Cross I, pp. 24–5: 'One of Mr Isaac Evans's most vivid recollections is that on the day of [Chrissey's marriage] he and his younger sister had a "good cry" together over the break up of the old home-life, which of course could never be the same with the mother and the elder sister wanting.'

pp. 7–8 *'disjointed specimens from history, ancient and modern . . .'*: GEL I, p. 29 (letter to Maria Lewis, Griff House, 4 September 1839).

p. 8 *'plunged in an abyss of books and preserves'*: GEL I, p. 59 (letter to Maria Lewis, Griff House, 20 July 1840).

p. 9 *her 'restless, ambitious spirit . . .'*: GEL I, p. 37 (letter to Martha Jackson, Griff House, 14 January 1840); *her 'walled-in world'*: GEL I, p. 71 (letter to Maria Lewis, Griff House, 27 October 1840); *'I have a world more to say . . .'*: GEL I, p. 92 (letter to Maria Lewis, Foleshill, Coventry, 20 May 1841); *she sent Maria a melancholy sonnet . . .*: GEL I, pp. 29–30 (letter to Maria Lewis, Griff House, 4 September 1839).

p. 10 *'When I hear of the marrying and giving in marriage . . .'*: GEL I, p. 6 (letter to Maria Lewis, Griff House, 18 August 1838); *Perhaps others could 'live in near communion with God'*: GEL I, p. 6 (letter to Maria Lewis, Griff House, 18 August 1838); *'anything but uninteresting . . .'*: GEL I, p. 51 (letter to Maria Lewis, Griff House, 26 May 26 1840); *'Every day's experience seems to deepen the voice of foreboding . . .'*: GEL I, p. 70 (letter to Martha Jackson, Griff House, 20 October 1840); *At a party she stood in a corner*: see GEL I, p. 41 (letter to Maria Lewis, Griff House, 13 March 1840).

p. 11 *'a deeply painful incident — it is like dying to one stage of existence'*: GEL I, p. 86 (letter to Martha Jackson, Griff House, March 1841); *'in any way that his wishes tend'*: see Haight, *George Eliot: A Biography*, pp. 146–7; *'I have had many thoughts . . .'*: GEL I, p. 240 (letter to Sara Hennell, Foleshill, Coventry, 13 October 1847).

p. 12 *'I love thee and I miss thee'*: GEL I, p. 209 (letter to Sara Hennell, Foleshill, Coventry, March 1846); *a young artist . . . asked her to embark on a courtship*: see GEL I, pp. 183–4 (Cara Bray to Sara Hennell, Coventry, 30 March 1845).

pp. 13–15 *a satirical story about being proposed to*: see GEL VIII, pp. 12–15 (letter to Charles Bray, Foleshill, 21 October 1846).

p. 16 *'with her hair over her shoulders . . .'*: William Hale White, letter to the *Athenaeum*, 28 November 1885; ***Herbert Spencer . . .caused her deeper heartbreak***: many biographers have suggested that Herbert Spencer treated Marian badly, but more sympathetic accounts of Spencer's role in their relationship are compelling: see Barbara Hardy, *George Eliot: A Critic's Biography* (London: Continuum, 2006), pp. 79–85; Robert Bates Graber, 'Herbert Spencer and George Eliot: Some Corrections and Implications', *George Eliot — George Henry Lewes Studies*, 22–3 (September 1993), pp. 69–83; *'Le coeur a ses raisons'*: see Blaise Pascal, *Pensées* (1670), art. 277: 'The heart has its reasons, which it does not know. We feel it in a thousand things'; *she sent Spencer a passionate letter*: GEL VIII, p. 57 (letter to Herbert Spencer, Broadstairs, July 1852)'.

p. 17 *He even 'hinted at the possibility of marriage'*: Herbert Spencer to E. L. Youmans, 3 February 1881, viewed in manuscript at the British Library and quoted in GEL VIII, p. 42; *Spencer began to take his friend George Lewes along*: Herbert Spencer to E. L. Youmans, quoted in GEL VIII, pp. 42–3; *'in a whirl . . .'*: LGHL I, p. 201 (George Lewes to Robert Chambers, 19 February 1852); *'the Prince of journalists'; 'the most amusing little fellow in the world . . .'*: see Rosemary Ashton, *G. H. Lewes: An Unconventional Victorian* (Oxford: Clarendon Press, 1991), pp. 4–5.

pp. 17–18 *He had 'always preached a doctrine of free love . . .'*: Ashton, *G. H. Lewes*, p. 58. The description of Lewes's appearance comes from a fictionalized sketch by Halcott Glover, written in 1945; the remarks about his morality and lifestyle are from the recollections of George Smith, who knew Lewes and Agnes when they were together in the 1840s.

p. 18 *'a very dreary wasted period of my life'; 'It was through him that I learned to know Marian . . .'*: Ashton, *G. H. Lewes*, pp. 120, 143.

p. 19 *'Mr Lewes' was making regular appearances in Marian's letters*: see GEL II, p. 68 (letter to Charles and Cara Bray, 142 Strand, London, 22 November 1852); p. 94 (letter to Sara Hennell, London, 28 March 1853); p. 98 (letter to Cara Bray, London, 16 April 1853); *'L'amour va son train'*: LGHL I, p. 227 (George Lewes to Frederick Ward, London, spring 1853); see also Ashton, *G. H. Lewes*, p. 140; *'a most kindly, genial, guileless person . . .'*: David Masson to Robert Vaughan, 8 May 1852, quoted in Ashton, *G. H. Lewes*, p. 137; *her friendship with Sara Hennell . . .foreshadowed her relation to Lewes*: in *Between Women: Friendship, Desire and Marriage in Victorian England* (Princeton, NJ: Princeton University Press, 2007), Sharon Marcus shows how Victorian novels reflect ideas about female friendship and marriage: 'In the plot of female amity, love between friends develops the emotional disposition necessary for companionate marriage . . . friendship between women precedes a happy marriage between a woman and a man.' Meanwhile, Marcus argues, 'the feminist bildungsroman deploys amity to help female protagonists acquire the autonomy that makes them equal to their husbands' (pp. 87–91).

p. 20 '*I am very happy . . .*': GEL II, p. 343 (letter to Mrs John Cash, Jersey, 6 June 1857); '*a flying leap into infinite space*': see Mrs Alexander Ireland, *Life of Jane Welsh Carlyle* (London: Chatto & Windus, 1891), p. 256 (letter from Jane Carlyle to Miss Barnes, 24 August 1859). Phyllis Rose describes how Jane Welsh took the leap into marriage to Thomas Carlyle in *Parallel Lives: Five Victorian Marriages* (New York: Vintage, 1983), pp. 21–44; Rosemary Ashton chronicles their entire marriage in *Thomas and Jane Carlyle: Portrait of a Marriage* (London: Vintage, 2003); '*Dear Friends — all three . . .*': GEL II, p. 166 (letter to Mr and Mrs Charles Bray and Sara Hennell, 21 Cambridge Street, London, 19 July 1854).

2. HONEYMOON

p. 21 *From Antwerp they travelled east . . .*: see GEL II, p. 171 (letter to Charles Bray, Weimar, 16 August 1854).

pp. 21–2 '*the second class carriage was so comfortable . . .*': *Journals*, p. 218: 'Recollections of Weimar 1854'.

pp. 22–3 *an account of that time by Madame de Staël*: see Madame de Staël, *De l'Allemagne* (Paris: Libraire de Firmin Didot Frères, 1852), pp. 74–5; p. 128. In his biography of Goethe, Lewes discusses Madame de Staël, and particularly her 1831 book *De l'Allemagne*: 'Goethe and Schiller, whom she stormed with cannonades of talk, spoke of her intellect with great admiration' — see *The Life and Works of Goethe*, vol. II, pp. 273–4; '*Here our feelings were deeply moved . . .*': *Journals*, pp. 235–6; *Whenever they walked up Schillerstrasse she was 'very much thrilled . . .*': *Journals*, pp. 234–5; *Thomas Carlyle had given Lewes a key to Weimar's high society*: see Ashton, *G. H. Lewes*, p. 148; *They quickly befriended Franz Liszt . . . a 'Grand Seigneur'*: GEL II, p. 171 (letter to Charles Bray, Weimar, 16 August 1854); see also LGHL I, pp. 232–5.

p. 24 *Marian recorded her 'startling' appearance*: *Journals*, p. 21; '*I sat near him so that I could see both his hands and his face . . .*': *Journals*, pp. 21–2; '*the first really inspired man I ever saw . . .*': GEL II, p. 171 (letter to Charles Bray, Weimar, 16 August 1854); '*Liszt is here, as you know . . .*': GEL II, p. 173 (letter to Bessie Parkes, Weimar, 10 September 1854).

p. 25 '*the animating spirit of a society . . .*': *Westminster Review*, July–October 1854 (London: John Chapman, 1854), vol. 62, p. 465.

p. 26 '*Love, wherever it is, is always the master . . .*': *Maximes de Madame de Sablé* (Paris: Librairie des bibliophiles, 1870), pp. 45–6 (*maxime* LXXIX); '*great ladies transformed all at once into writers . . .*': *Westminster Review*, July–October 1854, vol. 62, p. 454.

p. 27 '*Heaven forbid that we should enter on a defence of French morals . . .*': *Westminster Review*, July–October 1854, vol. 62, p. 451; '*the very sorrows — the heart-pangs and regrets . . .*': *Westminster Review*, July–October 1854, vol. 62, p.

452; *'intelligent observers of characters and events ...'*: *Westminster Review*, July–October 1854, vol. 62, p. 453.

p. 28 *'Let the whole field of reality be laid open to woman ...'*: *Westminster Review*, July–October 1854, vol. 62, pp. 472–3; *'exquisite enjoyment'; 'I am beginning to have that calm autumn feeling ...'; 'I am happier every day ...'*: GEL II, pp. 170, 173–4, 190 (letter to Charles Bray, Weimar, 16 August 1854; letter to Bessie Parkes, Weimar, 10 September 1854; letter to John Chapman, 30 August 1854; letter to John Chapman, Berlin, 9 January 1855).

p. 29 *she wrote up her recollections of those honeymoon weeks*: *Journals*, p. 220. 'Joy for ever' is a quotation from Keats's poem 'Endymion'; *George Combe ...had examined her 'very large brain'*: see Haight, *George Eliot: A Biography*, pp. 100–01; *'We are deeply mortified and distressed ...'*: GEL VIII, p. 129 (George Combe to Charles Bray, 15 November 1854); *Carlyle wrote to Lewes asking him 'to contradict ...'*: see Gordon Haight, 'The Carlyles and the Leweses' in *Carlyle and His Contemporaries*, ed. John Clubbe (Durham, NC: Duke University Press, 1976), pp. 191-2.

p. 30 *'I am sorry that you are annoyed with questions about me ...'*: GEL VIII, pp. 123–4 (letter to John Chapman, Weimar, 15 October 1854); *she alluded to new 'circumstances'*: see GEL VIII, p. 124 (letter to John Chapman, Weimar, 15 October 1854); Ashton, *G. H. Lewes*, p. 154.

pp. 30–31 *'I am ignorant how far Cara and Sara may be acquainted with the state of things ...'*: GEL II, pp. 178–9 (letter to Charles Bray, Weimar, 23 October 1854). Commenting on this passage, Rosemarie Bodenheimer writes: 'From her point of view, this formulation was a generous way to release Cara and Sara from association with a social outcast. From theirs, it was a further betrayal of the intimacy and confidentiality that Marian Evans had at least rhetorically sustained in her many letters to them during her sojourn in literary London — letters that often and affectionately returned to a distinction between real friends, who understood one's renegade nature, and the conventionally judging world' — *The Real Life of Mary Ann Evans. George Eliot: Her Letters and Fiction* (Ithaca, NY: Cornell University Press, 1994), p. 94.

p. 31 *'We have not heard of anything dreadful happening to Miss Evans ...'*: GEL VIII, p. 119 (Cara Bray to Mrs George Combe, Coventry, 23 September 1854).

pp. 31–2 *'When you say that I do not care ...'*: GEL II, pp. 181–2 (letter to Sara Hennell, Weimar, 31 October 1854).

p. 32 *Sara sent a warm letter signed 'Your ancient friend ...'*: GEL II, pp. 186–7 (Sara Hennell to Marian Evans, Coventry, 15 November 1854).

p. 33 *'We rise at eight; after breakfast read & work ...'*: LGHL I, p. 233 (George Lewes to Princess Caroline Sayn-Wittgenstein, Berlin, 16 December 1854); *Marian's most memorable encounter was with Christian Rauch*: *Journals*, pp. 41, 248.

p. 34 *'the love of beauty, the elevation of the soul ...'*: Madame de Staël, *De l'Allemagne*, p. 574; *'a double individual more powerful than the single'*: Spinoza's *Ethics, Translated by George Eliot*, ed. Clare Carlisle (Princeton,

NJ: Princeton University Press, 2020), p. 240; *'sees in the universe nothing but the manifestation of God'*: G. H. Lewes, 'Spinoza's Life and Works', *Westminster Review*, February–May 1843 (London: Samuel Clarke, 1843), vol. 39, p. 388.

p. 35 *the great poet's 'reverence' for Spinoza*: Lewes, *The Life and Works of Goethe*, vol. I, p. 103; vol. II, p. 394; *'we work hard in the mornings till our heads are hot . . .'*: GEL II, p, 186 (letter to Charles Bray, Berlin, 12 November 1854); *Their intellectual labours were entwined more closely than ever*: see *Journals*, pp. 35, 43; on Goethe and Jacobi, see Lewes, *The Life and Works of Goethe*, vol. I, pp. 281–2.

pp. 35–6 *'Science tells us that the world is always becoming . . .'*: Lewes, *The Life and Works of Goethe*, vol. II, p. 394.

p. 36 *'united to each other by a great need of friendship'*: Spinoza's *Ethics, Translated by George Eliot*, p. 276; *'Spinoza . . . cautiously approved of marriage'*: Spinoza's *Ethics, Translated by George Eliot*, p. 282; *One day Lewes was unwell*: *Journals*, p. 23.

p. 37 *Lewes judged it comparable to 'the masterpieces of Miss Austen . . .'*: Lewes, *The Life and Works of Goethe*, vol. II, p. 379.

p. 38 *'He was struck with it as a bit of concrete description . . .'*: *Journals*, p. 289: 'How I came to write Fiction', 6 December 1857. By contrast, Herbert Spencer encouraged Marian to write fiction in the early 1850s: 'It was, I presume, her lack of self-confidence which led her, in those days, to resist my suggestion that she should write novels. I thought I saw in her many, if not all, of the needful qualifications in high degrees — quick observation, great power of analysis, unusual and rapid intuition into others' states of mind, deep and broad sympathies, wit and humour, and wide culture. But she would not listen to my advice. She did not believe she had the required powers' — Spencer, *An Autobiography*, vol. 1 (London: Williams and Norgate, 1904), pp. 396, 398.

3. SANCTITY

p. 39 *a 'vague dream' to write a novel*: *Journals*, p. 289: 'How I came to write Fiction', 6 December 1857; *'writing hard, walking hard . . .'*: GEL II, p. 202 (letter to Charles Bray, East Sheen, 17 June 1855); *to address their letters 'to G. H. Lewes Esq'*: see GEL II, pp. 199–200 (letter to Charles Bray, East Sheen, 1 May 1855; letter to Bessie Parkes, 1 May 1855).

pp. 40–41 *'if there be any one subject on which I feel no levity it is that of marriage . . .'*: GEL II, p. 214 (letter to Cara Bray, East Sheen, 4 September 1855).

p. 41 *'I think we are nearer to each other than we could ever have been before . . .'*: LGHL III, p. 38 (letter to Cara Bray, Richmond, October 1856). See also Kathleen Adams, ' "Dear Cara": A Newly Discovered Letter', *George Eliot Review* 27 (1996).

p. 42 *She had also begun to write regular reviews for the Leader . . . a professional writer and critic*: see *Journals*, pp. 55–65; *£119 and 8 shillings for 1855*:

Journals, pp. 58, 64–5; '*I can't tell you how I value it* . . .': GEL II, p. 221 (letter to Charles Bray, Richmond, 21 November 1855); *some English critics complained* . . .: see Ashton, *G. H. Lewes*, pp. 167–8; Ashton, *George Eliot: A Life*, pp. 151–2. On the longer-term success of Lewes's biography, Ashton writes that '*The Life of Goethe* sold over 1,000 copies within three months. A second edition was called for in 1864, and a third in 1875, followed by many reprints in America and Britain'; *Reviewing a new English translation of Goethe's Wilhelm Meister's Apprenticeship* . . .: her review begins by drawing attention to 'Mr Lewes's *Life of Goethe*, which we now see advertised', and goes on to argue that Goethe's 'mode of treatment seems to us precisely that which is really moral in its influence. It is without exaggeration; he is in no haste to alarm readers into virtue by melodramatic consequences; he quietly follows the stream of fact and of life; and waits patiently for the moral processes of nature as we all do for her material processes. The large tolerance of Goethe, which is markedly exhibited in *Wilhelm Meister*, is precisely that to which we point as the element of moral superiority' — *The Leader*, vol. VI, no. 278 (21 July 1855), p. 703. Lewes's biography also discusses the morality of *Wilhelm Meister*: 'there is a complete absence of all *moral verdict* on the part of the author . . . *Wilhelm Meister* is not a . . . story written with the express purpose of illustrating one of the many maxims in which our ethical systems are expressed . . . [Yet] deep and healthy moral meaning lies in it' — *The Life and Works of Goethe*, vol. II, pp. 210–12; '*are taught by their own falls* . . .': *The Leader*, vol. VI, no. 278 (21 July 1855), p. 703.

p. 43 '*undermines all true moral development* . . .': *Westminster Review*, July 1855 (London: John Chapman, 1855), vol. 64, p. 295. These remarks appear in a brief review of Geraldine Jewsbury's novel *Constance Herbert* within the 'Contemporary Literature' section. Marian Evans criticizes the novel for both its moralism and its 'false view of life' — 'This is a grave question to enter on à-propos of a novel; but Miss Jewsbury is so emphatic in the enunciation of her moral, that she forces us to consider her book rather in the light of a homily than of a fiction — to criticize her doctrine rather than her story.' By coincidence, this edition of the *Westminster Review* leads with a substantial article on Spinoza by James Anthony Froude: see Carlisle (ed.), *Spinoza's Ethics, Translated by George Eliot*, pp. 27–33; on Spinoza's critique of rewards and punishments, see p. 159; '*the so-called moral dénouement*': *The Leader*, vol. VI, no. 278 (21 July 1855), p. 703. This remark echoes Spinoza's view that moralistic religion tends to project self-serving human judgements onto God. Here Marian Evans goes on to argue that novelists who contrive characters and plots as a sugary coating for a remedial 'moral dose' will inevitably bore their readers: 'Try this on the first child that asks you to tell it a story. As long as you keep to an apparently impartial narrative of facts you will have earnest eyes fixed on you in rapt attention, but no sooner do you begin to betray symptoms of an intention to moralise, or to turn the current of facts towards a personal application, than the interest of your hearer will slacken, his eyes will wander . . . One grand reason of this is that the child is aware you are talking *for it* instead of *from yourself* . . . Now, the moralising novelist produces the same effect on his mature readers'; *'We don't want a man with a wand . . .'*: *The Leader*, vol. VI, no. 269 (19 May 1855), p. 475. Here Marian Evans is discussing Charles Kingsley's novel *Westward Ho!*; *'Every great artist is a teacher . . .'*: *Westminster Review*, July 1855, vol. 64, p. 289. Again, she is discussing *Westward Ho!*, which she reviewed in the 'Arts and Belles Lettres' section of the *Westminster Review* as well as in the *Leader*; *'In making clear to ourselves what is best and noblest in art . . .'*: *Westminster Review*, April 1856, in a review of the third volume of John Ruskin's *Modern Painters* in 'Arts and Belles Lettres', vol. 65, p. 626; *'realism' — 'the doctrine that all truth and beauty . . .'*: *Westminster Review*, April 1856 (on Ruskin, London: John Chapman, 1856), vol. 65, p. 6. In her article 'The Natural History of German Life', published in the *Westminster Review* in July 1856 (London: John Chapman, 1856), she wrote, 'Art is the nearest thing to life; it is a mode of amplifying experience and extending our contact with our fellow-men beyond the bounds of our personal lot,' p. 54. This review is widely seen by scholars as offering 'a manifesto for moral realism': see George Levine's Introduction to *The Cambridge Companion to George Eliot*, ed. George Levine (Cambridge: Cambridge University Press, 2006) p. 8; *Ruskin encouraged painters and poets to 'manifest imaginative power . . .'*: John Ruskin, *Works*, ed. Cook and Wedderburn (London: Library Edition, 1903–12), vol. V, pp. 187, 63 (*Modern Painters*, vol. III).

p. 44 *For the Romantics it meant being faithful to your own heart . . .*: Darrel Mansell has argued that 'subjective truth' was important to George Eliot: see 'Ruskin and George Eliot's "Realism"', *Criticism*, vol. 7, no. 3 (1965), pp. 203–16. Mansell writes that 'In order for her novel to be "true", [an author] must remain true to her mental state by putting the story down as it comes to her . . . The novel is the mirror of her mind, and the reader is made aware in many ways that the author's mind is at work in the story, recollecting, selecting, arranging and commenting on what is happening' (pp. 213–15); *the 'genius' of her writing*: Marian's October 1855 *Westminster Review* article on the evangelical preacher John Cumming, which offered a Spinozist critique of moralistic Calvinism, convinced Lewes of 'the genius of her writing': see Cross I, p. 384 (Cross's source is Charles Lewes). For a discussion of this article and its connection to Spinoza, see Carlisle (ed.), *Spinoza's Ethics, Translated by George Eliot*, pp. 22–5; *he had published two mediocre novels*: Lewes's letters from May 1847 show his ambitions for his first novel, *Ranthorpe*: he sent a copy to Dickens, and tried to persuade John Blackwood to commission a review by Thackeray: see LGHL I, pp. 149–50. He tried fiction again in the spring of 1856, when he published 'Metamorphoses: A Tale' in *Blackwood's* magazine — see LGHL I, p. 244; *'wit, description, philosophy . . .'*: *Journals*, p. 289; *'Our friends — Herbert Spencer and others — used to say to me . . .'*: Collins (ed.), *George Eliot: Interviews and Recollections*, p. 51 (citing an 1877 letter from Margaret Holland); similar reports of Lewes's account of George Eliot's first foray into fiction are given by

Benjamin Jowett and Charles Eliot Norton: see Collins (ed.), *George Eliot: Interviews and Recollections*, pp. 50–51. While most biographers depict Lewes as selflessly encouraging Marian, Beverley Park Rilett has emphasized that Lewes's motivation was 'at least partly mercenary', and concludes that 'the crucible of Eliot's fiction writing career, which always has been construed as the perfect happiness of long-awaited loving companionship, was also a stressful time of financial need'. Rilett argues that this provides an interpretative key to George Eliot's novels: 'Lewes's focus on money and other signs of his less-than-altruistic encouragement of Eliot's "dream" provides an early insight into their diverging financial expectations and values ... These tensions ... become fully developed thematic concerns in her fiction', 'The Role of George Henry Lewes in George Eliot's Career: A Reconsideration', *George Eliot — George Henry Lewes Studies*, vol. 69, no. 1 (2017), pp. 2–34; pp. 4–5.

p. 45 *In May 1856 they set off for the seaside ...*: see *Journals*, pp. 59–60, 262; *clambered over rocks with him in her scruffiest dress*: see Ashton, G. H. Lewes, p. 174; *'We had a glorious hunt this afternoon ...'*: *Journals*, pp. 60–61; *'I never before longed so much to know the names of things ...'*: *Journals*, p. 272.

p. 46 *She eulogized the 'lovely' algae ...*: *Journals*, pp. 266–7; *'the lines all rectangular and mean ...'*: *Journals*, p. 264; *'In a flat country a house or town looks imposing ...'*: *Journals*, pp. 264–5; *These sentences found their way, hardly altered, into Lewes's first 'Sea-side Study'*: see G. H. Lewes, *Sea-side Studies* (Edinburgh: Blackwood, 1858), pp. 30–31. Gordon Haight notes this correspondence (see *George Eliot: A Biography*, p. 96) and Margaret Harris and Judith Johnston suggest that 'such lending corresponds to [Eliot's] assistance with translations and tabulations during [Lewes's] preparation of the Goethe book and is a rare (if not unique) instance in which their collaborations can be documented' –*Journals of George Eliot*, p. 261. I wonder if 'lending' is quite right: perhaps these reflections first arose in conversation as they walked round Ilfracombe, and thus came into being as a joint creation. See also Jeanette Samyn's fascinating article 'George Eliot, George Henry Lewes, and Parasitic Form', *SEL: Studies in English Literature 1500–1900*, vol. 58, no. 4, Autumn 2018, pp. 919–38), which explores the metaphor of 'parasitic cluster' that appears in these shared texts, tracing its significance through Lewes's science writing and George Eliot's fiction, particularly *The Mill on the Floss*. For Samyn, 'Parasites informed Lewes and George Eliot's thinking about what it meant to live among, alongside, and as part of others — not only to have needs and desires in common with one's intimates, but also, at least as often, to have them in conflict. From this shared understanding, however, the two writers moved in divergent directions'; *seismic theological questions*: sending one of his 'Sea-side' articles to John Blackwood, Lewes reassured him that 'there is no *Vestigian* heresy in what is said about Animals & Plants', a reference to Robert Chambers's controversial *Vestiges of the Natural History of Creation* (1844) — see LGHL I, p. 257 (George Lewes to John Blackwood, Richmond, December 1856).

p. 47 *'How lovely to look into that brilliant distance ...'*: *Journals*, p. 272; *'As I was lying in bed ...'*: *Journals*, pp. 289–90; *She had decided it would be the first in a series of 'Scenes of Clerical Life'*: *Journals*, p. 63; *'there remained the question whether I could command any pathos ...'*: *Journals*, p. 290.

p. 48 *'One day when I was going to town ...'*: Collins (ed.), *George Eliot: Interviews and Recollections*, pp. 51–2 (citing an 1877 letter from Margaret Holland; also reproduced in GEL IX, pp. 197–8); *'We both cried over it ...'*: *Journals*, p. 290; *'submitted to me by a friend' — a male friend, not a Silly Lady Novelist*: GEL II, pp. 269–70 (letter from George Lewes to John Blackwood, Richmond, 6 November 1856). Marian's latest *Westminster Review* article had mocked the far-fetched sentimentality with which women writers — excepting 'excellent' ones like Harriet Martineau, Charlotte Brontë and Elizabeth Gaskell — depicted religion, and asked, 'Why can we not have pictures of religious life among the industrial classes in England?' — 'Silly Novels by Lady Novelists', *Westminster Review*, October 1856, vol. 64, pp. 457, 460; *'My Dear Sir, I am happy to say ...'*: GEL II, p. 272 (letter from John Blackwood to George Lewes, Edinburgh, 12 November 1856); *'unusually sensitive'*: GEL II, p. 276 (letter from George Lewes to John Blackwood, Richmond, 22 November 1856).

p. 48–9 *sending Sara Hennell 'brusque' critiques*: see GEL II, pp. 267–71 (letters to Sara Hennell, Richmond, 18 October 1856; 5 November 1856; 8 November 1856). Marian reminds Sara that Kant rejected 'design arguments' for God's existence, and points out inconsistencies in her reasoning.

p. 49 *'a little bilious attack'*: GEL II, p. 273 (George Eliot to Sara Hennell, Richmond, 15 November 1856); *Lewes pressed the publisher for a warmer response*: GEL II, p. 273 (George Lewes to John Blackwood, Richmond, 15 November 1856); *'greatly restored the shaken confidence of my friend ...'*: GEL II, p. 276 (George Lewes to John Blackwood, Richmond, 22 November 1856); *'We are so long in this life ...'*: GEL II, p. 278 (letter to Sara Hennell, Richmond, 24 November 1856).

p. 50 *'It is a long time since I have read anything so fresh so humorous and so touching'*: GEL II, p. 283 (letter from John Blackwood to George Eliot, Edinburgh, 29 December 1856); *'Whatever may be the success of my stories ...'*: GEL II, p. 292 (letter to John Blackwood, Richmond, 4 February 1857).

p. 51–2 *'just like putting straw and fire together ...'*: see Thomas A. Fudge, 'Incest and Lust in Luther's Marriage', *The Sixteenth Century Journal* vol. 34, no. 2 (2003), pp. 319–45, especially pp. 324–5.

p. 52 *'All the ups and downs of comedy usually end in marriage ...'*: *The Correspondence of Erasmus*, vol. 11, p. 396 (letter to Frans van Cranevelt, 24 December 1525); see also p. 325 (letter to Daniel Mauch, 10 October 1525); *Luther spoke warmly of his 'pious, God-fearing, home-loving wife'*: see Trevor O'Reggio, 'Martin Luther on Marriage and the Family', *History Research* vol. 2, no. 3 (2012), pp. 195–218, p. 200; *More wrote hundreds of pages denouncing Luther's 'fylthy lyfe'*: Thomas More, 'A Dialogue concerning Heretics' in *The Complete Works of Thomas More*, vol. 6, p. 378; 'The Confutation of Tyndale's Answer' in *The Complete Works of Thomas More*, vol. 8, p. 496. See Eric Josef

Carlson, 'Clerical Marriage and the English Reformation', *Journal of British Studies* vol. 31, no. 1 (1992), pp. 1–31: pp. 10–11; Fudge, 'Incest and Lust in Luther's Marriage', pp. 338–44; *The 1548 Clerical Marriage Act* . . .: While Lutherans commended marriage as the highest expression of Christian love and (for women) obedience, its Anglican defenders were more pragmatic. They tended to follow St Paul in seeing chastity as the ideal state. But given the 'ardent and burnyng desire of nature', priests were permitted to take wives as 'an especiall and singular medicine' for the sin of fornication — Robert Barnes, 'That by God's word it is lawful for Priests that hath not the gift of chastity to marry Wives' in *The Whole Works of W. Tyndall, John Frith, and Doct. Barnes* (London: 1573), Part 2, pp. 310–11. See J. Yost, 'The Reformation Defense of Clerical Marriage in the Reigns of Henry VIII and Edward VI', *Church History* 50 (1981), pp. 155–8; Carlson, 'Clerical Marriage and the English Reformation', pp. 2–9. The 1548 Clerical Marriage Act states that it is better for priests to marry than to feign chastity, preserving the idea that genuine chastity was still preferable to marriage. When Mary I became Queen of England in 1553 this Clerical Marriage Act was repealed. Under Elizabeth I the 1559 Second Act of Supremacy once again abolished papal power in England; the Royal Visitation of 1559 declared clerical marriage lawful but required priests wishing to marry to seek both the permission of their bishop and the agreement of the woman's parents. Polemics against clerical marriage continued, but by 1563 'clerical marriage was a secure and unchallengeable feature of the Elizabethan church' and in 1571 the Thirty-Nine Articles, affirmed the clergy's right to marry (Article XXXII), thus 'again and finally' enshrining clerical marriage in English law: see Carlson, 'Clerical Marriage and the English Reformation', pp. 13, 28–9; *In England . . . marriage replaced monasticism*: see Lyndal Roper, 'Luther: Sex, Marriage and Motherhood', *History Today*, vol. 33 (December 1983), pp. 33–8; Merry Wiesner-Hanks, 'Martin Luther on Marriage and the Family', *Oxford Research Encyclopedia on Religion* (Oxford University Press online, 2016). Calvin wrote many biblical commentaries and sermons emphasizing that marriage was 'a holy covenant ordained by God': see John Calvin, *Sermons on Ephesians* (Edinburgh: The Banner of Truth Trust, 1974), pp. 564–76, 605–17; John Witte Jr and Robert M. Kingdon, *Sex, Marriage and Family in John Calvin's Geneva*, vol. 1: *Courtship, Engagement and Marriage* (Grand Rapids: Eerdmans, 2005), pp. 27–61.

p. 53 *The matrimonial rite* . . .: *The Book of Common Prayer*, 1559. See Stephanie Coontz, *Marriage: A History* (London: Penguin, 2005), p. 141.

p. 54 *'Tell a man he is not to be saved by his works* . . .': George Eliot, *Scenes of Clerical Life* (Oxford: Oxford University Press, 1988), pp. 169–70 (Chapter I); *'heart-piercing griefs'*: *Scenes of Clerical Life*, p. 199 (Chapter IV); *'wildly wishes herself dead'*: *Scenes of Clerical Life*, p. 204 (Chapter V); *'an unloving, tyrannous, brutal man* . . .': *Scenes of Clerical Life*, p. 239 (Chapter XIII); *'the young girl, proud in strength and beauty* . . .': *Scenes of Clerical Life*, p. 246 (Chapter XV).

p. 55 *'saving ignorance'*: *Scenes of Clerical Life*, p. 204 (Chapter V); *'Emotion is obstinately irrational'* . . . *'kindness is my religion'*: *Scenes of Clerical Life*, p. 235–7 (Chapter XII); *'surely, surely the only true knowledge . . .'*: *Scenes of Clerical Life*, p. 228–9 (Chapter X); *'well-filled lips . . .'*: *Scenes of Clerical Life*, p. 192 (Chapter III).

pp. 55–6 *'It seems a dreadful thing in life . . .'*: *Scenes of Clerical Life*, p. 274 (Chapter XXII).

p. 56 *'no one could feel that she was performing anything but a sacred office'*: *Scenes of Clerical Life*, p. 299 (Chapter XXVII); *'a sacred kiss of promise'*: *Scenes of Clerical Life*, p. 300 (Chapter XXVII); *'walked in the presence of unseen witnesses . . .'*: *Scenes of Clerical Life*, p. 301 (Chapter XXVIII).

p. 57 *'I have changed my name . . .'*: GEL II, pp. 331–2 (letter to Isaac Evans, Jersey, 26 May 1857); *financial arrangements*: in 1854 Marian had requested that her brother would 'in future' pay her income into the Coventry and Warwickshire Bank every six months, 'that I might order it to be sent to me wherever I wanted it, as he has sometimes sent me a cheque which I could not get cashed in London', and she asked Charles Bray to help her set up these arrangements — GEL II, p. 178 (letter to Charles Bray, Weimar, 23 October 1854). Ruby Redinger argues that Marian's reason for telling Isaac about her relationship with Lewes was primarily financial — see *George Eliot: The Emergent Self* (Bodley Head, 1976), p. 337; *Perhaps this was Lewes's idea*: George Eliot's letter to her brother Isaac of 26 May 1857, and her subsequent letter to his solicitor Vincent Holbeche (GEL II, p. 349), are both written in Lewes's hand — see Redinger, *George Eliot: The Emergent Self*, p. 340. Lewes might have copied her original letter to keep for their records; alternatively, the letter written by Lewes might be the first draft, which she copied and sent to Isaac. Whether or not Lewes initiated the correspondence, he was closely involved in its execution.

pp. 57–8 *'Now, let me ask you to open your eyes and look surprized'*: GEL II, p. 333 (letter to Fanny Houghton, Jersey, 26 May 1857).

p. 58 *quasi-parental quality*: such friends include Robert Brabant, George Combe and François D'Albert-Durade and his wife, with whom she lodged when she stayed in Geneva during the winter of 1849–50; *emphasize their age difference*: Kathryn Hughes notes that 'Since her thirties and possibly before, Marian had knocked a year off her age'; the birth date on her coffin was given as 1820 — see *George Eliot: The Last Victorian*, p. 482. I wonder if Marian wished (consciously or unconsciously) her relationship with Lewes to echo her close childhood relationship with her brother Isaac, who was born in May 1816, three and a half years before her; adjusting her own age by a year would create a similar age difference with Lewes, born in April 1817; *'your Brother is so much hurt . . .'*: GEL II, p. 346 (letter from Vincent Holbeche to Mrs Lewes, Sutton Coldfield, 9 June 1857).

p. 59 *'Our marriage is not a legal one . . .'*: There are two versions of this letter: one in GE's hand, and a draft in Lewes's hand — see Haight's note in GEL II, p. 349; *She became 'Marian Lewes' in these letters . . .*: Lewes was still referring to her as 'Miss Evans' in letters to their German friends in February and September 1857: see LGHL I, pp. 261–2, 267. In July 1859 Lewes explained to the journalist Robert Patterson that 'Miss Evans has ceased to bear that name for five years & I hope you will check anyone you may hear using it ... Miss Evans is Mrs Lewes now & knows no other names' — LGHL I, p. 288; around the same time, Marian wrote to Charles Bray 'My *name* is Marian Evans *Lewes*' — GEL III, p. 111 (letter to Charles Bray, 5 July 1859). By 1859, then, the Leweses were showing some impatience with friends who continued to call her Marian Evans, though the shift from Evans to Lewes was more complicated than they acknowledged; *'intensely agitated'*: see *Journals*, p. 69; *'Every form of disapproval jarred him painfully ...'*: *Scenes of Clerical Life*, p. 219 (Chapter VIII).

p. 60 *John Blackwood conveyed his doubts*: GEL II, p. 344 (John Blackwood to George Eliot, London, 8 June 1857); *she read several fine marriage novels*: see *Journals*, pp. 275, 279, 281 ('Recollections of the Scilly Isles' and 'Recollections of Jersey', 1857); *It was drawn from life*: on the 'real' Dempsters, see Haight's note in GEL II, p. 347.

p. 61 *'As an artist ...'*: GEL II, pp. 347–8 (letter to John Blackwood, Jersey, 13 June 1857); *'I was in raptures with Janet's Repentance ...'*: GEL II, p. 351 (George Lewes to John Blackwood, Jersey, 14 June 1857); *'In continuing to write for the Magazine ...'*: GEL II, pp. 352–3 (John Blackwood to George Eliot, London, 14 June 1857).

4. VOCATION

p. 63 *a 'miserably wet' Christmas Day*: *Journals*, p. 40; *'We ate our turkey together ...'*: *Journals*, p. 71; *During those winter evenings they read aloud by the fire*: *Journals*, p. 73; *'She was loving and kind to me ...'*: *Journals*, p. 297.

pp. 63–4 *'I never lost the impression of that afternoon ...'*: *Journals*, p. 296. See also GEL III, p. 176 (letter to Sara Hennell, Wandsworth, 7 October 1859).

p. 64 *'quiet depth of conviction'*: George Eliot, *Adam Bede* (London: Penguin Books, 1985), p. 71 (Chapter 2). Eliot writes that she conceived of Adam Bede by 'blending ... some recollections of my aunt in one story with some points in my father's early life and character ... The character of Adam, and one or two incidents connected with him were suggested by my Father's early life: but Adam is not my father, any more than Dinah is my aunt' — *Journals*, pp. 296–7. In an 1859 letter to Sara Hennell she expanded on the differences between Dinah Morris and Elizabeth Evans: her aunt was 'a tiny little woman, with bright, small dark eyes, and hair that had been black, I imagine, but was now grey — a pretty woman in her youth, but of a totally different physical type from Dinah. The difference — as you will believe — was not *simply* physical: no difference is. She was a woman of strong natural excitability ... But this vehemence was now subdued by age and sickness; she was very gentle and quiet in her manners — very loving — and (what she must have been from the very first) a truly religious soul, in whom the love of God and love of man were fused together' — GEL III, p. 175 (letter to Sara Hennell, Wandsworth, 7 October 1859). Marian emphasizes the difference between her aunt and Dinah because readers of *Adam Bede*, including Elizabeth Evans's children and grandchildren, had suggested that Dinah was a 'portrait' of her aunt — see GEL III, pp. 176–7 (letter to Sara Hennell, Wandsworth, 7 October 1859). Redinger suggests that the character of Adam Bede 'was not meant to stand as a realistic portrait of Robert Evans but arose out of what [George Eliot] had heard about him as a young man — her father as she had never known him. It is as if she wished to restore in the eyes of the world what she herself had cause to suspect her father lacked: manliness, especially in decisive thought and action within his own home. Adam is, above all else, manly,' *George Eliot: The Emergent Self*, p. 36; *'strong baritone'*: *Adam Bede*, p. 49 (Chapter 1); *'mellow treble tones'*: *Adam Bede*, p. 71 (Chapter 2); *'our marriage is not God's will'*: *Adam Bede*, p. 79 (Chapter 3).

p. 65 *'He was so delighted with the presentation of Dinah . . .'*: Journals, pp. 71, 297; *'subdued as it was . . .'*: Collins (ed.), *George Eliot: Interviews and Recollections*, pp. 39–40 (from Grace Greenwood, 'Three Great Women', 1881). See also Collins (ed.), *George Eliot: Interviews and Recollections*, p. 72: 'a voice clear and sweet and soft' (from George Smith's unpublished memoir). After Marian found fame as George Eliot, many people who met her commented on her 'beautiful' voice: Mrs Humphrey Ward recalled her 'low clear voice'; another acquaintance describes it as 'so low and soft . . . once heard it could never be forgotten'; in 1869 Henry James wrote to his father of her 'voice soft and rich as that of a counselling angel — a mingled sagacity and sweetness — a broad hint of a great underlying world of reserve, knowledge, pride and power' — see Haight, *George Eliot: A Biography*, pp. 417, 427, 429, 474; *'Her voice was a contralto . . .'*: Spencer, *An Autobiography*, vol. I, pp. 395–6; *'created a new voice for herself . . .'*: Mathilde Blind, *George Eliot* (London: W. H. Allen and Co., 1883), pp. 16–17. See also Hughes, *George Eliot: The Last Victorian*, pp. 23–4. George Eliot seemed to take some pride in the beauty of her voice: see Collins (ed.), *George Eliot: Interviews and Recollections*, p. 181 (citing Emma Nason).

p. 66 *the poet's Cumbrian accent*: on Wordsworth's accent, see Brennan O'Donnell, *The Passion of Meter: A Study of Wordsworth's Metrical Art* (Kent, OH: Kent State University Press, 1995), pp. 110–12; John Purkis, *A Preface to Wordsworth*, revised edition (London: Routledge, 1986), p. 40; *Marian's assured literary voice . . . does not match the needy diffidence described by Lewes*: Beverley Park Rilett has argued that Lewes was a 'dominant and controlling' partner who had a subduing effect on Marian, causing her to doubt herself: 'before Lewes assumed the role of strict mentor . . . Eliot had been fiercely independent in her opinions of her own work and the work of contributors' — 'The Role of George Henry Lewes in George Eliot's Career: A Reconsideration,' p. 6. While I agree that Lewes could be controlling, it is also possible that — independently of his influence — Marian was confident as a critic while being unsure of herself as a fiction writer. This would explain her reticence about writing fiction in her earlier life, despite her ambition to do so.

p. 67 *'renounced' the name Evans*: GEL II p. 384 (letter to Bessie Parkes, Richmond, 24 September 1857); see also p. 396 (letter to Charles Bray, Richmond, 30 October 1857); *She had recently begun a new part of her diary . . .*: Margaret Harris and Judith Johnston, the editors of George Eliot's journals, suggest that this sequence of entries document a 'rite of passage . . . about the making of George Eliot', and note that 'at this point she distances her account of her writing identity, the persona of "George Eliot" under which her fiction went into the world, from her daily record of activity', *Journals*, pp. 285–6.

pp. 67–8 *'This time last year I was alone, as I am now . . .'*: *Journals*, p. 72.

p. 68 *'that my writing may succeed and so give value to my life . . .'*: *Journals*, p. 292; *she wondered whether she would live long enough*: see Cross II, p. 2 (quoting from a journal entry, 2 January 1858), where Marian expresses doubt that she will be alive 'ten years hence'; *Dickens praised the 'exquisite truth and delicacy . . .'*: GEL II, pp. 423–4 (letter from Charles Dickens, London, 18 January 1858; *'a human book'*: GEL II, pp. 425–6 (letter from Jane Carlyle, Chelsea, 21 January 1858); *Dickens felt sure this author was a woman*: he wrote to Blackwood: 'As to Janet, in the last tale, I know nothing in literature done by a man like the frequent references to her grand form, and her eyes and her height and so forth; whereas I do know innumerable things of that kind in books of imagination by women. And I have not the faintest doubt that a woman described her being shut out into the street by her husband, and conceived and executed the whole idea of her following that clergyman. If I be wrong in this, then I protest that a woman's mind has got into some man's body by a mistake that ought immediately to be corrected' — GEL II, pp. 427–8 (Charles Dickens to John Blackwood, London, 27 January 1858).

p. 69 *'There can hardly be any climax . . .'*: GEL II, p. 424 (letter to John Blackwood, Richmond, 21 January 1858); *She devoted a page of the George Eliot part of her diary to a detailed account of Blackwood's visit*: *Journals*, p. 295 (the entry describes Blackwood's visits on 28 February and 4 March 1858, and was written some time between 4 March and 3 April).

p. 70 *'I drove to Richmond to see Lewes, and was introduced to George Eliot . . .'*: GEL II, p. 436 (John Blackwood to Mrs John Blackwood, London, 1 March 1858); *'He opened it, read the first page . . .'*: *Journals*, p. 295 (from an entry describing Blackwood's visits on 28 February and 4 March 1858, written some time between 4 March and 3 April); *'By a strange coincidence G. E. was with me . . .'*: GEL II, p. 439 (George Lewes to John Blackwood, Richmond, 13 March 1858); *Eliot '(very judiciously!) looks up to my critical opinion as oracular'*: GEL II, p. 295 (George Lewes to John Blackwood, Richmond, 11 February 1857); *'for you perceive his Pegasus is tender in the mouth . . .'*: GEL II, p. 448 (George Lewes to John Blackwood, Richmond, 3 April 1858).

p. 71 *'My heart is in the story'*: GEL II, p. 419 (letter to John Blackwood, Richmond, 9 January 1858); *She was impatient when she 'lost' two or three days' writing*: see *Journals*, p. 73; *'this is at present impossible to me . . .'*: GEL II, p. 428 (letter to Bessie Parkes, Richmond, 30 January 1858); *'I have given up writing articles . . .'*: GEL II, p. 431 (letter to Bessie Parkes, Richmond, 3 February 1858).

pp. 71–2 *'For thoughts are so great . . .'*: *Adam Bede*, pp. 135–6 (Chapter 8).

p. 72 *She later adapted Dinah's words in this scene*: GEL III, p. 185 (letter to John Blackwood, Wandsworth, 16 October 1859); *Aurora uses the word 'vocation' to describe her art*: Elizabeth Barrett Browning, *Aurora Leigh* (Oxford: Oxford University Press, 1993), p. 51; Book II, lines 55–6. In her 1870 dramatic poem 'Armgart', George Eliot echoes Browning's depiction of artistic vocation. Armgart, a gifted opera singer, says:

> I am an artist by my birth –
> By the same warrant that I am a woman:
> Nay, in the added rarer gift I see
> Supreme vocation.

See 'Armgart', Scene II, in *The Legend of Jubal and Other Poems* (Edinburgh and London: William Blackwood and Sons, 1874), p. 98; *'I know no book that gives me a deeper sense of communion . . .'*: GEL II, p. 342 (letter to Sara Hennell, Gorey, 5 June 1857); *'bursting through / The best of your conventions . . .'*: Browning, *Aurora Leigh*, Book II, pp. 51–2, ll. 469–73; *'For me / Perhaps I am not worthy . . .'*: Browning, *Aurora Leigh*, Book II, p. 52, ll. 485–97. In 1857 Marian's friend Barbara Leigh Smith quoted verses from *Aurora Leigh* in her radical pamphlet *Women and Work*:

> –Whoever says
> To a loyal woman, 'Love and work with me,'
> Will get fair answer, if the work and Love,
> Being good themselves, are good for her, the best
> She was born for. Women of a softer mood,
> Surprised by men when scarce awake to life
> Will sometimes only hear the first word, Love,
> And catch up with it any kind of work
> Indifferent, so that dear Love go with it.
> I do not blame such women, though for Love
> They pick much oakum.

See Barbara Leigh Smith, *Women and Work* (London: Bosworth and Harrison, 1857), p. 10.

p. 73 *Lewes was pursuing his scientific ambitions . . .*: see Ashton, *G. H. Lewes*, pp. 188–90; *Marian worked daily on Adam Bede, reading each new chapter aloud to her 'husband'*: see *Journals*, pp. 316–17; *'Mr. Lewes is in a state of perfect bliss . . .'*: GEL II, p. 454 (letter to Sara Hennell, Munich, 10–13 May 1858). See also LGHL I, pp. 276–7 (George Lewes to John Parker, Munich, 12 May 1858); *'People are so kind to us . . .'*: GEL II, p. 450 (letter to Sara Hennell, Munich, 17 April 1858); *Professor Liebig 'seems to have taken a benevolent liking to me . . .'*: GEL II, pp. 452–3 (letter to Sara Hennell, Munich, 10–13 May 1858); *Hofwyl, their boarding school in Switzerland*: Hofwyl had been proposed by Charles Bray or Sara Hennell as a suitable school for Lewes's sons: see GEL II, pp. 235–7 (letter to Charles Bray, Richmond, 1 April 1856; letter to Sara Hennell, Richmond, 6 April 1856). Kathryn Hughes remarks that 'It was perfect for the Lewes boys, offering the kind of liberal, wide-ranging and above all European education which had so distinctively shaped their father. It was also far enough away from London to keep them clear of painful gossip about their parents' situation' — *George Eliot: The Last Victorian*, p. 240.

p. 74 *'after I had suffered a great deal . . .'*: Journals, p. 318; *'general languor and sense of depression'*: Journals, p. 319; *'a charming journey'*: Journals, p. 324; *'a whole apartment of six rooms . . .'*: Journals, pp. 324–5; *they shared a carriage with an elderly couple*: Journals, p. 306; *'young fair heads of girls . . .'*: Journals, pp. 306–7.

pp. 74–5 *'how music that stirs all one's devout emotions . . .'*: Journals, p. 308.

p. 75 *'as if in a hurry to follow the sun'*: Journals, p. 309. pp. 74–5; *'I feel intensely the new beauty of the sky . . .'*: Journals, p. 311. *'I only know that it must make a deeply felt crisis in your life . . .'*: GEL II, pp. 464–5 (letter to Sara Hennell, Munich, 14 June 1858). Peggy Fitzhugh Johnstone's *Transformation of Rage: Mourning and Creativity in George Eliot's Fiction* (New York University Press, 1994) analyses George Eliot's novels in light of her separation from and loss of her mother.

pp. 75–6 *'a sort of awe . . .'*: Journals, p. 325; see also p. 317.

p. 76 *'she found it 'harder and harder to leave'*: Journals, p. 325.

p. 77 *unconscious easy grace . . .'*: Journals, pp. 317, 325; *'the rays that fall . . .'*: Adam Bede, p. 581 (Epilogue); *'other sorts o' teaching'*: Adam Bede, p. 583 (Epilogue). On Elizabeth Evans's decision to leave the Wesleyan Society when it no longer allowed women to preach, see GEL III, p. 175 (letter to Sara Hennell, Wandsworth, 7 October 1859); *'made all of grey, though in the usual Quaker form . . .'*: Adam Bede, p. 578 (Chapter 55); *Marriage and motherhood are now her vocation . . .*: in 1905 the sociologist Max Weber argued that the concept of vocation or calling is specifically Protestant, and traced it to Luther. According to Weber, Protestant Christians believe that 'the only way of living acceptably to God was not to surpass worldly morality in monastic asceticism, but solely through the obligations imposed on the individual through his position in the world. That was his calling [*Beruf*]' — *The Protestant Ethic and the Spirit of Capitalism*, trans. Talcott Parsons (London: Routledge 1992), p. 40. In his introduction to this text, Anthony Giddens notes that this is one of the most contested elements of Weber's analysis of capitalism (see p. xxiii).

pp. 78–9 *'My soul is so knit with yours . . .'*: Adam Bede, pp. 572, 576 (Chapter 54).

p. 79 *'What greater thing is there for two human souls . . .'*: *Adam Bede*, p. 576 (Chapter 54); *sent the manuscript to her publisher that very day*: *Journals*, p. 75; *'History of "Adam Bede"'*: *Journals*, p. 298.

pp. 79–80 *'The last day of the dear old year . . .'*: *Journals*, p. 75.

5. THE WORLD

p. 83 *'cases of inundation'*: *Journals*, p. 76, 12 January 1859; *'eerie stories'*: see 'Belles Lettres', *Westminster Review*, April 1856, vol. 65, p. 640; *'longing to die . . .'*: *The Lifted Veil* (Oxford: Oxford University Press, 1999), p. 15; *'double consciousness'*: *The Lifted Veil*, pp. 21, 42. See *Journals*, p. 336; Herbert Spencer, *An Autobiography*, vol. 1, p. 396. A few decades later, the American sociologist W. E. B. DuBois would use the phrase 'double consciousness' in *The Souls of Black Folk*, both echoing and altering the themes of *The Lifted Veil* (and of Marian's private self-description) in a very different social context: 'the Negro is . . . born with a veil, and gifted with second-sight in this American world — a world which yields him no true self-consciousness, but only lets him see himself through the revelation of the other world. It is a peculiar sensation, this double-consciousness, this sense of always looking at one's self through the eyes of others, of measuring one's soul by the tape of a world that looks on in amused contempt and pity.' — W. E. B. DuBois, 'Of Our Spiritual Strivings', *The Souls of Black Folks* (New York: Dover, 1944), p. 2.

p. 84 *'the fascination of an unravelled destiny'*: *The Lifted Veil*, p. 15; *'I shuddered — I despised this woman . . .'*: *The Lifted Veil*, pp. 19–20; *'a sort of crushing of the heart'*: *The Lifted Veil*, p. 31; *'We were front to front with each other . . .'*: *The Lifted Veil*, p. 32.

p. 85 *'a ridiculously desponding state'*: GEL III, p. 26 (letter to Sara Hennell, Wandsworth, 26 February 1859); *'It has ploughed up my heart'*: GEL III, p. 23 (letter to Cara Bray, Wandsworth, 24 February 1859); *they had trouble with their new servant*: moving from lodgings to a house posed this new domestic problem. On 19 February Marian wrote to Sara Hennell that 'we have only a temporary servant, and I shall not be quite at ease until I have a trustworthy woman who will manage without incessant dogging' — GEL III, p. 14 (letter to Sara Hennell, Wandsworth, 19 February 1859). On 22 February she wrote to Cara Bray for advice; Cara offered to place an advert in the *Coventry Herald*, to which Marian replied gratefully: 'Heaven and earth bless you for trying to help me . . . I need hardly tell you what I want — you know it so well: a servant who will cause me the least possible expenditure of time on household matters. *Cooking* is a material thing, not because Mr Lewes is epicurean (for he is stupid of palate) but because he is, amongst his other eminences, eminently dyspeptic . . . I wish I were not an anxious fidgetty wretch, and could sit down content with dirt and disorder. But anything in the shape of an *anxiety* soon grows into a monstrous vulture with me, and makes itself more present to me than my rich source of happiness, such as too few mortals are blessed with. You know me.' — GEL III, pp. 22–3 (letter to Cara Bray, Wandsworth, 24 February 1859). Lewes's journal also discusses their efforts to find a satisfactory servant: see GEL III, pp. 14, 19. The search continued throughout March and into April, and seemed to be resolved by 18 April — see GEL III, p. 53 (letter to Sara Hennell, Wandsworth, 19 April 1859, and George Lewes's journal, 18 April 1859); *'People who have been insepara-ble . . .'*: GEL III, p. 27 (letter to Charles Bray, Wandsworth, 28 February 1859); *was she proud to be needed by her husband?* Marian referred in a similar way to Lewes's authoritarian manner in a letter to Maria Congreve later that year: 'I am told peremptorily that I am to go to Switzerland next month . . . Mr Lewes commands me to say that he has just read the "Roman Empire of the West" [by Richard Congreve] with much interest, and is going now to flesh his teeth in the "Politique" [by Auguste Comte]' — GEL III, p. 101 (letter to Maria Congreve, Wandsworth, 27 June 1859). As in her letter to Charles Bray on 28 February, it is difficult to say whether she is grumbling or boasting about Lewes's insistence that she stay at home with him, or travel abroad with him (on this occasion she stayed in Lucerne alone while Lewes visited his sons at school). On their return home from Switzerland, Lewes declared that 'in spite of the fatigues of the journey Mrs Lewes is greatly benefited by the trip', though he also felt that 'except for the sight of the boys and the beauty of Lucerne, the trip was not worth the fatigue and time and money' — GEL III, p. 117 (George Lewes to John Blackwood, Wandsworth, 22 July 1859); *Chrissey died in March*: see GEL III, p. 38 (letter to Sara Hennell, Wandsworth, 21 March 1859). Chrissey had died on 15 March, and Marian received the news on 16 March; *'A work of true genius . . .'*: *Athenaeum*, 26 February 1859, p. 284 — sourced from the George Eliot Archive.

pp. 85–6 *'a first-rate novel . . .'*: *The Times*, 12 April 1859, p. 12 — sourced from the George Eliot Archive.

p. 86 *novels by male authors 'are more in keeping with the actual world . . .'*: *Economist*, 5 March 1859, pp. 256–7 — sourced from the George Eliot Archive; *Blackwood considered it a 'triumph'*: GEL III, p. 33 (John Blackwood to George Eliot, Edinburgh, 16 March 1859); *News of high sales and rave reviews reached her 'rather strangely'*: GEL III, p. 34 (letter to John Blackwood, Wandsworth, 17 March 1859) — written the day after she received news of Chrissey's death; *'the effect upon G. E. has been almost sad . . .'*: GEL III, p. 36 (George Lewes to John Blackwood, Wandsworth, 17 March 1859); *The Times printed a letter*: *The Times*, 15 April 1859, p. 10. The Liggins saga was a much longer story, dating back to May 1857: see Cross I, p. 449; *Lewes immediately wrote to The Times, in the name of George Eliot*: see *The Times*, 16 April 1859, p. 7; *'a perfect fever'*: GEL II, pp. 50–1 (George Lewes to the Editor of *The Times*, Wandsworth, 15 April 1859; John Blackwood to George Eliot, Edinburgh, 16 April 1859); *Comte proposed a 'religion of humanity . . .'*: Auguste Comte, *The Catechism of Popular Religion*, trans. Richard Congreve (London: John Chapman, 1858), pp. 319–20. Comte's theory of marriage is based on clearly defined gender roles. He argues that men and women have a mutually improving influence: women are emotionally and morally superior, being less selfish and more sympathetic, while 'the man is indisputably the superior in all that regards the character properly so called. And it is the character on which, in the main, depends command.' As for the intellect, Comte continues, 'in the man it is stronger and of wider grasp; in the woman it is more accurate and penetrating'. 'Everything then combines to show the mutual efficacy of the marriage union, which constitutes the highest form of friendship, with the additional charm of mutual possession' (pp. 319–20). Privately, Comte was a turbulent man who suffered phases of mental breakdown: he was very jealous of his wife and suspicious of her infidelities, though he himself fell passionately in love with Clotilde de Vaux and displayed a cultish devotion to her memory when she died.

pp. 86–7 *'It is rather unfortunate that they are so inseparable'*: see Haight, *George Eliot: A Biography*, pp. 299–300.

p. 87 *'houses full of eyes'*: *Journals*, p. 77; *'sweet, intelligent, gentle'*: GEL III, p. 53 (letter to Sara Hennell, Wandsworth, 19 April 1859); *'I usually wake up so entirely mistress of the situation . . .'*: quoted in Haight, *George Eliot: A Biography*, p. 300. Wanting to be told that people loved her was a perennial wish for Eliot: in 1875 she wrote to Georgiana Burne-Jones, 'I like not only to be loved, but also to be told that I am loved' (Cross III, p. 121, 11 May 1875); *'the belief that you do really care for me . . .'*: GEL III, p. 63 (letter to Maria Congreve, Wandsworth, 4 May 1859); *'Her friendship has the same date as the success of "Adam Bede"'*: *Journals*, p. 77; *'I sing my "Magnificat" in a quiet way . . .'*: GEL III, p. 44 (letter to John Blackwood, Wandsworth, 10 April 1859); *'sadder than usual'*: GEL III, p. 64 (letter to Barbara Bodichon, Wandsworth, 5 May 1859).

p. 88 *'that is written by Marian Evans . . .'*: GEL III, p. 56 (Barbara Leigh Smith Bodichon to George Eliot, Algiers, 26 April 1859); *'God bless you, dearest Barbara, for your love and sympathy . . .'*: GEL III, p. 63 (letter to Barbara Bodichon, Wandsworth, 5 May 1859); *'Dear Barbara, You're a darling . . .'*: GEL III, pp. 64–5 (letter to Barbara Bodichon, Wandsworth, 5 May 1859). Lewes added to Marian's next letter to Barbara two postscripts, the second of which was kept secret from Marian: 'P.P.S. *Entre nous*. Please don't write or tell Marian anything *unpleasant* that you hear unless it is important for her to hear it. She is so very sensitive, and has such a tendency to dwell on and believe in unpleasant ideas that I always keep them from her . . . She knows nothing of this second postscript, of course.' — GEL III, p. 106 (letter to Barbara Bodichon, Wandsworth, 30 June 1859). This was a response to Barbara's reports of gossip: people were speculating that 'Mrs Lewes' was George Eliot; 'from their way of talking it was evident they thought you would do the book more harm than the book would do you good in public opinion' — see GEL III, p. 103 (Barbara Bodichon to Marian Lewes, London, 28 June 1859). This letter may have been decisive in persuading Marian and Lewes to reveal George Eliot's identity publicly — though they had already shared the secret with Sara Hennell and the Brays on 20 June. On 30 June Lewes wrote to Barbara that 'we have come to the resolution of no longer concealing the authorship. It makes me angry to think that people should say that the secret has been kept because there was any *fear* of the effect of the author's name' — GEL III, p. 106; *'my Polly'*: Lewes called Marian 'Polly', a common nickname for Mary, from 1859 onwards (see Haight, *George Eliot: A Biography*, pp. 292–4). Mary Ann Evans calls herself 'Polly' in one of her first surviving letters, written to her friend Maria Lewis in 1838 (see GEL I, p. 8), but signing herself 'Polly' was the exception rather than the rule (see GEL I, pp. 26, 43, 47, 56, 64). The name resurfaces in correspondence with Sara Hennell during the 1840s: from 1844 onwards, she often signed herself 'Pollian' in her letters to Sara (see GEL I, p. 182; Haight, *George Eliot: A Biography*, pp. 79–80). Pollian was a pun on Apollyon, the 'monster' and 'foul fiend' of *The Pilgrim's Progress*. Apollyon is a destructive angel, 'hideous to behold: he was clothed with scales like a fish (and they are his pride); he had wings like a dragon, feet like a bear; and out of his belly came fire and smoke, and his mouth was as the mouth of a lion' — John Bunyan, *The Pilgrim's Progress* (London: Hurst, Robinson and Co., 1820) pp. 61–2.

p. 90 *The river would run through her novel . . .*: see Paul A. Makurath, 'The Symbolism of the Flood in Eliot's *Mill on the Floss*', *Studies in the Novel*, vol. 7, no. 2 (1975), pp. 298–300; *'in much anxiety and doubt . . .'*; *'certain new ideas have occurred to me . . .'*: *Journals*, p. 80 (18 September 1859; 7 October 1859). On their trip to Gainsborough, Lincolnshire, and rowing north down the Trent to its junction with the River Idle (at East Stockwith), see LGHL II, p. 21 (George Lewes to John Blackwood, London, 18 January 1861); Haight, *George Eliot: A Biography*, p. 305, quoting from Lewes's journal. Eliot found that the 'great success' of *Adam Bede* made her writing 'a matter of more anxiety than ever: I suppose there is a little sense of responsibility mixed up with a great deal of pride' — GEL III, p. 185 (letter to John Blackwood, Wandsworth, 16 October 1859); *childhood memories*: see Cross I, p. 17; *'easily moved to smiles or tears . . .'*: Cross I, p. 15.

p. 91 *'The child turns over the book . . .'*: Cross I, p. 18; *'I was constantly living in a world of my own creation'*: GEL II, p. 22 (letter to Maria Lewis, Griff House, 16 March 1839); *'absolute need of some one person . . .'*: Cross I, p. 15; *her mother had withdrawn into illness . . .*: see Cross I, p. 14, on Christiana Evans: 'shortly after her last child's birth she became ailing in health'. Cross's account of George Eliot's mother is not straightforward: he describes Christiana Evans, during Mary Anne's early childhood, as 'a shrewd practical person, with a considerable dash of the Mrs Poyser vein in her' (p. 13), making cheese and butter 'with great vigour' (p. 17). Why, then, were her children sent to boarding school so early? Kathryn Hughes offers interesting reflections on this question: in contrast to Rosemary Ashton's rosy view that Mr and Mrs Evans were 'merely seeking an education for their children' (Ashton, *George Eliot: A Life*, p. 17), Hughes suggests that Christiana Evans was 'a woman straining to cope with the demands of her family', perhaps suffering from 'the lassitude of bereavement, depression or physical exhaustion', and argues that 'the early withdrawal of her mother's affection' left George Eliot with 'a vulnerability to rejection that would last a lifetime' — see *George Eliot: The Last Victorian*, pp. 15–18. Brenda Maddox emphasizes

Christiana's depression after the deaths of her twin boys, and suggests that Mary Anne's mother 'did not love her' — see *George Eliot: Writer, Lover, Wife* (London: Harper Press, 2009), pp. 2, 5, 7. Nancy Henry considers the theory that Christiana Evans was an alcoholic, defended by Kathleen McCormack and Gay Sibley: Henry finds Sibley's argument that Mrs Poyser is a closet alcoholic convincing, while noting that Christiana might have been more like 'pill-popping Mrs Pullet [in *The Mill on the Floss*] or the opium addict Molly [in *Silas Marner*]' — see Henry, *The Life of George Eliot*, pp. 35–7; *'Childhood is only the beautiful and happy time in contemplation and retrospect . . .'*: GEL I (letter to Sara Hennell, Foleshill, 3 March 1844).

pp. 91–2 *'I was thy warmth upon thy mother's knee . . .'*: George Eliot, 'Self and Life', *The Legend of Jubal and Other Poems* (Edinburgh: William Blackwood and Sons, 1874), pp. 271–2. The poem ends by envisaging a marriage between Self and Life: 'Yea, I embrace thee, changeful Life! / Far-sent, unchosen mate! / Self and thou, no more at strife, / Shall wed in hallowed state. / Willing spousals now shall prove / Life is justified by love' (p. 275).

p. 92 *'inseparable playfellows'*: Cross I, p. 17; *'a deeply felt crisis . . .'*: Cross I, p. 21; *Her novel's opening scene moves on a 'mighty tide'*: George Eliot, *The Mill on the Floss* (London: Penguin Books, 1985), pp. 53–4 (Book First, Chapter 1); *Eliot . . . remained a 'little sister' in her imagination*: see the final stanza of her 1869 sonnet 'Brother and Sister': '. . . the twin habit of that early time / Lingered for long about the heart and tongue . . . / Till the dire years whose awful name is Change / Had grasped our souls still yearning in Divorce . . . / But were another childhood-world my share, / I would be born a little sister there' — George Eliot, *The Legend of Jubal*, p. 207; *Examining a cast of her head . . .*: from Charles Bray's *Phases of Opinion and Experience during a Long Life: An Autobiography* (pp. 74–5), quoted in Haight, *George Eliot: A Biography*, p. 51.

p. 93 *Her novel seems to say that survival comes at the cost of the past*: Rosemarie Bodenheimer's interpretation goes in a similar direction: 'It is as if the Marian Evans Lewes of 1859 were intent on filling up the rifts in her life with a persuasive defense of her power to adhere in memory, while demonstrating that an actual choice based on loyalty to the past would have killed her' — *The Real Life of Mary Ann Evans* (Ithaca, NY, and London: Cornell University Press, 1996), p. 104; *She cried as she wrote the novel's final scenes*: see GEL III, p. 269 (George Lewes to John Blackwood, Wandsworth, 5 March 1860).

p. 94 *She earnestly teaches the local gypsies about geography*: *The Mill on the Floss*, pp. 173–4 (Book First, Chapter 11); *Romanticism*: this is invoked in references to several Romantic works: Wordsworth's *Excursion*, Madame de Staël's *Corinne*, Bürger's *Leonore*, Novalis's *Heinrich von Ofterdingen*, Bellini's *Sonnambula*; *a new notion — 'the environment'*: see Etienne Benson, *Surroundings: A History of Environments and Environmentalisms* (Chicago: Chicago University Press, 2020).

p. 95 *Eliot had read Cuvier*: see GEL I, p. 246 (letter to John Sibree, Foleshill, 11 February 1848); *Journals*, p. 79 (19 July 1859); *each species 'becomes adapted to the conditions of life of its own region'*: Charles Darwin, *On the Origin of Species by Means of Natural Selection* (London: John Murray, 1859), p. 173. Darwin states that 'The expression of conditions of existence, so often insisted on by the illustrious Cuvier, is fully embraced by the principle of natural selection' (p. 206). Phrases such as 'conditions of life' and 'external circumstances' recur throughout the book. Its official publication date was 24 November 1859; in her journal, Eliot recorded starting it on 23 November, and reported to Charles Bray on 25 November that 'we are reading Darwin's Book on Species, just come out, after long expectation. It is an elaborate exposition of the evidence in favour of the Development Theory, and so, makes an epoch' — see GEL III, p. 214 (letter to Charles Bray, Wandsworth, 25 November 1859); *the concept of milieu, crystallized by Comte*: see Auguste Comte, *Cours de philosophie positive*, vol. 3 (Paris: Bachelier, 1838), pp. 288–9; *The Positive Philosophy of Auguste Comte*, trans. Harriet Martineau (London: John Chapman, 1853), p. 360. Martineau supplied the word 'environment' to gloss Comte's 'milieu'; it has no French correlate in the text. On the emergence of the concept of milieu, see Georges Canguilhem, 'The Living and Its Milieu', trans. John Savage, *Grey Room*, no. 3 (2001), pp. 6–31 (first published as 'Le Vivant et son milieu' in *La Conaissance de la vie* (Paris: Vrin, 1952)); *the ambitious new science of 'sociology'*: see Comte, *The Catechism of Popular Religion*, p. 219; *'The world within . . .'*: see Comte, *The Catechism of Popular Religion*, p. 95; *Journals*, p. 81 (25 October 1859); *it was here that . . . Herbert Spencer, first encountered Comte*: see Spencer, *An Autobiography*, vol. 1, p. 392; *Eliot herself had persuaded Spencer to read Comte's Cours de philosophie positive*: see Spencer, *An Autobiography*, vol. 1, p. 398; *Spencer proposed 'environment'*: Spencer popularized this term in English, but he came across it in Harriet Martineau's translation of Comte. It can be traced to Thomas Carlyle, who used the phrase 'environment of circumstances' to translate Goethe's *Umgebung*, or 'surroundings', in an 1828 review of Goethe's *Collected Works*, and used the word 'environment' in his own book *Sartor resartus* (1833–4). See Trevor Pearce, 'The Origins and Development of the Idea of Organism-Environment Interaction' in *Entangled Life: Organism and Environment in the Biological and Social Sciences*, eds. Gillian Barker, Eric Desjardins and Trevor Pearce (Dordrecht: Springer, 2014), pp. 13–32, and also his 'From "Circumstances" to "Environment": Herbert Spencer and the Origins of the Idea of Organism-Environment Interaction', *Studies in History and Philosophy of Biological and Biomedical Sciences*, 41 (2010), pp. 241–52; *relations 'between every living organism and the external world . . .'*: Herbert Spencer, *Principles of Psychology* (London: Longman, Brown, Green and Longmans, 1855), p. 376. Here Spencer defines 'environment' as 'all surrounding space with the coexistences and sequences contained within it' (p. 379); *'the broadest and most complete definition of life . . .'*: Spencer, *Principles of Psychology*, p. 374; *'Mr Lewes is nailed to the book . . .'*: GEL II, pp. 212–13 (letter to Sara Hennell, East Sheen, 24 August 1855). In his definitive philosophical work, *Problems of Life and Mind*, Lewes incorporated the concept of milieu into his definition of life: 'Life may be defined as *the mode of existence of an organism in relation to its medium*' — *The Physical Basis of Mind, Being the Second Series of Problems of Life and Mind* (London: Trübner & Co., 1877), p. 21; see also the section of this book titled 'Organism and Medium', pp. 40–50. Sally Shuttleworth discusses Lewes's interest in organicism and its influence on George Eliot in *George Eliot and Nineteenth-Century Science: The Make-Believe of a Beginning* (Cambridge: Cambridge University Press, 1984), pp. 1–23.

p. 96 *A new Anglican hymn*: 'All Things Bright and Beautiful' was first published in 1848. Another contemporary example of this optimistic worldview, referenced in *The Mill on the Floss* (p. 489), is the Bridgewater Treatises on natural theology, an edition of eight 'Treatises on the Power, Wisdom and Goodness of God, as Manifested in the Creation' published between 1833 and 1836; *human beings are no longer at ease in the world . . .*: see Genesis 3:16–24; *'labour of choice'*: see Bodenheimer, *The Real Life of Mary Ann Evans*, pp. 83–118, for an extensive discussion of George Eliot's construction of the 'labour of choice' in her letters and also in *The Mill on the Floss*. For Bodenheimer, 'George Eliot's representation of choice is about the essence of her experience, about how it was internally structured and how it was externally read and misread by others' (p. 87). She argues that 'if George Eliot's primary morality lies in her sense that characters must embrace choices in the face of relentlessly determining histories and circumstances' — i.e. what I am calling 'the world' — 'she is equally interested in the invisibility of such moralities to the naked eye' (p. 102). Bodenheimer points out that *The Mill on the Floss* 'has an especially intense relation to Marian Evans's life . . . The difficulty of the narrative lies in the fact that it is still caught up in the struggle it is attempting to depict' (pp. 102–3). She concludes that 'We may read the novel as an autobiographical account of [Marian Evans's] young and guilt-ridden struggle between loyalty and self-development, of all that kept her rooted to the spot in Warwickshire until her father's death. We may read it as a full rendering of the nostalgic desire for forgiveness, an apology for a felt betrayal of her past, even a wish to be released from the labour of a choice that altered the tone of every day of her life as Marian Evans Lewes. And we may read it as her declaration of a woman's life as a rich and strenuous process of choice, invisible to a world in which she is defined by requirements about conduct. All these readings would be true' — p. 111. Bodenheimer also discusses how other critics (Barbara Hardy, Janice Carlisle, Alexander Welsh) have interpreted the relationship between Maggie Tulliver's choices and Eliot's own life — see p. 102.

p. 97 *'There is no sense of ease . . .'*: *The Mill on the Floss*, p. 222 (Book Second, Chapter 1). George Eliot reinforces this allegorical dimension of the novel with significant references to *The Pilgrim's Progress: From This World, to That Which Is to Come*: the story of the Tullivers, like *The Pilgrim's Progress*, is narrated as a dream. Bunyan's parable of a brave Christian's moral journey through a treacherous fallen world had shaped Mary Anne Evans's imagination when she read it as a little girl; *'Character is destiny . . .'*: *The Mill on the Floss*, p. 514 (Book Sixth, Chapter 6); *'if the world had been left as God made it . . .'*: *The Mill on the Floss*, p. 69 (Book First, Chapter 3); *'This world's . . . too many . . .'*: *The Mill on the Floss*,

p. 464 (Book Fifth, Chapter 7); *'household gods'*: Mrs Tulliver exemplifies the 'fetishism' that Auguste Comte identified as the most primitive stage of human culture; as a child, Maggie Tulliver has a wooden doll that is described as a 'fetish'. In the mid-nineteenth century, the concept of fetishism was taken up by Marx to theorize a quasi-religious attachment to material commodities, and later by Freud to describe a form of sexual perversion. See Alan Bass, 'On the History of Fetishism: De Brosses and Comte', *The Undecidable Unconscious: A Journal of Deconstruction and Psychoanalysis*, vol. 2 (2015), pp. 19–45; Peter Melville Logan, *Victorian Fetishism: Intellectuals and Primitives* (Albany, NY: State University of New York Press, 2009), especially pp. 67–88; *'the objects among which her mind had moved . . .'*: The Mill on the Floss, p. 368 (Book Fourth, Chapter 2); *'a man who will make his way in the world'*: The Mill on the Floss, p. 205 (Book Second, Chapter 1).

p. 98 *'To render the world habitable . . .'*: Herbert Spencer, *Social Statics: Or, the Conditions Essential to Human Happiness* (London: John Chapman, 1851), p. 40. In October 1851 Eliot reported to Charles Bray that she had met 'a Mr Herbert Spencer who has just brought out a large work on "Social Statics" which Lewes pronounces the best book he has seen on the subject . . . I have been reading the copy which was to be sent to you' — GEL I, p. 364 (letter to Charles Bray, London, 4 October 1851). In February 1851 Lewes wrote in the *Leader* that 'We remember no work on ethics since that of Spinoza to be compared with it,' and he reviewed the book very positively in three successive *Leader* articles (15 March, 22 March and 12 April 1851); see Haight's note in GEL I, p. 364; *she inhabits a 'triple world . . .'*: The Mill on the Floss, p. 367 (Book Fourth, Chapter 2); *'excessive feeling'*: The Mill on the Floss, p. 486 (Book Sixth, Chapter 2); *the novel itself threatens to overflow its literary form*: see Lynne Tidaback Roberts, 'Perfect Pyramids: *The Mill on the Floss*', *Texas Studies in Literature and Language*, vol. 13, no. 1 (1979), pp. 111–24; *Two wealthy suitors*: Philip Wakem is the son of a lawyer and Stephen Guest is the son of the businessman: these successful fathers fit into the novel's symbolic economy as 'men of the world'.

p. 99 *'refashioning her little world . . .'*: The Mill on the Floss, p. 101 (Book First, Chapter 6).

pp. 99–100 *'everybody in the world seemed so hard . . .'*: The Mill on the Floss, pp. 319–20 (Book Third, Chapter 5).

p. 100 *'The world isn't made of pen, ink and paper . . .'*: The Mill on the Floss, p. 315 (Book Third, Chapter 5); *'There is something romantic in it . . .'*: The Mill on the Floss, p. 498 (Book Sixth, Chapter 3); *'What a wonderful marriage . . .'*: The Mill on the Floss, p. 620 (Book Seventh, Chapter 2); *'I went on with it in my own head . . .'*: The Mill on the Floss, p. 401 (Book Fifth, Chapter 1).

p. 101 *'I was never satisfied with a little of anything . . .'*: The Mill on the Floss, p. 428 (Book Fifth, Chapter 3); *'cool air as of cloisters . . .'*: GEL I, p. 278 (letter to Sara Hennell, Foleshill, 9 February 1849). Just as Scott's *The Pirate* functions in the novel as a token of Romantic literature, underpinned by allusions to many other Romantic works, so *The Imitation of Christ* is a token of devotional literature, underpinned by allusions to Jeremy Taylor's *The Rule and Exercise of Holy Living* (1650) and *The Rule and Exercise of Holy Dying* (1651), Richard Baxter's *Saints' Everlasting Rest* (1650), and Bunyan's *Pilgrim's Progress* (1678); '*contempt of the world*': Thomas à Kempis, *The Imitation of Christ*, Book I, Chapter 1.

p. 102 *playing with traditional gender roles* . . .: like many radical thinkers of this era, Schlegel tended to idealize women from a male point of view. While he advocated feminine independence, Lucinde herself is more a symbol of her author's ideals than a convincing character with a life of her own — see Margarete Kohlenbach, 'Lucinde 1799', in Christopher John Murray (ed.), *Encyclopedia of the Romantic Era, 1760–1850*, vol. 2 (New York: Fitzroy Dearborn, 2004), pp. 698–9; '*our decided disapprobation*': GEL III, p. 90 (George Lewes's Journal, 23 June 1859). Lewes added that this made Sara 'very unhappy'; a few days later Charles Bray reported to Eliot that 'we had Sara in stericks all the way home, because she had missed her final chance of explanation and advice from you' — GEL III, p. 94 (Charles Bray to George Eliot, Coventry, 26 June 1859). Here Bray is dismissive of Sara's work: '*I don't believe she can do better* and if she likes to amuse herself and spend her money in publishing, she can afford it and she does no one any harm and it may attract some *half-doz* congenial minds' — GEL III, pp. 94–5. Lewes continued his brutal critique of Sara's book after it was published, in a letter that he acknowledged was 'unpleasant' — while demanding her gratitude for the time and effort he took in writing it. Eliot described this letter as a 'missile', though she expected Sara to accept Lewes's 'candour' as 'the highest tribute' — see GEL III, pp. 318–22 (George Lewes to Sara Hennell, Wandsworth, 9 July 1860; George Eliot to Cara Bray, Wandsworth, 10 July 1860).

p. 103 '*Dear Friend, when all thy greatness* . . .': this poem, dated 21 June 1859, was found in the pocket of George Eliot's 1880 diary; quoted in Haight, *George Eliot: A Biography*, p. 288; '*after-sadness* . . .': GEL III, p. 90 (letter to Sara Hennell, Wandsworth, 24 June 1859); '*Mr Evans of Griff has been heard to say* . . .': GEL III, p. 98 (Sara Hennell to Marian Lewes, Coventry, 26 June 1859); '*From their way of talking* . . .': GEL III, p. 103 (Barbara Bodichon to Marian Lewes, London, 28 June 1859).

pp. 103–104 '*we have come to the resolution of no longer concealing the authorship* . . .': GEL III, p. 106 (letter to Barbara Bodichon, Wandsworth, 30 June 1859).

p. 104 '*this hard noisy world* . . .': GEL III, p. 109 (letter to Barbara Bodichon, Wandsworth, 2 July 1859); '*The other day I said to Mr Lewes* . . .': GEL III, p. 112 (letter to Maria Congreve, Wandsworth, 6 July 1859); '*but en revanche he sneezes powerfully* . . .': GEL III, p. 133 (letter to John Blackwood, Wandsworth, 17 August 1859). On Christmas Day, 1859, Eliot noted in her journal that 'We all, including Pug, dined with Mr. and Mrs. Congreve, and had a delightful day' — *Journals*, p. 83.

pp. 104–106 *One critic drew out this comparison* . . .: Anonymous, *Saturday Review*, IX, 14 April 1860, reprinted in *George Eliot: The Critical Heritage*, ed. David Carroll (London and New York: Routledge, 1971), pp. 117–19. This critic's remark about exhibiting ascetic religion as a temporary phase of development is astute, given Eliot's private joke about wanting to be a saint for a few months. His comparison with Brontë and Sand as novelists of passion echoes Eliot's own comparison of these two authors when she first read *Villette* — and was becoming acquainted with Lewes — in 1853: 'Lewes was describing Currer Bell to me yesterday as a little, plain, provincial, sickly-looking old maid. Yet what passion, what fire in her! Quite as much as in George Sand, only the clothing is less voluptuous' — GEL II, p. 91 (letter to Charles and Cara Bray, London, 5 March 1853).

p. 105 *George Lewes with the dog*: sadly this dog is probably not Pug, but a 'superb bulldog' named Ben, acquired to replace Pug, who was lost. Ben was 'dreadfully spoiled, & additionally dear to [Mrs Lewes] because he reminds her in so many ways of Pug'. Lewes wanted to name this second dog Savonarola, but decided that this 'would have been too much of a mouthful when one was angry' — see LGHL II, p. 57 (George Lewes to John Blackwood, The Priory, 8 March 1864).

p. 106 *The inward tragedy of The Mill on the Floss* ...: during the 1950s and 1960s literary critics debated this novel's tragic structure: see William R. Steinhoff, 'Intent and Fulfilment in the Ending of *The Mill on the Floss*', in *The Image of the Work*, eds. B. H. Lehman et al. (Berkeley: University of California Press, 1955), pp. 231–51; Jerome Thale, *The Novels of George Eliot* (New York: Columbia University Press, 1959), Chapter 2; Bernard J. Paris, 'Toward a Revaluation of George Eliot's *The Mill on the Floss*', NCF 11 (1956), pp. 18–31; Reva Stump, *Movement and Vision in George Eliot's Novels* (Seattle: University of Washington Press, 1959), chapters 5–6; George Levine, 'Intelligence as Deception: *The Mill on the Floss*', PMLA 80 (1965), pp. 402–9. Reviewing these debates in 1972, John Hagan persuasively argued that the relationship between Maggie and Tom is the central axis of the novel — and from a biographical perspective, this coheres with Eliot's reminiscence and recalibration of her relationship with Isaac Evans at this time: see 'A Reinterpretation of *The Mill on the Floss*', PMLA 87 (1972), pp. 53–63. Hagan argued that 'the whole of Maggie's story must be seen with reference to her tragic relationship with Tom' (p. 62), while William Steinhoff and Jerome Thale read it as 'a tragedy of repression and regression' (p. 53) and George Levine, Bernard Paris and Reva Stump emphasized Maggie's struggle to overcome her flawed character and argued that 'her destiny consists chiefly of this process of spiritual development' (p. 55).

6. MOTHERHOOD

p. 109 *'To Marian Evans Lewes* ...': see Haight's note in GEL III, p. 240.

p. 110 *'rock the cradle* ...': GEL III, p. 117 (George Lewes to John Blackwood, Wandsworth, 22 July 1859). See also GEL IV, p. 309 (letter to John Blackwood, London, 11 September 1866), where Eliot describes *Felix Holt* as her 'youngest born'; *'Magnificat anima mea!'*: Mary's song, in Latin translation, begins: *Magnificat anima mea Dominum*: 'My soul magnifies the Lord' — see Luke 1:46. Eliot's quotation leaves out 'Dominum', so it means simply 'my soul magnifies' or 'my soul praises'; *Lewes also had a book on the way*: *The Physiology of Common Life* was serialized in the *Cornhill Magazine* before being published in book form by Blackwood: see R. E. Smith, 'George Henry Lewes and His "Physiology of Common Life", 1859', *Proceedings of the Royal Society of Medicine*, vol. 53, no, 7 (1960), pp. 569–74; *'real holiday . . .'*: GEL III, p. 270 (George Lewes to Barbara Bodichon, Wandsworth, 6 March 1860); *'Ancient Bear . . .'*: LGHL I, p. 287 (George Lewes to Charles Lewes, Wandsworth, 7 July 1859); *The boys only learned of her existence in the summer of 1859*: see Haight, *George Eliot: A Biography*, p. 293; Ashton, *George Eliot: A Life*, p. 225. There is, however, one reference to 'Miss Evans' in a letter from Lewes to his eldest son Charles, written in November 1858. In this letter, sent for Charles's sixteenth birthday, Lewes writes: 'Miss Evans, who hopes you have not forgotten her more than she has forgotten you, gave me 5 francs for your *watch fund* the other day, as a birthday remembrance' — LGHL I, p. 280 (George Lewes to Charles Lewes, Richmond, 20 November 1858).

p. 111 *Lewes breezily filled letters to his sons with references to 'your mother'*: see, for example, GEL III, pp. 195–6 (George Lewes to his sons, Wandsworth, 10 November 1859); *'You are an excellent correspondent . . .'*: GEL III, p. 127 (letter to Charles Lewes, Wandsworth, 30 July 1859). It is interesting that she signed herself Marian Lewes in her letters to Charles; at this time, she insisted, to Charles Bray among others, that 'my name is Marian Evans Lewes' — see GEL III, p. 111 (letter to Charles Bray, Wandsworth, 5 July 1859); *'Good by, dear Charles . . .'*: GEL III, p. 179 (letter to Charles Lewes, Wandsworth, 7 October 1859).

p. 112 *'feeling a sort of rapture . . .'*: see Simcox, *A Monument to the Memory of George Eliot*, p. 82 (29 April 1879); *Eliot did not write about these reasons, nor about wanting a child*: see Ashton, *George Eliot, A Life*, pp. 161, 402–3. In addition to citing some evidence for the couple's use of birth control, Ashton notes that 'the one aspect about Marian's life with Lewes about which no evidence remains, as far as I know, is how much, if at all, she regretted that her anomalous position dictated childlessness to her.' She wonders whether George Eliot's depiction of *Silas Marner*'s Nancy Lammeter, a 'noble-hearted, childless woman' who experiences her childlessness as the 'one main thread of painful experience' running through her marriage, reflects Eliot's own experience (p. 252). In later years Eliot took on a maternal role in relation to a series of young women who revered her; she told one of these women that 'in proportion as I profoundly rejoice that I did not bring a child into the world, I am conscious of having an unused stock of motherly tenderness, which sometimes overflows' — GEL V, p. 52 (letter to Emilia Pattison, The Priory, 10 August 1869). On knowledge of, and attitudes to, birth control among the Victorian medical profession, see Michael Mason, *The Making of Victorian Sexuality* (Oxford: Oxford University Press, 1994), pp. 175–96; Mason notes that until the 1870s there was both significant 'ignorance' and 'violent fastidiousness' about contraception; *Menstruating women*: see Elaine and English Showalter, 'Victorian Women and Menstruation', *Victorian Studies*, vol. 14, no. 1 (1970), pp. 83–9. These authors emphasize 'taboos' surrounding menstruation, noting that 'even Victorians as open-minded as Florence Nightingale or John Stuart Mill maintain an almost complete silence on the subject' (p. 83). The process of ovulation was only beginning to be scientifically understood in 1845, and was widely represented — invariably by male experts — as incapacitating. In the middle years of the nineteenth century, 'scientific fact and scientific theory were being influenced by the prevailed social or ethical doctrine of women's inferiority'; the Showalters quote James MacGrigor Allan, an 'ardent anti-feminist' who in 1869 explained to the Anthropological Society of London that 'although the duration of the menstrual period differs greatly according to race, temperament, and health ... women are unwell, from this cause, on average two days in the month, or say one month in the year. At such times, women are unfit for any great mental or physical labour. They suffer under a languor and depression which disqualify them from thought or action, and render it extremely doubtful how far they can be considered responsible beings while the crisis lasts. Much of the inconsequent conduct of women, their petulance, caprice, and irritability, may be traced directly to this cause. It is not improbably that instances of feminine cruelty (which startle us as so inconsistent with the normal gentleness of the sex) are attributable to mental excitement caused by this periodical illness' (p. 85). It is not surprising that some modern feminists responded to this kind of moralizing by rejecting the idea that menstruation temporarily alters a woman's intellectual, emotional and physical condition, and thereby suppressing the experience of menstruation and refusing to let it intrude into the public or professional lives of pre-menopausal women. More earthy strands of feminist movement seek to reconnect modern women with their menstrual experience, and treat it as a source of distinctively feminine insight: see, for example, Alexandra Pope and Sjanie Hugo Wurltizter, *Wild Power: Discover the Magic of Your Menstrual Cycle and Awaken the Feminine Path to Power* (Carlsbad, CA: Hay House, 2017). Sheila Heti's 2018 novel *Motherhood* depicts an artist wrestling with the question of motherhood through different phases of her menstrual cycle.

p. 113 *'for twenty of the best years ...'*: G. H. Lewes, 'The Lady Novelists', *Westminster Review*, July 1852, quoted in Elaine and English Showalter, 'Victorian Women and Menstruation', p. 88. The Showalters suggest that since Lewes is discussing two childless female authors, Jane Austen and Charlotte Brontë, his remarks on women's 'broken' health allude to menstruation more than to motherhood; *'Your father and I ...'*: GEL III, p. 126 (letter to Charles Lewes, Wandsworth, 30 July 1859); *'I look forward to playing duets with you ...'*: GEL III, p. 125 (letter to Charles Lewes, Wandsworth, 30 July 1859); *Her second letter to Charles ...*: GEL III, p. 177 (letter to Charles Lewes, Wandsworth, 7 October 1859).

pp. 113–14 *'likely to be a poor correspondent ...'*: GEL III, p. 216 (letter to Charles Lewes, Wandsworth, 26 November 1859).

p. 114 *'Let us hope ...'*: GEL III, p. 242 (appendix to a letter from George Lewes to Charles Lewes, Wandsworth, 4 January 1860); *'make a new epoch in our domestic life ...'*: GEL III, p. 232 (letter to François d'Albert-Durade, Wandsworth, 6

December 1859); *'last bit of vagrancy . . .'*: GEL III, p. 238 (letter to Sara Hennell, Wandsworth, 30 December 1859). See also GEL III, p. 228 (letter to Barbara Bodichon, Wandsworth, 5 December 1859); *'We want to get away to Italy . . .'*: GEL III, p. 238 (letter to Sara Hennell, Wandsworth, 30 December 1859); p. 249 (letter to John Blackwood, Wandsworth, 12 January 1860).

pp. 114–15 *he wrote to Charles full of news . . .*: GEL III, pp. 273–5 (George Lewes to Charles Lewes, Wandsworth, 17 March 1860).

p. 115 *Even Lewes felt a twitch of anxiety*: a year later, he admitted that Eliot's relationship with his sons had been 'one of the rocks ahead' — GEL III, p. 421 (George Lewes to John Blackwood, Florence, 28 May 1861).

p. 116 *'hearts set on Italy and Italian skies'*: GEL III, p. 273 (George Lewes Lewes to Charles Lewes, Wandsworth, 17 March 1860); *'The human bustle and confusion . . .'*: *Journals*, p. 336 ('Recollections of Italy, 1860'). The journals' editors, Margaret Harris and Judith Johnston, note that Eliot 'constructs her Italian journey as a version of the Grand Tour inflected by English Romanticism. Her account acknowledges the class (aristocratic) and gender (male) implications of the Grand Tour, and is frequently cast in Romantic tropes of dream and transport . . . In a letter to John Blackwood she had described "the passage over the Mount Cenis, in the cramping diligence and traineau . . . with no food except a small loaf" [see GEL III, p. 285]. Such privations are ignored as [her "Recollections of Italy, 1860"] opens with the dramatic nocturnal scene in the Alps, launching an explicit account of crossing a boundary from the dullness of the mundane into the experience of heightened sensibility and romantic dream' (pp. 329–31); *'what gives beauty to every corner of the inhabited world . . .'*: *Journals*, pp. 338–40.

p. 117 *'there was nothing imposing to be seen'*: *Journals*, p. 342; *'the probable relations our "Rome visited" . . .'*: *Journals*, p. 341; *'from the depth of disappointment . . .'*: GEL III, p. 286 (letter to Maria Congreve, Rome, 4–6 April 1860); *'Oh, the beautiful men and women and children here! . . .'*: GEL III, pp. 287–8 (letter to Maria Congreve, Rome, 4–6 April 1860); *'Altogether, these ceremonies are a melancholy, hollow business . . .'*: GEL III, p. 288 (letter to Maria Congreve, Rome, 4–6 April 1860).

p. 118 *'sprinkled holy water . . .'*: from Lewes's journal, 7 April 1860. Quoted in Haight, *George Eliot: A Biography*, p. 324; *'perpetual noisy pic-nic'*: see GEL III, pp. 293–4 (letter to John Blackwood, Florence, 18 May 1860). On their use of guidebooks, see Anjte Anderson, 'Gendering Art History in the Victorian Age: Anna Jameson, Elizabeth Eastlake, and George Eliot in Florence' (MA thesis, University of Nebraska-Lincoln, 2020); *'As for me, I am thrown into a state . . .'*: GEL III, p. 294 (letter to John Blackwood, Florence, 18 May 1860); *'Polly at once caught the idea . . .'*: GEL III, p. 295 (George Lewes's journal, 21 May 1860).

p. 120 *Women were not allowed into the corridors and dormitories . . .*: see Anderson, 'Gendering Art History in the Victorian Age', pp. 151, 155; Andrew Thompson, 'George Eliot's Florentine Notes: An Edition of the Notebook Held at the British

Library', *George Eliot–George Henry Lewes Studies* vol. 70, no. 1, 2018, pp. 1–86, pp. 18–19.

p. 121 *following in the footsteps of . . . Anna Jameson*: Eliot had first read Anna Jameson in the 1840s: see GEL I, p. 36. In August and September 1861, when she was intensively researching *Romola*, she read Jameson's *Sacred and Legendary Art*: see *Journals*, pp. 100–101.

pp. 121–2 *'Has any woman in the world been so infringed upon . . .'*: S. Kierkegaard, *Fear and Trembling*, trans. Howard V. Hong and Edna H. Hong (Princeton, IN: Princeton University Press, 1983), p. 65.

p. 122 *the Book of Wisdom*: another Septuagint text, also associated with Mary, is from the Book of Sirach, or Ecclesiasticus: 'Wisdom will come to meet him like a mother, and receive him like a virgin bride' (15:1–2); *'a mother-goddess . . .'*: Anna Brownell Jameson, *Legends of the Madonna* (London: Hutchinson & Co., 1866), p. 4; *Many early worshippers of Mary were women*: in the fourth century, St Justina of Antioch sought Mary's protection when a powerful man tried to seduce her, and her prayers were answered; a migrant sect of Thracian women in Arabia, who offered honey cakes to Mary as if she were divine, were condemned as heretics by leaders of the Christian church: see *Legends of the Madonna*, pp. 5–6; *'hope in a higher as well as a gentler power . . .'*: *Legends of the Madonna*, p. 4; *'there she stands — the transfigured woman . . .'*: *Legends of the Madonna*, p. 34. Jameson found her response to the Sistine Madonna echoed in Wordsworth's poem 'The Virgin', from his 1822 *Ecclesiastical Sonnets*:

> Mother! Whose virgin bosom was uncrost
> With the least shade of thought to sin allied!
> Woman! Above all women glorified;
> Our tainted nature's solitary boast;
> Purer than foam on central ocean tost;
> Brighter than eastern skies at daybreak strewn
> With fancied roses, than the unblemish'd moon
> Before her wane begins on heaven's blue coast,
> Thy image falls to earth. Yet some I ween,
> Not unforgiven, the suppliant knee might bend,
> As to a visible Power, in which did blend
> All that was mix'd and reconcil'd in thee,
> Of mother's love with maiden purity,
> Of high with low, celestial with terrene.

p. 123 *an echo of our own mother's face . . .*: George Eliot gestures to this maternal beauty in *Daniel Deronda*, when Mirah describes her earliest memory: 'I remember my mother's face better than anything . . . I think my life began with waking up and loving my mother's face: it was so near to me, and her arms were round me, and she sang to me' — p. 210 (Chapter 20).

p. 124 *a week in Venice*: see Haight, *George Eliot: A Biography*, p. 329; *'Of all dreamy delights . . .'*: *Journals*, pp. 362–3; *Thornton, the most assertive of the three, had written to Lewes*: see Haight, *George Eliot: A Biography*, pp. 329–30; Bodenheimer, *The Real Life of Mary Ann Evans*, p. 198; *'It was a great delight to me . . .'*: GEL III, pp. 308–9 (George Lewes's journal, Geneva, 26 June 1860).

p. 125 *She had enjoyed being 'indulged' . . .*: GEL I, p. 328 (letter to Fanny Houghton, Geneva, 9 February 1850); see also pp. 316–17 (letter to Charles and Cara Bray, Geneva, 24 October 1849): 'I really can almost say I have never enjoyed a more complete bien-être in my life than during the last fortnight. For M. D'Albert I love him already as if he were a father and brother both,' she wrote after moving into their house. Before she lodged with the D'Alberts, Eliot stayed in a pension, where several older female guests doted on her in a motherly way — see GEL I, pp. 292, 296, 301, 307, 308; *'Does it ever happen to you now to think of a certain Englishwoman . . .'*: GEL III, pp. 186–7 (letter to François D'Albert-Durade, Wandsworth, 18 October 1859); *Tant que je vous connaissais*: GEL III, p. 186 (François D'Albert-Durade to George Eliot, 23 October 1859).

p. 126 *'I wish you were Mrs Lewes . . .'*: GEL III, p. 197 (Elizabeth Gaskell to George Eliot, Whitby, 10 November 1859); *Queen Victoria was re-reading Adam Bede*: see *Journals*, p. 87; Haight, *George Eliot: A Biography*, pp. 335–6; *'For the last six years I have ceased to be "Miss Evans" . . .'*: GEL III, p. 396 (letter to Clementia Taylor, London, 1 April 1861). Nancy Henry observes that letters such as these 'seem to make parenthood a moral value that gave Eliot a recognisable social position as mother of her husband's sons, normalising her irregular relationship with Lewes and recalling her own mother's role as stepmother to her father's children by his previous marriage' — *The Life of George Eliot*, p. 127; *'anxiety and trembling . . .'*: *Journals*, pp. 86–7.

p. 127 *It was a sensitive, even beautiful portrait*: John Blackwood thought it a good portrait of Eliot; he bought it from Laurence, and hung it in the back parlour of his office in Edinburgh. See Haight, *George Eliot: A Biography*, p. 339, and Haight's note in GEL III, p. 401; *remedial 'tonics'*: *Journals*, p. 87. Nineteenth-century tonics often contained iron or quinine; some of them were laced with cocaine.

p. 128 *she was 'weighed down' by anxiety . . .*: GEL III, pp. 313–14 (letter to François d'Albert Durade, Wandsworth, 3 July 1860); *'have so far done our duty by the boys . . .'*: *Journals*, p. 87; *'came across my other plans . . .'*: GEL III, p. 371 (letter to John Blackwood, 16 Blandford Square, 12 January 1861). See also GEL III, p. 382 (letter to John Blackwood, 16 Blandford Square, 24 February 1861); *Journals*, p. 87.

p. 129 *Silas Marner . . . has his treasured hoard stolen . . .*: George Eliot, *Silas Marner* (London: Penguin Books, 1994), p. 135 (Chapter 12); *a poem that likened books to 'chests of gold . . .'*: see GEL I, p. 28 (letter to Maria Lewis, 17 July 1830); Bodenheimer, *The Real Life of Mary Ann Evans*. p. 205; *'What an Autumn! . . .'*: GEL III, p. 211 (letter to Charles Bray, 21 November 1859); *'I have no memory of an autumn so disappointing . . .*': GEL III, p. 216 (letter to Charles Lewes, Wandsworth, 26 November 1859).

p. 130 *Silas is 'so confused . . .*': *Silas Marner*, p. 150 (Chapter 14). The symbolic equivalence — and the displacement — in this novel between child and gold, parental love and money, has far-reaching political implications. In her essay 'Love and Gold' the sociologist Arlie Russell Hochschild analyses the effects of global capitalism on women's lives, arguing that care for children has become a 'resource [extracted] from the Third World in order to enrich the First World' (p. 26) — see *Global Woman*, eds. Barbara Ehrenreich and Arlie Russell Hochschild (London: Granta, 2002), pp. 15–30; *The story's explicit moral . . .*: see *Silas Marner*, pp. 153–4 (Chapter 14). Nancy Henry observes that before the loss of his gold, Silas makes a 'fetish' of his money, and suggests that 'the figure of the miser revelling in his gold coins, which he keeps hidden and secretly takes out at night to finger and caress as a displacement for all other pleasures (sexual and communal) and beliefs (religious or moral), seems to epitomise the conflicted feeling Eliot had about her own growing wealth' — *The Life of George Eliot*, p. 126; *Silas gains infinitely more than he lost*: see *Silas Marner*, pp. 158–60 (Chapter 14). Stéphanie Drouet-Richet suggests that *Silas Marner* 'becomes a parable of the primacy of the life of the affections over a life of work and material goods' — 'Questioning Motherhood: Figures of Domesticity and Emancipation in George Eliot's Fiction', *Études anglaises* vol. 73 (2020), pp. 84–96. See also Henry, *The Life of George Eliot*, p. 127.

7. DISILLUSION

p. 135 *Blandford Square*: see Edward Walford, *Old and New London: Volume 5* (London: Cassell, Petter and Galpin, 1878), pp. 254–2. Marylebone Station was built on the site in the 1890s, and Blandford Square is now a small estate of 1960s brick flats next to the railway lines; *Eliot and Lewes often walked north-east . . . or south-east*: see GEL III, pp. 363–4 (letter to Maria Congreve, London, 7 December 1860); p. 381 (letter to Sara Hennell, 16 Blandford Square, 20 February 1861); p. 388 (letter to Barbara Bodichon, 16 Blandford Square, 11 March 1861); *the two women tried out services*: see *Journals*, pp. 98–9: during the summer of 1861 Eliot mentions attending the Unitarian Chapel in Little Portland Street; St Margaret's Church (in Westminster); St Peter's Church in Vere Street. See GEL III, p. 433 (letter to Sara Hennell, 16 Blandford Square, 2 July 1861): 'I can endure any amount of sitting in churches and chapels when I am not fidgetty about my companions, for I can dream and think without risk of interruption, and I should go to all sorts of places of worship if I could go alone.'; *two live-in servants*: it was normal for a small middle-class household to employ at least two servants. During the middle years of the nineteenth century servants were increasing in numbers, and a typical middle-class household with children employed 'the basic minimum of three domestics: cook, parlourmaid and housemaid, or cook, parlourmaid and nursemaid'; less affluent lower-middle-class families had to 'make do' with one general servant. See J. A. Banks and Olive Banks, *Feminism and Family Planning in Victorian England* (Liverpool: Liverpool University Press, 1964), p. 65; *'double solitude'. . .customary routine*: see GEL IV, p. 21 (letter to Sara Hennell, Blandford Square, 12 March 1862); p. 32 (letter to Cara Bray, 16 Blandford Square, 10 May 1862); *They bought a grand piano*: see *Journals*, p. 102 (3 October 1861): 'Today our new grand piano came — a great addition to our pleasures.'

p. 136 *Eliot did not like living in the city* . . .: GEL III, p. 450 (letter to Frau Karl Theodor Ernst von Siebold, 16 Blandford Square, 26 August 1861); p. 402 (letter to Barbara Bodichon, 16 Blandford Square, 9 April 1861); GEL IV, p. 4 (letter to François D'Albert-Durade, 16 Blandford Square, 2 January 1862). See also LGHL III, p. 43 (letter to François D'Albert-Durade, 16 Blandford Square, January 1861); *'much diminished by the gas and bad air'*: GEL III, p. 404 (letter to Sara Hennell, 16 Blandford Square, 12 April 1861); *For all the 'privileges' it conferred, London demanded 'sacrifices'*: GEL III, p. 404 (letter to Sara Hennell, 16 Blandford Square, 12 April 1861); *'to make a home for him . . .'*: GEL III, p. 449 (letter to Frau Karl Theodor Ernst von Siebold, 16 Blandford Square, 26 August 1861). This reflects the Victorian ethic whereby 'the middle-class mother was expressly enjoined . . . to devote herself to the moral development of her family'; to enable her to do so, domestic chores were delegated to household servants, i.e., working-class women — see Banks and Banks, *Feminism and Family Planning in Victorian England*, p. 62; *'we have all the blessings . . .'*: GEL IV, p. 4 (letter to François D'Albert-Durade, 16 Blandford Square, 2 January 1862); GEL III, p. 450 (letter to Frau Karl Theodor Ernst von Siebold, 16 Blandford Square, 26 August 1861); *'such domestic happiness . . .'*: GEL III, p. 421 (George Lewes to John Blackwood, Florence, 28 May 1861); *'As I often tell her . . .'*: GEL III, p. 420 (George Lewes to John Blackwood, Florence, 28 May 1861); *'could not tell how the feeling and knowledge came to her'*: GEL III, p. 427 (John Blackwood to his wife, London, 15 June 1861).

p. 137 *'too egoistic'*: *Journals*, p. 90 (19 June 1861); *Instead of writing her novel she devoured a history of Renaissance philosophy . . .*: see *Journals*, pp. 96–101; *'a painful way of getting knowledge'*: GEL III, p. 472 (letter to Theodosia Trollope, London, 10 December 1861). On Eliot's visits to the British Museum, see Susan David Bernstein, *Roomscape: Women Writers in the British Museum from George Eliot to Virginia Woolf* (Edinburgh: Edinburgh University Press), pp. 113–46. Bernstein notes the Reading Room's reputation as 'an unseemly collection of sneezes, wheezes, unscholarly women and lower-class men, a public space that was surely repugnant to George Eliot in late 1861'; she also speculates that Eliot's experience of 'dome consciousness' within this space was 'a blistering blend of imagined surveillance and judgement of both her writing and her lifestyle' (pp. 119–20). On panoptical architecture and surveillance, see Jeremy Bentham, *Panopticon, or, The Inspection House* (1791) and Michel Foucault, *Discipline and Punish* (1975); *She spent several afternoons there*: see *Journals*, pp. 105–9

(November 1861 to February 1862); *'buried' in old books*: GEL III, p. 430 (George Lewes to John Blackwood, 16 Blandford Square, 28 June 1861); GEL III, p. 435 (George Lewes to John Blackwood, 16 Blandford Square, 2 July 1861); *'trying to write, trying to construct . . .'*: *Journals*, p. 104 (31 October 1861); *she nearly decided to give up the Italian novel*: *Journals*, p. 104 (6 November 1861).

p. 137–8 *'Polly is still deep in her researches . . .'*: GEL III, pp. 473–4 (George Lewes to John Blackwood, 16 Blandford Square, 14 December 1861).

p. 138 *'flashes of hope . . .'*: *Journals*, p. 105 (8 December 1861); *'reproached' Eliot for procrastinating*: GEL III, p. 474 (John Blackwood to William Blackwood, London, 23 December 1861); *'I began my Novel of Romola'*: *Journals*, p. 107; *'the breath of cows and the scent of hay'*: GEL II, p. 387 (letter to John Blackwood, 17 October 1857); *the story . . .proposed by Lewes*: Susan M. Greenstein suggests that Eliot received Lewes's suggestion to write an historical novel about Savonarola as an 'assignment', and notes that 'from the first both George Eliot and Lewes saw the project in terms of an enormously successful genre, the historical romance', following the examples of Walter Scott and Edward Bulwer-Lytton — see 'The Question of Vocation: From *Romola* to *Middlemarch*', *Nineteenth-Century Fiction* vol. 35, no. 4 (1981), pp. 487–505, p. 495. However, Eliot and Lewes either conceived the project differently from the outset, or she quickly diverged from his view; when she finished *Romola*, Eliot said she had not intended it to be 'popular' — see GEL IV, p. 49 (letter to Sara Hennell, 16 Blandford Square, 14 July 1862). On the novels of Scott and Bulwer-Lytton as precursors to *Romola*, see Andrew Sanders, *The Victorian Historical Novel 1840–1880* (Basingstoke: Palgrave, 1978), pp. 168–8; Hugh Witemeyer, 'George Eliot's *Romola* and Bulwer-Lytton's *Rienzi*', *Studies in the Novel*, vol. 15, no. 1 (1983), pp. 62–73.

p. 140 *Plato's parable evokes a desire for truth*: see Jonathan Lear, 'Allegory and Myth in Plato's *Republic*' and 'The Psychic Efficacy of Plato's Cave' in *Wisdom Won from Illness: Essays in Philosophy and Psychoanalysis* (Cambridge, MA: Harvard University Press, 2017), pp. 206–43.

p. 142 *'dissidence between inward reality and outward seeming'*: George Eliot, *Romola* (London: Penguin Books, 1996), p. 525 (Chapter 64); *'Romola, you will look only at the images of our happiness . . .'*: *Romola*, pp. 200–201 (Chapter 20).

pp. 142–3 *'It was clear that their natures differed widely . . .'*: *Romola*, p. 244 (Chapter 27). Gillian Beer analyses Romola's avoidance of confrontation, writing that 'the failure to confront . . . is a strong temptation in marriage . . . In *Romola* George Eliot shows both how difficult is confrontation between intimates and for the first time relishes confrontation to the full: this empowers her imaginatively' — *George Eliot and the Woman Question* (Brighton: Edward Everett Root, 2019), pp. 121–5.

p. 143 *'She felt equal to any self-infliction . . .'*: *Romola*, p. 247 (Chapter 27); *'Poor Romola! . . .'*: *Romola*, p. 278 (Chapter 31).

p. 144 *'very important decisions have been made'*: Journals, p. 111 (23 May 1862); *'The going over to the enemy without giving me any warning . . .'*: GEL IV, p. 38 (John Blackwood to Joseph Langford, Sponden, 25 May 1862 and John Blackwood to William Blackwood). There is some snobbishness in this judgement about Lewes's 'voracity': Blackwood had inherited his wealth, and like others of his class he looked down on people who sought to make money. Lewes had a reputation for being greedy, at least among publishers. George Smith later recalled that 'Lewes was not so indifferent to money considerations as the woman of genius', and noted Lewes's 'disgust' when Eliot declined his £10,000 offer for artistic reasons — quoted in Collins (ed.), *George Eliot: Interviews and Recollections*, pp. 73–4. Lewes, however, told one friend that 'My main object in persuading her to consent to serial publication was not the unheard of magnificence of the offer, but the advantage to such a work of being read slowly & deliberately, instead of being galloped thro in three volumes' — LGHL II, p. 36 (George Lewes to W. M. W. Call, London, 5 July 1862); presumably this is one of the reasons he gave Eliot, as he tried to persuade her to accept Smith's offer. In 1859, on hearing a rumour that George Eliot had sold *The Mill on the Floss* to the publishers Lucas and Evans — who, like George Smith, first offered Lewes a publication contract before soliciting a work from George Eliot — Blackwood's colleague George Simpson had written, 'G.E. has sold herself to the highest bidder. I said very early that he was an avaricious soul, but even with this failing if he had known what dealing with Gentlemen was I think he would have explained the matter to Messrs B[lackwood] before accepting the offer of another party' — GEL III, pp. 203–4 (George Simpson to Joseph Langford, Edinburgh, 16 November 1859). A few days later, Simpson described Lewes's character as 'not high-minded' and his conduct as 'disingenuous' — GEL III, p. 209 (George Simpson to Joseph Langford, Edinburgh, 19 November 1859). At this time Lewes recorded in his journal that Eliot 'felt bound to give Blackwood the refusal' (GEL III, p. 203); John Blackwood felt that 'she is determined to stand by us' (GEL III, p. 233, John Blackwood to William Blackwood, London, 7 December 1859); *'This made me think about money . . .'*: Journals, p. 108 (23 January 1861); *'the most magnificent offer ever yet made for a novel' . . .*: GEL IV, p. 17 (George Lewes's journal, 27 February 1862); Journals, pp. 110–11 (27 February and 23 May 1862); Collins (ed.), *George Eliot: Interviews and Recollections*, p. 74; *'Nightmare of the Serial . . .'*: GEL III, p. 236 (letter to John Blackwood, Wandsworth, 20 December 1859).

p. 145 *'I cannot consent to begin publication . . .'*: Journals, p. 110 (1 March 1862); *he accepted the position of 'chief Literary Adviser . . .'*: GEL IV, p. 24 (George Lewes's journal, 8 April 1862); p. 29 (George Lewes's journal, 8 May 1862); p. 31 (George Lewes to Charles Lewes, London, 10 May 1862). The £600 salary is equivalent to about £55,000 today. *'If I join you my first thought naturally will be the strength of the Magazine . . .'*: LGHL II, pp. 33–4 (George Lewes to George Smith, London, 3 May 1862). Lewes prefaces these remarks by noting that he has 'not mentioned it to Mrs Lewes', and tells Smith 'Don't say a word about it' in front of her when he comes to visit later that week; *'one of the softest and most agreeable voices . . .'*: Collins (ed.), *George Eliot: Interviews and Recollections*, p. 73 (quoting from George Smith's recollections); *After a long walk with Lewes . . .*: On 18 May Lewes noted in his journal that they walked to Hampstead, discussing Smith's offer; on 19 May 'Smith called, and we finally settled about the publication of *Romola* which is to begin in July' — see GEL IV, p. 35.

p. 146 *'in the perfect spirit of gentlemanliness and good feeling'*: *Journals*, p. 111 (23 March 1862); *'under all the circumstances she had felt . . .'*: GEL IV, p. 44 (John Blackwood to William Blackwood, London, 18 June 1862); *'that subjection to her husband's mind . . .'*: *Romola* (Chapter 27), p. 246; *'as a loving woman must . . .'*: *Romola* (Chapter 27), p. 247.

p. 147 *'the triumphs of this century . . .'*: *Romola* (Chapter 5), pp. 52–3.

p. 147–8 *'bruised, despairing'*: *Romola* (Chapter 32), p. 283.

p. 148 *'subdued'; 'quivering'*: *Romola* (Chapter 27), p. 248; *'all that sense of power over a wife . . .'*: *Romola* (Chapter 31), p. 276; *'the desolation of her life . . .'*: *Romola*, pp. 315–16 (Chapter 36). George Eliot's description of the church bells' 'demonic peal of triumph' at Romola's misery echoes Eliot's description, shortly after finishing the novel, of the city's effects on her mental health: 'The wide sky, the *not*-London, makes a new creature of me in half an hour. I wonder then why I am ever depressed — why I am so shaken by agitations. I come back to London, and again the air is full of demons' — GEL IV, p. 102 (letter to Barbara Bodichon, 16 Blandford Square, 19 August 1863); *'the most learned woman in the world . . .'*: *Romola*, p. 322 (Chapter 36). Cassandra Fedele was active as a scholar, writer and orator when she was a young woman, between 1487 and 1498; *Romola* opens in 1492, and it is 1494 when Romola contemplates travelling to Venice to learn from Fedele. Fedele married in 1498, when she was thirty-four, and after this wrote very little — see *Cassandra Fedele: Letters and Orations*, ed. and trans. Diana Robin (Chicago, ILL: University of Chicago Press, 2000); *seeking a 'new life . . .'*: *Romola*, pp. 328, 330 (chapter 37); *'no human presence . . .'*: *Romola*, p. 355 (chapter 40).

pp. 148–9 *'You are Romola de' Bardi, wife of Tito Melema . . .'*: *Romola*, pp. 355–6, 360, 362 (Chapter 40). See Greenstein, 'The Question of Vocation: From *Romola* to *Middlemarch*', pp. 487–505.

p. 149 *'Father, I will be guided . . .'*: *Romola*, p. 319 (Chapter 36). Mary Gosselink De Jong observes that 'As a woman in a sexist society [Romola] has learned to be passive and submissive; even her suicide is such ("Romola could not directly seek death . . . She could only wish that death would come")' — '*Romola*: A Bildungsroman for Feminists?', *South Atlantic Review* vol. 49, no. 4 (1984), pp. 75–90, p. 79; *'inexorable external identity'*: *Romola*, p. 324 (Chapter 36); *One night they argue in the street . . .*: *Romola*, p. 405–6 (Chapter 46).

pp. 149–50 *'She looked up at him with that submission in her glance . . .'*: *Romola*, pp. 411–12 (Chapter 48).

p. 150 *'Marriage must be a relation either of sympathy or of conquest'*: *Romola*, pp. 413–14 (Chapter 48); *'need of direction even in small things'*: *Romola*, p. 363 (Chapter 41); *'something like a rope . . .'*: *Romola*, p. 389 (Chapter 44); *too much swayed by her feelings*: Nancy L. Paxton — for whom Romola is 'in many respects Eliot's most feminist hero' — connects these themes with John Stuart Mill's philosophy: 'In her presentation of Romola's private life with Tito, Eliot anatomizes the operation of that "passion or inclination" that is, according to J. S. Mill, "permanently incompatible" with woman's "moral power" in marriage, that impulse which renders women powerless in the patriarchal family that Comte — and [Herbert] Spencer — would normalize . . . By invoking this example from Florentine history, Eliot suggests how civil laws governing marriage have enhanced the authority of the husband at the wife's expenses, even when she possesses Romola's "large intelligence" and "penetrating moral vision".' On Tito's sale of Romola's father's library, Paxton argues that 'In describing how marriage laws buttress Tito's power and prevent Romola from talking any legal action to preserve her father's bequest, Eliot repeatedly characterises his exploitation as typical of "husbands," thus highlighting the patriarchal nature of the marriage laws in Renaissance Italy, laws which remained essentially intact, as Victorian feminists argued, in nineteenth-century England' — *George Eliot and Herbert Spencer: Feminism, Evolutionism, and the Reconstruction of Gender* (Princeton, NJ: Princeton University Press, 1991), pp. 123, 130. Susan Greenstein highlights Tito's efforts to 'control' Romola by a 'calculated attack on [her] reason . . . Like Gwendolen [Harleth, heroine of *Daniel Deronda*] later on, Romola learns that the wife who will not obey must be mad' — 'The Question of Vocation: From *Romola* to *Middlemarch*', p. 500; *'no compensation for the woman . . .'*: *Romola*, p. 500 (Chapter 61); *'orphaned'*: *Romola*, p. 504 (Chapter 61).

p. 151 *realism . . .which she had compared to seventeenth-century Dutch paintings*: see *Adam Bede*, Chapter 17; Daniel P. Gunn, 'Dutch Painting and the "Simple Truth" in *Adam Bede*', *Studies in the Novel* vol. 24, no. 4 (1992), pp. 366–80; Hugh Witemeyer, *George Eliot and the Visual Arts* (Yale, CN: Yale University Press, 1979); *a symbolist work*: see Felicia Bonaparte, *The Triptych and the Cross: The Central Myths of George Eliot's Poetic Imagination* (New York, NY: New York University Press, 1979): '[*Romola* is] a symbolic narrative in which every character, every event, every detail — every word, in fact — is an image in an intricate symbolic pattern' (p. 10); *a lonely Madonna*: The 'womanly labours' of caring for the poor and sick do not come naturally to Romola; in fact, they exhaust her and make her ill. Noting this, Nancy Paxton suggests that 'Romola assumes the role of Madonna . . . because her culture offers it as the only admissible one which will allow her to move freely about the city and still be regarded with respect . . . she ultimately recognises that this role, like that of Tito's "angel wife," simply disguises the actual reality of her powerlessness in Florentine society' — *George Eliot and Herbert Spencer*, p. 135; *a dark-skinned, black-eyed Jewish baby boy*: the baby is the son of Portuguese migrants who are fleeing the Inquisition. Since he is named 'Benedetto' (meaning 'blessed') the allusion to Spinoza is unmistakeable, Benedetto being the Italian equivalent of Spinoza's Hebrew and Latin names, Baruch and Benedict. Probing this allusion, Moira Gatens notes that in 1847 Marian Evans described Jesus as a 'Jewish philosopher' — see 'George Eliot's "Incarnation of the Divine" in *Romola* and Benedict

NOTES

Spinoza's '"Blessedness": A Double Reading', *George Eliot–George Henry Lewes Studies*, no. 52/53 (2007), pp. 72–92; p. 89; *'absently on the distant mountains...': Romola*, p. 581 (Epilogue); *a domestic tableau*: Nancy Paxton gives an optimistic reading of the closing scene: 'Finally, Romola creates a family that transcends the law of the father and recognizes a basis for moral resistance beyond it ... [She] claims the right to effect change, achieving and articulating a vision of moral law and social duty which honors not only the memory of Savonarola's acts of heroic resistance but also the sacredness of the maternal in herself' — *George Eliot and Herbert Spencer*, p. 140. However, David Kurnick emphasizes Romola's 'abstraction', which persists even in the Epilogue, noting that Romola's 'ideal state' is generally 'an absence from her own unfolding story' — see 'Abstraction and the Subject of the Novel: Drifting through *Romola*', *NOVEL: A Forum on Fiction* (2009), vol. 42, no. 3, pp. 490–96. Mary Gosselink De Jong is more willing to criticize George Eliot herself: 'Like countless women in her own and later times, Eliot apparently assumed that Romola must choose between love and work' — '*Romola*: A Bildungsroman for Feminists?', p. 84. As Gosselink De Jong points out, 'a reader's response to Romola's adoption of these dependents and abandonment of a public life tells that reader something about the kind of feminist he or she is'; her own proposal that Romola take Tito's family to Venice 'where she could work to support them' reflects the 1980s ideal of the 'career woman'; *'the Great Mother'* or *'the Kingdom of God'*: see *Romola*, pp. 504, 549 (chapters 61, 67). George Eliot's naming of cosmic divinity as 'the Great Mother' is striking; this echoes Anna Jameson's linking of Mary to pre-Christian goddesses in *Legends of the Madonna* and resonates with the critique of patriarchal religion put forward in the 1860s by the feminist Frances Power Cobbe: 'We have had enough of *man's* thoughts of God — of God first as the King, the "Man of War", the Demiurge, the Mover of all things, and then, at last, since Christian times, of God as the Father of the World ... But the woman's thought of God as the "Parent of Good, Almighty", who unites in one the father's care and the mother's tenderness, *that* we have never yet heard' — *Essays on the Pursuits of Women* (London: Emily Faithfull, 1863); *free to mourn at last*: when we are introduced to Romola early in the novel, we are told that she has 'inherited nothing but memories — memories of a dead mother, of a lost brother, of a blind father's happier times — memories of far-off light, love, and beauty' (p. 59, Chapter 6)); after her marriage battle is over, Romola relinquishes the 'burden of choice' and surrenders to grief: 'Memories hung upon her like the weight of broken wings that could never be lifted' (p. 504, Chapter 61). *Piero di Cosimo, a 'strange freakish painter'*: see Giorgio Vasari, *Lives of the Most Eminent Painters, Sculptors and Architects*, vol. IV, trans. Gaston du C. de Vere (London: Macmillan and Co. and the Medici Society, 1912–14), pp. 125–34. Lewes bought Eliot a copy of Vasari's book in October 1861 (see *Journals*, p. 102) and she used it for her portrayal of Piero di Cosimo.

p. 152 *Eliot and Lewes probably visited his Mary Magdalene Reading*: Eliot mentions visiting the Barberini Palace, which houses this painting, in her 'Recollections

323

of Italy': see *Journals*, p. 345. When she saw Frederic Leighton's first sketch of Romola for the *Cornhill* (see 'The Blind Scholar and His Daughter', above), she told him that 'I meant the hair to fall forward from behind the ears over the neck' — as it is in Piero di Cosimo's *Santa Maria Maddalena* — GEL IV, p. 40 (letter to Frederic Leighton, 16 Blandford Square, 4 June 1862). In Chapter 3 of *Romola*, the barber Nello shows Tito a sketch of three masks by Piero di Cosimo, one of which is 'a sorrowing Magdalen'; Barbara Hardy thinks this is a 'faint image' of Romola's face — see *The Novels of George Eliot* (London: Athlone Press, 1959), p. 176.

p. 153 **Tito as Virgil's Sinon**: see *Aeneid*, Book 2; Dante describes Sinon as 'the false Greek' and places him in the eighth circle of the Inferno among the 'falsifiers of words' (see *Romola*, p. 600).

p. 154 **When Romola visits Piero's house . . .**: see *Romola*, pp. 254–7 (Chapter 28); **Romola shares some of her characteristics with Eliot the woman**: many critics have identified George Eliot with Romola. Bonaparte describes *Romola* as a 'spiritual and intellectual autobiography' — *The Triptych and the Cross*, p. 54; Diane Sadoff suggests that Romola embodies George Eliot's suppressed desire to be free of male dominance — see *Monsters of Affection: Dickens, Eliot and Brontë on Fatherhood* (Baltimore, MD: Johns Hopkins University Press, 1982), pp. 92–4; Sadoff draws on Laura Comer Emery's analysis of *Romola* in *George Eliot's Creative Conflict: The Other Side of Silence* (Berkeley, CA: University of California Press, 1976) — see pp. 78–104 of Emery's book. In her psychoanalytic study *Transformation of Rage: Mourning and Creativity in George Eliot's Fiction* (New York, NY: New York University Press, 1997), Peggy Fitzhugh Johnstone suggests that Romola and Tito project separated psychological aspects of their author: 'they reflect the defensive processes of splitting and projection against the rage that followed from what I believe to be the author's renewed sense of loss following her family's estrangement, her sister Chrissey's death, and her new family's move into London' — see pp. 86–110 for the full interpretation; **'the spiritual blight that comes with No-faith'**: GEL IV, pp. 64–5 (letter to Barbara Bodichon, 16 Blandford Square, 26 November 1862). Carole Robinson argues that the dead father figures in *Romola* represent 'the ultimate absent authority, the banished God of Victorian agnosticism' — '*Romola*: A Reading of the Novel', *Victorian Studies* vol. 1, no. 6 (1962), pp. 29–42, p. 40.

p. 155 **'Dover Beach', written during this period**: the poem is thought to have been written during the 1850s, though it was not published until 1867.

p. 156 **'that force of outward symbols . . .'**: *Romola*, pp. 324–5 (Chapter 36); **'meditating' her unwritten novel**: Eliot described herself as 'meditating' *Romola* in November 1860: see *Journals*, p. 87 (28 November 1860).

p. 157 **'Heavy and good for nothing . . .'**: see *Journals*, pp. 114–17 (quoted entries at 17 December 1862; 25 June 1863). Susan Greenstein traces a parallel between the subject of the novel — Romola's 'vocational crisis' — and its author's experience of writing it: 'Notorious as the most arduously produced of George Eliot's novels, *Romola* suggests a crisis of vocational doubt . . . Together with the debilitating trials of *Romola*'s composition, the contours of the finished novel give evidence of a writer questioning the value of her work, struggling to convince herself of her authority to perform it, and considering the price that will be exacted from her in the loss of her maternal self if she perseveres' — 'The Question of Vocation: From *Romola* to *Middlemarch*', pp. 488–90. *Frederic Leighton . . .'knew Florence by heart . . .'*: GEL IV, p. 37 (George Lewes to Charles Lewes, 16 Blandford Square, 21 May 1862); p. 49 (letter to Sara Hennell, 18 Blandford Square, 14 July 1862); *Miss Evans (or Mrs Lewes) has a very striking countenance*: see Haight, *George Eliot: A Biography*, pp. 356–7; *'I am more gratified, I think . . .'*: GEL IV, p. 40 (letter to Frederic Leighton, 16 Blandford Square, 26 May 1862).

p. 158 *She described to Leighton the 'misery . . .'*: GEL IV, pp. 55–6 (letter to Frederic Leighton, 16 Blandford Square, 10 September 1862); *Sara Hennell . . .found Romola 'very, very beautiful . . .'*: GEL IV, pp. 103–4 (Sara Hennell to Marian Lewes, Coventry, 22 August 1863); *'No one speaks about her books to her, but me . . .'*: GEL IV, pp. 58–9 (George Lewes to Sara Hennell, 16 Blandford Square, 12 September 1862); *'snatched up' at least one letter . . .*: GEL IV, pp. 60–61 (letter to Sara Hennell, 16 Blandford Square, 5 October 1862); *'Very slight things make epochs in married life'*: *Romola*, p. 274 (chapter 31); *she did not intend Romola to be 'popular . . .'*: GEL IV, pp. 48–9 (letter to Sara Hennell, 16 Blandford Square, 14 July 1862).

p. 159 *'wonderful piece of painting . . .'*: Richard Holt Hutton, 'Romola', *Spectator*, 18 July 1863, pp. 17–19; *'of course if I had been called on to expound my own book . . .'*: GEL IV, pp. 96–7 (letter to Richard Holt Hutton, 8 August 1863); *'where the duty of obedience ends . . .'*: *Romola*, pp. 457, 468 (chapters 55, 56); *'it is a man's place to rule . . .'*: S. A. Sewell, *Woman and the Times We Live In* (Manchester: Tubbs and Brook, 1869), p. 28.

8. SUCCESS

p. 163 *the 'roar of London' was just a 'faint murmur'*: Collins, *George Eliot: Interviews and Recollections*, p. 95 (quoting from Henriette Field's *Home Sketches in France, and Other Papers*, 1875). See GEL V, p. 73: 'this N. W. region . . . is very healthy, there is a wider sky, and there are stations of the Underground Railway at short distances from each other. In a word, it is detestable; but less detestable than most parts of London and its suburbs' (letter to Emmanuel Deutsch, London, 18 December 1869); *Eliot's writing room . . .*: see Collins, *George Eliot: Interviews and Recollections*, pp. 233–4 (quoting Elizabeth Bruce, writing in the *Christian Leader*, 1881); *Owen Jones, the pioneering architect*: see George Eliot, 'The Grammar of Ornament' (review of Owen Jones's book of this title), *Fortnightly Review*, 15 May 1865, pp. 124–5. On the great expense of decorating The Priory, see LGHL II, pp. 48–9: 'Owen Jones is making a lovely thing of the Priory,' writes Lewes, 'But I trouble to think of the [illegible] Bill. The way he sacrifices furniture & walls is enough to make one's bankers book leap in its desk' (George Lewes to George Smith, November 1863).

p. 164 *a 'severe lecture' from Jones*: GEL IV, p. 116 (letter to Maria Congreve, The Priory, 28 November 1863); *'men and women of rank and reputation'*: Collins, *George Eliot: Interviews and Recollections*, p. 53 (from Frederic Harrison, 'Reminiscences of George Eliot', 1901); pp. 88–9 (from Julia Clara Byrne, *Gossip of the Century*, 1899). An illustration of the Priory drawing room appeared in *Harper's Monthly Magazine*, December 1880–May 1881, p. 918; *Every Sunday afternoon they were 'at home'* . . .: Collins (ed.), *George Eliot: Interviews and Recollections*, p. 90 (from Charles Walston, *Truth: An Essay in Moral Reconstruction*, 1919); *Illustrious visitors came* . . .: Collins (ed.), *George Eliot: Interviews and Recollections*, p. 88 (quoting Frederic Harrison's *Autobiographic Memoirs*, 1911); *'Lewes paced the floor the whole time* . . .': Collins (ed.), *George Eliot: Interviews and Recollections*, p. 99 (from Sophia Kovalevskaia, 'A Memoir of George Eliot'); *Many guests reported a similar sequence of impressions on meeting her* . . .: see Collins (ed.), *George Eliot: Interviews and Recollections*, pp. 76, 79, 81, 82, 94; *'a nervous intensity of expressive power* . . .': Collins (ed.), *George Eliot: Interviews and Recollections*, pp. 56, 62, 68; see also p. 92, where the writer Philip Gilbert Hamilton describes debating with her about Comte's philosophy and feeling the effects of her 'singular power'.

p. 165 *'religious services'*: GEL V, p. 29 (George Lewes to John Blackwood, The Priory, 7 May 1869); *his ugliness 'redeemed'*: Collins (ed.), *George Eliot: Interviews and Recollections*, p. 91; *'worship', 'adoration' and 'devotion'*: Collins (ed.), *George Eliot: Interviews and Recollections*, pp. 67, 69, 91, 99.

pp. 165–6 *One visitor thought the drawing room itself was like a shrine*: Collins (ed.), *George Eliot: Interviews and Recollections*, pp. 99, 69.

p. 166 *'She was his chief topic of conversation* . . .': Collins (ed.), *George Eliot: Interviews and Recollections*, p. 99.

p. 167 *'outrageously egotistical* . . .': Collins (ed.), *George Eliot: Interviews and Recollections*, p. 85; *tactless, vain and a little vulgar*: Collins (ed.), *George Eliot: Interviews and Recollections*, p. 78; *'where his tail ought to be'*: Lewes wrote to his mother during a visit to Berlin, 'If your son comes back "with his head where his tail ought to be" you must not be surprised; in any case you must expect him to have his head *turned* from all the flattery and attention which is momently paid him here. After writing to you on Tuesday, I went to the University Festival of which I spoke, and there found myself seated apart from the public among the Princes, Professors, Ambassadors, and persons covered with stars and decorations . . . [At the opera] we had seats in the box set apart for the Diplomatists at the House of Parliament' — GEL V, pp. 83–4 (George Lewes to Mrs Willim, Berlin, 28 March 1870). Lewes was especially impressed by royalty and aristocracy — see his triumphant account of a garden party he attended at the home of Henrietta Stanley, Countess of Airlie, in 1867: 'Nothing could exceed the attention with which I was treated. As the servant announced my name I heard a woman's voice say "Here he is", so that they had been talking about me. Lady

Amberley and Lady Airlie seemed anxious to introduce me to everyone, first to their whole family and then to all the more distinguished guests, so that I had to bow to more Lords and Ladies than I ever met before. Lady Stanley expressed great pleasure in seeing me, having as she said, read all my works, subscribed to the *Fortnightly* as soon as it appeared, and gave it up directly I gave it up' — quoted in Haight, *George Eliot: A Biography*, p. 392. In 1875 Lewes met the Queen of Holland at another of Lady Airlie's garden parties, and gloated to at least four correspondents that 'the Queen had expressed a special wish that I should be presented to her', while mocking the Queen's tedious conversation — see GEL VI, pp. 154–5, 157, 160 (George Lewes to Mary Cross, Alexander Main, John Blackwood, George Holyoake, July–August 1875); *they sniffed out her 'peasant' roots . . .*: George Smith wrote that 'She came of peasant parents, and there survived perhaps a peasant strain in her' (Collins (ed.), *George Eliot: Interviews and Recollections*, p. 82). 'Peasant' was of course an exaggeration: Robert Evans was a prosperous artisan who rose to the middle classes. But Smith's remark indicates a perception among some people that Eliot and Lewes had risen beyond their natural social level. *'Biology — the science of Life . . .'*: G. H. Lewes, *Studies in Animal Life* (London: Smith, Elder & Co., 1862), p. 2. As Lewes explained in his later work *Problems of Life and Mind*, the term 'biology' was 'proposed independently yet simultaneously in Germany and France, in the year 1802, by Treviranus and Lamarck . . . Yet only of late years has it gained general acceptance in France and England' — *The Physical Basis of Mind, Being the Second Series of Problems of Life and Mind*, p. 6 (London: Trübner and Co., 1877).

p. 168 *'Life is the dynamical condition of the organism . . .'*: G. H. Lewes, *Aristotle: A Chapter in the History of Science* (London: Smith, Elder & Co., 1864), pp. 230–31; *the Fortnightly Review, a highbrow journal . . .*: see Ashton, *G. H. Lewes*, pp. 224–8 *an essay on rationalism and witchcraft*: this is a review of W. E. H. Lecky's *History of the Rise and Influence of the Spirit of Rationalism in Europe*, in which Eliot pays particular attention to witches and persecution: see *The Fortnightly Review*, ed. George Henry Lewes, vol. I (London, Chapman and Hall, 1865), pp. 43–55; *'flatly received by the general public . . .'*: LGHL II, p. 46 (George Lewes's journal, 21 August 1863; George Lewes to George Smith, August 1863). *Romola* was highly praised by the progressive theologian F. D. Maurice, and also admired by Tennyson, Robert Browning and Richard Monckton Milnes (later Lord Houghton), among other eminent contemporaries; *the Cornhill had not made money on Romola*: the novel's lukewarm reception by the reading public also affected the *Cornhill*'s reputation and circulation: see LGHL II, pp. 49–50 and pp. 70–72, where Lewes discusses the 'steady decline in sale' of the magazine: 'I think if "Romola" had been an English story we should already have solved the problem. It has unfortunately not been so generally popular as I hoped & believed its intrinsic beauty would have made it' (George Lewes to George Smith, London, 1863, and 6 August 1864); *'painful disappointment . . .'*: *Journals*, p. 110 (23 May 1862).

p. 169 *'careless, slow and inefficient'*: George Lewes's journal, 17 May 1862; see Haight, *George Eliot: A Biography*, p. 34; *'the thought of marriage is always a solemn and melancholy thought to me . . .'*: GEL IV, pp. 154–5 (George Lewes's journal, 23 June 1864; George Eliot to François D'Albert-Durade, The Priory, 24 June 1864); *'Sometimes it requires an effort to feel affectionately . . .'*: GEL IV, p. 312 (letter to Sara Hennell, The Priory, 29 September 1866); *'at once amiable and troublesome . . .'*: GEL IV, p. 117 (letter to François D'Albert-Durade, The Priory, 28 November 1863); *dreaming of joining anti-imperialist freedom fighters abroad*: see Nancy Henry, *George Eliot and the British Empire* (Cambridge: Cambridge University Press, 2002), pp. 52–9.

p. 170 *Lewes looked forward to him earning an annual salary of £1200*: see Henry, *George Eliot and the British Empire*, p. 44; LGHL II, p. 41 (George Lewes to W. M. W. Call, London, January 1863); *'coarse men engaged in guerrilla warfare . . .'*: GEL IV, p. 117 (letter to François D'Albert-Durade, The Priory, 28 November 1863); *'nightmare of uncertainty'*: GEL IV, p. 106 (letter to Cara Bray and Sara Hennell, 16 Blandford Square, 1 September 1863); *'Conceive us, please, with three boys at home . . .'*: GEL IV, p. 94 (letter to Clementia Taylor, London, 30 July 1863); *'a dear companion . . .'*: GEL IV, p. 106 (letter to Cara Bray and Sara Hennell, 16 Blandford Square, 1 September 1863); *'He failed . . .'*: GEL IV, p. 117 (letter to François D'Albert-Durade, The Priory, 28 November 1863). See also p. 101 (letter to Barbara Bodichon, 16 Blandford Square, 19 August 1863); p. 105 (letter to Sara Hennell, 16 Blandford Square, 23 August 1863).

pp. 170–71 *'the relations of England with her colonies . . .'*: Caroline Bray, *The British Empire* (London: Longman, 1863), p. 34. See GEL IV, p. 120, for Eliot's response to Cara's book.

p. 171 *'a serious deterioration of the race . . .'*: Bray, *The British Empire*, pp. 348–51; *Dickens . . . sent four of his six sons . . . to the colonies*: see Henry, *George Eliot and the British Empire*, pp. 61–3. Anthony Trollope's second son was also sent to the colonies: he emigrated to Australia when he was eighteen. Henry writes that 'Like Eliot and Lewes, Trollope and Dickens had read a great deal about the colonies, but their sons were as ill-prepared for colonial careers as were the Lewes boys'; she suggests that during the 1850s and 1860s (when all these boys were sent to British colonies) the need to prepare middle-class sons for emigration was not yet recognized as a national problem (pp. 48, 61). See Patrick A. Dunae, 'Education, Emigration and the Empire: The Colonial College, 1887–1095' in *'Benefits Bestowed'? Education and British Imperialism*, ed. J. A. Mangan (Manchester: Manchester University Press, 1998), pp. 193–210; *Lewes thought about sending Thornton to Canada . . .*: GEL IV, p. 112 (George Lewes's journal, 1 November 1863).

pp. 171–2 *Cara Bray's textbook informed Victorian readers that Natal . . .*: Bray, *The British Empire*, pp. 34–5. On the economic and political volatility of Natal in the early 1860s, see *The Cambridge History of the British Empire*, ed. Eric A. Walker, vol. VIII, pp. 426–9. The word 'Kafir' — now considered an offensive racist term in South Africa — was at that time in common use. As Bray explains, 'Kafir is an Arabic word, meaning "infidel", and was applied originally by the Arabian traders of the Indian seas to the people dwelling on the east coast of Africa; and was adopted afterwards by the Portuguese, Dutch and English' (p. 349). The district between Cape Colony and Natal was called British Kaffraria.

p. 172 *'at last' shipped off to Natal*: GEL IV, p. 111 (George Lewes's journal, 1–13 November 1863). Thornton left England on 16 October (see GEL IV, p. 109); *'He went in excellent spirits . . .'*: GEL IV, p. 109 (letter to Sara Hennell, 16 October 1863); *Bertie, who had been 'backward' at school . . .*: GEL VIII, p. 153; see Bodenheimer, *The Real Life of Mary Ann Evans*, pp. 198–9; *'At last we have gained our quiet domesticity . . .'*: GEL IV, p. 117 (letter to François D' Albert-Durade, The Priory, 28 November 1863).

p. 173 *'by overwork and over-confidence'*: GEL VI, p. 85 (George Lewes to Elma Stuart, London, 26 October 1874); *'transcendent' skies*: Eliot and Lewes both used the adjective 'transcendent' in their letters from Spain: see GEL IV, pp. 346, 347, 350, 351; LGHL II, pp. 115–18. On the gypsy captain, see LGHL II, p. 118; *'A young maiden . . .'*: Cross III, pp. 42–4, from Eliot's notes on *The Spanish Gypsy*.

p. 174 *the same period as Romola*: both *Romola* and *The Spanish Gypsy* begin in 1492. For an analysis of the significance of that year, see Sylvia Wynter, '1492: A New World View' in *Race, Discourses and the Origins of the Americas*, eds. Vera Lawrence Hyatt and Rex Nettleford (Washington and London: Smithsonian Institute Press, 1995), pp. 5–57; *poetry, then seen as the highest literary art . . .*: see Henry, *The Life of George Eliot*, p. 174; *'for the first time in my serious authorship . . .'*: Journals, p. 122 (1 January 1865); *He had lost patience with the lengthening poem*: see Journals, p. 123; GEL IV, p. 412 (letter to John Blackwood, The Priory, 30 December 1867): '[Mr Lewes] urged me to put the Poem by (in 1865) on the ground of monotony'; *'in deep depression feeling powerless'*: Journals, p. 123 (25 March 1865); *'Dear George is all activity . . .'*: Journals, pp. 123–4 (25 March 1865); *'miserable over a new novel'*: Haight, *George Eliot: A Biography*, p. 383 (quoting from T. A. Trollope, *What I Remember*, 1887).

p. 175 *a new Divorce and Matrimonial Causes Act . . .*: in a letter written during her blossoming relationship with Lewes in the spring of 1853, Eliot mentions the 1853 Commission which led eventually to this reform of the divorce laws — see GEL II (letter to Sara Hennell, London, 28 March 1853): 'Lewes, as always, genial and amusing. He has quite won my liking, in spite of myself . . . Of course, Mr Bray highly approves the recommendations of the Commissioners on *Divorce*.' The juxtaposition hints that at this time she might have hoped new laws would enable Lewes to divorce. On the double standard enshrined in the 1857 Divorce Act, see Margaret Woodhouse, 'The Marriage and Divorce Bill of 1857', *American Journal of Legal History*, vol. 3, no. 3 (1959), pp. 260–75; Ann Sumner Holmes, 'The Double Standard in the English Divorce Laws, 1857–1923', *Law and Social Enquiry* vol. 20, no. 2 (1995), pp. 601–20. Holmes shows how such a double standard was implicit or explicit in many contributors to the parliamentary debates on the Bill pertaining to divorce and remarriage in 1857, and concludes that 'the belief that men were physically incapable of chastity made a husband's adultery more justifiable than a wife's' (p. 611). Those who argued for equality between the sexes at this time — an expedient alliance of feminists and moralists — insisted that men should be held to the same high moral standards as women, rather than that female adultery should also be tolerated. Divorce legislation was made more equal in the Matrimonial Causes Act of 1923, which allowed women to sue for divorce on the grounds of adultery alone, though husbands were still able to sue a co-respondent for damages while women were not; *'guilty of incestuous Adultery ...'*: the 1857 Divorce and Matrimonial Causes Act, Section 27, quoted in Holmes, 'The Double Standard in the English Divorce Laws, 1857–1923,' p. 602.

p. 176 *a specifically sexual guilt that must be proved in court*: discussing the theory advanced by Haight, and repeated by other biographers, that Lewes could not legally divorce Agnes because he had condoned her adultery by recognizing her first child by Thornton Hunt as his own, Henry notes that 'no biography offers evidence to prove that registering Edmund's birth constituted "condonation" of adultery' — Henry, *The Life of George Eliot*, pp. 98–101. Also see Haight, *George Eliot: A Biography* p. 132; Ashton, *G. H. Lewes*, pp. 99–100; Ashton, *George Eliot: A Life*, p. 102. The source of the suggestion that divorce was precluded because Lewes had condoned Agnes's adultery may be Eliza Lynn Linton's fictionalized memoir, *Autobiography of Christopher Kirkland* (1885). Linton, who tended to be critical of Eliot and Lewes, remarked that Lewes 'who afterwards posed as the fond husband betrayed by the trusted friend [Hunt], was, in the days when I first knew them all, the most pronounced Free-lover of the group, and openly took for himself the liberty he expressly sanctioned in his wife. [Lewes could not] go into the Divorce Court for his personal relief, because of that condonation and his own unclean hands ...' (p. 280). 'We can be certain', writes Henry, 'that no one (Lewes, Agnes, Hunt, Eliot) wished to be dragged through the courts and into the public limelight, exposing sensitive and ambiguous questions of sexual conduct and paternity that would be embarrassing to all parties and harmful to the many children now involved, not to mention the new author George Eliot, who came into being the same year as the Matrimonial Causes Act of 1857' (p. 101). *Lewes rightly thought it inferior ...*: GEL IV, p. 265 (George Lewes's journal, 1 June 1866); *John Blackwood took it for £5,000*: see GEL IV, p. 240; *'a failure'*: GEL IV, p. 274 (Joseph Langford to William Blackwood, London, 13 June 1866); *'I will take this yearning self ...'*: The Spanish Gypsy (Edinburgh and London: William Blackwood and Sons, 1879), p. 163.

p. 177 *'a race more outcast ...'*: The Spanish Gypsy, p. 112; *'worship'*: The Spanish Gypsy, p. 180; *'to be the angel ...'*: The Spanish Gypsy, p. 147; *'I belong to him who loves me ...'*: The Spanish Gypsy, p. 156; *'He would not go away ...'*: The Spanish Gypsy, p. 374; *'All love fears loss ...'*: The Spanish Gypsy, p. 155; *'There is no question as to its being good ...'*: GEL IV, p. 370 (John Blackwood to William Blackwood, 19 June 1867).

p. 178 *praising the beauty of its 'language and thoughts'*: GEL IV, p. 402 (John Blackwood to George Eliot, Edinburgh, 29 November 1867); *'fit for a*

Drawing-Room Table': GEL IV, p. 439 (George Simpson to William Blackwood, Edinburgh, 9 May 1868); '*admire what my husband is . . .*': GEL IV, p. 438 (letter to Cara Bray, The Priory, 7 May 1868); see also GEL IV, p. 355 (letter to John Blackwood, The Priory, 21 March 1867): '[I]t is not a work to get money by, but Mr Lewes urges and insists that is shall be done.' '*My poem has been a great source of added happiness . . .*': Journals, p. 133; '*I am a woman of about the same age . . .*': GEL IV, p. 417 (letter to Arthur Helps, London, 12 January 1868); '*as rich in blessings . . .*': Journals, p. 133.

p. 179 '*Times are still so bad . . .*': GEL VIII, pp. 343–5 (Thornton Lewes to George Lewes, Tent Hotel, Sand Sprint, 12 June–12 August 1865); '*This country is so fearfully unsettled . . .*': GEL VIII, pp. 351–2 (Thornton Lewes to George Lewes, Ladismith, 24 February 1866); '*almost eaten up by flies*': GEL VIII, pp. 368–9 (Thornton Lewes to George Lewes, Rouxville: a village on the Orange River, [Orange] Free State, 24 February 1866).

p. 180 '*given up the best fourth of their country . . .*': GEL VIII, p. 376 (Thornton Lewes to George Lewes, Ladismith, 2 June 1866); *Poor Bertie . . . found George Eliot's novels*: see Henry, *George Eliot and the British Empire*, p. 1 (Herbert Lewes to George Lewes, Cape Town, 14 October 1866); '*The Free State Govt. has broken its promises . . .*': GEL VIII, p. 390 (Thornton Lewes to George Lewes, Durban, 9 December 1866); *their 'magnificent mud mansion' burned to the ground*: see Henry, *George Eliot and the British Empire*, p. 71 (Thornton Lewes to George Eliot and George Lewes, 12 July 1867); '*in agony*'; '*so weak*': see Henry, *The Life of George Eliot*, p. 175 (Thornton Lewes to George Lewes, 16 September 1867); *a 'homeopathic cure . . .*': see Henry, *George Eliot and the British Empire*, p. 72 (Thornton Lewes to George Lewes, 9 March–26 April 1868). See also Henry, *The Life of George Eliot*, p. 175; '*There is still war in the Free State . . .*': see Henry, *George Eliot and the British Empire*, p. 72 (Herbert Lewes to George Eliot and George Lewes, 27 October 1867); '*our family is very prosperous . . .*': GEL IV, p. 419 (letter to François D'Albert-Durade, London, 30 January 1869).

p. 181 '*I am gradually wasting away . . .*': GEL VIII, p. 433–4 (Thornton Lewes to George Lewes, Wakkerstroom, 12 October 1868); *When Henry James turned up*: see Henry James, *The Middle Years* (New York: Charles Scribner's Sons, 1917), Chapter V.

p. 182 *His pain could be so excruciating . . .*: see GEL V, pp. 34–5, 46 (George Lewes's journal, 10–13 May 1869); Ashton, *G. H. Lewes*, p. 250; *Paget pronounced his case 'very serious*': GEL V, p. 40 (George Lewes's journal, 18 May 1869); '*our days have been broken into small fragments*': GEL V, p. 44 (letter to Cara Bray, 13 June 1869); *their life had resumed much of its usual routine*: see Journals, pp. 136–8: Eliot's reading during this time included Lucretius, Victor Hugo, Theocritus, Plato, Aristophanes and Shakespeare, as well as books on the history of French literature and the history of medicine; she also wrote eight sonnets, and 100 verses of *The Legend of Jubal*, as well as three chapters of *Middlemarch*, between June and September 1869. These journal entries complicate Rosemary

Ashton's claim that both Eliot and Lewes nursed Thornton 'day and night' (*G. H. Lewes*, p. 250); Ashton's biography of George Eliot similarly does not mention that Eliot was working hard throughout the period of Thornton's illness. '*A Novel called Middlemarch*': *Journals*, p. 134 (1 January 1869); '*interruptions*' *from Thornton . . .*: *Journals*, pp. 137–8; '*drifting away*': Ashton, *G. H. Lewes*, p. 250; '*Through the six months of his illness . . .*': *Journals*, p. 139; '*buried alive*': GEL VIII, p. 491 (Herbert Lewes to George Eliot, Wakkerstroom, 23 December 1870).

p. 183 *Bertie . . .was not encouraged to come home*: see Bodenheimer, *The Real Life of Mary Ann Evans*, pp. 225–7. In October 1875, a few months after Bertie's death, Eliot explained to her old friend François D'Albert-Durade that 'He had for some time been in delicate health, and we were afraid of urging him to come to England because his disease was of a nature to be encouraged by our fitful climate' — GEL VI, pp. 173–4 (letter to François D'Albert-Durade, The Priory, 13 October 1875); *Agnes Lewes was virtually erased from the family narrative*: Collins's *George Eliot: Interviews and Recollections* contains a reminiscence by Mary Huddy, who worked for Lewes's mother, Mrs Willim, suggesting that Agnes and her younger children (fathered by Thornton Hunt) were not allowed to visit Mrs Willim, 'that being the condition — as I was told afterwards — under which George Eliot would be introduced to her. The old lady extended a welcome to her son's clever companion, but to the end of her life . . . she regretted the loss of her daughter-in-law's loving attentions' (p. 60); '*a calamity . . .*': Collins, *George Eliot: Interviews and Recollections*, p. 58 (quoting from Moncure Daniel Conway's *Autobiography*, 1904). I have borrowed the phrase 'marriage resister' from Adrienne Rich's 'Compulsory Heterosexuality and Lesbian Existence', pp. 651–2; *perhaps they were genetically disposed to the illnesses that killed them*: Eliot herself suggested this in a letter to Sara Hennell: see GEL VI, p. 191. Several biographers take up this explanation for the deaths of Thornton and Bertie. '*That is how families get rid of troublesome sprigs*': *Middlemarch*, p. 380 (Chapter 38 — the 'troublesome sprig' in question is Will Ladislaw).

p. 184 '*must be borne with resignation . . .*': see GEL VI, p. 165 (letter to John Cross, Rickmansworth, 14 August 1875); Bodenheimer, *The Real Life of Mary Ann Evans*, p. 228; '*dual egotism*': see Simcox, *A Monument to the Memory of George Eliot*, p. 82 (29 April 1879).

9. PHILOSOPHY

p. 187 *Eliot donated £50*: see Haight, *George Eliot: A Biography*, pp. 396–7. The College for Women which opened in 1869 had five students; the college moved to Girton in 1873. Women were allowed to sit university examinations, but could not receive degrees until 1948. From 1872 until her death, Eliot also made a 'little subscription' (£2.2/- per year) to the Working Women's College, established in 1864 at Queen Square, Bloomsbury, by the feminist Elizabeth Malleson, a friend of Eliot — see LGHL III, pp. 46, 64; *Until the 1860s . . .*: Cambridge colleges began to allow Fellows to marry in the 1860s; Oxford passed a University Test Act in 1871 which permitted married men to become college Fellows. *'She lavished almost a mother's love . . .'*: GEL V, p. 69 (George Lewes to Thomas Trollope, London, 22 November 1869).

p. 188 *'The number of our birthdays to come . . .'*: GEL V, p. 68 (letter to Sara Hennell, London, 15 November 1869); p. 70 (letter to Barbara Bodichon, London, 25 November 1869); *'It seemed the light was never loved before . . .'*: *The Legend of Jubal and Other Poems*, p. 8. The last three lines quoted here are inscribed on the manuscript of the poetry collection published by Blackwood in 1874, prefaced by the words, 'To my beloved Husband, George Henry Lewes, whose cherishing tenderness for twenty years has alone made my work possible to me' — see Haight's note in GEL VI, p. 38; *'the stings of new ambition . . .'*: *The Legend of Jubal and Other Poems*, pp. 9–10; *'I think too much . . .'*: GEL V, p. 110 (letter to Charles Lewes, July 1870); *'make a few lives near to us . . .'*: GEL V, p. 76 (letter to Oscar Browning, January 1870); *'how diffusive your one little life can be'*: GEL V, p. 83 (letter to Jane Senior, March 1870). In 1873 Jane Senior joined the Civil Service as an inspector of workhouses, wrote a reforming report for the government, and co-founded an organization to support young working-class women, with the help of Eliot's friends Barbara Bodichon and Bessie Belloc (formerly Bessie Parkes) — see Sybil Oldfield, *Jeanie, an 'Army of One': Mrs Nassau Senior 1828–1877, The First Woman in Whitehall* (Hightown: Sussex Academic Press, 2008).

pp. 188–9 *the 'hungry ambition' and 'strong egoism . . .'*: GEL V, p. 125 (letter to Maria Congreve, December 1870).

p. 189 *At present the thought of you*: GEL V, pp. 106–7 (letter to Edith Bulwer-Lytton, Harrogate, 8 July 1870). Five years later, Eliot returned to this idea of an 'independent' delight in sunshine, but now it was interestingly modified to exclude certain dependencies: 'Sunshine becomes more and more of an independent joy to me — independent of everything but husband and health, which are rather weighty provisos' — GEL VI, p. 134 (letter to Elma Stuart, The Priory, 24 March 24 1875).

p. 190 *news of France and Prussia invading each other*: in September 1870 they spend several hours each day reading newspaper reports about the Franco-Prussian War — see GEL V, pp. 114–17. By mid-October, however, Eliot seemed fed up with their news consumption: 'Thoughts about the war are not sanitary, and they urge themselves through every other subject', she complained to Oscar Browning — GEL V, p. 118. *Jowett . . .sent Eliot and Lewes part of the manuscript*: see GEL V, p. 112 (letter to Sara Hennell, Limpsfield, 12 August 1870); *Lewes began revising his Biographical History of Philosophy*: see GEL V, p. 118 (letter to Oscar Browning, The Priory, 18 October 1870); p. 122 (letter to Sara Hennell, The Priory, 18 November 1870); Isobel Armstrong, 'George Eliot, Hegel, and *Middlemarch*', 19: *Interdisciplinary Studies in the Long Nineteenth Century* no. 29 (2020), pp. 5–11.

p. 191 *Hegel's works disclosed 'a world of relations'*: see G. H. Lewes, *The History of Philosophy from Thales to Comte*, vol. II, fourth edition (London: Longmans, Green and Co., 1871), p. 595; *his 'entirely rewritten' chapter*: see GEL V, p. 169 (letter to Cara Bray, Shottersmill, 25 July 1871). A few years later, Lewes described his relief at getting 'away from hated metaphysics into dear Biology and Psychology' — GEL VI, p. 125 (George Lewes to Alexander Main, The Priory, 12 February 1875); *'leaves all the questions for which Science is useful ...'*: G. H. Lewes, *The History of Philosophy from Thales to Comte*, vol. II, p. 597; *weighed the value of knowledge on a utilitarian scale*: in 1826 Henry Brougham founded the Society of Useful Knowledge, and the 1829 Royal Charter that established my own university, King's College London, refers to 'useful knowledge' and 'useful education'; *'In Astronomy, Physics ...'*: G. H. Lewes, *The History of Philosophy from Thales to Comte*, vol. II, p. 598. See also LGHL II, pp. 166–7: 'the radical worthlessness of Hegelianism lies in the complete absence of any pathway from the abstract to the concrete so that verification is impossible in general, & it is only when by accident Hegel is caught venturing into the scientific range that one can appreciate how absurd he is' (George Lewes to William Robertson Smith, Shottermill, 16 August 1871). *'I triumph or I fail ...'*: 'Armgart', *The Legend of Jubal and Other Poems*, p. 73; *'too much ambition ...'*: 'Armgart', *The Legend of Jubal and Other Poems*, pp. 75–6.

p. 192 *'almost total despair of future work'*: *Journals*, p. 141. On 4 August 1870, Eliot recorded beginning 'Armgart' 'under much depression'; on 27 October she wrote that since finishing the poem 'I have been continually suffering from headache and depression, with almost total despair of future work. I look into this little book now to assure myself that this is not unprecedented.'

p. 193 *Celia ...is a keen observer*: George Eliot accentuates Celia's empiricism: 'her marvellous quickness in observing a certain order of signs generally prepar[ed] her to expect such outward events as she had an interest in' (Chapter 5); Dorothea complains that Celia 'will look at human beings as if they were mere animal with a toilette' (Chapter 2); *'Here was a man who could understand ...'*: *Middlemarch*, pp. 22, 25 (chapters 2 and 3); *She notices his 'two white moles ...'*: *Middlemarch*, pp. 20, 48 (chapters 2 and 5).

pp. 193–4 *'It would be my duty to study ...'*: *Middlemarch*, p. 29 (Chapter 3).

p. 194 *'the glow of proud delight ...'*: *Middlemarch*, p. 45 (Chapter 5); *'something funereal'*: *Middlemarch*, p. 49 (Chapter 5); *'continually sliding into inward fits ...'*: *Middlemarch*, p. 197 (Chapter 20).

p. 195 *'by politely reaching a chair for her ...'*: *Middlemarch*, p. 198 (Chapter 20); *'How was it that in the weeks since her marriage ...'*: *Middlemarch*, pp. 195–6 (Chapter 20); *an 'irreproachable husband'*: *Middlemarch*, p. 199 (Chapter 20). 'And the deeper [Casaubon] went in domesticity the more did the sense of acquitting himself and acting with propriety predominate over any other satisfaction. Marriage, like religion and erudition, nay, like authorship itself, was fated to become an outward requirement, and Edward Casaubon was bent on fulfilling unimpeachably all requirements' (p. 280 (Chapter 29)).

p. 196 *'quite sure that no one could justly find fault with her'*: *Middlemarch*, p. 593 (Chapter 58).

pp. 196–7 *a short essay on Mary Wollstonecraft . . .*: 'Margaret Fuller and Mary Wollstonecraft', *The Leader* vol. VI, no. 290 (13 October 1855), pp. 988–9. Eliot's quotations from Mary Wollstonecraft refer to her 1792 work *The Vindication of the Rights of Woman* (New York: A. J. Matsell, 1833), pp. 182, 208.

p. 197 *Hegel's Phenomenology of Spirit*: see Armstrong, 'George Eliot, Hegel, and *Middlemarch*', which makes a compelling case for the profound influence of Hegel's *Phenomenology of Spirit* on both Eliot and Lewes. Armstrong notes that in February 1871 — when Eliot was putting together the previously separate elements of *Middlemarch* — Lewes realized, too late for his revised chapter on Hegel, the importance of the *Phenomenology* (p. 1). She then presents a close reading of *Middlemarch* that demonstrates both its affinity with Hegel's analysis of 'Lordship and bondage', and its 'highly critical and demystifying reading' of the *Phenomenology* (pp. 13–22). Armstrong perceives a development from Eliot's treatment of the 'sheer motiveless violence of domestic abuse' in *Janet's Repentance* to the intelligible exposition of marital violence achieved in *Middlemarch*, where 'the Hegelian structure of oppression makes this violence readable'; she argues that Eliot's 'innovation — to read the master/slave through the passional relations of modern marriage and its manifold economic and other subjugations . . . shifts the context of Lordship and Bondage from a political to a psychological or existential register' (pp. 15, 18). Of course one might argue that, precisely because of these power dynamics, marriage is as 'political' as any other social relationship.

pp. 197–8 *'Lydgate, forgetting everything else . . .'*: *Middlemarch*, pp. 301–2 (Chapter 31).

p. 198 *Laure, an actress who actually murders her husband*: when Lydgate begins to be alienated from Rosamond he associates her with Laure: 'His mind glancing back to Laure while he looked at Rosamond, he said inwardly, "Would *she* kill me because I wearied her?"' (*Middlemarch*, p. 592 (Chapter 58)). Later he calls Rosamond his basil plant, because 'basil was a plant which had flourished wonderfully on a murdered man's brains' (p. 835, Finale); *a 'life-and-death struggle . . .'*: G. W. F. Hegel, *Phenomenology of Spirit* (Oxford: Oxford University Press, 1979), §187; see Armstrong, pp. 19–20; *'Mercifully grant that we may grow aged together'*: *Middlemarch*, p. 741 (Chapter 74); see the Book of Tobit, Chapter 8, Verse 7. *George Eliot examines the interplay of philosophical and erotic passions*: for both Dorothea and Lydate, philosophical passion conflicts with erotic passion. In Dorothea's case, philosophical passion overrides erotic passion, and thus she marries Casaubon; in Lydgate's case, erotic passion overrides philosophical passion, and thus he marries Rosamond. Both passions prove to be self-destructive, and also damaging to their chosen partners. Neither character is offered the choice of leaving their partner. The difference between their fates seems to be decided merely by fortune: Dorothea gets a second chance at a more life-enhancing relationship, while Lydgate does not.

p. 199 *her 'vivid sympathetic experience returned to her . . .'*: *Middlemarch*, p. 788 (Chapter 80); *'imagined otherwise'*: *Middlemarch*, p. 469, Chapter 47. Barbara Hardy discusses this theme in a chapter titled 'Possibilities', and draws attention to the phrase 'imagined otherwise'. Hardy finds in all George Eliot's novels a tendency to keep a character's 'alternative life in mind, having a ghostly presence within the actuality of an event, and playing some part in the final impression'. Hardy recognizes that 'the unplayed possibilities emerge everywhere in *Middlemarch*', and argues that 'the world of unrealised possibility is most prominent in *Daniel Deronda*' — see *The Novels of George Eliot*, pp. 135–54, especially pp. 135, 144, 147–8.

p. 200 *The biblical myth about the origin of sin*: see Genesis 2:4 to 3:6. Until 2:5 the description of God making the 'earth and heavens' is wholly affirmative, then suddenly the focus shifts to what is missing — there are no plants, no rain and no one to work the ground — and this awareness of what is *not* seems to lead directly to the creation of a man, Adam (2:5–7). Again, though, something is missing — 'it is not good for the man to be alone' — so God makes a woman, Eve, out of Adam's rib (2:18–22). This episode concludes with a justification of marriage: 'This is why a man leaves his father and mother and is united to his wife, and they become one flesh' (2:24); *a 'ceaseless activity' of form in flux*: see Hegel, *Phenomenology of Spirit*, Preface, §2.

p. 201 *'A friend, to whose revision this chapter is much indebted . . .'*: G. H. Lewes, *The History of Philosophy from Thales to Comte*, vol. II, p. 598; *Oxford Hegelians*: see Armstrong, 'George Eliot, Hegel, and *Middlemarch*', pp. 8–10; *'Do not imagine his sickly aspect . . .'*: *Middlemarch*, p. 123 (Chapter 13). These insights on negation and linguistic form in *Middlemarch* are indebted to Debra Gettelman's talk on this topic '*Middlemarch*'s Negations', which I heard at the George Eliot Bicentenary Conference at the University of Leicester in 2018: Gettelman cited this sentence about Bulstrode, as well as the novel's closing sentences, but there are many other examples to be found in *Middlemarch*. *'I will not even refer to Dido or Zenobia'*: *Middlemarch*, p. 550 (Chapter 55).

p. 202 *'the growing good of the world . . .'*: *Middlemarch*, p. 838 (Finale). See above, and GEL V, p. 76 (letter to Oscar Browning, The Priory, January 1870). Likewise, George Eliot's description of Dorothea's 'diffusive' goodness echoes her advice to Jane Senior about her 'diffusive . . . little life' cited earlier in this chapter. This was, Eliot suggested, the ethic she was trying to follow: 'One lives by faith in human goodness, the only guarantee that there can be any other sort of goodness in the universe' — GEL V, p. 83 (letter to Jane Senior, The Priory, March 1870); *'but still — it could not be fairly called wooing . . .'*: *Middlemarch*, p. 633 (Chapter 62).

p. 203 *'never tempt her deliberate thought . . .'*: *Middlemarch*, p. 580 (Chapter 57); *Sir James Chettam feels jealous*: near the end of *Middlemarch*, Sir James feels 'a jealous repugnance hardly less in Ladislaw's case than in Casaubon's' (p. 818, Chapter 84) — in other words, he is almost as jealous as he was at the beginning of the novel, when he was a single man who hoped to marry Dorothea; *diverging opinions on widows who marry again*: see *Middlemarch*, pp. 548–51 (Chapter 55). Mrs Cadwallader refuses to rule out a speedy second marriage in front of her husband — 'It might be a necessary economy' — and contrasts the Christian propriety of second marriage with Hindu practice of *sati* (whereby a grieving widow throws herself on her husband's funeral pyre), outlawed in 1829–30 by British governors of Indian provinces, and banned by proclamation by Queen Victoria in 1861. Mrs Cadwallader wants Dorothea to marry again, and cites as cautionary tales the fates of Dido and Zenobia, widows who did not remarry, and ended their lives in suicide and slavery respectively. Sir James Chettam, by contrast, finds 'something repulsive in a woman's second marriage'.

pp. 203–204 *'Marriage is so unlike everything else . . .'*: *Middlemarch*, p. 797 (Chapter 81). For 'another presence', see p. 661 (Chapter 64).

p. 204 *'When a tender affection . . .'*: *Middlemarch*, p. 580 (Chapter 57).

p. 205 *'I meant everything to be different . . .'*: *Middlemarch*, pp. 764–6 (Chapter 76). See also p. 737 (Chapter 73): 'He had meant everything to turn out differently', and p. 835 (Finale): '[H]e had not done what he once meant to do'; *'there was always something better . . .'*: *Middlemarch*, p. 821 (Chapter 84) and p. 835 (Finale). *Lydgate's fleeting comparisons between Dorothea and his wife*: see *Middlemarch*, pp. 592–3 (Chapter 58): Lydgate's thoughts pass from Rosamond to 'another woman', Dorothea; he recollects her voice of 'deep-souled womanhood' as 'a music from which he was falling away', before this reverie is interrupted by Rosamond's 'silvery neutral' voice politely offering him his tea. Several contemporary reviewers noted the ghost marriage plot that seems to haunt the novel: the *Edinburgh Review*, for example, remarked that 'Each volume, up to the very last, left open the question whether the real hero and the real heroine of the book could not by some means be brought together; and we are not sure that the failure of this expectation will be easily got over' — *Edinburgh Review*, January 1873, p. 264; *'"But what should we have been then? . . ."'*: *Middlemarch*, p. 536 (Chapter 54); *echoes of Lewes in Celia's practical kindness . . .*: John Cross suggests that Celia Brooke was modelled on Marian's sister Chrissey: see Cross I, p. 25.

p. 206 *'like two secluded owls . . .'*: GEL V, p. 150 (letter to Clementia Taylor, Shottermill, 6 June 1871); see also pp. 158, 177 for Eliot's accounts of reading scientific books to Lewes in the evenings. *Each morning Lewes 'sifted' her post*: see GEL V, pp. 184, 202; *'housekeeper, secretary and Nurse all in one'*: GEL V, p. 197 (letter to Cara Bray, The Priory, 6 October 1871); *he suggested changes to the structure of 'Miss Brooke'*: see GEL V: 'Mr Lewes has been saying that it may perhaps be well to take in a portion of Part II at the end of Part I. But it is too early for such definite arrangements' — p. 168 (letter to John Blackwood, Shottermill, 24 July 1871); 'We have added on to the end of part I that portion of part II which closes with the scene at the miserly uncle's — a capital bit to end with' — p. 184 (George Lewes to John Blackwood, London, 7 September 1871); *(illustration caption) Owen Jones advised on the final cover design*: see GEL V, p. 196; *He negotiated simultaneous publication . . .*: see GEL V, pp. 152, 190–1,

199; pp. 146, 179, 185; *a 'perfect' work of art*: 7 March 1873, *The Times*, 1873, p. 3.

p. 207 *'It is a mercy he was not drowned'*: GEL V, p. 200 (John Blackwood to George Lewes, Edinburgh, 11 October 1871); *Main sent Eliot long, ardent and rather intimate letters*: see Kathleen Adams, 'The Gusher: A Portrait of Alexander Main', *George Eliot Fellowship Review* 14 (1983), pp. 65–73; Rebecca Mead, *My Life in Middlemarch* (New York, NY: Crown Publishing, 2013); *'what Shakespeare did for the Drama . . .'*: Alexander Main (ed.), *Wise, Witty and Tender Sayings, in Prose and Verse, Selected from the Works of George Eliot* (Edinburgh and London: William Blackwood and Sons, 1872), p. ix. The title of this anthology was suggested by Lewes: see GEL V, p. 194 (George Lewes to John Blackwood, London, 29 September 1871). On Main's anthologies (he also compiled a *George Eliot Birthday Book* in 1878), see Alexis Easley, ' "A Thousand Tit-Bits": George Eliot and the New Journalism' in *George Eliot: Interdisciplinary Essays*, eds. Jean Arnold and Lila Marz Harper, pp. 19–40.

p. 208 *'I would take out the allusion to morality . . .'*: GEL V, p. 212 (John Blackwood to William Blackwood, St Andrews, 2 November 1871); *'for ever sanctified the Novel . . .'*: Main (ed.), *Wise, Witty and Tender Sayings*, p. ix; *Effusive letters accompanied hand-made gifts*: see Haight, *George Eliot: A Biography*, p. 452; *John Cross, a handsome young banker*: see Kathleen Adams, 'Short Biography of John Walter Cross', *George Eliot Fellowship Review*, no. 10 (1979), pp. 14–18, and *George Eliot Review Online*, accessed 13 January 2022; *colonial speculations*: see Henry, *George Eliot and the British Empire*, p. 97; Haight, *George Eliot: A Biography*, p. 458.

p. 209 *'half a man'*: Simcox, *A Monument to the Memory of George Eliot*, p. 4; see Rosemary Bodenheimer, 'Autobiography in Fragments: The Elusive Life of Edith Simcox', *Victorian Studies*, 2002, pp. 399–422; *Middlemarch . . . marked a new 'epoch' in literature . . .*: Simcox (writing as H. Lawrenny), *The Academy*, no. 63, 1 January 1863. See GEL V, p. 149: 'There may not be in this first part what are considered popular incidents'; p. 168: 'there will be complaints of the want of the continuous interest of a story, but this does not matter when all is so fresh and true to life' (John Blackwood to George Eliot, 2 June 1871 and 20 July 1871); *They worshipped her . . .*: see GEL IX, p. 303 (Edith Simcox to George Eliot, London, 28 March 1880): 'Do you see darling I can only love you three lawful ways, idolatrously as Faber the Virgin Mary, in romance wise as Petrarch, Laura, or with a child's fondness for the mother one leans on.' Frederick Faber, a member of Newman's Oxford movement, had converted to Catholicism and written a book on Mary; such Marian devotion was regarded as idolatrous by Anglican and Protestant Christians.

pp. 209–10 *'What is better than to love . . .'*: GEL V, p. 171 (letter to Edith Bulwer-Lytton, Shottermill, 25 July 1871). See also GEL VI, p. 64 (letter to Mrs William Smith, 1 July 1874): 'what you say of the reasons why one may wish even for the anguish of being *left* for the sake of waiting on the beloved one to the end — all that goes to my heart of hearts. It is what I think of almost daily.' Around this time, the sudden death of Lewes's friend Lady Amberley prompted him to sympathize with her husband and reflect that 'Such ruptures give every married pair a pang of anticipation'– LGHL II, p. 205 (George Lewes to Charles Lewes, 1 July 1874).

p. 210 *the ethic of vigilance*: while she was working on *Middlemarch*, Eliot offered some rather ambiguous reflections on 'married constancy' — see GEL V, pp. 132–3 (letter to Sara Hennell, The Priory, 2 January 1871); *'we never know who are to influence our lives'*: GEL V, p. 167 (John Blackwood to George Eliot, St Andrews, 20 July 1871); *'Destiny stands by sarcastic . . .'*: *Middlemarch*, p. 95 (Chapter 11).

10. DESTINY

p. 213 *Gambling turns out to be a metaphor for marriage*: see *Daniel Deronda*, p. 441 (Chapter 36): 'It would by-and-by become a sort of skill in which she was automatically practised, to bear this last great gambling loss with an air of perfect self-possession' — this 'gambling loss' is her marriage to Grandcourt, and here 'the losing was not simply a *minus*, but a terrible *plus* that had never entered into her reckoning' (p. 598, Chapter 48).

p. 214 *'the Jewish question'*: Marx's essay 'On the Jewish Question' was published in 1844 in *Deutsch-Französische Jahrbücher*. It was a response to Bruno Bauer's 'The Jewish Question', published the previous year. *'What in the midst of that mighty drama . . .'*: *Daniel Deronda*, p. 125 (Chapter 12). Eliot's phrasing echoes Carlyle's dramatization of two different life-views — 'the Everlasting No' and the 'Everlasting Yea' — in *Sartor Resartus*.

p. 215 *an old Jewish joke*: *Daniel Deronda*, p. 743 (Chapter 62); *'Key to All Psychologies'*: GEL V, p. 291 (Lewes to John Blackwood, 13 July 1872); see Ashton, *G. H. Lewes*, p. 259; *Eliot and Lewes found this a 'painful sight'*: GEL V, p. 314 (letter to John Blackwood, Homburg, 4 October 1872). See Jane Irwin (ed.), *George Eliot's Daniel Deronda Notebooks*, p. xxvii; Kathleen McCormack, *George Eliot in Society: Travels Abroad and Sundays at the Priory* (Columbus, OH: Ohio State University Press, 2013), pp. 111–13; Henry, *The Life of George Eliot*, p. 216. In her letter to Blackwood, Eliot describes 'Miss Leigh' as 'Byron's grand niece', while in his diary Lewes describes her as 'Byron's granddaughter' — see GEL V, p. 314 (26 September 1872); her grandmother was Augusta Mary Byron Leigh, Byron's half-sister, who had a scandalous affair with Byron. *'A sky as vast as ours'*: *George Eliot's Daniel Deronda Notebooks*, pp. 16–17, 22. On the Leweses' friendship with John Tyndall, and his influence on their work, see LGHL III, p. 155; *to tutor Eliot in Hebrew*: Eliot started learning Hebrew in the 1840s, when she was translating Strauss's *Life of Jesus*, but she renewed and extended her studies after meeting Deutsch in the 1860s. See William Baker, *George Eliot and Judaism*, pp. 21–2.

p. 216 *They contemplated a trip to Palestine . . .*: see GEL VI, p. 319 and note (Lady Strangford to George Eliot, 30 May 1874; letter to Elizabeth Stuart Phelps, The Priory, 16 December 1876); LGHL III, p. 80 (letter to Lucy Smith, The Priory, 23

October 1874). 'Unless we could go to the East — which infirmities forbid — England is now richer to us than any other part of Europe,' Eliot wrote to Lucy Smith. *'Town, with its necessity of receiving numerous visitors . . .'*: GEL VI, p. 46 (letter to Edith Griffiths, The Priory, 9 May 1874). See also LGHL II, p. 159: 'Mrs Lewes never seems at home except under a broad sweep of sky and the *greenth* of the uplands around her' (George Lewes to Anne Gilchrist, Shotter Mill, May 1871); *they spent several Christmases with them in Weybridge*: see GEL VI, p. 56; *'a house with undeniable charms . . .'*: GEL VI, p. 55 (letter to Anna Cross, Earlswood Common, 14 June 1874); p. 57 (letter to John Blackwood, Earlswood Common, 16 June 1874). See also p. 54 (letter to Kate Fields, Earlswood Common, 5 June 1874). In 1872 Eliot and Lewes considered buying land and having a house built on it, and John Cross was also involved in this project — see GEL V, p. 340 (letter to John Cross, The Priory, 11 December 1972).

p. 217 *'her Hebrew and Oriental studies'*: GEL VI, p. 79 (George Lewes to Elma Stuart, Earlswood Common, 25 August 1874); *'brewing' and 'simmering' Daniel Deronda*: GEL VI, pp. 58–60 (letter to John Blackwood, Earlswood Common, 16 June 1874); p. 91 (John Blackwood to George Eliot, Edinburgh, 19 November 1874); *She copied out Auguste Comte's entire Positivist Calendar*: see *George Eliot's Daniel Deronda Notebooks*, pp. 186–94. Comte's thirteen months are named Moses, Homer, Aristotle, Archimedes, Caesar, Saint Paul, Charlemagne, Dante, Gutenberg, Shakespeare, Descartes, Frederick (after Frederick the Great, King of Prussia) and Bichat (after the scientist Xavier Bichat). *'Topography of Arthurian Legend'*: *George Eliot's Daniel Deronda Notebooks*, p. 243; *Gwendolen, she discovered . . .*: see *George Eliot's Daniel Deronda Notebooks*, p. 446; *towers of books on Jewish history and philosophy*: George Eliot's notes for *Daniel Deronda* include references to Abraham Berliner's *Aus dem Leben der deutschen Juden im Mittelalter*, Franz Delizsch's *Zur Geschichte der jüdischen Poesie*, Johann Eisenmenger's *Entdektes Judenthum*, G. H. A. von Ewald's *Geschichte des Volkes Israel*, Abraham Geiger's *Das Judenthum und seine Geschichte* and *Sadducäer and Pharisäer*, Heinrich Graetz's *Geschichte der Juden*, Jacob Hamburger's *Real-Encyclopädie des Judentums*, R. Hirschfeld's *Das innere Leben des modernen Judenthums*, Hyam Isaacs's *Ceremonies, Customs, Rites and Traditions of the Jews*, Abraham Kuenens's *The Religion of Israel to the Fall of the Jewish State*, Giuseppe Levi's *Parabelen, Legenden und Gedanken aus Thalmud und Midrasch*, Abraham Löwy's *Miscellany of Hebrew Literature*, Henry Milman's *The History of the Jews*, Salomon Munk's *Palestine*, Wolf Pascheles's *Sippurim: Eine Sammlung jüdischerVolkssagen*, James Picciotto's *Sketches of Anglo-Jewish History*, David Rothschild's *Der synagogale Cultus in historisch-kritischer Entwicklung*, Moritz Steinschneider's *Jewish Literature from the Eighth to the Eighteenth Century*, Abraham Tendlau's *Sprichwörter Redensarten deutsch jüdischer Vorzeit* and Johann Wagenseil's *Belehrung der jüisch-teutschen Red-und Schreibart*, among other works relating to Judaism. See Avrom Fleischman, 'George Eliot's Reading: A Chronological List', *George*

Eliot — George Henry Lewes Studies, no. 54–5 (September 2008), pp. 1–106; **notes on the Kabbalah**: see *George Eliot's Daniel Deronda Notebooks*, p. 454, where George Eliot's notes emphasize the Neo-Platonic source of Kabbalistic teachings; **an unknowable, indescribable God**: see Avinoam Fraenkel, *Nefesh HaTzimtzum: Rabbi Chaim Volozhin's Nefesh HaChaim with Translation and Commentary* (Jerusalem: Urim Publications, 2015), vol. 1, pp. 40–41; Arthur Green, *These Are the Words: A Vocabulary of Jewish Spiritual Life* (Nashville, TN: Jewish Lights Publishing, 2013), p. 14. Fraenkel emphasizes that God's essence cannot be spoken of at all, and 'Ein Sof' is not a name or a description, just 'a reference' to the highest level that can be referred to in any way. Green suggests that 'Eyn Sof' is best understood as an adverb, i.e., as 'endlessly'. English spellings vary from 'Ein Sof' (Fraenkel), 'Eyn Sof' (Green) and 'En-Soph' (George Eliot, following Heinrich Graetz and Christian Ginsberg). For George Eliot's notes on 'En-Soph', see Irwin (ed.), *George Eliot's Daniel Deronda Notebooks*, pp. 173, 455. I am grateful to Rabbi Dov Bard for guidance on the Kabbalah. **'Individuals in the lower world . . .'**: *George Eliot's Daniel Deronda Notebooks*, pp. 173–4.

p. 218 **'Man's life like the shadow . . .'**: *George Eliot's Daniel Deronda Notebooks*, p. 458; **'every fixed star is a sun . . .'**: Bernard le Bovier de Fontenelle, *Conversations on the Plurality of Worlds*, trans. Elizabeth Gunning, ed. Jerome de la Lande (London: T. Hurst and T. Ostell, 1803), pp. 110–13. See *George Eliot's Daniel Deronda Notebooks*, pp. 258–9; Eliot's notes on Fontenelle's text refer to the French edition. The idea of multiple worlds also appears in her notes on the Kabbalah, which mention '4 Worlds. 1. The *Atzilatic*, or world of emanations . . . 2. The Briatic world, further removed . . . 3. The Jetziratic World, called the world of formation, & of Angels . . . 4. The Assiatic World called the world of action & the world of *matter*' — *George Eliot's Daniel Deronda Notebooks*, p. 455. As Fraenkel explains, there are myriad worlds, and these four are 'world levels', each one a 'grouping containing countless levels' — *Nefesh HaTzimtzum*, p. 40; **'all religious theories, schemes and systems . . .'**: *George Eliot's Daniel Deronda Notebooks*, p. 311. Tyndall's inaugural lecture was delivered in Belfast on 19 August 1874, published in *Nature* the following day, and read by Lewes and Eliot on 23 August; see *Nature* 10 (1874), pp. 308–19; **Lewes . . . was already convinced**: Lewes criticized other aspects of Tyndall's lecture: see GEL VI, p. 79 (George Lewes to Alexander Main, Earlswood Common, 8 September 1874).

p. 219 **'Nothing here is trivial . . .'**: this theme is anticipated by Dorothea Brooke's youthful hope that her married life will hold 'nothing trivial': 'Everyday-things with us would mean the greatest things' (*Middlemarch*, p. 29 (Chapter 3)). For different interpretations of the significance of the Kabbalah in *Daniel Deronda*, see William Baker, 'The Kabbalah, Mordecai, and George Eliot's Religion of Humanity', *The Yearbook of English Studies*, vol. 3 (1973), pp. 216–21, and Peter J. Capuano, *Changing Hands: Industry, Evolution and the Reconfiguration of the Victorian Body* (Ann Arbor: University of Michigan Press, 2015), pp. 164–73; **'chooses a companion soul . . .'**: see *George Eliot's Daniel Deronda*

Notebooks, p. 455; Baker, 'The Kabbalah, Mordecai, and George Eliot's Religion of Humanity', p. 217; Christian Ginsburg, *The Kabbalah: Its Doctrines, Development and Literature* (1863), published together with *The Essences: Their History and Doctrines* (London: Routledge and Kegan Paul, 1955), pp. 124–5. Eliot's notes are a close paraphrase of Ginsburg's text.

pp. 219–20 *'That is really the highest good of a wife ...'*: GEL VI, pp. 116–17 (letters to Emily Cross and Francis Otter, London, 13 January 1875). Emily and Francis Otter would name their daughter Gwendolen.

p. 220 *'Pinched' and 'crushed' ... 'That white hand ...'*: *Daniel Deronda*, pp. 423, 427 (Chapter 35). See also p. 565 (Chapter 45): '[S]he was as frightened at a quarrel as if she had foreseen that that it would end with throttling fingers on her neck'; *'as with a dream-change ...'*: *Daniel Deronda*, p. 606 (Chapter 48); *'Constantly she had to be on the scene as Mrs Grandcourt ...'*: *Daniel Deronda*, pp. 548, 587 (chapters 44, 48); *Grandcourt waits outside*: *Daniel Deronda*, p. 549 (Chapter 44); *'rebuked' or 'punished'*: *Daniel Deronda*, pp. 557, 590, 611 (chapters 45, 48).

p. 221 *'like a white image of helplessness ...'*: *Daniel Deronda*, p. 448 (Chapter 36); *'It followed that he turned her chin and kissed her ...'*: *Daniel Deronda*, p. 597 (Chapter 48); *'shocks of humiliation ...'*, *'proud concealment ...'*: *Daniel Deronda*, p. 423 (Chapter 35); *'this handsome, fair-skinned English couple ...'*: *Daniel Deronda*, p. 681 (Chapter 54); *'If this white-handed man ...'*: *Daniel Deronda*, pp. 593–4 (Chapter 48). Gwendolen is also an emblem of whiteness: she is often described as pale, and Eliot's notes on her name mention its association with the moon and state that '*Gwen* is used in Welsh in the double sense of the colour white & of a woman, perhaps for the same reason that "the fair" so often stands for a lady in poetry' — see *George Eliot's Daniel Deronda Notebooks*, p. 446. Capuano analyses the meaning of hands in *Daniel Deronda*, though with a focus on Jewish hands: see *Changing Hands, Industry, Evolution and the Reconfiguration of the Victorian Body*, pp. 152–82.; *'galley-slave'*: *Daniel Deronda*, p. 695 (Chapter 56); *'those fatal meshes ...'*: *Daniel Deronda*, pp. 668, 672 (Chapter 54). This metaphor for marriage — a mesh woven more tightly on the inside than on the outside — develops the metaphors of webs and weaving that recur through George Eliot's novels. For example, *Middlemarch*'s narrator describes his task as 'unravelling certain human lots, and seeing how they are woven and interwoven'. *Daniel Deronda*'s conjugal 'mesh' highlights a difference between the inside and the outside of a marriage — between the way it is experienced by the couple, and the way it appears to others.

pp. 221–2 *symptoms of various nervous disorders*: after she becomes Mrs Grandcourt, Gwendolen is often described as cold and immobile, frozen like a statue; confronted with food, she does not eat, and is thin, pale and shivery. The term *anorexia nervosa* was established by the English physician William Gull in 1873 in a ground-breaking paper, and in the same year Ernest-Charles Lasègue's paper *De l'Anorexie Hystérique* was published in both French and English. Gull noted that anorexia nervosa was most commonly found in young women aged between sixteen and twenty-three, and identified symptoms of fatigue and low body temperature as well as weight loss — see W. W. Gull, 'Anorexia nervosa (apepsia hyserica, anorexia hysterica)', *Transactions of the Clinical Society of London*, 1873; Antoni Niedzielski, Natalia Kazmierczak and Andrzej Grzybowski, 'Sir William Withey Gull', *Journal of Neurology* vol. 264, no. 2 (2017), pp. 419–20; W. Vandereycken and R. van Deth, 'A tribute to Lasègue's description of anorexia nervosa (1873), with completion of its English translation', *British Journal of Psychiatry* vol. 157 (1990), pp. 902–8. On Gwendolen's symptoms in the context of Victorian psychiatry, see Athena Vrettos, 'From Neurosis to Narrative: The Private Life of the Nerves in *Villette* and *Daniel Deronda*', *Victorian Studies* vol. 33, no. 4 (1990), pp. 551–79; Jill L. Matus, 'Historicizing Trauma: The Genealogy of Psychic Shock in *Daniel Deronda*', *Victorian Literature and Culture* vol. 36, no. 1 (2008), pp. 59–78.

p. 222 *'fits of spiritual dread . . .'*: *Daniel Deronda*, p. 63 (Chapter 6). *'an undefined feeling of immeasurable existence . . .'*: *Daniel Deronda*, pp. 63–4 (Chapter 6); *'It came over me that when I was a child . . .'*: *Daniel Deronda*, p. 695 (Chapter 56). On the theme of incest in *Daniel Deronda*, see Henry, *The Life of George Eliot*, pp. 225–8, where Henry links Shelley's verse drama *The Cenci* (1819), lauded by Lewes in an 1841 essay for the *Westminster Review*, with the scandal about Byron and his half-sister; *'a sort of physical repulsion'*: *Daniel Deronda*, p. 70 (Chapter 7); *'with a vague fear'*: *Daniel Deronda*, p. 327 (chapter 29); *'was it some dim forecast . . .'*: *Daniel Deronda*, p. 357 (chapter 31); the *'momentous discovery . . .'*: Freud, 'The Aetiology of Hysteria' (1896), pp. 192–3, in *The Standard Edition of the Complete Psychological Works of Sigmund Freud*, vol. III. In the 1870s and 1880s Freud read and admired George Eliot's novels, including *Middlemarch* and *Daniel Deronda*, and may well have been influenced by them — see Ernest Jones, *The Life and Work of Sigmund Freud*, vol. 1 (Oxford: Basic Books, 1953), pp. 131, 168, 174; Carl T. Rotenberg, 'George Eliot, Proto-Psychoanalyst', *American Journal of Psychoanalysis*, vol. 59, no. 1 (1999), pp. 257–70.

p. 223 *'making no break in her more acknowledged consciousness . . .'*: *Daniel Deronda*, p. 606 (Chapter 48); *'like so many women petrified white'*: *Daniel Deronda*, pp. 358–9 (Chapter 31). See also my note above, on the meaning of the name Gwendolen.

p. 224 *Now she feels a tender solidarity*: see *Daniel Deronda*, p. 554 (Chapter 44); *'the nameless something . . .'*: *Daniel Deronda*, p. 677 (Chapter 54); *'the wonderful union . . .'*: David Kaufmann, *George Eliot and Judaism*, translated by J. W. Ferrier (Edinburgh and London: William Blackwood and Sons, 1877), pp. 13–14; *'among his own people'*: Haight, *George Eliot: A Biography*, p. 470 (quoting from Emily Strangford, *Literary Remains of the Late Emanuel Deutsch* (New York: Henry Holt and Company, 1874), pp. x–xi); *'a land and a polity . . .'; 'a man's country is where he is well off . . .'*: *Daniel Deronda*, pp. 527, 532 (Chapter 42).

pp. 224–5 *'a German Jew . . .'*: G. H. Lewes, 'Spinoza', *Fortnightly Review*, no. 22 (1 April 1866), pp. 385–7.

p. 225 *'our own better future ...'*: *Daniel Deronda*, p. 538 (Chapter 42); *successive reforms*: see H. S. Q. Henriques, 'The Political Rights of English Jews', *The Jewish Quarterly Review* vol 19, no. 2 (1907), pp. 298–341. The 1858 Oaths Act and Jewish Relief Act allowed Jews to omit the words 'upon the true faith of a Christian' from the oath sworn by those taking office under the British Crown; the 1871 Promissory Oaths Act made the wording of Oaths of Allegiance even more flexible for non-Christians (pp. 333–4). From 1867 'every office, the throne alone excepted, could legally be filled by a Jew' (p. 339). The 1872 Ballot Act made special provision for voters 'of the Jewish persuasion' to record votes in an election held on a Saturday in a manner that did not breach their Sabbath observance (p. 324); *'Do you mind about the Conservative majority? ...'*: GEL VI, p. 14 (letter to Barbara Bodichon, The Priory, 9 February 1874); *'quiet steady government'*: GEL VI, p. 19 (John Blackwood to George Eliot, Edinburgh, 18 February 1874); *'no believer in Salvation by Ballot'*: GEL VI, pp. 21–2 (letter to John Blackwood, The Priory, 20 February 1874); *Disraeli was a novelist ...*: Eliot read Disraeli's Young England trilogy, charting the course of the 'New Generation', when she was in her twenties and still Mary Ann Evans. The trilogy culminates in *Tancred, or The New Crusade*, which describes an Englishman's journey to Jerusalem and emphasizes European culture's debt to Judaism. Reading it in the 1840s, Eliot could not share Disraeli's enthusiasm for 'the fellowship of race'; she was more drawn to a Wordsworthian communion with 'the ocean and the sky and the everlasting hills' — GEL I, pp. 246–8 (letter to John Sibree, Foleshill, Coventry, 11 February 1848). She dug out her copy of *Tancred* as she compiled material for *Daniel Deronda*, and copied a passage from the novel alongside notes on the Kabbalah and the principles of gambling; *a policy of 'fasting' from contemporary fiction*: see GEL VI, pp. 123, 418. In 1861 Lewes remarked that 'Mrs Lewes as a matter of hygiene *very* rarely reads stories', which suggests that once she became a novelist she preferred to keep her mind uncluttered or uncontaminated by new fiction — LGHL II, p. 26 (George Lewes to John Blackwood, London, 1 October 1861). *Eliot was plotting a different diagnosis ...*: she summarized her representation of Jews in *Daniel Deronda* as follows: 'precisely because I felt that the usual attitude of Christians towards Jews is — I hardly know whether to say more impious or more stupid when viewed in the light of their professed principles, I therefore felt urged to treat Jews with such sympathy and understanding as my nature and knowledge could attain to. Moreover, not only towards the Jews, but towards all oriental peoples with whom we English come in contact, a spirit of arrogance and contemptuous dictatorialness is observable which has become a national disgrace to us. There is nothing I should care more to do, if it were possible, than to rouse the imagination of men and women to a vision of human claims in those races of their fellow-men who most differ from them in customs and beliefs ... To my feeling, this deadness [of supposedly educated English people] to the history which has prepared half our world for us, this inability to find interest in any form of life that is not clad in the same coat-tails and flounces as our own lies very close to the worst kind of irreligion. The best that can be said of it is, that it is a sign of the intellectual narrowness — in plain English, the stupidity, which is still the average mark of our culture' — GEL VI, pp. 301–2 (letter to Harriet Beecher Stowe, The Priory, 29 October 1876). For scholarly analyses of *Daniel Deronda*'s engagement with Judaism, see Cynthia Scheinberg, ' "The Beloved Ideas Made Flesh": *Daniel Deronda* and Jewish Poetics', *ELH*, vol. 77, no. 3 (2010), pp. 813–39; Amanda Anderson, *The Powers of Distance: Cosmopolitanism and the Cultivation of Detachment* (Princeton, NJ: Princeton University Press, 2001), pp. 119–46.

p. 226 *'rank and wealth'*: *Daniel Deronda*, p. 143 (Chapter 13); *One November afternoon they walked to Blackfriars Bridge*: George Lewes's diary, 15 and 18 November 1874; see Carol A. Martin, *George Eliot's Serial Fiction* (Columbus, OH: Ohio State University Press, 1994), p. 213; *from 'the simmering' to 'the irrevocable'*: see GEL VI, p. 91 (John Blackwood to George Eliot, Edinburgh, 19 November 1874); *Eliot 'hung her head low . . .'; 'perfectly charming and all about English Ladies and Gentlemen . . .'*: GEL VI, p. 136 (William Blackwood to John Blackwood, London, 21 April 1875). Similarly, Lewes later wrote to John Blackwood that 'the new book like "Middlemarch," is a story of English life bit *of our own day*, and dealing for the most part in a higher sphere of Society' — GEL VI, p. 193 (George Lewes to John Blackwood, 22 November 1875). In this letter Lewes advised Blackwood on how to advertize *Daniel Deronda*, and his wording was printed almost verbatim in the *Athenaeum* on 27 November. *John Blackwood had declined to publish Problems of Life and Mind*: see GEL V, pp. 400, 410–11, 413–14; Ashton, *G. H. Lewes*, p. 260. When Blackwood declined the book, Lewes immediately secured its publication by his friend Nikolaus Trübner; *'face of horror and fright . . .'*: GEL VI, p. 136 (William Blackwood to John Blackwood, London, 21 April 1875).

p. 227 *She returns to questions of voice and vocation . . .*: in *Daniel Deronda* the simply rustic moral purpose of *Adam Bede*'s hero and heroine give way to upper-class ennui, and Dinah's clear treble tones are replaced by voices that are frail, fallible and often rather desperate. Gwendolen fails to realize her dream of becoming a singer instead of a wife, and her moral voice is 'throttled into silence' (p. 669, Chapter 54) by her marriage to Grandcourt; Mirah's voice is too weak for a large stage; Mordecai's prophetic voice fades as his consumptive lungs struggle for breath; *uncanny clairvoyant powers*: Chapter 38 opens with an authorial comment about 'second sight' which is then linked to Mordecai, but equally well applies to Gwendolen: 'there are persons whose yearnings, conceptions . . . continually take the form of images which have a foreshadowing power . . . the event they hunger for or dread rises into vision with a seed-like growth' (p. 471). *Alcharisi shares her struggle to escape patriarchal power*: Alcharisi tells Daniel: 'I did not want a child . . . I did not want to marry. I was forced into marrying your father — forced, I mean, by my father's wishes and commands; and besides, it was my best way of getting some freedom' (p. 626, Chapter 51); 'you can never imagine what it is to have a man's force of genius in you, and yet to suffer the slavery of being a girl. To have a pattern cut out — "this is the Jewish woman; this is what you must be; this is what you are wanted for; a woman's heart must be of such a size and no larger, else it must be pressed small, like Chinese feet; her happiness is to be made as cakes are, by a fixed recipe"' (p. 631, Chapter 51).

p. 228 *'Whether it will rival Middlemarch . . .'*: LGHL II, p. 210 (George Lewes to John Blackwood, The Priory, 12 January 1875); *Jewish rootlessness*: Chapter 3 opens with Gwendolen's rootlessness: 'Pity that Offendene was not the home of Miss Harleth's childbirth, or endeared to her by family memories! A human life, I think, should be well rooted in some spot of native land . . .' (p. 22): this invokes both modern cosmopolitanism and the old trope of the 'Wandering Jew', and prefigures the Jewish search for a 'native land' that shapes the entwined destinies of Daniel, Mirah and Mordecai; *for the first time, George Eliot makes her heroine marry for money*: Barbara Hardy points out that *Felix Holt: The Radical* anticipates this theme, since its heroine Esther Lyon is 'a Gwendolen who escapes her Grandcourt' — *The Novels of George Eliot*, p. 227.

pp. 228–9 *'sold her truthfulness . . .'*: *Daniel Deronda*, p. 669 (Chapter 54).

p. 229 *'Pray wear this ring . . .'*: *Daniel Deronda*, p. 312 (Chapter 28); *forced to wear his 'poisoned' diamond necklace*: *Daniel Deronda*, p. 556 (Chapter 45) — this is described as a 'submission to a yoke'; *'hurting herself with the jewels . . .'*: *Daniel Deronda*, p. 610 (Chapter 48); *'taken up and used by strangers'*: Gwendolen and Mirah are both taken from their mothers; they both suffer traumas that drive them to despair; they both learn to conceal their shameful feelings; they are both 'used' in the double sense of being exploited, and of becoming accustomed to it. On the female artist as prostitute, see Catherine Gallagher, 'George Eliot and *Daniel Deronda*: the Prostitute and the Jewish Question' in Ruth Bernard Yeazell (ed.), *Sex, Politics and Science in the Nineteenth-Century Novel* (Baltimore, MD: Johns Hopkins University Press, 1986), pp. 39–62. Gallagher shows how *Daniel Deronda* 'repeatedly emphasises the close connection between selling oneself as a sexual commodity and selling oneself as an artist' (p. 53), and believes, as I do, that the intertwining of art, marriage and money throughout the novel is linked to George Eliot's 'particular experiences in the realm of exchange' and her 'fears of authorship' (p. 59); *'must learn her part . . .'*: *Daniel Deronda*, pp. 732–3 (Chapter 61); *a 'commodity disdainfully paid for . . .'*: *Daniel Deronda*, pp. 222, 558 (chapters 20, 46); see also p. 631 (Chapter 51).

p. 230 *in the 1870s he began to refer to her as 'Madonna'*: see GEL VI, pp. 120–21, 157, 169, 374, 389, 391; LGHL II, pp. 218, 232–3, 238, 239, 244; LGHL III, pp. 77, 90, 91–3, 104, 109, 111, 114, 119, 123, 128, 133, 135–6. In 1872 Eliot signed herself 'Madonna' at the bottom of a letter from Lewes to their friend Elizabeth Benson — see LGHL II, pp. 176–7. In *Daniel Deronda*, the poor yet happy (and usually all-female) Meyrick household is a kind of sacred space in which devotion to the arts is uncontaminated by money; Mrs Meyrick is an idealized mother, presiding over daughters who seem to be set apart from the economy of sexual desire; *Eliot agonized about the price of her new poetry collection*: Eliot broached the subject of a poetry collection by writing to Blackwell about 'a small collection of my poems which Mr. Lewes wishes me to get published in May (GEL VI, letter to John Blackwood, The Priory, 6 March 1874, p. 25), and they had an ongoing correspondence about how much the book should cost: see GEL VI, pp. 38, 41, 42, 57. In *Daniel Deronda*, Daniel and Mordecai have an interesting conversation about the price of a second-hand book (Solomon Maimon's *Autobiography*): '"What is the price of this book?" ... "What are you disposed to give for it?" ... "Don't you know how much it is worth?" ... "Not its market-price. May I ask, have you read it?"' (p. 386, Chapter 33). For sales figures of *Middlemarch*, see GEL VI, pp. 9–10 (John Blackwood to George Lewes, Edinburgh, 17 January 1874); pp. 114–15 (John Blackwood to George Lewes, Edinburgh, 11 January 1875). *Eliot's earnings were still sent to Lewes, and deposited in his bank account*: see Haight, *George Eliot: A Biography*, p. 523. This has been disputed by Harriet F. Adams, who argues that as an unmarried woman Eliot was legally able 'to keep her own earnings, as she, in fact, had done' — 'George Eliot's Deed: Reconciling an Outlaw Marriage', *Yale University Library Gazette* vol. 75, no. 1 (2000), p. 54. However, Adams provides no evidence that Eliot received payments in her own name or in her own bank account, and during the 1870s John Blackwood consistently sent cheques and royalty statements for George Eliot's works to Lewes — see GEL V, pp. 80, 263, 298, 330, 347–8, 364, 369–70; GEL VI, pp. 9, 14, 328–9, 349; GEL VII, p. 7. A banker's draft dated 2 August 1876 credits 'G. H. Lewes' for £2,000, sent by Blackwood as partial payment for *Daniel Deronda*, and one of Blackwood's letters makes it explicit that his cheque is made out to Lewes: see LGHL II, p. 229 and GEL VI, pp. 328–9 (John Blackwood to George Lewes, 12 January 1877). In the 1860s Blackwood sometimes sent cheques directly to Eliot, but letters accompanying some of these cheques indicate that they were made out to Lewes: see GEL VIII, p. 290 (John Blackwood to George Eliot, Edinburgh, 25 September 1861) and GEL IV, p. 318 (John Blackwood to George Eliot, Edinburgh, 13 December 1866). One letter, however, records a cheque payable to Eliot for *The Mill on the Floss* — see GEL III, p. 395 (John Blackwood to George Eliot, Edinburgh, 1 April 1861). Other evidence that Lewes dealt with income from George Eliot's novels is provided in his letters to John Cross asking him to buy or sell stocks and bonds: see GEL V, pp. 368, 402; *she does not write unless I make her do it*': Collins, *Interviews and Recollections*, p. 128 (quoting a letter from Alexander Ewing to Ethel Smyth);*worked harder than any carthorse*': p. 170 (quoting Rudolf Lehmann, *An Artist's Reminiscences*, 1894); *eager and gesticulating man ...*': *Daniel Deronda*, pp. 738–9 (Chapter 62). Eliot wrote of Lewes, 'how very quick and light his step was' — GEL VI, p. 342 (letter to Emilia Pattison, The Priory, 18 February 1877). Lapidoth also resembles Lewes in being a former actor and playwright.

p. 231 *last great gambling loss*': *Daniel Deronda*, p. 598 (Chapter 48); *in helpless humiliation*': *Daniel Deronda*, p. 20 (Chapter 2); *fire and will*': *Daniel Deronda*, p. 25 (Chapter 3).

p. 232 *I am cruel ...*': *Daniel Deronda*, pp. 805–7 (Chapter 69); *Never again ...*': Collins, *Interviews and Recollections*, p. 170 (quoting Lehmann, *An Artist's*

Reminiscences, 1894); *Lewes 'fidgets her . . .*': GEL VI, p. 253 (John Blackwood to William Blackwood, London, 18 May 1876); *'the passion of the moment . . .*': GEL VI, p. 233 (letter to John Blackwood, The Priory, 18 March 1876); *'spiritual children*': GEL VI, p. 246 (letter to Harriet Beecher Stowe, The Priory, 6 May 1876); *advertized as a tale of modern English life*: see GEL VI, pp. 192–3 (George Lewes to John Blackwood, 22 November 1875); Martin, *George Eliot's Serial Fiction*, p. 211; *Lewes declared it her greatest work*: see GEL VI, p. 226 (George Lewes to Alexander Main, The Priory, 1 March 1876).

p. 233 *'Mr Lewes carefully protects me . . .*': GEL VI, p. 230 (letter to Elma Stuart, The Priory, 3 March 1876). See also p. 244: 'you know I am well taken care of by my husband and am saved from getting my mind poisoned with print about myself' (letter to Alexander Main, The Priory, 2 May 1876); p. 318: 'I hardly ever read anything that is written about myself — indeed, never unless my husband wishes me to do so by way of exception. I adopted this rule many years ago as a necessary preservative against influences that would have ended by nullifying my power of writing. Mr Lewes reads anything about me that comes in his way and occasionally gives me reports of what he reads if it happens to shew an unusual insight or an unusual ineptitude' (letter to Elizabeth Stuart Phelps, The Priory, 16 December 1876). In 1872, during the serial publication of *Middlemarch*, Lewes 'told her of tho wouldn't let her *read*' a rave review in the *Telegraph* — LGHL II, pp. 178–9 (George Lewes to Charles Lewes, Red Hill, 19 June 1872). Lewes explained their policy in 1876: 'Mrs Lewes never reads what is written about herself & her works, however favourable it may be. This is a matter of moral & intellectual hygiene which is particularly necessary in one of her extreme sensitiveness, & one I try to get all authors & artists to adopt (without success I am bound to add!) However although she does not read articles, I always tell her when there is anything I think she will be especially pleased to hear' (George Lewes to Edmund Yates, The Priory, 2 February 1876) — LGHL II, pp. 219–20. This appeal to 'hygiene' echoes his rationale for Eliot's avoidance of contemporary fiction: see Note 61 above; *her Jewish characters were not well received*: see GEL VI, p. 336: 'She has been pained to find many dear friends and some of her most *devoted* readers, utterly dead to all the Jewish part . . . it is in vain that she abstains from reading what is written about her; there is always enough reaching her by indirect routes to tell her how her purpose has been misunderstood or met with indifference' (George Lewes to Edward Dowden, London, February 1877). To John Blackwood, Lewes wrote frankly of 'disappointment' at *Daniel Deronda*: 'There seems to be so general a sense of disappointment — so much deadness to the Jewish element — that my only hope for a large sale until the public has learned to get over its first disappointment is in the Jewish public and they can only, I fear, be caught by the cheap edition. (Don't allude to the disappointment in any letters to me — she only knows that Judaism is unpopular not what is said otherwise about the book.) I remember that "Romola" was received with a universal howl of discontent — and now it is the book most commonly placed at the head of her works — or at any rate after "Middlemarch." If Deronda is what I take it to be we shall see a revival or rather a reversal of opinion' — GEL VI, p. 312 (George Lewes to John Blackwood, The Priory, 22 November 1876). See also *Journals*, pp. 146–7, December 1876. On the reception of *Daniel Deronda* and its impact on George Eliot's work on the remainder of the novel, see Martin, *George Eliot's Serial Fiction*, pp. 211–37. Henry James's response to *Daniel Deronda* is entertaining: see 'Daniel Deronda: A Conversation', *Atlantic Monthly* (December 1876), vol. XXXVIII (Boston: H.O. Houghton and Company; New York, NY: Hurd and Houghton; Cambridge, MA: The Riverside Press, 1876), pp. 684–94; *'mermaid witch'*: see GEL VI, p. 144 (John Blackwood to George Eliot, London, 25 May 1875); *'This is better than the laudation of readers . . .'*: GEL VI, p. 290 (letter to Barbara Bodichon, London, 2 October 1876). One letter of appreciation came from England's Chief Rabbi, Hermann Adler — see GEL VI, p. 275. On the split readership between the English and Jewish parts of the novel, see also LGHL II, p. 227; *'free command over editions and prices'*: GEL VI, p. 303 (George Lewes to John Blackwood, The Priory, 29 October 1876). Lewes's correspondence with Blackwood on the complete works was not straightforward: see GEL VI, pp. 298–303. Blackwood initially offered £4,000 for a new ten-year lease on George Eliot's works, noting that 'the size and price of the works' would be 'at our [i.e. the publisher's] discretion' (p. 298). *Lewes probably raised the possibility of offering the rights to a different publisher*: Blackwood made his initial offer (see previous note) on 19 October, and on the 23rd Lewes wrote that they were 'in a fluctuating state, and we must have another week before finally deciding' — GEL VI, p. 299 (George Lewes to John Blackwood, The Priory, 23 October 1876). Here Lewes assures Blackwood that they are keen for the books to 'continue to appear under the old flag', which at least hints that this was not entirely taken for granted. If this hint was simply part of Lewes's negotiating strategy, it may still have caused Eliot some misgivings. 'Mrs Lewes begs me to add', Lewes continues, 'that she is quite sure there will be no difference in our views whatever the ultimate arrangement may be', and there is perhaps a trace of Eliot's obstinacy here.

p. 234 *She told him how much she owed him . . .*: GEL VI, p. 293 (John Blackwood to William Blackwood, St Andrews, 11 October 1876): '[S]he had been looking over my old letters and cannot resist writing to say how much she owes me, in fact pretty much that she could not have gone on without me. You may conceive this in her language. It is the greatest compliment that a man in my position could possibly receive, and that and the context about herself brought warm tears to my eyes.' George Eliot's letter to Blackwood has not been found. *'Tears came into my eyes . . .'*: GEL VI, p. 294 (John Blackwood to George Eliot, St Andrews, 12 October 1876); *'the context about herself'*: GEL VI, p. 293 (John Blackwood to William Blackwood, St Andrews, 11 October 1876).

p. 235 *their country house . . .*: see GEL VI, pp. 313–14, 320, 322. The Leweses bought the house in December 1876 for £4,950; *Alfred Tennyson, the Poet Laureate, lived nearby*: GEL VI, p. 393 (George Lewes to Elma Stuart, the Heights, 12 July 1877); *'a gentle hill . . .'*: Cross III, pp. 298–9; *After a decade of long journeys . . .*: see McCormack, *George Eliot in Society*, pp. 124–5; *'a land of pine-woods . . .'*:

Cross III, pp. 298–9; *'paradise'*...*his own woods*: GEL VI, p. 389 (George Lewes to John Blackwood, the Heights, 20 June 1877); p. 393 (George Lewes to Elma Stuart, the Heights, 12 July 1877); GEL VII, p. 39 (George Lewes to Elma Stuart, the Heights, 10 July 1878); *'quite renovated*...*'*: *Journals*, p. 147 (10 November 1877). See also GEL VI, p. 417 (letter to Clementia Taylor, London, 10 November 1877); LGHL II, p. 236 (George Lewes to John Blackwood, 9 October 1877); *'Something should be born here.' She seemed to agree with him*: GEL VI, p. 390 (John Blackwood to William Blackwood, London, 25 June 1877).

pp. 235–6 *an 'enlarging vista*...*'*: *Journals*, p. 148 (31 December 1877).

p. 236 *'Which would you choose?*...*'*: GEL VI, p. 415 (letter to John Cross, 6 November 1877).

11. THE OTHER SHORE

p. 239 *'For God's sake, tell her not to have the photograph reproduced!'*: GEL VI, p. 321 (letter to Cara Bray, London, 21 December 1876); *'rather a horror of photography'*: GEL III, p. 307 (letter to John Blackwood, Berne, 23 June 1860). The photograph was taken by John Mayall on 26 February 1858 — see *Journals*, p. 73. The Leweses later denied its existence to people who requested a photograph of George Eliot — see LGHL II, pp. 163–4, 170: 'I would send you [a photograph] of Mrs Lewes were there such a thing in existence — but there isn't' (George Lewes to James Lowell, 20 June 1871); 'I wish I could send you a photo of [Mrs Lewes] but she has never had one taken' (George Lewes to James Lowell, 3 October 1871); GEL V, pp. 271, 377: 'I have no photograph of myself, having always avoided having one taken' (letter to Harriet Beecher Stowe, 24 June 1872); 'she has always refused to be photographed' (George Lewes to Elma Stuart, 19 February 1873). *'It needs the friendly eyes*...*'*: GEL VI, p. 321 (letter to Cara Bray, London, 21 December 1876). *During the 1870s Eliot's thoughts often turned to the question of biography*: see Bodenheimer, *The Real Life of Mary Ann Evans*, pp. 236–41; on her interest in biography and autobiography throughout her career, see Henry, *The Life of George Eliot*, pp. 7–16; *'risen so high'*: GEL VI, p. 295 (John Blackwood to George Eliot, St Andrews, 12 October 1876).

p. 240 *'horror of being interviewed and written about'*: GEL VII, p. 19 (letter to Lord Houghton, The Priory, London, 9 April 1878); *'sated with praise'; 'the stability of her fame'*: Collins, *Interviews and Recollections*, p. 193. The source is Lord Acton, an eminent politician and historian, who got to know George Eliot in the late 1870s. His sense that she was anxious about the stability of her fame is linked to her preceived ambition: 'She was intensely ambitious. Doubted as to her own fame. Cared only for the future, but cared for it with meaty interiority'; *afraid of 'spoiling' them*: 'To write indifferently after having written well', she remarked, 'is like an eminent clergyman's spoiling his reputation by lapses and neutralising all the good he did before' — GEL VI, p. 76 (letter to John Blackwood, Earlswood Common, 8 August 1874). Quoting Eliot's remark that Mary Wollstonecraft's death 'came in time to hinder [her] joys from being spoiled', Bodenheimer notes 'Marian Lewes's habitual notion that her own career might be retrospectively "spoiled" by some future event' — *The Real Life of Mary Ann Evans*, p. 234.

p. 241 *biographies of great writers* — *Blake, Scott, Wordsworth, Keats, Byron*: see GEL V, p. 54; VI, p. 389; VII, p. 65; VIII, p. 481; *Journals*, p. 214; LGHL II, p. 159; *'The world of thought and passion lay beyond his horizon ... '*: G. H. Lewes, 'Dickens in Relation to Criticism', *Fortnightly Review* no. 11 (February 1872), pp. 146–52. See Ashton, *G. H. Lewes*, pp. 256–8. Understating the vehemence of Lewes's critique of Dickens, Ashton asks, 'How could Lewes avoid judging other novelists by the standard he saw his remarkable wife setting for the English novel as an imaginative expression of psychological realism?' (p. 257). As she explains, Lewes's article provoked Forster to attack him in the third volume of his biography of Dickens, which came out in 1874. Years earlier, in 1853, Lewes had criticized Dickens by presenting a detailed scientific refutation of *Bleak House*'s spontaneous combustion plot in two *Leader* articles: see LGHL I, pp. 208–26. *'Is it not odious ...'*: GEL VI, p. 23 (letter to John Blackwood, The Priory, 20 February 1874). See also p. 67 (letter to George Bancroft, Earlswood Common, 15 July 1874): 'I think it one of the abuses of print and reading that the mass of the public will read any quantity of trivial details about a writer with whose works they are very imperfectly, if at all, acquainted.'

p. 242 *'any influence I have ...'*: GEL VI, p. 289 (letter to Haim Guedalla, The Priory, 2 October 1876); *'My writings are public property ...'; she especially insisted that Lewes should not be involved*: GEL VI, p. 167 (letter to Elma Stuart, Rickmansworth, 2 September 1875): 'Neither Mr Lewes nor I must have anything to do with it ... And I particularly object to Mr Lewes having any cognizance of what you choose to say'; see also p. 190. *'Hardly anything could have happened ...'*: *Journals*, p. 143 (1 January 1873); *She worried that ... she might diminish George Eliot's legacy*: see Bodenheimer, *The Real Life of Mary Ann Evans*, pp. 240–42; *'more and more timid ...'*: GEL VI, pp. 216–17 (letter to Joseph Payne, The Priory, 25 January 1876). See also GEL VII, p. 44 (letter to Clementia Taylor, the Heights, 18 July 1878): 'My function is that of the *aesthetic*, not the doctrinal teacher — the rousing of nobler emotions, which make mankind desire the social right, not the prescribing of special measures, concerning which the artistic mind, however strongly moved by social sympathy, is often not the best judge.'

p. 243 *'a Lock-up book for her Autobiography'*: GEL V, p. 123 (George Lewes's diary, 22 November 1870); *'impossible for her to write an autobiography ... judging herself and showing how wrong she was'*: GEL VIII, p. 465 (Emily Davies to Jane Crow, London, 21 August 1869); *'repugnance to autobiography ...'*: GEL VI, p. 371 (letter to Sara Hennell, The Priory, 15 May 1877); see also pp. 310–11 (letter to Sara Hennell, 22 November 1876); p. 353 (letter to Cara Bray, The Priory, 20 March 1877)).

pp. 243–4 *wishing she had never 'said a word to anybody ...'*: GEL VI, pp. 351–2 (letter to John Blackwood, The Priory, 20 March 1877).

p. 244 *'The beings closest to us . . .'*: Daniel Deronda, p. 672 (Chapter 54); *'extinct, rolled up, mashed . . .'*: GEL III, pp. 64–5 (letter to Barbara Bodichon, Wandsworth, 5 May 1859); *this writing self, diffused into its art*: John Cross recalled Eliot telling him that 'in all that she considered her best writing, there was a "not herself" which took possession of her, and that she felt her own personality to be merely the instrument through which this spirit, as it were, was acting' — Cross III, p. 424.

p. 245 *a child of both Romanticism and conservative Middle England*: see Henry, *The Life of George Eliot*, pp. 239, 243; *'consciousness is chiefly of the busy, anxious metropolitan sort . . .'*: Impressions of Theophrastus Such, p. 42; *has failed as an author . . .*: Impressions of Theophrastus Such, pp. 8–10; *'self-ignorance' and 'self-betrayal'*: Impressions of Theophrastus Such, p. 6.

p. 246 *Isaac Casaubon's Greek and Latin edition of Theophrastus's Characters*: see R. C. Jebb, *The Characters of Theophrastus* (London and Cambridge: Macmillan & Co., 1870), p. 5. On the genre of the *Characters*, see pp. 15–47; on Theophrastus's influence on early modern writers, including Jean de la Bruyère, see pp. 48–72.

pp. 246–7 *'Life is very sweet to us . . .'*: GEL VII, p. 5 (letter to Elma Stuart, The Priory, 5 January 1878).

p. 247 *'Madonna is very "jolly" . . .'*: LGHL II, p. 239 (George Lewes to John Blackwood, December 1877); *'My Little Man . . .'*: GEL VII, p. 34 (letter to Elma Stuart, the Heights, 27 June 1878); *'Madonna I grieve to say . . .'*: GEL VII, p. 39 (George Lewes to Elma Stuart, the Heights, 10 July 1878). See also p. 43: 'Mrs Lewes is not very well, but has improved the last few days' (George Lewes to William Blackwood, the Heights, 17 July 1878); *'I wish I could tell you better news . . .'*: GEL VII, p. 54 (letter to Elma Stuart, the Heights, 8 August 1878); *'I can't work at all . . .'*: GEL VII, p. 50 (George Lewes to John Blackwood, the Heights, 6 August 1878). On 12 August Lewes was well enough to spend the afternoon at Tennyson's house, and that day Eliot took her turn at being ill with 'sick headache' — see GEL VII, p. 57 (George Lewes's diary, 12 August); *'and I as usual have taken his place . . .'*: GEL VII, pp. 61-2 (letter to Cara Bray, The Heights, August 26th 1878).

pp. 247–8 *they managed to receive visits . . .*: see GEL VII, p. 64 (George Lewes to Charles Lewes, the Heights, 26 August 1878); Simcox, *A Monument to the Memory of George Eliot*, p. 39.

p. 248 *Sometimes John Cross came over from Weybridge . . .*: see Cross III, pp. 333–4; Simcox, *A Monument to the Memory of George Eliot*, p. 66; *'The shadow of trouble . . .'*: Cross III, pp. 240; *'love is never without its shadow of anxiety'*: Cross III, p. 233 (letter to John Cross, December 13th 1877); *'This place is getting lovelier . . .'*: GEL VII, p. 73 (George Lewes to Charles Lewes, the Heights, 15 October 1878); *'Do you remember . . .'*: GEL VII, p. 72 (letter to Sara Hennell, the Heights, 15 October 1878); *'I miss so much the hope . . .'*: GEL VII, p. 71 (letter to Barbara Bodichon, the Heights, 15 October 1878); *'imprudently drove out . . .'*: GEL VII, p. 80 (letter to John Blackwood, The Priory, 23 November 1878); *'deep trouble'*: GEL VII, p. 81 (letter to Sara Hennell, The Priory, 24

November 1878); *'a deep sense of change within'*: GEL VII p. 84 (letter to Barbara Bodichon, The Priory, 25 November 1878).

p. 249 *'O how nice!'*: see GEL VII, pp. 80–81 (letter to John Blackwood, The Priory, 23 November 1878); pp. 93–4 (letter to John Blackwood, The Priory, 13 January 1879); *Lewes died at dusk*: see Simcox, *A Monument to the Memory of George Eliot*, p. 52: 'He died at a quarter to six' on 30 November. *Often sadness and fear overwhelmed her . . .*: see Simcox, *A Monument to the Memory of George Eliot*, pp. 52, 65, 68–70 (1 December, 13 January, 30 January, 4 February, 17 February); *She could talk only about Lewes*: see Simcox, *A Monument to the Memory of George Eliot*, p. 57 (12 December 1878); *she resolved to 'carry out his wishes' . . .*: see Simcox, *A Monument to the Memory of George Eliot*, p. 52 (2 December 1878). The first book, the *Problems of Life and Mind: First Series*, published in 1874, was titled *The Foundations of a Creed*; the second book, the *Problems of Life and Mind: Second Series*, published in 1877, was titled *The Physical Basis of Mind*; *a Cambridge studentship . . .*: £5,000 in 1879 is equivalent to about £500,000 today; *she read poetry about death and loss . . .*: see *Journals*, p. 155 (1 January 1879). From Chaucer's *Book of the Duchess* she copied, 'For I am sorrow and sorrow is I'; from Izaak Walton's *Life and Death of Dr Donne* she copied, 'She now being removed by death a commensurate grief took as full possession of him as joy had done.' *'Finished second reading of M.S . . .'*: see *Journals*, pp. 156–8 (January 1879).

p. 250 *'Some little happiness . . .'*: see *Journals*, p. 155 (1 January 1879). The original couplet, from Browne's *Brittania Pastorals* (1613), reads: 'Some little happiness have thou and I / Since we shall die ere we have wished to die'. Eliot placed brackets around the second line, and added her own version beneath it; *'Kneeling before this ruin . . .'*: see *Journals*, p. 156; *King John*, Act 4, Scene 3, ll. 65–72. In the play, the last two lines of Salisbury's speech are 'Till I have set a glory to this hand, / By giving it the worship of revenge.' See Robert Macfarlane, *Original Copy: Plagiarism and Originality in Nineteenth-Century Literature* (Oxford: Oxford University Press, 2007), pp. 120–26 for an analysis of the copied and altered passages in George Eliot's journal during the weeks after Lewes's death. *'Wrote verses to Polly'*: *Journals*, p. 159 (23 January 1879).

p. 251 *she made significant changes*: see *Journals*, p. 166 (11 March 1879): 'Read chapter on the affective states Problem III and wrote new page'; *'aggressive and defensive impulses . . .'*: see K. K. Collins, 'G. H. Lewes Revised: George Eliot and the Moral Sense', *Victorian Studies* vol. 21, no. 4 (1978), pp. 491–2. Collins traces some of the most significant revisions that George Eliot made to the third series of *Problems of Life and Mind*, focusing especially on sections of a chapter on 'The Moral Sense' and situating this material in the context of contemporary philosophical debates. The paper includes an appendix which juxtaposes Lewes's original versions of key sections with the published versions edited by George Eliot; *'the consciousness of dependence . . .'*: G. H. Lewes, Problems of Life and Mind, Third Series, pp. 386–7; see Collins, 'G. H. Lewes Revised: George Eliot and the Moral Sense', pp. 491–2.

p. 252 *The first friend she saw . . .was John Cross*: see *Journals*, p. 163 (23 February 1879); *During the spring Eliot saw her grandchildren, and many friends*: see *Journals*, pp. 165–74 (March to May 1879).

p. 253 *Now she might be Beatrice*: see GEL VII, p. 212 (letter to John Cross, the Heights, 16 October 1879); *struggle and crisis*: see *Journals*, pp. 169, 172, 174 (3 April, 7 April, 2 May, 16 May 1879); *'Decisive conversation'*: *Journals*, p. 179 (21 August 1879); *choices*: *Journals*, pp. 183, 184, 186 ('Joy came in the evening', 8 October; 'Choice of Hercules', 9 October; 'Meditation on difficulties', 17 October, 'Another turning-point', 25 November); *'a solemn time . . .'*: GEL VII, p. 211 (letter to John Cross, the Heights, 16 October 1879). *One of her few surviving letters to Cross . . .*: GEL VII, p. 212 (letter to John Cross, the Heights, 16 October 1879). Nancy Henry describes this letter as 'overwrought, scattered . . . bizarre and contradictory', and wonders whether it was written under the influence of the daily pint of champagne that Eliot's doctor had prescribed for her at this time — see *The Life of George Eliot*, p. 260.

pp. 253–4 *On the anniversary of Lewes's death . . .*: *Journals*, p. 187 (29 November 1879) — this was a Saturday, and Eliot was reckoning the anniversary 'by the days of the week' rather than by the date (28 November 1878).

p. 254 *'Cold in the earth . . .'*: see *Journals*, pp. 188–9 (17 December 1879); *'I kissed her again and again . . .'*: Simcox, *A Monument to the Memory of George Eliot*, p. 117 (9 March 1880); *'much oppressed with difficulties . . .'*: GEL IX, p. 300 (letter to Miss Beneke, The Priory, 19 March 1880).

p. 255 *Edith . . .was certainly eager to take on the task*: see Simcox, *A Monument to the Memory of George Eliot*, pp. 139–49. Here Simcox describes beginning research for Eliot's biography immediately after her funeral on 29 December 1880: she gathered letters, visited her birthplace in the Midlands, and visited many of her old friends, including Sara Hennell, 'a little grey haired pleasant faced old lady' (p. 144). Then on 20 January 1881 John Cross told her 'he had made up his mind to write the life himself . . . I cannot help being envious' (pp. 148–9). Martha Vicinus discusses the relationship between Eliot and Simcox in the context of other nineteenth-century 'erotic friendships' between women: see *Intimate Friends: Women Who Loved Women, 1778–1928* (Chicago, ILL: University of Chicago Press, 2004), pp. 121–6; *They would sign new wills*: see Haight's note in GEL VII, p. 268. *Eliot wished to be buried there*: see Haight, *George Eliot: A Biography*, p. 548: John Tyndall wrote to the Dean of the Abbey that he had been told — presumably by John Cross — that it was 'the expressed wish of George Eliot to be buried in Westminster Abbey'.

p. 257 *Its title page displayed her married status*: see Cross I, p. v. *One day she suggested that he should 'do some one work . . .'*: see Simcox, *A Monument to the Memory of George Eliot*, p. 148.

p. 258 *'A great momentous change . . .'*: GEL VII, p. 269 (letter to Georgiana Burne-Jones, The Priory, 5 May 1880). See also p. 270 (letter to Maria Congreve, The Priory, 5 May 1880): 'A great, momentous change is going to take place in my life,' wrote Eliot, not specifying what this change was; Charles would visit Maria to explain in a few days; *taken by surprise*: see GEL VII, pp. 308–9 (letter to Clementia Taylor, the Heights, 2 August 1880): 'Do not reproach me for not telling you of my marriage beforehand. It is difficult to speak of what surprises ourselves, and the decision was sudden, though not the friendship which led to the decision.' *'All this is a wonderful blessing . . .'*: GEL VII, p. 291 (letter to Barbara Bodichon, Verona, 1 June 1880); *'something like a miracle-legend'*: GEL VII, p. 296 (letter to Maria Congreve, Venice, 10 June 1880). *'The great event that has happened in my life . . .'*: GEL VII, p. 276 (John Cross to Elma Stuart, Paris, 11 May 1880).

p. 259 *'heart-loneliness'*: see Cross III, p. 387: 'Accustomed as she had been for so many years to solitude *à deux*, the want of close companionship continued to be felt very bitterly.' *'I shall be a better, more loving creature . . .'*: GEL VII, p. 291 (letter to Barbara Bodichon, Verona, 1 June 1880); *'I would still give up my own life . . .'*: GEL VII, p. 283 (letter to Charles Lewes, Grenoble, 21 May 1880); *'finally decided'*: Cross III, p. 387; *'mutual dependence'*: Cross III, p. 387; an *'imagined otherwise' while Lewes was still alive*: Ashton reports that Frederic and Ethel Harrison, the Leweses' Positivist friends, 'privately told friends that they believed George Eliot "had got tired of Mr Lewes & had liked Mr Cross before [Lewes] died."' Ashton's source is a letter from Edward Beesley to Herbert Spencer. Beesley adds that he does not believe this, and understands why Eliot accepted Cross: 'Loneliness, a longing to have her real name & position like other and inferior women, gratitude to the warmhearted man who wanted to give her name and home and everything, — affection for him of a right and good kind: Why are these not enough?' — *George Eliot: A Life*, p. 373.

pp. 259–60 *'nearly 20 years' difference . . .'*: GEL VI, p. 398 (letter to Barbara Bodichon, the Heights, 2 August 1877).

p. 260 *'in some dim form'*: Simcox, *A Monument to the Memory of George Eliot*, p. 121; *'had twice broken it off . . .'*: Simcox, *A Monument to the Memory of George Eliot*, p. 121; *'violent emotions'*: see Collins, *George Eliot: Interviews and Recollections*, p. 23, quoting notes made by Lord Acton after visiting François D'Albert-Durade in the 1880s. *They were both very anxious . . .*: see GEL VII, p. 308 (letter to Barbara Bodicon, the Heights, 1 August 1880); Simcox, *A Monument to the Memory of George Eliot*, p. 128.

p. 261 *'chronicle of our happy married life'*: GEL VII, p. 272 (letter to Eleanor Cross, Paris, 9 May 1880); *'We crossed the Channel delightfully . . .'*: *Journals*, p. 203 (7 May 1880); *'many years younger . . . almost a magical effect'*: Cross III, pp. 417–18; *a curriculum of shared reading that returned to old loves*: in his biography of Goethe, Lewes had judged *Hermann und Dorothea* 'the most perfect of his poems' — *The Life and Works of Goethe*, vol. II, p. 221. *'Looking at pictures or sculpture . . .'*: Cross III, p. 418. Cross wrote to his sister that he ought to 'become very wise' in the company of his new wife, 'guide, philosopher, and friend' — GEL IX, p. 311 (John Cross to Mary Cross, Verona, 1 June 1880). *'Johnnie has entered with great interest . . .'*: GEL VII, pp. 298–9 (letter to Mary, Eleanor and Florence Cross, Venice, 13 June 1880). Eliot later suggested that 'lack of muscular exercise' — or possibly 'unsanitary influences' including a Scirocco wind from the Sahara and 'bad smells' under their hotel window — had caused Cross's 'attack of illness' in Venice: see GEL VII, p. 301.

p. 262 *Police . . .recorded the incident as a suicide attempt*: see Brenda Maddox, *George Eliot: Novelist, Lover, Wife*, pp. 215–17; *Cross was supposed to 'watch over' her*: GEL VII, p. 341 (letter to Cara Bray, the Heights, 28 November 1880); see also p. 287 (letter to Isaac Evans, Milan, 26 May 1880): 'his affection has made him choose this lot of caring for me rather than any other of the various lots open to him'. According to Eliot's friend Lord Acton, 'At Venice she thought him mad, and she never recovered the dreadful depression that followed' — quoted in Haight, *George Eliot: A Biography*, p. 544; *'tried to drown himself'*: see Collins, *George Eliot: Interviews and Recollections*, p. 217 (citing a letter from Caroline Jebb to her sister, 7 September 1880); *The 'old story' . . .*: see Edith Simcox, *A Monument to the Memory of George Eliot*, p. 127 (30 June 1880). Kathryn Hughes connects the 1854 and 1880 marriage scandals, suggesting that gossips who said Cross jumped out of the window to escape sex with an old woman were following 'a line of reasoning which reprised all those old jokes from 1854 about Marian being a nymphomaniac whose incontinent lusts broke through every legal and social constraint. In the original 1854 rumour Lewes had been viewed as Marian's partner in crime, a man whose urge to sexual misconduct was matched only by her own. In the 1880 version Cross was cast as the naïve virgin, and per- haps even unacknowledged homosexual, chased around the bed by a hideous, lascivious woman demanding sex' — *George Eliot: The Last Victorian*, p. 479; *'choosing her trousseau'*: Collins, *George Eliot: Interviews and Recollections*, p. 217 (citing a letter from Caroline Jebb to her sister, 7 September 1880).

pp. 262–3 *Caroline Jebb . . .met Mr and Mrs Cross*: Collins, *George Eliot: Interviews and Recollections*, p. 217 (citing a letter from Caroline Jebb to her sister, 7 Sep- tember 1880).

p. 263 *a note of congratulation*: see GEL VII, p. 280 (Isaac Pearson Evans to George Eliot, Griff House, 17 May 1880). It is a brief note, as follows: 'My dear Sister, I have much pleasure in availing myself of the present opportunity to break the long silence which has existed between us, by offering our united and sincere congratulations to you and Mr Cross, upon the happy event of which Mr Holbe- che [his solicitor] has informed me. My wife joins me in sincerely hoping that it will afford you much happiness and comfort. She and the younger branches unite with me in kind love and every good wish. Believe me, Your affectionate brother, Isaac P. Evans.' The letter was forwarded to Eliot in Milan, and she replied quickly: 'it was a great joy to me to have your kind words of sympathy, for our long silence has never broken the affection for you which began when we were little ones. My Husband too was much pleased to read your letter . . . He is of a most solid, well tried character and has had a great deal of experience' — GEL VII, p. 287 (letter to Isaac Evans, Milan, 26 May 1880). Eliot had instructed her solicitor to inform her brother's solicitor of her marriage to Cross: see GEL IX, pp. 307–8; *'It is difficult to give you materials for imagining my "world" . . .'*:

Cross III, p. 313 (letter to Cara Bray, 28 November 1880); *the beginning of some story*: see Simcox, *A Monument to the Memory of George Eliot*, p. 149; *'this new House we meant to be so happy in . . .'*.

p. 264 *arranged on new shelves in the same order as before*: GEL VII, p. 351 (John Cross to Elma Stuart, 4 Cheyne Walk, 23 December 1880).

LAST WORDS

p. 267 *her 'notorious antagonism to Christian practice . . .'; 'She cannot eat her cake and have it too'*: see Haight, *George Eliot: A Biography*, p. 549, quoting Thomas Huxley. T. H. Huxley makes a cameo in Lytton Strachey's *Eminent Victorians* as a member of the Metaphysical Club, a group of distinguished intellectuals who gathered to discuss moral and religious questions 'after a comfortable dinner' at the Grosvenor Hotel in Westminster.

p. 269 *A stone was laid for her in Poets' Corner*: it was unveiled by Gordon Haight, editor of the complete edition of George Eliot's letters and author of a landmark biography published in 1968.

p. 270 *'vent wisdom'*: Collins *George Eliot: Interviews and Recollections*, p. 215 (quoting Georgiana Burne-Jones, *Memorials of Edward Burne-Jones*, 1906); *'It is almost too great happiness . . .'*: GEL VII, p. 276 (John Cross to Elma Stuart, Paris, 11 May 1880); *a traumatic experience*: see Bodenheimer, *The Real Life of Mary Ann Evans*, p. 113.

p. 271 *if she 'hadn't been human . . .'*: Collins, *George Eliot: Interviews and Recollections*, p. 215 (quoting Georgiana Burne-Jones, *Memorials of Edward Burne-Jones*, 1906); *'The secret of his lovableness . . .'*: Simcox, *A Monument to the Memory of George Eliot*, pp. 53, 67 (2 December 1878; 19 January 1879); *his biography would be much maligned for making George Eliot too respectable*: see, for example, Virginia Woolf, 'George Eliot', *The Times Literary Supplement*, 20 November 1919 — this was the *TLS*'s lead essay, appearing two days before the centenary of Eliot's birth; *his bursts of temper*: see Anthony Trollope's obituary in the *Fortnightly Review*, 1 January 1879, pp. 16–24. Trollope recalls how Lewes's face often 'blazed up' suddenly 'in strong indignation', but his smile would quickly return.

p. 272 *'The place that may belong to her . . .'*: Cross III, p. 440; *'loved her lover-wise'*: see Simcox, *A Monument to the Memory of George Eliot*, p. 146 (18 January 1881).

Index

INDEX OF COMMENTATORS, THEORISTS, SCHOLARS